A HANDBOOK OF FIRE TECHNOLOGY

A Handbook of Fire Technology

for fire officers, safety and security officers
and students of fire engineering

R.S.Gupta
former director,
National Fire Service College, Nagpur

Universities Press

A HANDBOOK OF FIRE TECHNOLOGY (2ND EDITION)

UNIVERSITIES PRESS (INDIA) PRIVATE LIMITED

Registered Office
3-6-747/1/A & 3-6-754/1, Himayatnagar,
Hyderabad 500 029, Telangana, India
info@universitiespress.com; www.universitiespress.com

Distributed by
Orient Blackswan Private Limited

Registered Office
3-6-752 Himayatnagar, Hyderabad 500 029, Telangana, India

Other Offices
Bengaluru, Chennai, Guwahati, Hyderabad,
Kolkata, Mumbai, New Delhi, Noida, Patna

First published by Orient Longman Private Limited 2009
Second Edition 1993
Reprinted 1997, 2005, 2007
First Universities Press impression 2009
Reprinted 2021, 2026

502283

ISBN 978-81-7371-686-7

Printed in India at
Kensington Printing & Packaging, Noida 201 301

Published by
Universities Press (India) Private Limited
3-6-747/1/A & 3-6-754/1 Himayatnagar,
Hyderabad 500 029, Telangana, India

Foreword

For the progressive study of Fire Technology, students are largely dependent on the works of foreign authors as also on studies and reports of practices and methods followed in other countries.

Although, some efforts have been made recently to publish journals and papers reflecting some original thoughts and ideas of our engineers and scientists, a requirement still exists for material that will not only serve to improve the competence of the serious-minded Fire Engineers, but, at the same time, meet the practical needs of those concerned with planning of resources to meet emergent situations.

A Handbook of Fire Technology which I understand is the first work of this nature to be published in India, should fill a long standing void. It covers a wide spectrum in the field of Fire Technology and Fire Engineering and should provide a lead to other potential authors.

Shri R.S. Gupta, with his considerable experience both in the operational and the administrative departments of the Fire Services, and later, as Director of the National Fire Service College, Nagpur, has produced a systematic presentation of the three important elements, which he has highlighted in the preface. This book also contains much useful practical advice on topical matters, which are of interest to all students of Fire Engineering and professional firemen. I commend that it should be widely read.

Sd/- Lt. Gen. E. G. PETTENGELL, P.V.S.M,
Director General Civil Defence

1 October 1975

Ministry of Home Affairs
Express Building, 2nd Floor
Bahadur Shah Zafar Marg, New Delhi 110 001

Preface to the Second Edition

The first edition of this book was written in 1974 and was published in 1976. It was written especially for the students of fire engineering who found it difficult to follow the very limited number of overseas publications available on the subject.

The book deals with three basic subjects of fire engineering: (i) chemistry of combustion including heat, (ii) electricity in relation to fire hazards, and (iii) hydraulics and water supplies for firemen. The style and approach to the subjects are simple and they are written in such a way that these can be easily understood by all.

Since the publication of the first edition there have been tremendous changes in the science of fire technology. New extinguishers have been developed which are very fast in action. New theories of fire extinction have been defined. The latest appliances for fire-fighting and for rescue work widely differ from the old ones in efficiency and speed. No less is the success in the field of automatic fire detection using nuclear radiation, infra-red or ultraviolet ray technology or laser beams, which have revolutionized the system of automatic fire detection.

The basic units of measurement have also changed with the result that all mathematical problems regarding hydraulics, heat, general physics and mensuration are now being worked out in S.I. units instead of in the F.P.S. system. All the illustrative examples in the first edition of the book, which were worked out in the F.P.S. system, have now been worked out in S.I. units for the students of fire engineering intending to sit for professional examinations. Along with this, other chapters have also been revised to make the book up-to-date.

In the revised edition, I have retained the essentials of each topic, which can be easily understood and remembered. Most of the problems on hydraulics, electricity, chemistry, heat and mechanics have been fully worked out. No other book available on this subject provides so much information in one volume.

I shall consider my efforts successful if students find the new edition useful and if it is accepted by the fire officers and others concerned with fire safety in different institutions and industries. I strongly feel that they will benefit from the technical information, data and charts and also from the solutions given to a large number of problems.

I acknowledge my indebtedness to the authors of the books mentioned in the bibliography. This moment of happiness brings to my mind thoughts of my wife who had inspired me to take up this task, and who is no longer in this world to see the new publication.

Calcutta 1992 R.S.Gupta

Preface to the First Edition

A Handbook of Fire Technology contains the basic information on three important subjects: (i) Chemistry of Combustion; (ii) Electricity in relation to Fire Hazards and (iii) Hydraulics and Water Supplies for Fire Officers, apart from other useful informations for a Fire Engineer.

From my long experience in the National Fire Service College, Nagpur, as its Director, I have found that the trainee officers from our country or from abroad, who go there for a course, generally find it difficult to follow the instructions clearly in these three subjects, which are indeed the stepping stones for attaining proficiency in Fire Engineering. So far, there had been no suitable book, written by any Indian author on these subjects from a fireman's point of view and in the language of a fireman. I believe, this handbook will fill up the gap that had been existing so long.

Apart from meeting the needs of a trainee officer preparing for professional examinations in the science of fire-fighting, this handbook contains some useful hints and suggestions for all those connected with fire prevention and protection, either in the fire brigades or in the various trade or commerce, whose duties mainly involve prevention of fire and its extinction and elimination of life risk, such as the fire prevention methods for high-rise buildings in U.K. and in this country, summary of certain basic requirements for some of the commonly used fire appliances, equipments and fire-fighting media, storage risks of certain industrial materials, finished products, etc.

Fires due to electricity roughly account for about 20 to 25 per cent of all the fires in this country. With rapid urbanization and industrialization and the extension of electrification schemes, the potential fire hazards and with the risks due to electricity have increased. This handbook contains basic informations and broad guidelines for Safety Engineers, Security Officers, or Civil Engineers as well, connected with the safety in industrial establishments.

The subject of Hydraulics is quite important for all fire officers, as water is the life blood to a fireman, who has to depend on the availability of the requisite supply of water, pump, and the appropriate type of hose and branch pipe. Unless he knows the characteristics of his pumps and hose and the desired output from his branch at the requisite pressure, he will not be able to do the job. The technique of water relay from a long distance to the place of fire is a specialized subject and requires experience and knowledge in the operation. This handbook will give him a valuable guidance.

There are also certain other important points, which may be useful for the purpose of reference in the day-to-day work of a fire protection officer, with a host of other materials, covered under the Appendices, including Metrication and the Conversion of the hydraulic formula from the F.P.S. system into metric units. For the benefit of the students in Fire Engineering, a number of problems have also been solved in metric units.

The presentation of the subject-matter has been made in such a manner as to serve the practical needs of a fire or Civil Defence Officer and others having some background on the subjects, highlighting the points of practical importance. I hope the book will be useful to those seeking more information on the three subjects, on which this handbook has been prepared.

Finally, I thank all who have given me the inspiration to write this small book, particularly my students, who have requested me to write something that might be useful to them.

My thanks are also due to my son Shri S.N. Gupta, M.Sc., who was sometimes a Lecturer in Physics and who took the trouble of revising the entire manuscript.

I also acknowledge my indebtedness to the authors of the books mentioned in the bibliography, at the end for this handbook and the information contained in them.

Calcutta
12 September 1975

R.S. GUPTA

Contents

Part 2: Electricity in Relation to Fire Hazard

Part 3: Hydraulics and Water Supplies for Firemen

To my mother
Late Smt Sarojini Devi
and to my wife
Late Smt Bonolata Gupta

CHAPTER 1

Part 1: Chemistry of Combustion: A. Essential Prerequisites

Different states of matter

There are three kinds of bodies in this universe, viz. solids, liquids and gases, and theym ay exist in the form of an element or a compound, being combined chemically with more than one element, or in the form of a mechanical mixture of several substances.

Element

An element is a substance which cannot be resolved or split up into simpler substances by any chemical means. Thus, substances like hydrogen, oxygen, copper, iron, sulphur etc. are elements and cannot be broken up into substances simpler than themselves. It is interesting to note that over 90% by weight of the earth's crust is made up of twenty elements leaving about eighty other elements to account for the remainder.

Chemical compound

On the other hand, a compound is a substance produced of two or more elements in definite proportions by weight by chemical combination. The substance produced will have properties entirely different from those of the reacting elements or substances. Both carbon dioxide gas and lime may react together in definite proportion to produce chalk which has got quite different properties than either of CO_2 gas or lime. Similarly, two volumes of hydrogen combine with one volume of oxygen to produce water, which has properties entirely different from those of hydrogen and oxygen. These are examples of chemical compounds.

Mechanical mixture

A mechanical mixture is the result of bringing together two or more elements or compounds in any proportion by weight without producing any change in their individual properties.

In the case of ordinary air, there are two main gases in it, viz. oxygen and nitrogen, along with a few other gases in small amount. Oxygen is consumed and nitrogen is breathed out along with carbon dioxide. Air is a simple mixture of several gases like oxygen, nitrogen etc. which can be easily separated into their constituents and the constituents may not always be present in a fixed proportion in the atmosphere. The percentage of oxygen or other gases may vary slightly. Such substances are called mechanical mixtures.

Chemical reaction and catalysts

A chemical reaction involves the transformation of the reacting substances into one or more new substance brought about by chemical methods such as combination, decomposition, or displacement etc. and produces a permanent change. When magnesium is burnt in air, it combines directly with the oxygen of the air producing magnesium oxide. Chemical reaction takes place by physical contact between the different constituents present in a fixed proportion and it is accelerated by heat and pressure or by electrical discharges. Sometimes the mere presence of a foreign substance may either increase or retard the speed of a chemical reaction. Such substances do not take part in the chemical reaction and remain unchanged in mass as also in chemical and physical properties during the course of the reaction. These substances are called catalytic agents or catalysts. Positive catalysts are those which increase the velocity of a chemical reaction and negative catalysts are those which retard it.

Properties of matter—density and specific gravity

Every substance has its own mass and volume. The density of a substance is its mass per unit volume. Water has the density of 1 gm per cc, meaning thereby that one cu.m of water would weigh 1 kg.

The specific gravity of a substance, on the other hand, is the ratio of the mass of unit volume of the substance to the mass of unit volume of water at 4^0C. It can also be defined as the ratio of the density of the body to the density of water at 4^0C.

Since the density of water in C.G.S. units equals 1 gm per cc, the specific gravity = density (C.G.S. units).

Vapour pressure and molecular attraction

The vapour pressure of a liquid is the pressure exerted by the vapour of the liquid at any given temperature, at which the vapour and liquid phases of the substance are in equilibrium in a closed container. A high vapour pressure indicates a high rate of evaporation, as it is with certain volatile inflammable liquids like ether, petrol etc.

As stated previously, matter is composed of solids, liquids and gases. In solids molecular attraction is the highest, the molecule being the smallest particle of a substance capable of independent existence without losing the characteristics of the substance. On account of the molecular attraction, solids retain their shape and size and unless heat, which is a form of energy, is applied, solids do not change their shape. In liquids the molecular attraction is very much less than that in solids, and as such, liquids have no definite shape of their own. They take the shape of the container. In gases molecular attraction is the least and that is the reason why they are mobile and tend to occupy a greater space, covering the entire space available.

Vapour density and molecular weight

In the case of gases, it is very important to know the vapour density in relation to air because it gives an idea as to whether the gas is lighter than air so as to distribute itself in the available atmosphere, forming an inflammable and explosive mixture such as hydrogen, coal gas, or acetylene, or if it is heavier than air, e.g. ether or petrol vapour, when it can settle at the bottom, rendering that particular place explosive and dangerous. The density of any gas may be measured with air or hydrogen taken as a standard substance. In fire service, the measurement is generally taken with regard to air. Vapour density, when measured in terms of air, is the ratio of the mass of a given volume of the vapour to the mass of an equal volume of air under the same temperature and pressure. Vapour density is equal to half the molecular weight of the substance since the molecular weight of any gas is twice its density in relation to hydrogen which has 2 atoms in one molecule, i.e.

$$D = \text{Molecular weight}/2$$

Since, the vapour density of air is 14.5 (approx), if the result arrived at by the aforesaid formula is divided by 14.5 and if it is less than 1, it indicates that the vapour or gas is lighter than air; if it is greater than 1, then it is heavier than air.

The vapour density of CO_2 gas is found to be 1.53, air being the unit. Now air is 14.4 times as heavy as hydrogen. Hence, the density of gases, taking hydrogen as the unit, is multiplied by 14.4. The density of a gas with hydrogen as the unit = wt. of 1 litre of the gas/wt. of 1 litre of H_2 measured at the normal temperature and pressure (N.T.P.), i.e. at 0^0C and 760 mm of mercury. Since the weight of 1 litre of hydrogen = 0.98986 gm, the weight of 1 litre of any gas at N.T.P. can be found to be equal to its density × 0.089 gm, i.e. its density × 0.09 gm (roughly).

Diffusion of gases

All gases diffuse and tend to mix with one another till a uniform mixture is formed. The natural process by which one gas is thus disseminated through another is called 'gaseous diffusion'. Lighter gases having lower density diffuse more quickly than heavier gases having greater density. This property of gaseous diffusion has important significance during rescue operations or fighting a gas fire in a closed space with restricted ventilation, where different types of gases like ammonia, chlorine, petroleum vapour, ether etc. might be encountered.

Graham's Law of Diffusion states: *The velocities of diffusion of gases (at constant temperature and pressure) are inversely proportional to the square root of their densities*, viz. $v_1\sqrt{D_1} = v_2\sqrt{D_2}$, where v_1 and v_2 are the velocities of diffusion and D_1 and D_2 are the densities of the two gases.

Atoms and molecules

As stated previously, matter may exist in the form of elements or compounds. An atom is the ultimate particle of an element, capable of taking part in chemical reactions, whereas a molecule of a substance, produced by the union of atoms, is the ultimate particle of matter capable of existing in the free state, retaining the properties of the substance.

Atomic and molecular weight

As the magnitude of the atoms and molecules is extremely small, their weight or their number in a substance cannot be determined by directly weighing or counting them. Their weights are found in relation to a standard, as relative atomic weights or molecular weights. Hydrogen being the lightest, the weight of its atom is taken as unity with reference to which all atomic and molecular weights are expressed. The molecular weight of a substance is therefore the number which expresses how many times a molecule of it is heavier than an atom of hydrogen. The atomic weight of an element on the other hand is the number which expresses the ratio of the average weight of an atom of the element to the weight of an atom of hydrogen.

Molecular weight and gram-molecular volume

The molecular weight of a gaseous substance = $2D$, where D is its vapour density. It is also the weight of the substance, which occupies in the gaseous state the same volume (viz. 22.4 litre) as two parts by weight of hydrogen at N.T.P. Thus, the molecular weight of any gas, expressed in grams, always occupies 22.4 litre at N.T.P. The expression N.T.P. signifies normal temperature and pressure and this is taken as 0^0C and 760 mm of mercury.

Chemical reaction and valency

The atoms of many elements cannot exist alone, but seek partners with another atom of either the same or different elements. It is this urge or tendency to link up with other atoms as a result of chemical affinity which gives rise to chemical reactions with all its practical consequences. The capacity of an element for combining with other element is known as the valency of that element. The valency of an element is measured by the number of hydrogen or chlorine atoms which combine with or are displaced by one atom of the element.

Chemical reactions – exothermic and endothermic reactions

Whenever there is any chemical reaction, heat is either liberated or absorbed from the reacting substances. In the former case, it is called an exothermic reaction and in the latter case it is called an endothermic reaction.

Heat of formation

Heat of formation is the energy, measured as heat, which is given off or lost when a given reaction takes place. In endothermic reactions, the substances formed contain more energy than the reacting substances, whereas exothermic reactions produce substances with less energy than that contained in the reacting materials.

In case of combustion involving a carbonaceous fuel and oxygen, CO_2 gas is generally produced, with the liberation of heat. This may be expressed in terms of chemical equation as

$$C + O_2 = CO_2 + 39,2920 \text{ joule}$$

where C and O represent the symbols for carbon and oxygen and the members attached to the symbol represent the number of atoms.

The above equation means that 12 gm of carbon react with 32 gm of oxygen to produce 22.4 litre of CO_2 at N.T.P. or 44 gm of CO_2, with the liberation of 27,44,280 calorie of heat, which is the heat of formation. Thus, the calorific value of heat generated per gram of carbon burnt to CO_2 equals 1/12th of 27,44,280 calorie.

In absence of sufficient oxygen, the CO_2 gas produced above reacts with the red hot carbon to produce CO gas as follows:

$$C + CO_2 = 2CO - 10{,}98{,}720 \text{ calorie}$$

i.e. 12 gm of carbon react with 44 gm of CO_2 to produce 2×22.4 litre of carbon monoxide at N.T.P. with the absorption of 10,98,720 calorie of heat. The condition leading to the formation of carbon monoxide occurs very frequently in practice on the fire ground, i.e. whenever red hot carbon and carbon dioxide gas meet in the absence of free oxygen in an unventilated space. This occurs in every bed of burning solid fuel such as coal, coke or charcoal, which is more than a few inches thick. The production of carbon monoxide gas, in this way, is quite dangerous to a person, leading to his collapse and ultimate death due to oxygen starvation. The carbon monoxide thus produced forms a stable compound with red blood corpuscles, known as carboxyhaemoglobin, when inhaled by anybody for a sufficiently long time in an unventilated space.

Water Gas and Producer Gas

Another endothermic reaction that takes place is stated below. When steam comes in contact with red hot carbon— a phenomenon quite common in a fire due to a fire stream striking against burning carbonaceous substances—the following reaction takes place:

$$C + H_2O = CO + H_2 - 82{,}152 \text{ calorie for 12 gm of carbon.}$$

Bright red heat is necessary for carbon to react with the oxygen of water— a temperature nearing 955^0C.

The mixture of carbon monoxide and hydrogen produced by the decomposition of steam by red-hot carbon is called Water Gas. It is inflammable.

Another type of gas called Producer Gas is also produced by passing a regulated supply of air through a red-hot stack of hot coke and is used as fuel or for heating furnaces in iron and steel industry for its high calorific value. The hydrogan gas is principally a mixture of carbon monoxide, and nitrogen.

Temperature and heat

Temperature indicates how hot or cold a body is whereas heat is the energy that can be utilized to do a work and can always be transformed into another form of energy.

For measurement of temperature we generally use either the centigrade or the fahrenheit scale, though celsius, which is the name for the centigrade scale, is also used. In the centigrade scale the freezing point of water is taken as 0^0 and the boiling point of water as 100^0, whereas, in the Fahrenheit scale the freezing point is taken as 32^0 and the boiling point as 212^0. In other words, 100 divisions of the centigrade scale correspond to 180 divisions of the fahrenheit scale, which can be expressed as:

$$\frac{C}{100} = \frac{F-32}{180}$$

or

$$\frac{C}{5} = \frac{F-32}{9}$$

or

$$C = \frac{5}{9} \times (F-32).$$

Calorie and British Thermal Unit

For measurement of heat, there are two units, viz. the calorie and the British Thermal Unit, under the to C.G.S. and F.P.S. unit respectively. The unit of heat in SI units is joule. The quantity of heat required to raise the temperature of 1 gram of water through 1^0C is called a calorie; whereas the quantity of heat required to raise the temperature of 1 lb of water through 1^0F is called a British Thermal Unit (252 calories are equivalent to 1 B.Th.U.) It may be remembered that 1 calorie = 4.18 J and 1 B.Th.U = 1.055 kJ.

Specific heat and heat capacity

The heat required to raise the temperature of a body depends upon its specific heat which may be defined as the ratio of the quantity of heat required to raise the temperature of a given mass of a substance through a given range to the quantity of heat required to raise the temperature of an equal mass of water through the same range. In other words, the specific heat denotes the quantity of heat required to raise the temperature of one gram of substance through one degree centigrade. It is interesting to note that the specific heat of all other substances is less than that of water and some are very much lower. The specific heat of water is 1 whereas ice has a specific heat of 0.5 and steam has a specific heat of only 0.48. Organic substances such as petrol, alcohol etc. have low specific heat. This means that such substances, when exposed to a given quantity of heat, show a much greater rise of temperature than water – a factor of considerable importance to a fire officer from the point of view of fire propagation. The quantity of heat required to raise the temperature of a body through 1^0C, on the other hand, is the heat capacity of that body and it is the product of the mass of the body and its specific heat (i.e. $m \times s$).

The SI unit of heat capacity is the joule per degree centigrade (J/^{0}C). In the SI system, the specific heat capacity of a substance is measured in joules per kilogram per ^{0}C (J/kg per ^{0}C). Water has the maximum specific heat capacity, viz. 4200 J/kg (4.2 kJ/kg) per ^{0}C. This may also be seen from the chart below:

	Material	Specific heat capacity (J/kg per ^{0}C)
1.	Water	4200
2.	Iron	460
3.	Aluminium	900
4.	Copper	400
5.	Mercury	140
6.	Glass (ordinary)	670
7.	Ice	2100
8.	Earth, rock etc.	840
9.	Carbon tetrachloride	850
10.	Methylated spirit	2400
11.	Benzene	1720
12.	Glycerol	2560

Substances with low specific heat capacity heat up more rapidly in a fire situation than those of high specific heat capacity, and are of special importance in promoting fire risks.

Latent heat of fusion

Apart from specific heat, water in the form of ice has much higher latent heat of fusion and latent heat of vaporization than other common substances. It requires more energy to change ice to water and boiling water to steam than to change other substances like paraffin, wax etc. from their solid to liquid or liquid to vapour state.

If heat energy is removed from water by cooling, the molecules of water, which are capable of considerable mobility, become sluggish and at a certain temperature lose their freedom of movement as a liquid and freezes to a solid state called ice. Now, to melt this ice to water without changing the temperature, energy in the form of heat is required. This is called the latent heat of fusion of ice and equals 80 calorie per gram. Hence, 'Latent Heat of Fusion' of ice may be defined as the quantity of heat required to convert one gram of ice to water at 0^0C without any rise of temperature. It requires 336000 J to convert 1 kg of ice at 0^0C to water at the same temperature.

Latent heat of vaporization

To convert water at 100^0C to steam at 100^0C, it requires more heat energy than that required to convert ice at 0^0C to water at 0^0C. To make a liquid boil, it requires an almost complete loosening of the bonds linking the molecules together and hence a large addition of energy. The necessary energy—the latent heat of vaporization—amounts to 540 calorie per gram of water at the normal boiling point. Latent heat of vaporization may be defined as the number of units of heat required to change one gram of a liquid into vapour, at the boiling point, without raising its temperature.

Experiments show that 2260000J are required to convert one kilogram of water at its boiling point into steam at the same temperature and 860000J are required to convert 1 kg of alcohol into vapour at the same temperature. These are known as the latent heats of vaporization.

Boiling point of water and atmospheric pressure

It should be noted that freezing occurs at a fixed temperature and the latent heat of a substance is, therefore, constant. Vaporization, on the other hand, can occur at all temperatures up to the critical temperature, at which, the distinction between gas and liquid disappears. The boiling point is merely the temperature at which a liquid emits vapour at a pressure equal to the existing atmospheric pressure. If water is evaporated at 100^0C, 540 calorie of heat will be required per gram. It may be remembered that the amount of heat required to change boiling water to steam (the latent heat of vaporization) is 6 times the amount required to bring the same quantity of cold water, say at 10^0C, to boiling point at 100^0C. The amount of heat, on the other hand, required to bring 1 gm of water at 0^0C to 100^0C is equal to 100 calorie per gram, the specific heat of water being 1. It again absorbs 540 cal/gm in conversion to steam at the boiling point. Thus, water, on account of its high heat absorbing capacity in being converted to steam and for the ease of its availability, is considered as the ideal extinguishing medium for most of fires.

Effect of change of pressure on boiling point

Water boils at 100^0C when the external atmospheric pressure of 760 mm of mercury is 1.013 bar. If the external atmospheric pressure is raised, the boiling point is also raised, and if the external pressure is lowered, the boiling point is also lowered. The effect of raising the boiling point is to increase the quantity of heat required to raise the temperature of cold liquid to the new boiling point and to decrease the latent heat of vaporization.

Effect of heat

Heat being a form of energy, is liberated as a result of work. Heat and work are mutually convertible. The effects of heat on a body are the following:

i) Increase in size (length, area and volume); *ii*) Increase in pressure (with regard to gases); *iii*) Change of the body from one form to the other (i.e. from solid to liquid or from liquid to vapour); *iv*) Production of glow or change in colour of the substance involved; *v*) Generation of small electric current (thermo-electric effect) in some cases.

Coefficient of expansion

Bodies increase in length, area and volume due to heating effect. The increase in length per unit length for one degree rise in temperature is defined as the coefficient of linear expansion. The coefficient of linear expansion is used when dealing with solids and the coefficient of cubical expansion is used for liquids and gases. These coefficients are generally calculated with regard to the centigrade scale.

The amount of expansion can be expressed as original length × coefficient of linear expansion × rise in temperature. Thus a 20 ft beam of iron after a 1000^0C rise in temperature in a fire will increase its length by $20 \times 1000 \times 0.0000122 = 0.244$ ft $= 2.928$ inches or nearly 3 inches, which is likely to cause the collapse of a wall.

The formula for finding out the increased length is $l_t = l_0(1+\alpha t)$ where l_t denotes the increased length at t^0C, l_0 denotes the length at 0^0C, α = the coefficient of linear expansion, and t is the rise in temperature.

Expansion for nickel – iron alloy (Invar)

This is an alloy of iron containing 36% of nickel (i.e. 64% iron and 36% nickel) with a coefficient of linear expansion of 0.0000001 per ^{0}C, i.e. less than 1% of that of steel and is almost negligible in most cases. Invar is used for the manufacture of measuring rods and tapes.

Superficial and volumetric expansion

It was said earlier that the effect of heat is not to change the length only. It causes an increase in the area of the substance and also the volume. The relationship between the coefficients of linear, superficial and volumetric expansion of a substance may be shown as $\beta = 2\alpha$ and $\gamma = 3\alpha$, i.e. the coefficients of superficial and volumetric expansion are twice and thrice the coefficient of linear expansion, respectively. From this the increase in area and the increase in volume of a substance due to a rise in temperature can be calculated by multiplying the initial area of a substance by twice the coefficient of linear expansion of the substance and the rise in temperature, and the initial volume of the substance by thrice the coefficient of linear expansion of the substance and the rise in temperature, respectively.

Combustion and the points relating to it – triangle of combustion

Ordinary combustion is a chemical reaction between a fuel and oxygen in presence of heat. In other words, it may be stated that three things are essential for combustion which can be represented by the three arms of a triangle, viz. heat, combustible substance and the supporter of combustion or oxygen. A fire cannot take place in absence of any one of these three factors.

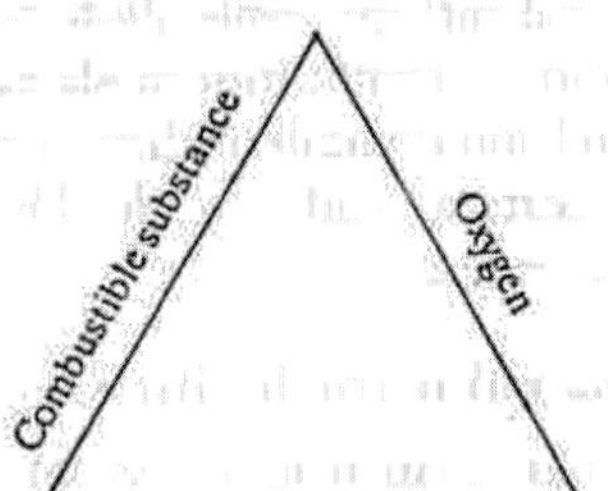

Fig.1 Triangle of combustion

In extinguishing a fire, all that is done is to break any of the arms of the 'Triangle of Combustion', i.e. heat may be removed and brought below the ignition point of the substance involved by pouring water (i.e. by cooling), or supply of oxygen to the fire may be stopped by smothering the fire by foam or dry sand (smothering), or the fire may be extinguished by removing the combustible substance from the scene of the fire (i.e. by isolation). Thus, whatever may be the equipment or the extinguishing media for fire-fighting, cooling, smothering and isolation or starvation are the three processes for fire extinction.

TETRAHEDRON OF FIRE

While the combustion process is extraordinarily complex and is the subject of much research, sufficient information has been gained to make it possible to visualize it with slight difference.

In a fire there are two different phases in which combustion proceeds, viz. the surface combustion mode and the flaming mode. The surface combustion mode incorporates the three essential elements of fire as represented by the triangle of combustion, viz. heat, oxygen and combustible substance. The flaming mode, on the other hand, incorporates four basic requirements, viz. heat, oxygen, combustible substance and in addition, another factor called the uninhibited chain reaction of combustion process. This is called the tetrahedron of combustion.

These two modes may occur either singly or in combination. Flammable liquids or gases burn in the flaming mode only. Examples in which both the modes exist are solid carbonaceous fuels such as coal, wood, vegetable fibres etc. With these materials, the early stages of combustion start with the flaming mode with a gradual transition towards the surface combustion mode, during which both the modes are simultaneously in action. Ultimately, the flaming mode is terminated with the residual surface combustion mode existing alone. Examples in which the surface combustion mode exists alone are fires involving pure carbon and other readily oxidizable non-metals such as sulphur, phosphorus and certain readily oxidizable metals like magnesium, aluminium, uranium etc.

Flash point and ignition temperature

Thus, apart from the supply of oxygen, the combustible substance has to be raised to the ignition temperature for the fire to occur. The notion of flash point and ignition temperature is important to every fire officer.

The flash point of an inflammable substance may be defined as the lowest temperature at which it gives off sufficient vapour so as to form a momentary flash with air on application of a small flame in the prescribed manner in the flash point apparatus. The ignition temperature of a substance is the temperature at which spontaneous ignition can take place. The self-ignition point (sometimes called the auto-ignition point or the combustion point) also refers to the temperature at which a substance must reach before it will ignite in the absence of a flame. Different substances have different flash points and auto-ignition temperatures, a range of which appear in the appendix.

Fire point

The lowest temperature at which the heat from combustion of a burning vapour is capable of producing sufficient vapour to enable combustion to continue is known as fire point. It is generally above the flash point.

Spontaneous combustion – overheating due to absorption of oxygen

Spontaneous combustion occurs as a result of the heat generated by the reacting substances themselves, e.g. when hot glycerine is poured on to crystals of potassium permanganate, the substances soon begin to fume and afterwards they burst into flame. Apart from this, the absorption of oxygen by certain vegetable oils, such as by unboiled linseed oil soaked in cotton, or by certain animal oils and fats, as also the 'absorption' of oxygen by certain substances, e.g. pyrites present in coal, may lead to such an increase in temperature as to bring forth spontaneous ignition. Apart from what has been stated above, there are many other chemical reactions which produce:

i) heat and light and which come under the definition of combustion though oxygen does not take part in these reactions, e.g. burning of powdered metals like iron, magnesium, aluminium, or hydrogen in an atmosphere of chlorine gas.

ii) combustion (without heat and light) – oxidation or rusting of iron is accompanied without rise in temperature and without a flame.

iii) combustion (without heat) – moist yellow phosphorus emits a bluish glow of light without evolution of much heat. This is known as Phosphorescence.

Types of combustion

According to its nature, combustion may be classified as follows:

i) Slow or incipient combustion – one in which the amount of heat and light emitted is feeble.

ii) Rapid or active combustion — one in which a considerable amount of heat and light are emitted within a short time.

iii) Deflagration — a case of combustion which takes place with considerable rapidity evolving heat and light.

iv) Explosion — a very rapid combustion accompanied by a loud report within an extremely short time, with generation of very high pressure and temperature.

Specific surface and rate of combustion

Generally, combustion starts at the surface during the first phase of the fire between the combustible substance and the supporter of combustion. After the fire is initially started at the surface, it goes deeper and deeper inside till it engulfs the entire substance. This is specially true of chemicals on fire. For ordinary combustible things like wood, a protective covering of charcoal is formed outside, safeguarding the inside cover. The more the area exposed the greater is the hazard. In other words, it can be said that the rate of combustion, among other things, depends on the specific surface of the substance. Specific surface denotes the area of a substance in terms of square centimetres for each gram of it. It does not denote the weight or the mass of the substance but it is the area per unit weight of the body only. Due to their large specific surface, substances like paper, dry straw, or grass are more susceptible to quick spread of fire than ordinary wood, coal etc.

Spread of fire

Apart from specific area, the spread of fire also depends on certain physical and chemical characteristics of the substance. Of these characteristics, the amount of heat generated or given off by the burning substance, the ability of the substance to conduct heat away, and the heat generated during combustion are the important points for consideration. The main factors on which the spread of a fire would depend are:

i) the area of the substance exposed;

ii) the amount of heat generated or given off by the burning substance;

iii) the ability of the substance to conduct the heat away from the zone of combustion;

iv) the atmospheric humidity and the wind velocity.

Effects of humidity, temperature and atmospheric pressure on combustion

Atmospheric humidity plays a major part in combustion in moisture absorptive materials such as wood and paper but it has no effect on the combustion of substances like celluloid, gasoline etc. However, in carbonaceous substances like green vegetable matter, cotton, wood etc., the greater the amount of moisture content in such fuels, the greater will be the amount of heat that goes into evaporating and driving off the water, and as such, it is more difficult to raise the temperature to the ignition point in such substances.

Temperature is also important in accelerating the spread of combustion which, like other chemical reactions, proceeds much more rapidly at high temperature. Fires generally start at a slow speed first, but gradually as the temperature rises, the rate of burning is accelerated, creating still higher temperatures and the fire burns progressively faster. In spite of this, there is a practical limit to the temperature produced in fires due to the heat being dissipated away by radiation which increases as the fourth power of absolute temperature. A greater portion of the heat produced goes into heating up the nitrogen in the air and other inert materials in fire area and there is a theoretical limit to the maximum generation of temperature. The temperature in fires may range between 1650^0C and 2760^0C, but it seldom goes above 1650^0C (approx).

Atmospheric pressure at elevations of over 3048m is so much less than the normal pressure that it affects the combustion of ordinary materials which becomes slower than that at sea level and as the air pressure is further decreased, a point is eventually reached when combustion may not occur. On the contrary, where air pressures are increased above normal, as in underwater tunnel digging, combustion is greatly accelerated.

The velocity of air also has an important effect in combustion. An increase in air velocity brings oxygen to the surface more rapidly and accelerates combustion. Moving air also produces a cooling effect. An excess flow of air may therefore cool the burning substance in such a way that the fire may not continue.

Surface spread of flame

According to spread of flame over the surface of different materials as per prescribed test for this purpose, there are four classifications:

Class I : Surface of very low flame spread— refers to surfaces on which not more than 19 cm spread of flame occurs.

Class II : Surface of low flame spread— refers to those surfaces on which during the first 1.5 minutes of test, the spread of flame is not more than 30 cm and no matter how long the heat source is applied, it does not exceed 60 cm.

Class III: Surfaces of medium flame spread— refers to those surfaces on which during the first 1.5 minutes of test, the spread of flame is not more than 30 cm and during the first 10 minutes of test, the spread of flame is not more than 83 cm though it may spread further after 10 minutes.

Class IV: Surfaces of rapid flame spread — those surfaces on which during the first 1.5 minutes of test, the spread of flame is more than 12 cm, or during the first 10 minutes of test is more than 83 cm.

MODE OF TEST

The material under test is placed on a vertical plane, i.e. at right angles to a radiating surface and is subjected to flame as well as radiant heat which is high at one end of the specimen under test and is progressively reduced along its length. Specimens under test are of standard dimensions and are tested on both surfaces.

Ignition temperature of the gases

Flammable gases, as are commonly used in industries, have ignition temperatures generally below 700^{0}C. They can be ignited by naked flames having temperatures as high as 1100^{0}C by incandescent bodies or by sparks glowing at temperatures above dull red heat (700^{0}C app.). Gases, with ignition temperatures below 500^{0}C can be ignited by surfaces at black heat. The ignition temperature of acetylene is 335^{0}C, butane is 428^{0}C, and propane is 466^{0}C. Town gas (mostly coal gas) used for heating or lighting has of course slightly higher ignition temperature, viz. in the vicinity of 538^{0}C. The relative fire hazards may be appreciated from the above.

Tinder, kindling and bulk fuel

On the basis of specific surface and fire susceptibility, all combustible solids may be classified under three categories as (*i*) tinder, (*ii*) kindling and (*iii*) bulk fuel. Tinder may be defined as material which can be ignited by an ordinary lighted match. Materials such as wood, cardboard, paper, textiles etc. may be classed as tinder, provided they have a specific surface of not less than 20 sq. cm/gm. Dusts may have a specific surface greater than 1000 sq. cm/gm so that in the case of combustible dusts, it is not surprising that, when mixed with air in the correct proportion, they are able to experience oxidation at rates so rapid as to constitute explosion. Thus for a combustible solid to be classified as tinder, it should have a specific surface of 20 sq. cm or above. Kindling can be a substance having specific surface between 2 to 20 sq. cm/gm and bulk fuel may be a substance having specific surface between 0.04 to 2 sq. cm/gm of the substance.

Fire resistance

From the point of view of the spread of fire, it is important for a fire officer to know the fire resistance of individual materials and elements of structures.

The term fire resistance denotes the capacity of an element to withstand heating of specified severity, while performing its normal functions, thus restricting the spread of fire in a building for a definite time. In other words, it gives the length of timeduring which a construction offers resistance to a standard fire. The basis for the standard fire is the time–temperature curve, which is accepted internationally.

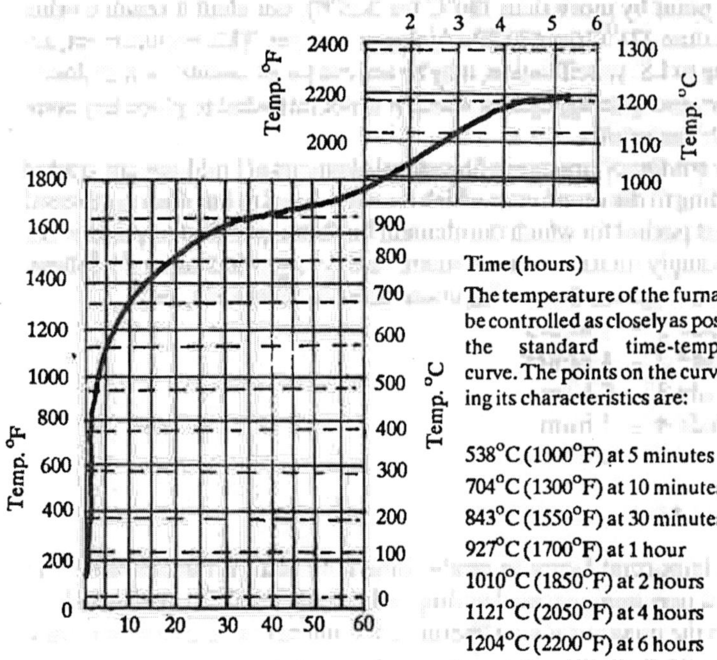

The temperature of the furnace shall be controlled as closely as possible to the standard time-temperature curve. The points on the curve defining its characteristics are:

538°C (1000°F) at 5 minutes
704°C (1300°F) at 10 minutes
843°C (1550°F) at 30 minutes
927°C (1700°F) at 1 hour
1010°C (1850°F) at 2 hours
1121°C (2050°F) at 4 hours
1204°C (2200°F) at 6 hours

Fig.2 Time–temperature curve

A graphical representation of the time–temperature curve has been reproduced in Fig. 2. The curve has resulted from observations from a series of fires as well as from measurements at test fires.

FACTORS FOR DETERMINING FIRE RESISTANCE

The factors for determining the fire resistance of a structural element as a result of the tests will depend upon the first critical point, denoting failure of the specimen to act as a barrier to the spread of fire, viz.

(*i*) collapse of the structure by excessive deflection;

(*ii*) occurrence of cracks or other openings through which flames or hot gases might pass;

(*iii*) a rise in temperature at the non-heated surface of the structure such as flammable materials present which could set fire or smoulder.

The I.S. Specification 1641-1960 Code of practice for fire safety in buildings clarifies the aforesaid paragraph under (*iii*) by stating that the average temperature of the non-heated surface shall not increase by more than 139°C (250°F) above the initial temperature and that the temperature of the unexposed face (i.e. non-heated) shall not increase at any point by more than 180°C (or 325°F), nor shall it reach a value higher than 221°C (or 430°F) whichever is lesser. This requirement, according to I.S. specification, may be waived for elements such as doors, shutters and glazing, against which it is not intended to place any combustible materials.

Fire grading of structures: Structural elements of buildings are graded according to the time factor which is nearly equal to but does not exceed the test period for which the element fulfils its specified requirements. Accordingly, all structural elements have been graded under the following five categories depending upon their fire resistance, viz.

Grade 1 – 6 hours
Grade 2 – 4 hours
Grade 3 – 2 hours
Grade 4 – 1 hour
Grade 5 – 0.5 hour.

Fire load

An important factor in establishing the basis for the assessment of fire risk pertaining to any building is the concept of 'fireload' which indicates the quantity of heat liberated per unit of floor area when a building and its contents are completely burnt. All occupancies/buildings etc. can be graded according to their fire hazard and to be provided for with suitable fire precautions on the basis of the fire load. Hence, grading of building according to both fire load and fire resistance can be made. The formula for calculating fire load is stated below:

$$\text{Fire load (kcal/m}^2\text{)} = \frac{\text{combustibles in k} \times \text{calorific value in kcal/k}}{\text{oor area in square metre}}$$

The calculation of fire load is the basis for determining the classification of occupancies for fire grading of buildings.

Classification of occupancies

The Fire Offices Committee (U.K.), in its report of fire grading of building in 1946, has recognized three main classes of occupancies on the basis of fire load. This conforms to the relevant I.S. specification also and may be stated as:

i) Occupancies of low fire load: such as ordinary buildings for residential purpose, hotels, offices, schools etc, or occupancies having fire load not exceeding 2,75,000 kcal/m^2 of net floor area of any compartment, nor exceeding an average of 550,000 kcal/m^2 on limited isolated area. (For reference, maximum for this type in F.P.S. system is 1,00,000 B.Th.U./sq.ft).

The fire resistance required by building of this category to withstand the complete burn-out of their contents without collapse is one hour as has been found after tests. Extensive investigations carried out in Switzerland and Germany have shown that the fire load in offices varies from 10kg to 30kg/m^2 equivalent to 43,356 to 130,068 kcal/m^2 whereas this type of occupancy has one hour rating with a maximum fire loading upto 270,978 kcal/m^2 equivalent to 60kg/sq. m.

ii) Occupancies of moderate fire load: such as retail shops, bazars, stalls, factories, etc. Here the fire load exceeds 2,75,000 kcal/m^2, and is upto 550,000 kcal/m^2. This is equivalent to the fire load of 275,000 kcal/m^2, not exceeding an average of 1,100,000 kcal/m^2 on limited isolated area as per relevant I.S specification. Occupancies of this type should have a fire resistance of 2 hours.

iii) Occupancies of high fire load: godowns, warehouses, etc. This category as per I.S. specification exceeds the fire load by 550,000 kcal/m^2, but does not exceed an average of 1,100,000 kcal/m^2 of floor area. A fire resistance of 4 hours for these types of occupancies is considered sufficient.

During a fire, heat is liberated and this heat raises the temperature of the adjoining structure or of the materials stored nearby. Heat is transmitted from one body to the other (which is comparatively colder)to raise the body to a higher temperature, which might finally result in ignition due to the gradual rise in temperature from the source of heat. (The maximum for this type in F.P.S. system is 4,00,000 B.Th.U/sq.ft, exceeding an average of 2,00,000 B.Th.U./ sq. ft).

Transmission of heat

Heat is transmitted by three processes, viz. (*i*) conduction, (*ii*) convection, and (*iii*) radiation.

CONDUCTION

If an iron bar is heated at one end, the other end will gradually become hot. What happens here is that heat travels from particle to particle in the direction of decreasing temperature, till it reaches the other end. In this process, the particles do not change their position. They convey the heat from the hot region to the cold region. According to the kinetic theory of matter, the molecules of a substance are supposed to be oscillating and the motion becomes more vigorous as the temperature rises. Owing to oscillations, the molecules at the hot end share their energy with their slower moving neighbour and these in turn carry energy to the next layer, and thus a rise of temperature travels down the bar, although the molecules themselves do not move from their mean position. Transmission of heat by this process takes place only in solids and it is called conduction. Thus, by conduction heat passes from the hotter to the colder parts of a body or from one hot body to a colder body in contact with it without transference of any material particles.

Thermal conductivity

Substances which allow heat to be conducted have different rates of thermal conductivity which is defined as the *quantity of heat that flows through a slab of the material of unit thickness, unit cross section, in unit time (i.e. 1 second) when the difference of temperature between two faces is* 1^0*C.* The conductivity of iron is 0.14 calorie per cm per second per degree centigrade. It means that if the temperature of two faces of a cube of iron of 1 cm in each dimension differs by 1^0C, then in one second 0.14 calorie of heat will pass from the hot face to the cold face. Thermal conductivity of glass is 0.0025 and that of aluminium is 0.5.

There are many cases of spread of fire from one room to the other due to conductivity of heat through steel girders or walls. The thermal conductivity is expressed as:

$$Q = K \frac{A(\theta_2 - \theta_1)t}{d}$$

where Q = the total quantity of heat passing through a cube; A = the area of any face; $(\theta_1 - \theta_2)$ = the difference of temperature between the two faces; d = the thickness of the cube. The following example will be useful.

Example : Find the difference in temperature between the two sides of a boiler plate 20 mm thick having thermal conductivity 0.2 C.G.S. units, when transmitting heat at the rate of 600 kcal per square metre per minute.

600 kcal = 600 × 1000 cal and one square metre = 10,000 sq. cm. Also one minute = 60 seconds; 20 mm = 2 cm

Now substituting the values in formula

$$Q = K \frac{A(\theta_2 - \theta_1)t}{d}$$

we have,

$$600 \times 10 \quad \frac{0.2 \times 10000(\theta_2 - \theta_1) \times 60}{2}$$

$$(\theta_2 - \theta_1) \; \frac{600 \times 1000 \times 2}{0.2 \times 10000 \times 60} = 10^0\,C$$

CONVECTION

In this process the heated particles go up and move in the air or the liquid in a cycle called convection current, carrying their heat with them from a hotter to a colder place and by frequent collisions with the colder particles; the rise in temperature is diffused throughout the whole mass. Convection currents can occur only in liquids and gases.

The air over any hot surface has its temperature raised and consequently expands, becoming less dense than the surrounding air; it rises above, carrying its heat energy with it and its place is taken by the surrounding colder and heavier air from the sides. A process such as this is called convection. Here the heat is transmitted by the movement of the heated particles themselves.

Heat is thus transmitted by convection when particles of a material conveying the heat are carried from one point to the other from a hotter to a colder place. In a fire, convection currents can convey hot gases produced by combustion upwards through stairwells or open lift shafts, thereby spreading fire to the upper parts of a building.

RADIATION

In conduction and convection heat is propagated through the intervention of particles of matter. In radiation, heat travels through space from which all matter might be removed. There is no necessity of any material medium unlike the other two processes for transmission of heat. Radiated heat does not heat the intervening medium through which it passes.

The sun's rays pass through the air without appreciably heating it. If they are allowed to fall on the bulb of a thermometer, the temperature as indicated by a thermometer rises. If the bulb be covered by lamp black, the rise of temperature is greater than if the bulb is of clear glass. Radiated energy reaching the thermometer from the sun has travelled through the air without having increased its temperature in the form of waves and has been transferred into heat on reaching the thermometer bulb. Thermal radiation can also pass through vacuum.

Heat, in this case, travels in straight lines and is known as radiant energy and the process of its transference is called radiation. Radiant heat can be reflected, refracted or polarized and it obeys the laws of light. The amount of heat radiated from a given source varies as the fourth power of the absolute temperature of the source, other conditions being unchanged. In radiation, heat is transmitted through wave motion and it travels in straight lines while in conduction and convection heat travels in any path. Radiation of a particular wavelength is absorbed and others transmitted through material substances.

There are some substances through which radiant energy passes unchanged in amount. In the case of other substances, some or all of the radiant energy is transformed into heat. Such substances are said to absorb the radiation they receive and their temperature is raised by this absorption. Heat energy is thus transmitted by radiation when it passes from one point to another without raising the temperature of the medium through which it travels.

The amount of heat radiated from a fire increases considerably with a rise in temperature of the fire but its intensity at a surface decreases the further the surface is from the fire. A waterspray absorbs heat and can therefore be used to protect property from radiant heat and the consequent ignition and also for the protection of the personnel engaged in fire-fighting.

Newton's law of cooling : *The rate of loss of heat by a body is proportional to the difference between the temperature of the body and its surroundings.*

Emissive power

The rate at which a body loses heat by radiation may depend (*i*) on the nature of the surface; (*ii*) on the temperature of the body and its surroundings; and (*iii*) on the material of which the body is composed of.

When heat radiation passing through air falls on a surface, some of the heat waves may merely be turned back or reflected. This is specially the case when the surface is bright. A good reflector is therefore a bad absorber. But reflection takes place equally when the waves are travelling from the interior of the substance towards the air. Hence, if the surface is a good reflector, most of the heat is returned to the interior. Thus good reflectors emit very little radiation.

A substance which absorbs all the radiation falling upon it is called a perfectly black body. The ratio of the quantity of radiation emitted per second by a square centimetre of a surface to the quantity emitted by a square centimetre of a perfectly black body under similar conditions is called the emissive power of the surface.

Thermal conductivity and ignition temperature

Ignition of a combustible material occurs only when there is sufficient temperature and sufficient heat present to initiate the reaction. Fire cannot continue if the heat produced is carried away faster than its production, as in that case the substance will very soon go down below its ignition temperature and a substance can lose heat only by the three processes, viz. (*i*) conduction; (*ii*) convection and (*iii*) radiation.

Substances which easily and readily conduct heat are called good conductors, e.g. metals, wheareas substances which do not do so are called bad conductors, e.g. glass, wood, gas. On the other hand, substances which do not allow heat to pass are called insulators, e.g. mica. The amount of heat transferred in solids depends mostly upon their thermal conductivity.

The transmission of heat, on the other hand, cannot be completely stopped by any heat-insulating material which has low heat conductivity. If the rate of heat conductivity through the insulating material is greater than its rate of dissipation, the temperature of the combustible material may increase to the point of ignition. Fires have actually taken place in the wooden joists, underneath defective types of hearth, and in old buildings. It has also been found that fires had occurred by transmission of heat over a long period, through as much as a 0.6m thick solid concrete.

Principle of measurement of heat

Heat flows from a body at higher temperature to the one at lower temperature till the two bodies attain the same temperature. In this process the heat lost by a hot body is the heat gained by the cooler body, till finally both the bodies attain the same temperature. Heat lost or gained by body = mass of the body × specific heat of the body × difference of temparature $= m \times s \times t$. The specific heat is the thermal capacity per unit mass $= s$, when m is unity and the rise in temperature is only one degree centigrade.

Sufficient heat to cause ignition may be produced from a number of sources, either chemical, electrical or mechanical. Compression of a gas produces heat but the actual combustion or occurrence of a fire depends on the factors stated before.

Ignition by radiation

Many cellulose materials such as those made of wood, paper and many textiles liberate combustible gases when they are heated to 70^0 to 80^0C. The combustible gases will ignite spontaneously at about 480^0C even when no ignition source is present. In laboratory test, intensities of heat necessary to permit ignition by a pilot flame or to cause spontaneous ignition have been measured. The intensities are expressed in terms of the number of calorie per sq. cm/second falling on the surface of the specimen. Wood of any variety requires a minimum intensity of 0.3 cal/cm^2/second for pilot flame and 0.8 cal/cm^2/sec for spontaneous ignition. These intensities correspond respecitvely to about eighteen and forty times that of summer sun at latitude 52^0. Fibre insulating board, a frequently used board and valuable building material, may ignite in the presence of a pilot flame when it receives only 0.15 cal/cm^2/sec.

In cases of wood, paper and other cellulose materials, the duration of exposure for the ignition to occur can be calculated for any given intensity of heat when the density, specifice heat and thermal conductivity of the material are known. Spontaneous ignition of wood, paper or cotton, when exposed to a heat intensity above 0.3 cal/cm^2/second, may take place within 2 minutes.

Intensity of radiation

The intensity of radiation, I, is related to absolute temperature, T, according to the well known law, viz, $I = \sigma T^4$, where σ is the Stefen-Boltzman constant = 5.7×10^{-5}erg/cm^2/sec.

Thus the amount of heat radiated per second per unit area is directly proportional to the fourth power of the absolute temperature. The temperature of a burning copartment will obviously have an important effect on the heat radiated since this depends on a fourth-power relation.

Effect of ventilation on fires

The temperature of the fire depends on the rate of burning and fires may be considered as divided into two types:

(*i*) those in which the ventilation is restricted and the rate of burning depends on the size of the window, and

(ii) those in which the window area is comparable with the floor area, where the rate of burning depends on the fire load, its surface area and arrangement, and not on the window area. Such fires may be said to be fully ventilated.

It can be shown that for practical purposes the effect of ventilation on the rate of burning in the two types may be disregarded and that for both the types, the radiating intensity tends to an upper limit of 4 cal cm^{-2} sec^{-1} and the intensity is reduced if the fire load is small.

TYPE 1: FIRES WITH RESTRICTED VENTILATION

The maximum temperature reached in a compartment on fire is a function of $A\sqrt{H}$, where A is the area of the single window opening and H is the height of the window. $A\sqrt{H}$ is the important parameter affecting the rate of burning irrespective of compartment size.

The temperatures attained increase with ventilation, the results tending to a limiting value of less than 1100^0C which corresponds to a theoretical maximum radiating level of 4 cal cm^{-2} s^{-1} and can be taken as the maximum intensity for this type of fire. For most buildings, a fire may always be capable of reaching temperatures of 1100^0C.

There are two conditions where the temperatures are significantly less than 1100^0C.

(*i*) compartments with $A\sqrt{H}$ less than $5m^{5/2}$,

(*ii*) compartments with a small fire-load, i.e. where the fire load/unit floor area is 25 kg/m^2 or less, the fire does not last long enough for the compartment itself to become sufficiently hot and the radiating intensity is significantly less than 4 cal cm^{-2} sec^{-1}

TYPE 2: FULLY VENTILATED FIRES

When the window is comparable with or larger than the floor area, the fires burn at a rate which is largely independent of $A\sqrt{H}$ and the intensity emitted for a given size of compartmer' is found experimentally to be related to the rate of burning. The intensity of radiation gives a better correlation with the rate of burning per unit window area than the rate of burning per unit floor area, and the rate of burning in fully ventilated fires is approximately related to the amount of fuel.

For cubical compartments with large windows, the intensity of radiation is 2 cal $cm^{-2}sec^{-1}$ for a fire-load per unit floor area of about 25 kg/m^2 and this has been taken as the secondary standard, lower than the primary standard of 4 cal cm^{-2} sec^{-1}. Fires with less than 25 kg/m^2 fire-load per unit floor area would give temperatures less than the approximate value of 800^0C, which corresponds to an intensity of radiation of 2 cal cm^{-2} sec^{-1}.

Hence, for the purpose of devising regulations for fire-break or space separation, the intensity of radiation of 4 cal cm^{-2} sec^{-1} is taken as the normal standard, and 2 cal cm^{-2} sec^{-1} for fire-loads per unit floor area of less than 25 kg/m^2 is considered as the secondary standard.

Range of flammability and flash point

In the case of flammable vapours, there is a minimum and a maximum concentration of vapour in air, below or above which propagation of flame does not occur. These limiting mixtures of vapour with air are known as the lower and higher limits of flammability and are usually expressed in terms of percentage by volume of vapour and air. Within the limits of flammability lies a narrow range, confined by the explosive limits, which mark the minimum and maximum concentration of vapour in air for the propagation of flame with a speed and violence sufficient to constitute explosion. The concentration at which a gas or vapour may be explosive is in most cases, and roughly, the mean of its upper and lower explosive limits, i.e. at the concentration at which an oxygen balance is achieved for complete combustion. It is interesting to consider mixtures of petrol vapour with air as examples of the significance of these ranges.

If petrol vapour is less than 1% (app.) when mixed with air, the mixture cannot be ignited, for it is too lean. Petrol vapure between 1 and 1.75% (app.) mixed with air can be ignited and flame will pass through it with a whooshing noise, which becomes louder the richer the mixture in petrol vapour is.

Between 1.75 to 3% of petrol vapour mixed with air, the mixture will propagate flame so rapidly that a noise equivalent to a bang or detonation results, the detonation being loudest and with the most destructive effect at about 2.25% of petrol vapour in air.

Between 3 to 6% (app.) of petrol vapour mixed with air, the mixture can be ignited and enflames with a whooshing noise, which becomes less audible the greater the percentage of flammable vapour is. Over 6% of petrol vapour mixed with air cannot be ignited, as it is too rich and, so, incombustible.

Since a flammable vapour–air mixture will not propagate flame until the lower limit of flammability has been attained, it follows that in effect the flash point of a substance does not only represent the temperature at which that substance first evolves flammable vapour in sufficient quantities to support and propagate flame, but also it coincides with the lower limit of range of the flammability.

It may also be stated that a liquid which burns not only presents an explosion hazard at temperatures above its flash point, but is a fire hazard at temperatures above the flash point. It, therefore, follows that there is no risk of a vapour fire or explosion provided that the liquid is stored at a temperatures below its flash point.

Successive explosions

An explosion of a flammable gas or vapour in a vessel does not result in complete combustion and the vessel thereafter does not become safe contrary to the common belief.

A vessel containing a gas or vapour can suffer successsive explosions without addition of fresh gas, if the first explosion occures with a gas concentration close to the upper explosion limit. All the gases, it may by noted, are not necessarily burnt in the first explosion; what remains can often be in concentration above the lower explosive limit, i.e. within the explosive range.

Dust explosion

Combustible dusts, if finely divided and when suspended in air in suitable concentration, consisting of particles below 0.3 mm in diameter, behave like flammable vapour– air mixture and are liable to explode even by a spark.

Almost all combustible dusts, including dusts of many metals in a state of fine sub-division, when mixed with air in a proper proportion, can be ignited to cause violent explosion. Dust suspended in air is far more dangerous than settled dust.

LOWER RANGE OF FLAMMABILITY

The force of the explosion depends on, among other things, the density of the dust cloud. Usually the lowest concentration of dust which will allow an explosion to propagate is around 20 to 40 gm/m^3.

PRESSURE GENERATED

The pressure generated in dust explosions is of the order of 690 kN/m^2 and as a brick wall can only withstand 3.5 kN/m^2, it is quite likely that even a massive brick wall be completely disintegrated by dust explosions.

One of the most distinctive aspects of dust explosion is that a small primary explosion can produce pressure waves which, by dispersing settled layers of dust into the air, spread secondary explosions through a whole factory.

CAUSES

Dust explosions most commonly occur in grinding and pulverizing mills and in cyclones. Dusts are formed and collected in the grinding or pulverizing process by the accidental inclusion of foreign bodies or particles of steel or stone, resulting in heat or sparks. Most of the flammable dusts are, however, ignited by spark energy much less than 50 milli joules, and in the case of zirconium dust, only 5 milli joules are required.

PREVENTION

Apart from taking steps for prevention of foreign materials from entering grinding mills by magnetic or gravity separation, and prevention of build-up of electrostatic charges by proper earthing, the following provisions are important from safety point of view:

(*i*) Inhibiting ignition of dusts by inerting the atmosphere near about the source of release of dust with carbon dioxide or nitrogen gas.

(*ii*) Good housekeeping and cleanliness to prevent accumulation or deposition of dusts.

(*iii*) Limiting the effects of explosion by segregation of the hazardous processes and by provision of auxiliary ducting and explosion vents in the plants on an average of 0.09 m^2 for every 0.57 m^3 of plant for carbonaceous dusts and 0.28 m^3 for metal dusts.

B. Product of Flame and its Characteristics

A flame is a zone in which chemical reaction takes place between gases with the evolution of heat and light accompanied by vigorous combustion. The characteristic of flame, its size, its changing shape, and its colour give an idea of the nature of the combustibles and the temperature produced.

A solid substance which does not evolve gaseous flammable products, when heated, does not exhibit flame while burning. Thus, when carbon burns, the combustion takes place on a reacting surface which glows; while in the case of a gas, not only a much larger surface is in contact with the oxygen of the air, but also the union between the combustible and the supporter of combustion takes place over a larger area.

Flames may be divided into two classes: (*i*) luminous flame, producing heat and light, e.g. the flame of a burning oil, an oil lamp, a candle, and (*ii*) non-luminous flame, producing heat and very little light, e.g. burning hydrogen or burning carbon monoxide.

Again, since gases must be present in order that flame may be produced, burning solids, such as iron, charcoal etc., although emit both heat and light, emit no flame.

Flames vary in structure according to (*a*) the nature of the combustibles and (*b*) conditions under which combustion takes place. Flames may be studied as follows:

Zones of combustion

1. Two-zone structure: The flame produced by burning hydrogen or carbon monoxide is very simple. It consists of only two zones or mantles, one surrounding the other. The inner zone consists of unburnt gas, and in the outer zone a single chemical reaction takes place due to combustion, with the evolution of heat and light.

2. Three-zone structure: The flame of ammonia (NH_3) burning in oxygen consists of three zones—an inner zone of unburnt gas, surrounded by a second yellow zone in which ammonia decomposes into its elements, and the outer-most pale greenish-yellow zone where hydrogen is burnt and converted into H_2O (water). Flames of hydrogen sulphide vapour and cyanogen have similar structures.

3. Four-zone structure: Hydrocarbon flames—these flames are more complicated and have four zones. The candle flame or the coal gas flame are the common examples.

The candle flame or the coal gas flame is found to consist of the following four zones as shown in Fig. 3.

(*i*) The dark blue zone 'd' of unburnt and partly decomposed gases or vapours surrounding the wick or issuing out of the burner jet—the zone of no combustion, with the smallest amount of heat as compared to the heat in the other zones (temperature range 300^0-350^0C).

(*ii*) The next region is a bright bluish-green zone 'c' of partially unburnt gas. The gases from the lower zone are partially decomposed and oxidized forming free carbon, carbon monoxide, carbon dioxide, hydrogen, and water vapour (temperature range 500^0-1540^0C).

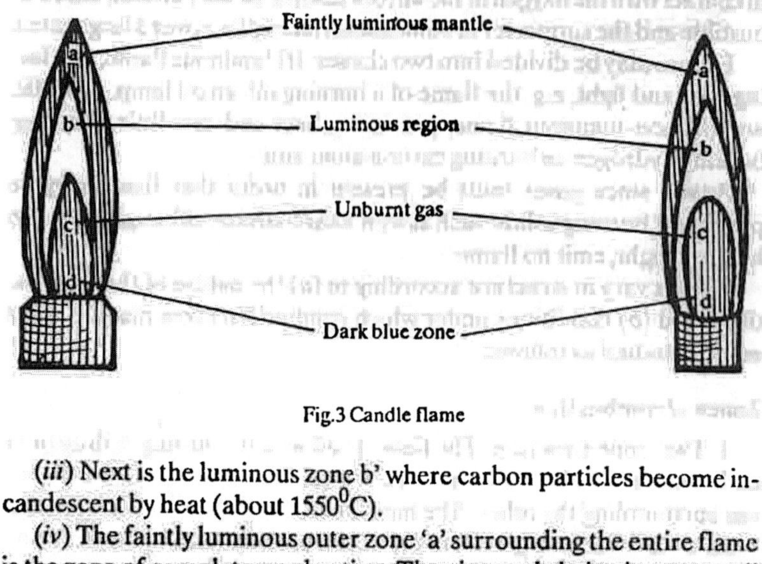

Fig.3 Candle flame

(*iii*) Next is the luminous zone b' where carbon particles become incandescent by heat (about 1550^0C).

(*iv*) The faintly luminous outer zone 'a' surrounding the entire flame is the zone of complete combustion. The air supply being in excess, all CO, H_2 and free carbon from lower zones are completely oxidized, producing the maximum amount of heat. Hence, this outermost zone is the hottest part of the flame (temparature range 1500^0 to 1570^0C).

Causes of luminosity of flame

Luminosity of flame is due to highly heated incandescent particles of carbon which separate by the decomposition of the combustible matter. It is also due to the following:

(*a*) The temperature of the flame gases: Luminosity increases by heating the interacting gases, while it decreases by cooling the gas mixture.

(*b*) The density of the flame gases : It increases with the increase of pressure (i.e. density of gases) and decreases with a decrease of pressure.

(*c*) The presence of solid particle in the flame. Flames containing solid particles are brighter.

Non-luminous flames

Many gases produce luminous or non-luminous flames during their burning. The following may be noted:

Hydrogen or carbon monoxide – faint blue.

Methane and ammonia – faint yellow.

Hydrogen sulphide – blue as in burning sulphur.

The vapours of certain volatile liquids like carbon disulphide and alcohol burn with flames which are only slightly luminous, while in the flames of ether and acetone, there being comparatively little separation of carbon, giving no soot, the flame is generally bluish and non-luminous.

Flame colour of some of the metals whileburning in air

Metal	Colour of flame
Calcium (silver-white metal, density 1.53, melts at 842 – 8^{0}C	Burns with a brick red flame
Aluminium (specific gravity 2.7, melts at 660^{0}C)	Burns with a brilliant white flame, producing a white deposit of aluminium oxide Al_2O_3
Sodium (soft silver-white metal, density 0.97, melts at 97^{0}C)	Burns with a brilliant golden-yellow flame
Potassium (more hazardous than sodium, melts at 62^{0}C, density 0.86)	Burns readily in air with a lilac flame
Magnesium (silver-white metal, specific gravity 1.74, melts at 651^{0}C)	Burns with a dazzling white light (rich in actinic rays) forming light powder of magnesium oxide (MgO) and mixed with magnesium nitride (Mg_3N_2)
Zinc (Bluish-white metal, specific gravity 7.14, melts at 419.4^{0}C)	Burns in air (when strongly heated) with a greenish-blue flame, producing clouds of white zinc oxide (ZnO).

Metal	Colour of flame
Barium (silver-white soft metal, specific gravity 3.5, melt at 850^{0}C)	Bottle green
Copper (redmetal, specific gravity 8.95, malleable and ductile, melts at 1085^{0}C)	Dark green
Strontium (reactive metalresembling purple red, specific gravity 2.6, melts at 757^{0}C	Purple red

Flame temperature

Appearance of flame	Temperature in ^{0}C
First visible red	535
Dull red	700
Cherry red	900
Dull orange	1100
Orange-yellow	1200
White	1300
Bright white	1400
Dazzling white	1500

C. Practical Application of Thermal Expansion

THERMOSTATS

If two strips of different metals are fastened together length-wise, thereby preventing them from moving independently, a change in temperature will cause distortion in shape, resulting in a curve, with the formation of an arc of a circle.

If one end of such a bimetallic strip is fixed, a variation in temperature will cause the other end to move. The movement of this free end can be made to close an electric circuit, e.g. to cause an alarm to be operated, or conversely, it may be designed to open an electric circuit and switch off a heating appliance automatically without any manual effort. This is called a thermostat. In short, it may be defind as an instrument for maintaining a constant temperature by the use of a device which cuts off the supply of heat when the required temperature is exceeded, and automatically restores the supply when the temperature falls below what is required.

THERMISTOR

A thermistor, on the other hand, is a semiconductor, the electrical resistance of which decreases rapidly with increase in temperature, e.g. the resistance may be of the order of 10^5 ohm at 20^0C and only 10 ohm at 100^0C.

Thermistors are used as a sensitive temperature-measuring device and to compensate temperature variations of other components in a circuit.

Effect of increase in temperature on density

Since the density of a substance is the ratio of its mass and its volume, an increase of temperature results in a decrease of density. The volume of a given mass of the substance increases as its temperature rises. Water, however, behaves in a peculiar way. Its expansion is not uniform. The expansion between 30°C and 50°C being double that between 10°C and 30^0C. On cooling below 10^0C, water contracts until its temperature reaches 4^0C. On further cooling, it expands until its volume at 0^0C is 0.00012 times greater than its volume at 4°C. It expands further when it freezes.

Water in ponds and lakes freezes from the top downwards and once the temperature on the surface has fallen to 4^0C, further cooling of the lower level can only occur by conduction and the process is slow because water is a poor conductor.

Basic combustion process

When ordinary combustibles like charcoal, wood, cotton, or flammable gases are burnt in air, they give out heat during the process of combustion; this is known as exothermic reaction. The quantity of heat produced per unit weight of fuel is the calorific value of the fuel, i.e. the heat of combustion.

Flame is the visible part of an exothermic vapour phase reaction zone consisting of two or more gases, one of which is usualy oxygen. Sufficient heat is released to raise the reactants and their products to a temperature at which they are incandescent. Reaction rates at these temperatures (commonly between 1500°C and 2000°C) are extremely high and a great deal of energy is released.

Activation energy

For the majority of substances, combustion cannot occur at room temperature because the reacting molecules repel each other. To react, they must possess sufficient energy to overcome the initial mutual repulsion and come together to form an activated complex for the combustion to occur. The energy required to overcome the mutual repulsion is known as the activation energy

Auto-ignition temperature and thermal run-away

As the temperature increases the number of molecules that possess sufficient energy to form an activated complex increase rapidly. There is a critical temperature above which enough molecules possess sufficient energy for the process to become self-propagating, leading to flammable combustion. This critical temperature is called the Auto-Ignition Temperature (A.I.T.).

Above the A.I.T. the energy released by the reacting molecules is sufficient to activate even larger number of molecules and there is an ever-increasing rate of production of heat energy less the heat lost due to radiation and other factors. The temperature rises and the mixture enters a stage of thermal run-away, which rapidly becomes a flaming combustion (a thermal explosion).

For a thermal run-away to occur, the system must gain thermal energy, i.e. the rate of heat gain must be positive. The rate of heat gain is proportional to the exothermic reaction rate, which increases very rapidly at higher temperatures.

EFFECT OF OXYGEN AND PRESSURE ON A.I.T.

In an atmosphere with low oxygen concentration, the A.I.T. is higher; conversely, the A.I.T. will be lower if the fuel is burnt is pure oxygen. Increasing the pressure of a fuel–air mixutre will decrease the A.I.T. of the flammable mixture.

AUTO-INGITION TEMPERATURE OF CERTAIN COMMON MATERIALS

Coal	125°C – 130°C	Jute	193°C
Hay	172°C	Cotton	228°C
Newspaper	184°C	Rayon	234°C
Saw-dust	192-220°C	Magnesium	507°C

Spontaneous heating and ignition

Apart from spontaneous heating as a result of surface oxidation and gradual rise in temperature, such as in coal, unboiled linseed oil and others (viz. rags containing spilt-oil or paint in a factory being thrown over into a heap and lying in a corner for sometimes) fibrous materials of vegetable origin, such as cotton or hay, are also liable to undergo spontaneous combustion.

If the moisture content of hay is just right for the biological process to continue with the help of certain thermophilic bacteria like yeast or fungi, there will be a temperature rise in the interior of the haystack which is well-insulated against the dissipation of heat. The optimum temperature for the growth of the organisms is about 40°C and they die at temperatures above 65°C. Once the temperature is above 30°C the thermophilic bacteria start their activity. The optimum temperature for them is 60°C and they can survive up to about 75°C. The ignition temperature of hay is, however, 172°C. This is where the surface oxidation takes over. The rate of oxidation in such cases is higher than it would be for uncontaminated hay because the micro-organisms leave behind some substances that are readily oxidizable.

Coal has the unusual ability for a solid material to heat up from room temperature to its ignition point solely as a result of surface oxidation. Similarly, paint and a number of animal and vegetable oils are capable of surface oxidation and heating up if a large surface area is exposed to air.

Almost all other combustible materials are capable of spontaneous heating only when their temperature has been increased to a point near the ignition temperature. A common example of spontaneous heating at elevated temperature in chemical industries is the lagging fires in pipe lines. When a hot liquid or steam is being transferred through a pipe line, say from one plant in a chemical works to another, the pipe line will be lagged or insulated by a layer of 5cm or more of asbestos, mineral wool, glass fibre, or a similar fibrous or cellular material to prevent heat loss. The lagging is protected by an outer coating or some impervious material which gets frequently cracked due to a variety of reasons. It is at this stage that some spilled combustible liquid like fuel oil, which are being processed in the plant, may penetrate into the lagging and come in contact with a heated surface, and after an initial delay of perhaps several weeks, the contaminated lagging will be smouldering, causing a serious fire hazard.

Basic combustion process

Flame is the visible part of an exothermic vapour-phase reaction zone. Temperature, pressure and mixture ratio amongst the reactants should be right for a flame to continue. Combustion reactions can be maintained in a flame, only when sufficient heat is being transferred to the unburnt gases to bring them up to the flame temperature. This fresh gas entering the flame can then react. The fuel–air mixture thus occuring should be correctly balanced to make the flame self-sustaining and if the mixture is ideal, the combustion will produce the hottest flame with great flare-up.

In the case of methane, where the range of flammability is between 5.3 to 14%, a mixture containing 9.1% methane is the ideal mixture for the hottest flame to continue and this is called the stoichiometric mixture.

It is worth noting that, for methane, the lower flammability limit is roughly half the stoichiometric mixture and this is true for a large number of fuels. Thus, stoichiometric mixture for a flammable gas is the ideal concentration of gas–air mixture for the combustion to continue with the maximum effect and with the production of the hottest flame.

Process of ignition – minimum amount of energy required

The basic requirement for ignition is that a certain minimum amount of energy must be applied to a certain minimum volume of pre-mixed gases before a flame can propagate through a mixture. The minimum volume for the ignition to propagate in a methane–air mixture is about 1cu mm. For stoichiometric mixtures of most hydrocarbon vapours with air, the minimum ignition energy is about 0.2 mJ. Other organic fuels do not differ very much from this, but, for hydrogen–air mixture, it is exceptional with a minimum value of 0.02mJ. Values are much less for mixtures with oxygen and the minimum for most hydrocarbon–oxygen mixtures is 0.002 mJ. These values were obtained through laboratory tests.

Ignition due to electric sparks

Electric sparks in the form of static discharge can also be an ignition source. There are two kinds of sparks, viz. a capacitative spark and an inductive spark. A capacitative spark is usually a single discharge of very short duration and is more efficient because, first, the temperature of this spark, compared to the inductive spark, is higher, since the energy is released very quickly. Secondly, this type of spark can create some chain carriers by discharging hot gaseous molecules. On the other hand, an inductive spark is usually oscillatory. It continues to pass for sometime in one direction and then in the other. It is usually thicker than a capacitative spark and less bright.

Capacitative sparks (electrical discharges from condensers) being more powerful are more likely to cause an ignition as against inductive sparks from electric motors although the capacity in the former may be low; the charge may be at many thousand volts, so that the energy ($\frac{1}{2} CV^2$) can be well above the minimun to ignite a gaseous mixture. Hazardous charges are also produced by the pumping of hydrocarbons exceeding certain speed, the flow of powders, and the discharge of steam.

Radiation energy

Radiated heat on combustible surfaces, and particularly on wood, is a common cause of fire spread. The radiation intensity needed to ignite wood depends on the type of wood, its shape, the moisture content, and the ambient conditions. The minimum radiation that, after a very prolonged period, could result in the release of flammable vapours from wood is about 1.7 W/cm^2. The vapours thus released could be ignited by a flame, which under right condition may cause the complete combustion of the wood.

The minimum radiation for spontaneous ignition from the smouldering surface of the wood is about 2.9 W/cm^2, as against the maximum radiation intensity of 0.06 to 0.08 which radiates from the sun. This would have to be increased about fifty times to ignite wood and this can happen if the sunlight is focussed into a small area by a lens or even by a glass bottle.

An intensity of 1 W/cm^2 on the skin can be quite painful after a few seconds, and this is an useful check on the conditions that could lead to the ignition of wood (minimum energy required 0.4 cal/cm^2/sec). Some materials, notably fibre board, can be ignited by radiation more readily than wood.

In a fire involving ordinary carbonaceous materials, the chances of fire spreading from one building to the other due to radiation is low. To ensure that there would be no spread of fire by radiation under any circumstances, all the buildings should be 100m apart. Even then sparks have been known to start a fire 400m away from their origin, and fires can spread over greater distances due to blazing flammable liquids.

It may however be noted that heat transferred to wood at the minimum radiation intensity for ignition, viz. 2.9 W/cm^2 could be completely removed by the application of water at 0.1 mg/cm^2/sec.

Branching chain reactions and burning of fires

The chemical reactions in a flame take place very quickly at a very high temperature, and in a very small volume. All flame reactions depend largely on the activities of stray bits of molecules of the reacting substances. These little fragments are very reactive, very unstable, and can exist for a fraction of a second; also, these molecules are extremely mobile.

When hydrogen burns in oxygen, the reaction may be written as:

$$2H_2 + O_2 = 2H_2O$$

In this reaction, hydrogen atoms (H), oxygen atoms (O) and hydroxyl radicals (OH) react in the form of completely free ions. In a flame they have sufficient concentration and the series of reactions that may possibly take place may be represented by $\dot{O}^{*} + H_2 \rightarrow OH^{*} + \dot{H}$. The arrow indicates that it is a part of the complete process and not a balanced reaction, and the asterisks are used to indicate the molecular fragments or free radicals.

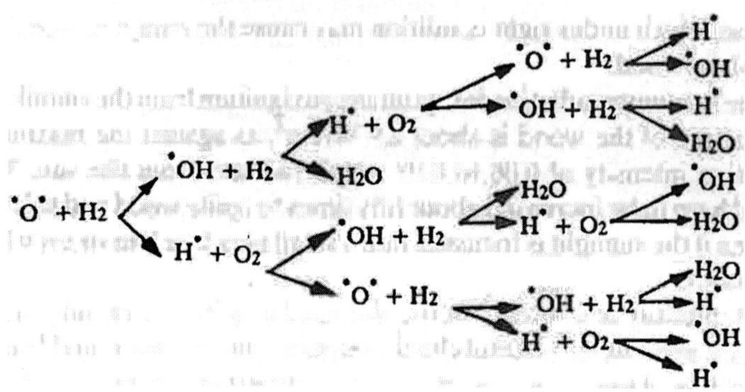

Fig.4 Branching chain reaction

In the above process, an hydrogen atom colliding with an oxygen molecule reacts in the same way, again producing two active fragments, viz. $\dot{H}^{*} + O_2 \rightarrow \dot{OH}^{*} + \dot{O}$ and finally the $\dot{OH}^{*}$ reacts like this, producing only one new fragment $^{*}OH + H_2 \rightarrow H_2O + H^{*}$.

Thus the combustion of hydrogen is not the direct reaction shown in the very first chemical equation, but it happens in a series of separate steps, i.e. chain reactions and the complete process of combustion occurs in what is called as a branching chain reaction, because, in two of the steps of reaction we get two chain carriers in exchange for one as shown in Fig 4.

Diffusion flame

All combustion processes are vapour-phase reactions and they happen when the mixture of fuel vapour and air is within the limits of flammability. In an ordinary fire, the fuel vapour and air meet and are mixed by a process called diffusion within the reaction zone. At high temperature, this mixing of the fuel with air takes place very quickly and the mixing within the reaction zone is very efficient. Flames in which the reactants are mixed by diffusion in this way are called diffusion flames. Nearly all the flames tackled by the firemen are of this kind.

Premixed flames

Unlike the diffusion flame, where the flammable vapour and air enter the reaction zone in suitable concentration and mix by diffusion and burn, a pre-mixed flame is one where the flame would occur due to the flammable vapour having been already mixed with air in the requisite concentration before the ignition source is applied.

In the case of a flammable gas, such as natural gas and air burning in a glass tube which is about 8 mm in diameter, the bright blue inner cone, which is a true pre-mixed region, can be seen surrounded by a paler diffusion flame.

Pre-mixed flames and explosions

Pre-mixed flames are far less frequently seen by a fireman than diffusion flames, but they are of considerabe importance, because, a propagating pre-mixed flame is an explosion which can be hazardous.

Burning velocity

If an explosive mixture in the vapour space of methanol tank is ignited, a pre-mixed flamc will begin to travel away from the source at a characteristic speed called the burning velocity. If the source is small the flame will be roughly spherical and it will also be very thin probably with a bright blue colour. As it spreads through the explosive mixture there will be a rise in pressure. The rate at which pressure rises will increase during an explosion. The pressure increase, however, is comparatively slow at the beginning of an explosion and it is this fact that makes possible the Explosion Suppression technique, i.e. by dctecting and extinguishing an explosion before the pressure reaches a dangerous level.

Expansion ratio for gases

This refers to the maximum explosion pressure of a flammable mixture with air, as compared to the normal initial atmospheric pressure. For gasoline and for most hydrocarbons, the maximum explosion pressure of the mixture with air, initially at atmospheric pressure, is about 8 bar.

Flash over

This happens when a solid flammable substance has been smouldering in a closed room in insufficient air. Unburnt flammable vapours resulting from the pyrolysis of fuel may mix with air away from the source of ignition. This may happen when a window breaks or a door in the closed room where the fire might be burning is suddenly opened. As a result, an explosion might occur and propagate from an ignition source. The mixture is usually ignited as soon as it enters the flammable range.

Explosions involving solid fuels from dusts and sprays

Vapour–air explosions can occur when any solid fuel like wood or coal or plastic is heated sufficiently, or when any normally safe liquid like tar or fuel oil is heated above its flash point. Explosions can also propagate in suspensions of fine dusts and sprays. These flames really are a special example of rather coarse pre-mixing. These particles can react very rapidly with the oxygen in the air because the total surface is very great.

For dusts there is a fairly well-defined lower limit, but the upper limit is difficult to determine. Burning velocities for dust are generally lower than that for vapour–air mixture, but the maximum explosion pressures reached are quite high as can be seen from the table below:

Fuel	Lower limit kg/cu.m	Maximum explosion pressure (bar)
Coal	0.035	7.8
Sulphur	0.035	2.8
Starch	0.045	11.0
Aluminium	0.035	6.5
Polyethylene	0.025	5.7

If the droplets in a mist are less than 10 micron in diameter, the mist will burn in exactly the same way as the corresponding vapour–air mixture. This is due to the droplets being vaporized by radiated heat before they enter the flame front. Larger drops may be overtaken by the flame and continue to burn behind it. This results in the reduction of the burning velocity as also in the maximum explosion pressure.

Unconfined vapour cloud explosion (U.V.C.E)

In chemical industries, flammable liquids may be processed or stored at temperatures above their boiling points. A sudden uncontrolled release of such liquids in atmosphere can readily vaporize creating an explosive mixture diffusing in air. Fine mist from such a release remains suspended in air which readily ignites in droplet sizes from 0.5 to 10 micron. Invariably such vapours are denser that air and drift over a wide area covering plant, equipment, and buildings.

Where the releases have been massive, ignition occurs within 15 to 20 seconds from the periphery of the cloud (where the vapour–air mixture is just flammable). Rapid flame propagation through vapour–air mixture in the form of a pre-mixed flame travelling very rapidly through the cloud, attains deflagration velocity (sub-sonic) with severe shock wave from blast, resulting in wide spread damages. On the other hand, there are also instances of such clouds becoming sufficiently diffused below flammable limit without any effect.

However, the effect of shock waves from the blasts due to the unconfined vapour cloud explosion are severe with disastrous results. The pressure waves from the blasts have disastrous effects on locations far from the plant. Even from a medium blast pressure of 34 kPa at 60m, a person can become deaf without realizing rupture of his ear drum. At the same pressure persons have been bodily lifted and thrown, vessels partially filled have collapsed, and buildings got demolished. U.V.C.E. shock waves have been recorded as double this pressure (equivalent to 20 tonne of T.N.T.), if not more, to smash, drag, and haul heavy structures, causing destruction and setting a number of fires instantaneously.

Boiling liquid expanding vapour explosion (B.L.E.V.E.)

Due to the effect of U.V.C.E, the shock wave generated can cause fracture of piping which are above ground, vessels develop profuse leak, rip out insulation igniting the liquid released. As a result of the flame impingement at some place of the storage vessel, the tensile strength of the material can be sufficiently reduced so as to yeild under vapour pressure to cause the vessel to fail before the relief valve of the vessel can open. The released liquid will boil in atmosphere and vaporize rapidly to develope a B.L.E.V.E. Already ignted from fire the B.L.E.V.E. can become a huge fire-ball, tending to move down the wind with intense heat radiation with a huge combustion pressure wave.

There are instances of fatal burns from B.L.E.V.E. at a distance of 400 m; blistering of paints in houses at 1000m and serious burns to spectators more than 1200m away have also been reported.

It may be noted that in case of sudden release of a flammable liquid (above its boiling point) from a storage tank, if the vapour produced does not light up, but drifts and ignites subsequently, then it will cause U.V.C.E. and not B.L.E.V.E. It is the time lag of ignition which is important for differentiating between the two though the effect of each is more or less the same.

Deep-seated fires

Fibrous materials like cotton, jute, hemp, flax, kapok will readily form deep-seated fires, specially when these materials are stored in heaps. This is because these materials are good insulators; and also, air is loosely trapped within the heaps. Fire-fighting becomes a difficult problem in such cases. A normal surface fire spreading through a stack of bales involving these materials will rapidly penetrate into the individual bales and become deep-seated.

If this happens in a ship's hold, the surface flames can be extinguished by the local application of water or CO_2 or by an inert gas system. But in the totally enclosed space it is very difficult to extinguish the deep-seated fires. Water may not be able to easily penetrate into the bales and its use may also be undesirable because it will cause the bales to swell.

Even though the inerting system can reduce the oxygen concentration in the hold to well below what is needed to support a flame, this may not be sufficient to stop the smouldering. However, the rate of heat release will be considerably reduced by the dilution of air and will become less as the air is further vitiated by the combustion products. The fire may thus be controlled, but smouldering can continue for several weeks till the whole mass slowly cools down to a temperature at which the fuel surface is no longer reactive. However, if the affected bales are taken out of the hold and broken open, resulting in the exposure of a hot reactive material to a copious supply of oxygen, ignition would be very rapid with a cloud of burning fibres being blown out.

Depending upon the nature of the material and its specific surface the time taken for a deep-seated fire to grow would vary from 10 minutes or more for a fire involving a pile of newspapers to 20 seconds if the same paper is shredded, giving it more specific surface. Deep-seated fires can be easily extinguished by breaking the stacks where possible and attackingthe seat of the fire with fine spray of water. But, this is not always possible, specially in ship's hold or other confined space where the only way is to cool down the entire atmosphere by water spray and to inject an inhibiting gas like CO_2 for a considerable time.

Limits of flammability, flammability envelope, peak concentration and the effects of pressure and temperatures on the limits of flammability and peak concentration

As stated previously, the limits of flammability denote the percentage by volume of the fuel to air. The limit of flammability of n-hexane (gasoline) in air are 1.2 to 7.4% and the stoichiometric mixture is about 2.2%. The limits are largely determined by the fact that as we move away from the stoichiometric point to either the weak or the rich limit, there is an increasing amount of either air or fuel in the mixture that cannot react. This excess material passes through the reaction zone where it is heated but contributes nothing to the energy release. If the mixture ratio approaches either limit, the flame temperature gets less, and so does the amount of excess energy that is available for the continuous ignition of the fresh unburnt gases. If this energy falls below a certain critical level, the flame can no longer propagate. The mixture is outside the limits of flammability. The effect of an increase in temperature and pressure is to widen the limits of flammability.

Hazardous chemicals

The presence of certain groups of atoms in a molecule may indicate that the substance is potentially hazardous, particularly, if its formation is endothermic. It may be useful to indicate some of the unstable structures. The undermentioned groups can be found in any high explosives:

nitrate	$-ONO_2$
nitro	$-NO_2$
nitramine	$=N-NO_2$ or $-NH-NO_2$

The more sensitive primary explosives often contain these groups:

nitroso	$-NO$
diazo	$-N=N-$
halogen amines	$=N-X$ (where X is the halogen)
azide	$-N_3$

Peroxides and acetylides are also hazardous:

acetylenic	$-C\equiv C-$
peroxide	$-O-O-$

Unstable chemicals

They are usually materials that contain a large amount of locked-in energy. This is released as heat when they decompose. The rate of decomposition increases with temperature; if the heat cannot be dissipated fast enough the rapidly accelerating reaction may become a detonation.

The most notorious of these compounds are the organic peroxides. They contain unstable peroxide group which can oxidize the hydrocarbon part of the molecule. Acetyl, benzoyl, lauroyl peroxides are all used in the plastics industry as polymerization initiators. The first two are very sensitive and may be readily detonated. They are usually supplied in solution, the solvent acting as a stabilizer and small quantities may be supplied simply moistened with water. Even then, they are dangerous in a fire. They are powerful oxidizing agents and form hazardous, sometimes sensitive, mixtures with combustible organic materials.

CHAPTER 2

A. Elements and their Compounds; Properties and Hazards

Out of the one hundred and five elements in the periodic table, which exist freely in the solid, liquid and gaseous stages, some are metals like sodium, potassium, iron, copper etc. Some are non-metals like oxygen, nitrogen, hydrogen etc. and some have been classified as metalloids like arsenic and antimony because they possess properties of both metals and non-metals.

It is the general practice to denote metallic elements by the letters um at the end e.g. Sodium, Calcium, Magnesium etc. While the letters -in,-ine, -on etc. are found at the end in the case of non-metallic elements e.g. hydrogen, Bromine, silicon, iodine etc. There are, however, exceptions to this rule.

Prefixes are used to indicate the number of atoms of a particular element contained in a molecule of a compound. The prefixes used in this way are mono, di, tri, tetra and penta, meaning one, two, three, four and five respectively. Examples of the use of these prefixes are:

Carbon monoxide (CO)	Meaning one atom of carbon and one atom of oxygen.
Carbon dioxide (CO_2)	Meaning one atom of carbon, but two atoms of oxygen .
Sulphur trioxide (SO_3)	Meaning one atom of sulphur and three atoms of oxygen..
Carbon tetrachloride (CC_4)	Meaning one atom of carbon and four atoms of chlorine.
Phosphorus pentoxide (P_2O_5)	Meaning two atom of phosphorus and five atoms of oxygen.

Allotropy

The property possessed by some elements of existing in different forms, differing more or less in physical and in some chemical properties is known as allotropy. Thus diamond, graphite, charcoal, lamp black are the allotropic modification of carbon. Phosphorus also has allotropic modification in red and white phosphorus. Some of these elements, existing under different allotropic modifications, have their own fire risks under certain conditions and have different ignition temperatures.

The various elements and compounds, such as acids, oxides, peroxides, nitrates, chlorates, picrates, alcohols, ethers, acetates, esters, etc. have, however, their special hazards apart from other flammable substances.

Classification of hazardous chemicals

The broad classification of hazardous chemicals may however be made as follows:

(*i*) Explosives (including propellants, pyrotechniques, war gases);

(*ii*) Compressed, dissolved, permanent and liquified gases;

(*iii*) Substances reacting dangerously with air and/or water giving (*a*) flammable vapours ; (*b*) toxic vapours and (*c*) corrosive vapours or residues ;

(*iv*) Substances evolving flammable vapours at ordinary temperature and pressure;

(*v*) Corrosive substances like acids or caustic alkalies, which may also generate hydrogen in contact with certain metals;

(*vi*) Poisonous substances;

(*vii*) Substances of specific fire hazards, viz. oxidizing agents or strong supporters of combustion, as also substances liable to spontaneous combustion and readily combustible substances.

Organic and inorganic compounds

Amongst the different chemical compounds, a division has been made between the organic and inorganic compounds. The organic compounds are those which contain carbon atom in their molecules.

Aliphatic and aromatic hydrocarbons

Organic compounds such as the derivatives of the various petroleum are known as aliphatic hydrocarbons like benzine, petrol, turpentine. Organic compounds obtained from coal and its derivatives are called aromatic hydrocarbons, like benzene, toluene, xylene, naphtha. It may also be noted here that all volatile organic solvents have a low flash point and high vapour pressure at ordinary temperature. The vapour pressure increases with rise in temperature.

Acids

Acids may be either inorganic or organic. The most common members of the inorganic group are the mineral acids like hydrochloric nitric and sulphuric and the organic group are formic, acetic and butyric acids, which are important to fire officers. Acid may be defined as a compound which contains replaceable hydrogen atom, a part or whole of which can be replaced by metals or groups of elements acting like metals to produce a salt.

Salts

Salts are formed due to reaction of acid with an alkali and are named after the acid from which they are formed. In the case of acids having both hydrogen and oxygen atoms in the molecule, if the names of the acid end in -ic, the name of the salt will end in -ate and if the name of the acid ends in -ous, the name of the salt will end in -ite, i.e.

-ic acids give -ate salts.

-ous acids give -ite salts.

Sulphuric acid gives sulphate and nitrous acid gives nitrite salts.

In the case of acids containing hydrogen and other nonmetallic elements or element, but not oxygen, e.g. hydrochloric acid (HCl), hydrocyanic acid (HCN), the terminal -ic is hanged to - ide; thus hydrochloric acid will give chloride, hydrocyanic acid will give cyanide.

pH value and its significance

In aqueous solution, an acid dissociates into +ively charged H-ions (hydrogen ions). This property of the acids is called ionization. Different acids give different H-ions and the strength of acids depends upon the concentration of these H-ions. It is to be remembered that the strongest acid gives the largest number of H-ions in equivalent solution. The strenght of an acid in solution is determined by how much it will ionize in solution. This varies with different acids. Similarly, for alkalies, the concentration of negatively charged OH ions in equivalent solution determines its strength. The pH of a solution is the negative exponent of its H-ion concentration and pH numbers are powers of the dilution which one gram equivalent of H-ion has undergone. Hence, pH = 1 indicates a very strong acid and pH = 14 a very strong alkali and a solution with pH = 7 is neutral, i.e. neither acidic nor alkaline.

The concentration of an acid however, depends upon the amount of water in which it is dissolved. Acetic acid may be very concentrated having little water in it, but it will still be a weak acid because it is only slightly ionized.

General properties of acid

(*i*) It turns blue litmus red;
(*ii*) It has a sour taste;
(*iii*) It reacts vigorously with alkalies, producing salts and water and neutralizing the same;
(*iv*) It has a corrosive action on skin;

Causes of fire

When in contact with combustible materials certain inorganic acids may cause fire. Strong nitric acid causes fire when it is brought in contact with dry straw or dry saw-dust, paper etc. The fire starts from 35 to 45 minutes in such cases to about 3 hours time for more dilute nitric acids after bringing the acid in contact with such substances. Concentrated sulphuric acid, on the other hand, which is heavier than water, when brought in contact with water will immediately produce a great degree of heat which might crack the glass carboy and lead to the spillage of acid, producing more heat and thereby charring wood, textiles, paper and setting fire to them under suitable circumstances. Strong mineral acids should not be brought in contact with oxidizers like chlorates, picrates etc.

The heavier organic acids resemble hydrocarbons in character and are not soluble in water. They are sometimes referred to as fatty acids, as some of them occur naturally in animal fats. The general formula of an organic acids is R (COOH), where R stands for any radical like CH_3, C_2H_5 etc. The fire hazard of organic acids is due to their combustible nature. The flash points of the following organic acids are given below:

Acetic acid : 46^0C.
Butyric acid : 78^0C.

Base and alkali

As opposed to acids, a base is a compound, usually the oxide or the hydroxide of a metal (or a group of elements acting as a metal) which can react with an acid to produce salt and water. An alkali is a strong base soluble in water. Caustic soda, caustic potash etc. are examples of alkalies, whereas ammonia is an example of a base.

General properties of a base

General properties of a base are as follows:

(*i*) In aqueous solution, a base produces hydroxyl ions, (OH) groups charged with negative electricity;

(*ii*) It turns red litmus blue, or phenolphthaline solution in alcohol base to pink;

(*iii*) It has a characteristic sharp taste;

(*iv*) It neutralizes acids, producing salt and water.

While acids are used by almost all industries either in concentrated or in liquid form, alkalies are generally used in soap, paper, textiles, rayon, dyes, glass and in a number of other industries.

The caustic alkalies referred to above are found both in solid and liquid form. The liquid form is sold in various concentrations varying from about 50 to 73% by weight of caustic soda. The solid form may be in cake, flake, ground or powdered variety. The huge requirement of caustic soda in this country is met mostly by internal production by elelctrolysis of brine.

HAZARDS

Caustics should be kept in a dry location, not below ground level, and unless kept in water-tight sealed containers, they should not be stored under automatic sprinklers. Caustic soda, caustic potash etc. are non-combustible but react with water to generate heat. The most severe hazard is their destructive effect on living tissues caused by contact of the caustic solution on the skin.

Solution of the caustic alkali may generate hydrogen in contact with zinc, galvanized metals, or aluminium and this may result in a hydrogen explosion if a source of ignition is present.

Fire-fighting

In general copious amount of water in the form of fine spray are to be used for fire-fighting involving acids and alkalies, which thus become more and more diluted and lose their strengh till they become harmless.

In case of small spillage involving acids, dirt, sand, talc etc. may be employed when there is no water available. Flooding or indiscriminate use of water is not recommended in the laboratory or in the store room, where the water used might react with other substances to cause a chemical reaction.

In fires involving either acids or alkalies, the area is to be ventilated quickly and gas masks should be used where any toxic gases or elements are suspected to exist or be liberated.

Important properties of certain acids and alkalies

Before concluding the portion on acids and alkalies, it would be interesting to note certain particular characteristics of the following mineral acids and the caustic alkalies.

1. SULPHURIC ACID (H_2SO_4)

Sulphuric acid is a colourless and odourless oily liquid of specific gravity 1.8. It is very hygroscopic and miscible with water in all proportions. Oleum is fuming sulphuric acid. It is very strong and active. Inhalation of vapours causes extreme damage to lung tissue. It reacts violently with water, particularly when a small quantity of water meets a large quantity of acid. Sulphuric acid, when heated above 290°C, is decomposed into choking fumes of SO_2.

At higher temperature, the acid is decomposed even more and in addition to poisonous fumes of SO_2, free oxygen is liberated.

$$2H_2SO_4 = 2H_2O + 2SO_2 + O_2$$

Dilute and concentrated sulphuric acid have different reactions with metals.

Although cold concentrated H_2SO_4 is inactive towards metals, when heated, it reacts vigorously with most of them. The gas evolved is normally SO_2 as indicated below:

$$Cu + 2H_2SO_4 = CuSO_4 + 2H_2O + SO_2$$

$$Zn + 2H_2SO_4 = ZnSO_4 + 2H_2O + SO_2$$

$$S + 2H_2SO_4 = 2H_2O + 3SO_2$$

Cold concentrated acid does not attack iron, copper, lead, mercury, tin, silver. Hence iron vessels can be used in transporting the cold concentrated acid.

Cold dilute sulphuric acid acts upon iron, zinc, magnesium etc., with the liberation of hydrogen and formation of the corresponding salts.

$$Fe + H_2SO_4 = FeSO_4 + H_2$$

$$Mg + H_2SO_4 = MgSO_4 + H_2$$

Sulphuric acid acts as an oxidizing substance also, producing SO_2 (sulphur dioxide) or CO_2 gas, when it reacts with non-metallic substance like sulphur or charcoal respectively.

Owing to its great affinity for water, sulphuric acid is hygroscopic in nature. Sulphuric acid (conc) should never be kept exposed as it will absorb water and become hot. The acid has a highly corrosive action upon the skin and animal tissues. Sugar, saw-dust, paper are charred, i.e. carbonized in contact with sulphuric acid and free carbon is liberated.

The burning action of H_2SO_4 on cloth, paper is due to a similar dehydrating action on the cellulose ($C_6H_{10}O_5$).

Sulphuric acid reacts with metallic chlorides and nitrates to form hydrochloric and nitric acids respectively.

$NaCl + H_2SO_4 = NaHSO_4 + HCl$

$NaNO_3 + H_2SO_4 = NaHSO_4 + HNO_3$

The properties of this acid can be summarized as follows :

(*i*) It is heavier than water; (*ii*) It is hygroscopic in nature; (*iii*) Heat is evolved when mixed with water; (*iv*) It chars sugar by absorbing the elements of water from it and leaving a voluminous mass of charcoal; (*v*) It chars paper, wood and sawdust; (*vi*) It has no action on zinc, iron, lead and copper with cold cocentrated acid; (*vii*) Concentrated hot acid evolves choking and irritating SO_2 gas by coming in contact with copper, zinc, iron, tin, etc; (*viii*) Cold and dilute acid evolves H_2 gas which is flammable on coming in contact with most of the metals like zinc, iron, tin etc; (*ix*) It liberates nitric acid from a nitrate and hyd rochloric acid from a chloride on being strongly heated; (*x*) It is decomposed by heat into SO_2 and O_2 gas.

Uses

This acid is widely used in the manufacture of a number of heavy chemicals, such as in the manufacture of hydrochloric and nitirc acid, phosphorus, some manures (super phosphate of lime), sulphates, explosives, paints etc. and in dying industry, for refining petroleum, in bleaching operations, in the manufacture of ethylene and accumulators.

A fire officer is expected to coine across large storage of sulphuric acid in any chemical industry fertilizer factory or in an oil refinery.

2. HYDROCHLORIC ACID (HCl)

It is a colourless gas with a pungent, suffocating smell, being heavier than air and is highly soluble in water, forming a strong acid solution.

The gas is neither flammable nor a supporter of combustion. The acid solution reacts with most metals, their oxides, hydroxides and carbonates. The dry HCl gas combines with ammouia, producing white fumes of ammonium chloride. Burning sodium combines with it to produce hydrogen and solid sodium chloride:

$2Na + 2HCl = 2NaCl + H_2.$

This acid on being mixed with strong and concentrated nitric acid in the proportion of 3:1 ($HCl:HNO_3$) forms Aqua Regia, which dissolves the noble metals like gold and platinum which cannot be dissolved by other acids. The concentrated acid evolves chlorine gas when it comes in contact with crystals of potassium permangnate ($KMnO_4$) or potassium dichromate ($K_2Cr_2O_7$). Cold hydrochloric acid will attack most metals like zinc, iron, magnesium to form a chloride of the metal and to evolve free hydrogen; thus,

$Mg + 2HCl = MgCl_2 + H_2$

$Zn + 2HCl = ZnCl_2 + H_2$

Uses

Hydrochloric acid is mostly used in dying industry, in the manufacture of colours, phosphates, metallic chlorides and chlorine.

3. NITRIC ACID (HNO3)

Nitric acid is a colourless liquid with a peculiar smell, strongly fuming in air, hygroscopic and having specific gravity of 1.52. The pure acid decomposes on boiling. It decomposes into NO_2, O_2 and water, when it is dropped over heated stone or passed through a heated clay pipe.

$4HNO_3 = 4NO_2 + 2H_2O + O_2$.

Nitric acid is a strong oxidizing agent. Dry saw-dust or straw is nitrated leading to fire. Cotton, if treated with strong nitric acid in presence of sulphuric acid produces a dangerous explosive like gun-cotton. Concentrated nitric acid dropped on warm charcoal produces a violent reaction; the charcoal burns brilliantly and CO_2 is produced.

Action of nitric acid on organic compounds

Strong nitric acid is extremely corrosive, causing serious and painful wounds on the skin. The dilute acid also stains the skin yellow. Other organic materials such as silk, feather, leather and vegetable tissues turn yellow-brown due to the formation of xantho proteic acid. Turpentine bursts into flame on coming into contact with strong nitric acid.

Cotton (cellulose) is attacked by concentrated HNO_3 in presence of concentated H_2SO_4, producing nitro-cellulose or gun-cotton. Glycerine, under similar conditions, produces nitro-glycerine and carbolic acid produces picric acid, which are all violently explosive substances.

Action on metals

Nitric acid acts on most metals even in the cold state and, unless the acid is very dilute, toxic fumes of nitrogen peroxide are usully evolved. In a number of cases, NO (nitric oxide) is given off, but as this gas immediately reacts with atmospheric oxygen to form nitrogen peroxide, the resultant danger is identical.

$2NO + O_2 = 2NO_2$

The reactions of nitric acid vary according to whether the acid is concentrated, i.e. no water, or strong with 35% of water, or dilute with 80% water mixed. As stated above, it can generally be accepted that the final result of most reactions with nitric acid is NO_2 gas, but in some cases, as in zinc, varying degrees of concentration may cause the evolution of NH_3 (ammonia) or even nitrous oxide (N_2O). One important deviation from the rule is that of magnesium and manganese, which with cold and dilute nitric acid evolve hydrogen.

$Mg + 2HNO_3 = Mg(NO_3)_2 + H_2$

When concentrated HNO_3 comes in contact with iron, aluminium, or chromium, a very thin film of metallic oxide is formed and it serves to protect these metals from further attack. They are then described as 'passive' but dilute acid, but will, however, react vigorously with them, as with most metals. With dilute acids:

$3Cu + 8HNO_3 = 3Cu(NO_3)_2 + 4H_2O + 2NO.$

With strong acid:

$Cu + 4HNO_3 = Cu(NO_3)_2 + 2H_2O + 2NO_2.$

$Mg + 4HNO_3 = Mg(NO_3)_2 + 2H_2O + 2NO_2.$

Finally, nitric acid reacts with all solid non-metallic elements to evolve NO_2 gas. Thus with sulphur and carbon, the reaction are:

$S + 6HNO_3 = H_2SO_4 + 2H_2O + 6NO_2.$

$C + 4HNO_3 = 2H_2O + CO_2 + 4NO_2$

Uses

Nitric acid is mostly used in the manufacture of dyes, explosives and for etching designs on copper, brass, or bronze articles and by goldsmiths for refining gold.

CAUSTIC SODA AND CAUSTIC POTASH

Caustic soda (NaOH) and caustic potash (KOH) are the most common caustics used in various industries to manufacture soap, pulp, paper, textiles, rayon, manufacture of reclaimed rubber, dyes, and glass. A fire officer is likely to come across these two very important chemicals, more often, than other chemicals. They are obtained either in solid or in liquid form. The liquid comes in various concentrations varying from about 50% to 73% by weight for caustic soda. The solid form may be in cake, flaked, grounded, or powdered variety.

Storage

They should be stored in a dry loaction not below the ground level. The storage building should preferably be made of noncombustible or fire resistant material to avoid the need to employ fire hose streams in areas where these materials are kept. They should always be kept away from acids, moisture, explosives, trichloroethylene and combustible materials.

HAZARDS OF ALKALIES

Caustic soda, caustic potash etc. are non-combustible but they react with water to produce heat. This is also true of the concetrated solutions. Deep and painful burns are caused when strong alkalies come in contact with skin. The affected part should immediately be washed with plenty of water and some soothing oil like olive or coconut oil be applied immediately. If caustic soda or potash come in contact with eyes, it may cause blindness. A fireman should be careful in handling acids and alkalies. In contact with water, solid caustic soda will react to produce heat, which may be sufficient to ignite combustible materials under certain conditions.

Solutions of the caustic alkalies produce hydrogen in contact with zinc, galvanized metals, or aluminium, which may result in a hydrogen explosion if a source of ignition is present.

$$Zn + 2NaOH = Zn(ONa)_2 + H_2 \uparrow$$

$$Zn + 2KOH = Zn(OK)_2 + H_2 \uparrow$$

GENERAL PROPERTIES

Caustic soda is a white deliquescent crystalline solid, rapidly absorbing moisture from the air. By a prolonged exposure, it also absorbs CO_2 from air and foms Na_2CO_3 (sodium carbonate). It melts but does not decompose on heating. It is highly soluble in water with the evolution of heat. The solution has a strongly alkaline reaction turning red litmus blue and phenolphthalein pink. It is soapy to touch and has a corrosive (caustic) action upon the skin. Caustic soda being a strong alkali neturalizes acid to form a salt and water. It liberates NH_3 from ammonium salts and precipitates hydroxides of metals from their salt solutions.

$$NH_4Cl + NaOH = NaCl + H_2O + NH_3$$

$$CuSO_4 + 2NaOH = Cu(OH)_2 + Na_2SO_4$$

B. Alkali Metals

Lithium, sodium, potassium, rubidium, caesium are known as alkali metals, which are all light in weight, having a low specific gravity. They are all silver white, ductile and react vigorously with water to form hydroxides. Most of these metals are kept under kerosene or naphtha (particularly sodium and potassium) to avoid accidental exposure to air which may cause ignition of the metal due to rapid oxidization. The choking white fumes are toxic. The rection with water is as follows:

$2Na + 2H_2O = 2NaOH + H_2$

Sodium is used in petroleum refining and also as a heat-transfer medium in the reactors and in the manufacture of fireworks and in other chemical works. Like caustic soda or caustic potash, metals of this group should not be stored under the basements, nor in rooms, where they may be exposed to water.

They should be stored separately from acids, flammable liquids, combustibles, explosive and oxidizing materials.

Hazards

Alkali metals are readily flammable at relatively low temperatures and some like sodium, potassium and rubidium ignite when moist. Lithium resembles sodium (melting point 186^0C) and has a severe fire hazard when exposed to heat or flame. It reacts violently with water, acids and oxidizing agents and produces hydrogen due to reaction with water or steam.

Alkali metals decompose water violently to yield hydrogen and in the case or potassium (K), rubidium (R), and sodium (Na), they ignite explosively due to the combustion of hydrogen produced at the high temperature.

Caesium reacts with oxidizing agents and can ignite spontaneously in moist air, libetrating hydrogen. Caesium is a silver white ductile metal with melting point of 28.5^0C and it is used in photo-electric cells. It produces a dangerous fire, particularly in contact with water and forms an explosion hazard. Fumes, in the form of finely divided caustic, are given off on being hydrolyzed, and they irritate nose, throat and skin. Sodium melts at 95.5^0C whereas potassium melts at 62^0C. Potassium is more hazardous and it may form an explosive compound in contact even with CO_2.

Fire-fighting

Water, foam, soda acid, carbon dioxide should never be used on fires involving sodium, potassium or the other alkali metals. CO_2 gas in any form as well as carbon tetrachloride will react violently with hot sodium. Where the metal is submerged in liquid hydrocarbon (kerosene), the fire can be extinguished by CO_2 and there will be no re-ignition because the blanket of solvent vapour prevents the sodium from catching fire.

Since the material tends to melt and flow, when involved in fire, care must be exercised even in applying dry powders so as not to cause any splattering of the molten liquid. Sodium fires can best be extinguished by dry common salt, powdered graphite or by fine, dry soda-ash powders or by dry chemical powders of the special type. This is to be thrown in liberal quantities over the burning material just to smother the fire. Dry sand can also be used. If sodium and potassium are kept under kerosene in airtight containers in a proper fire-resistive building or cabinet, there is no likelihood of their offering any problem in fire-fighting. Water could be used as usual to extinguish fire in other portions of the building.

Fire risks involving certain metals

Aluminium and magnesium metals are hazardous, particularly in finely divided forms. They are liable to burn in air and present serious explosion hazards. Aluminium particles will burn, when in dust, powder or in flake form. As a dust cloud or in ribbon form, it can be ignited almost instantly. Loose machine turnings ignite fairly readily. Heavy magnesium castings are somewhat difficult to ignite. The metal has a very high heat conductivity and, in fact, the heat is carried away and dissipated before the burning point is reached. However, if the fire is well started, it is sure to consume all the magnesium contained in the pile.

Water should never be used for fighting fires in aluminium or magnesium. It will accelerate the burning. Other extinguishing agents such as foam, CO_2, soda acid will be of no use. The recommended extinguishing agents for such metal fires are the special heat-resistant chloride-based dry chemical powders (Eutectic chlorides), viz. a mixture of sodium chloride, potassium chloride and barium chloride in appropriate proportions. Certain special characteristics of magnesium and aluminium and a few other metals are mentioned below:

ALUMINIUM

A light, ductile metal of good electrical conductivity and resistance to corrosion. It melts at 660^0C and at a high temperature, when burning.

It decomposes water, like magnesium, producing hydrogen. Aluminium is mostly used for making cooking utensils, for transmission of electric current through cables made of aluminium, and for manufacture of light alloys such as magnalium (alloy of aluminium and magnesium) and duralumin (alloy of aluminium, copper, magnesium, manganese and silicon) in the ratio of Al (93.5 to 95.5%), Cu (3.5 to 4.5%), Mg (0.4 to 0.7%), Mn (0.4 to 0.7%) and Si (upto 0.7%). Duralumin is an important alloy of aluminium, which is about as hard as steel, but 1/3rd its weight. It is mostly used in the construction of aircrafts. Aluminium foil is also used for covering cigarettes, chocolates etc.

MAGNESIUM

It is a brilliant white metal and is soft, ducitle, and malleable like aluminium. The melting point is 649^0C. Dust or flakes of magnesium are liable to ignite readily. It reacts violently with water when heated, producing hydrogen, though at ordinary temperature also, it reacts with water, but very slowly, to produce very small amount of hydrogen. There is, however, a severe risk of ignition of magnesium in machine operation, and as dust, the explosion hazard is very great. Magnesium ignites when dispersed in air at 519^0C.

TITANIUM

This is a strong white metal, lighter than steel, and used in alloys with steel to give high working temperature. Its melting point is 2000^0C. Titanium is easily ignited in the form of thin chips, drillings, or turnings, though larger pieces present only a slight fire hazard, except in heat treatment battery. It offers a severe dust explosion hazard, being ignitable in cloud form (480^0C). It even reacts with CO_2, nitrogen, sand, carbon tetrachloride and water.

ZIRCONIUM

The melting point of this metal is 1900^0C. It resembles titanium in certain aspects though the fire and explosion hazards are much more severe. It ignites as a dust cloud at a temperature of 20^0C.

ZINC

Zinc has a very high resistance to atmospheric corrosion. It is used as a protective coating (e.g. in galvanized iron) and is also used in sheets and as a constituent of alloys with aluminium, copper and magnesium. The melting point is 419^0C. The metal can, however, be ignited, though it is considered to have no fire risk. In the form of dust, it offers an explosion hazard.

Pyrophoric metals

Hafnium, plutonium, thorium, titanium, uranium and zirconium are all highly combustible metals. The hazards of this group are similar to those of magnesium and similar safeguards should be applied. In powder form, they present severe dust explosion possibilities. Some are pyrophoric and ignite spontaneously, when dispersed in air. They burn readily in pure nitrogen or CO_2 gas and explode in contact with oxidizing agents. Some of the above-stated metals also heat spontaneously in air and should be stored and handled in a non-reactive liquid or gas. In the molten state or when burning, all these metals react vigorously with water, foam, CO_2, vaporizing liquids and may explode. Special dry chemical extinguishers could only be used, very carefully, to blanket small fires. The extinguishing media should not be applied directly on the burning materials.

CHAPTER 3

Some common Salts and their Fire Hazards

Certain chemical compounds are discussed below from the point of view of their special fire hazards and storage risks.

Sodium and potassium chlorate ($NaClO_3$ and $KClO_3$)

Chlorates are the salts of chloric acid and contain ClO_3 group. They are colourless crystals or fine white powders and are usually soluble in water. Chlorates tend to liberate oxygen violently under influence of friction, shock, concussion or heat. All chlorates and particularly potassium chlorate are highly explosive and dangerous. Chlorates are strong oxidizing agents, and when mixed with organic materials, form very flammable mixtures (e.g. spraying of chlorate solutions on weeds). When mixed with finely divided organic matter, such as dust on a loading wharf, such mixtures may ignite, when stepped on.

Sodium or potassium chlorates are the most dangerous oxidizing agents. Intimate contact with organic substances, sulphur and sulphides, powdered metals, phosphorus or ammonium compounds can cause fire and explosions. Ordinary combustible materials like dried vegetation or clothing become highly flammable if contaminated with it. Slight heat or friction or even a small spark may be sufficient to cause a rapid burning fire or explosion. Containers may explode when involved in fire.

All chlorates, when brought in contact with sulphuric acid (or other strong mineral acid) are liable to cause fire or explosion, evolving explosive chlorine peroxide gas. When mixed with ammonium salts, chlorates are liable to decompose spontaneously and ignite.

Chlorate mixtures containing sulphur and sulphides are extermely sensitive to blows or friction and are used as explosives. Explosion may occur when breaking up chunks of chlorate. When chlorates are mixed with potassium cyanide, oxygen evolves with explosive violence.

STORAGE

Sodium or potassium chlorate should be stored in metal container in detached buildings or in a room separated from other parts of the premises by fire resistant walls and floors. No combustible materials or acids should be kept in the store and the store should be kept scrupulously clean.

Sodium chlorite ($NaClO_2$)

Chlorites are the salts of the chlorous acid, containing ClO_2 group. They are bleaching agents, which react like hypochlorites, but their decomposition requires higher temperatures and the resulting explosion is more violent. They are powerful oxidizers, so that same precautions should be taken as for chlorates.

Potassium cyanide (KCN)

It is a salt of the hydrocyanic acid (HCN). When acted upon by acids or moisture, some cyanides give off hydrocyanic acid (HCN) which is deadly poisonous and flammable. All cyanides are extremely poisonous and should not be handled with bare hands. Open vats of cyanide solutions should not be kept in the same room with open vats of sulphuric or hydrochloric acid, as the cyanide solution, on coming in contanct with acids may produce deadly toxic hydrocyanic acid vapours. Also the hydrochloric acid may give off HCl gas, which if mixed with cyanide vapours, forms HCN, specially if the air is moist.

Though cyanides are not usually combustible, at high temperature, they become molten and yield small amounts of flammable vapours. The principal concern to fire-fighters is the deadly toxic vapour emitted and for which rubber gloves and respiratory protection (breathing apparatus) are recommended. However, HCN gas being lighter than air and highly soluble in water, tends to offset the toxic hazards to some degree. For this reason, fog or finely diffused spray are recommended for fires involving cyanides.

CO_2 extinguishers should not be used where dry cyanides are involved, particularly if the air is moist or where water spray is also being used, as the carbonic acid formed tends to accelerate the evolution of hydrocyanic acid which is highly toxic and lethal.

EXPLOSION HAZARDS OF CYANIDES

Cyanide baths are used for heat treating and case hardening of certain machine parts made of steel. The floors of such baths should be kept dry as the cyanide may explode, when dropped on wet floors. Cyanides should never be added to molten nitrate or nitrate baths (or vice versa) for a disastrous explosion may result. A small nitrate bath can explode even at 233^{0}C (app.) with a terrific explosion.

Sodium hydrosulphide (NaHS)

This group includes sulphahydrils, thio alcohols, thiols or mercaptans. Sodium hydrosulphide in the form of colourless needles is soluble in water.

Hydrosulphides are generally flammable liquids, e.g. ethyl mercaptan (ethy1 sulphahydrate) has a flash point of -40^{0}C.

Sodium hydrosulphite or sodium hyposulphite ($Na_2S_2O_4$)

These are salts of hyposulphurous acid, containing S_2O_4 group. Sodium hydrosulphite is a yellowish or greyish-white powder and is used as a bleaching agent and for removing dyes from fabrics. The dry anhydrous salt is only stable in dry air. It is highly soluble in water.

SAFETY

It is classed as a flammable solid and requires the yellow label as an indication of its hazard. It oxidizes in air and even more readily in the presence of moisture, giving off irritating SO_2 gas. Sodium hydrosulphite is combustible and is liable to ignite if allowed to become damp. It should be stored in a cool dry place away from other materials.

Calcium hypochlorite ($Ca(ClO)_2$)

Hypochlorites are compounds containing the group $(COl)^-$, the most common of which are the hypochlorites of calcium, sodium and potassium. Sodium hypochlorite hydrate consists of greenish-yellow crystals which are liable to explode when warmed or placed in contact with organic matter.

Calcuim hypochlorite is not by itself combustible but at high temperatures, liberates oxygen to support combustion. Hence, it should be stored in a cool, dry place, away from combustible materials and acids. Since chlorine is freely released when exposed to the air or moisture, it should not be stored near containers of turpentine or other hydrocarbons, the vapours of which will spontaneously explode when diffused with chlorine. If mixed with organic materials or flammable liquids, friction against the packing may lead to heating and spontaneous ignition.

In fighting a fire where this material is involved, ventilation is important and respiratory protection devices should be worn if the pungent odour of chlorine is noticeable. Water spray is recommended as the preferred extinguishing agent and it can be used for cooling the exposed drums of the chemical. If a container of calcium hypochlorite is exposed to excessive heat or the direct rays of the sun, the gas liberated may develop sufficient pressure to rupture the container. Chlorine, the most irritating gas, is liberated from this material when it is subjected to heat or moisture.

Sodium hypophosphite (NaH_2PO_2)

These are the salts of orthophosphorus acids or hypo-orthophosphorus acids. The hypophosphites of sodium, potassium and calcium are white crystals, which melt but decompose when heated to form phosphene (PH_3), a spontaneously inflammable and poisonous gas, along with other products. Hypophosphites burn at high temperatures and form powerful explosives when mixed with nitrates, chlorates, and other oxidizers.

Ammonium nitrate (NH_4NO_3)

It is an inorganic salt of nitric acid with ammonia. Ammonium nitrate (NH_4NO_3) is a light yellow crystalline or granular powder which evolves nitrous oxide when heated; it increases the intensity of the fire in combustible materials. It explodes when kept in a confined space or under pressure and at higher temperature. A sudden heat may result in an explosion. Ammonium nitrate is highly soluble and it absorbs moisture to form a hard cake. It is therefore stored in multi-wall, sealed paper bags and not in bulk.

In view of the hazardous nature of the commodity, bags of NH_4NO_3 should be stored in piles not more than 3.6 m in width, with a clearance of 76 cm from the walls, and with aislespace between the piles of the same width. A clearance of 1 m from the eaves of the roof should also be left.

Ammonium nitrate should not be stored in a structure containing explosive organic chemicals, flammable liquids, corrosive acids, chlorates, permanganates, finely divided metals, sulphur or other combustible material. Storage piles must be at least 9 m away from these materials and they should be stored on clean concrete floor, at least 1 m away from any steam pipe, electric wiring, switches etc.

FIRE-FIGHTING

Copious amount of water must be used but care should be taken that neither the molten nitrates nor the solution containing the nitrate comes in contact with any organic substance, which might be hazardous on being dried up with a layer of the nitrate on its body.

Sodium nitrate ($NaNO_3$)

Sodium nitrate is a hygroscopic crystalline material and is a typical example of the other inorganic nitrates like lead nitrate, silver nitrate, ferric nitrate, copper nitrate etc. which are all the salts of nitric acid.

Sodium nitrate is not combustible, but as a strong oxidizing agent, it may cause combustible material that has been in contact with it to burn violently on ignition. When heated, sodium nitrate releases oxygen which intensifies the flame.

STORAGE

Nitrates should be stored in fire-resistive or non-combustible buildings away from fire or any source of heat. They should also be stored in such a way that they do not come in contact with combustible material or with easily oxidizable substances like sulphur, charcoal, sugar etc., to avoid explosion or fire.

FIRE-FIGHTING

The building affected should be ventilated to get rid of the toxic gases evolved and breathing apparatus should be worn by firemen. Water should be applied in large volumes in such a way as to avoid scattering of the material. Vaporizing liquid extingusher, CO_2, dry chemicals and foam extinguishers are ineffective.

The fire area should be cordoned off and care should be taken to see that the fused mass or the molten substance in liquid form does not flow and come in contact with the organic substances which are combustible in nature.

After the fire has been extinguished, unsalvageable nitrate should be disposed off by burying them in the ground or submerging them into deep water. Wooden floors, which have been contaminated, should be watered well and scrubbed as otherwise, on drying, their burning rates will be increased considerably if a source of ignition should cause them to be ignited.

Potassium perchlorate ($KClO_4$)

Perchlorates are the salts of perchloric acid containing the ClO_4 radical in the molecule. They are powerful oxidizing agents and form slightly less powerful explosive mixtures than the chlorates. Perchlorates are less sensitive to impact and friction. They do not form a free acid in the presence of moisture; instead they offer greater safety in the event of accidental contact with weak acids, which form the main ingredient of many of the gums, such as rosin, used in pyrotechnic mixture.

Perchlorates are usually stored in wooden boxes, kegs, barrels and sometimes in iron drums. They should not be stored in the same room with explosives, acids, flammable liquids or combustible materials, e.g. sulphur, charcoal or cotton. Potassium perchlorate liberates oxygen at about 400^0C. It should be stored in a dry place and segregated from acids and combustible materials.

Potssium permangante ($KMnO_4$)

Permanganates are the salts of the permanganic acid and are strong oxidizing substances. Mixtures of permanganates an comustible material are subject to ignition by friction or may ignite spontaneously if acted upon by corrosive liquid acids. Potassium permanganate is sponatneously inflammable and violently reactive with glycerol and certain glycols. Less violent reactions occur with acetic anhydride, benzaldehyde, creosote etc. Potassium permanganate liberates O_2 when warmed in a solution or when dry at about 240^0C.

Permanganates should not be stored with explosives, acids, glycerol, formaldehyde or other organic materials or with charcoal, sulphur and similar substances.

FIRE-FIGHTING

As with other solid oxidizers, fires involving permanganates should be tackled with large volumes of water using caution not to spread the chemical with a strong jet. The solutions of permanganate, a purple-coloured strong oxidizing agent produced during fire-fighting, should preferably be buried underground instead of allowing it to pass into a public drain.

Metallic hydrides

Calcium hydride, lithium hydride, aluminium hydride and sodium hydride are the most important of metallic hydrides that are generally formed by heating the metals in hydrogen. Their use is mainly confined to the chemical industry but are also used in other fields. Calcium and lithium hydrides are used as drying agents, as reagents in chemical manufacture and as easily portable sources of hydrogen.

The metal hydrides are usually obtained in the from of powders. Once ignited, they are difficult to extinguish and as a further danger, hydrogen is evolved if they come in contact with water.

Sodium hydride and lithium aluminum hydride react violently with water. The hydrogen evolved ignites sponatneously and may explode. Explosions can occur even in a damp atmosphere. Calcium and lithium hydrides react with water but the hydrogen evolved does not ignite spontaneously. In the presence of a fire, however, water applied in any form to the hydrides may cause an explosion. Burning sodium hydride is so dangerous that it can even extract combined water from concrete and explode.

Hydrides are nromally stored in sealed cans or under an inert hydrocarbon liquid. In storage and handling, it is necesary to keep water or air away from the hydrides.

Instead of water, solutions of ethyl acetate or ethyl alcohol in a hydrocarbon solvent may sometimes be also employed for storage. The hydrides are, however, decomposed by such solutions, evolving some hydrogen in the process. The hazards associated with highly inflammable hydrogen are accompanied by a flammable liquid hazard when this method is used and it should be done very carefully by skilled men only.

CHAPTER 4

Study of a Few Gases from the Point of Fire Hazard

Any gas when subjected to a high pressure in a cylinder may be dangerous. Even compressed air or carbon dioxide gas contained in a cylinder can violently burst its container due to an abnormal rise of pressure inside when exposed to a high temperature or involved in a fire for a long time. Gases can be flammable, toxic, or both. They may also support combustion and be toxic or both. They may be divided into following groups from a fire officer's point of view:

Classification	Common examples
(A) Flammable	Hydrogen
(B) Toxic	Sulphur dioxide and methyl bromide
(C) Flammable and toxic.	Ammonia, hydrogen sulphide
(D) Supporter of combustion	Oxygen and nitrous oxide
(E) Poisonous and supporter of combustion	Chlorine and nitrogen dioxide

General principles of storage of gases

(*i*) Gases which support combustion must be kept entirely away from gases which will burn. Hence chlorine, fluorine, nitrous oxide, oxygen and compressed air must never be stored with flammable gases like ammonia, hydrogen, acetylene and hydrogen sulphide.

(*ii*) No gas cylinder should ever be stored among combustible materials where it may be subjected to heat in case of a fire.

(*iii*) Cylinders containing flammable or toxic gases should not be stored in basements where they may endanger the lives of firemen and cause an extremely difficult situation for fire-fighting or salvaging.

(*iv*) It is always preferable to store flammable and poisonous gases outside any building in a shaded enclosure with sufficient ventilation on all sides.

Fire-fighting

(*i*) Where the nature of the gas is unknown, a self-contained breathing apparatus, preferably of the closed-circuit type, should be worn before entering the gaseous atmosphere.

(*ii*) Approach should be made from the windward side, where possible.

(*iii*) All people to be evacuated, starting from the leeward side.

(*iv*) If the gas is leaking from the cylinder without burning, action should first be taken to stop the leak. Where the gas is soluble in water, such as ammonia or sulphur dioxide, and the use of water will not cause serious damage, then the fog or spray can be effectively used to help clear a path to the location for closing down the main valve.

(*v*) If the gas is already burning, it may be dangerous to extinguish the flame and the gas should be allowed to flow and burn, as otherwise an explosive mixture may be formed with air, which, if ignited, may cause far greater damage than if the original fire had been allowed to burn. The best method of extinguishing gas fires is to stop the flow of gas. Extinguishing the flame with CO_2 or dry chemical may be desirable to enable shutting off the gas supply valves.

Individual gases

HYDROGEN

It is the lightest of all the elements and is colourless, odourless and highly flammable and explosive. The ignition temperature is 585^{0}C with a range of flammability of 4.9 to 74.2% in air. It is non-toxic, but suffocating in a confined space.

Generation of the gas

Hydrogen may be prepared by bringing dilute sulphuric acid in contact with zinc, iron, tin. It may also be formed due to the reaction of water with sodium, potassium, calcium, lithium, aluminium or magnesium.

Caustic alkalies at a boiling point may also produce this gas on coming in contact with zinc, aluminium or tin. Water on coming in contact with red hot iron will also produce hydrogen gas.

Hazards

When a tightly closed valve of a hydrogen cylinder is suddenly opened or when the gas under high pressure is leaking from a joint in a hydrogen system, it may catch fire immediately. The reason is that the electrical charges produced on small dust particles or minute droplets of moisture by friction ignite the hydrogen–air mixture as it leaves the vessel. Hydrogen is spontaneously explosive with its equal volume of chlorine in bright sunlight.

Battery charging rooms sometimes (lead-acid storage battery) build up as high as 5.3% of hydrogen by volume in the air if not properly ventilated; several cases of such explosions have been reported.

The leakage of this gas, which is colourless and odourless, cannot be readily detected without the use of explosimeter. It creates a very dangerous situation when there is leakage of this gas, as an explosion might occur with disastrous consequences, specially, where this gas is used in bulk such as in factories producing hydrogenated fats and oils.

As noted previously, hydrogen burns in air or in oxygen, producing a very high temperature. Two volumes of hydrogen combine with one volume of oxygen in presence of heat with an explosive violence. The peak pressures developed by explosion of vapour–air mixture are of a high order and have been estimated at 14–21 bar for 40 litre of liquid hydrogen in test block houses 113.25m^3 volume. It may be remembered that hydrogen cannot burn on its own and there must be air or oxygen to support the combustion. The addition of 16.5 parts by volume of nitrogen or 10.2 parts by volume of CO_2 to one part by volume of hydrogen is said to render the latter non-flammable.

The gas has industrial applications in the production of hydrogenated fats and oils and for preparing ammonia synthetically, apart from its limited application in producing oxy-hydrogen flame or cooling the coils of big H.T. transformer. It is used as a reducing agent also.

OXYGEN

A colourless and odourless gas with vapour density of 16(H = 1). Oxygen is non-flammable but is a strong supporter of combustion. It is filled in steel cylinders, at a pressure of 152 bar at normal temperature. It is chemically stable and not shock-sensitive and will not decompose.

Oil or grease in the presence of oxygen under pressure may ignite violently. Oxygen cylinders should never be used for the storage of any other gas, even temporarily. The valves in the cylinder must be kept free from oil or grease as self-ignition might occur when oxygen is released.

Cylinders must not be stored in proximity to those containing flammable liquids or gases.

Generation

Oxygen is formed when chlorates like potassium chlorate or peroxides like BaO_2 (barium peroxide) or H_2O_2 (hydrogen peroxide) or nitrates like lead nitrate, potassium nitrate etc. are strongly heated. It is also formed when sodium or potassium peroxides are treated with water. Permanganates or dichromates like potassium permanganate or potassium dichromates also yield oxygen on being strongly heated. Concentrated sulphuric acid or nitric acid on being dropped over hot pumice stone yield oxygen.

Hazards

Liquid oxygen (B.P.–182.5^{0}C) has a pale blue colour. It has to be handled very carefully because of its hazardous nature. Substances, which burn when mixed with liquid oxygen (specially rocket fuels), represent an explosion hazard. These mixtures can even be exploded by static electricity, mechanical shock, and electric spark. The ordinary burning of rocket fuels or other combustible materials, when mixed with liquid oxygen, may progress to a detonation. Every fire involving liquid oxygen is an explosion hazard.

When a fire results from a leak or flow of liquid oxygen in contact with wood, paper, waste or similar materials, the first action should be to stop the flow if possible. For small spills or after the flow of liquid oxygen has stopped, copious quantities of water should be applied to extinguish the fire quickly.

Characteristics

Oxygen does not burn but supports combustion. A minimum of 20% of oxygen is required for a fire to burn; as the concentration is reduced below this figure, the intensity of a fire gradually diminishes and an ordinary fire extinguishes below 15% of oxygen concentration, unless oxidizers or substances containing their own oxygen (viz. explosives) are involved. There can be no fire without oxygen. It is possible only in certain cases, like magnesium burning in CO_2 gas, or paraffin wax burning in an atmosphere of chlorine. Substances rich in oxygen, such as peroxides, chlorates, permanganates, nitrates, chromates, picrates are quite hazardous, especially when they come in contact with organic substances, and they are called 'oxygen carriers' or oxidizers. Both oxidizers and oxidizables should never be stored together. It may be noted that materials that burn in air will burn more vigorously in oxygen. Even some of the most conventional flame-resisting paints, clothing, lubricants etc. will burn violently in oxygen. Thus, the strongest precaution must be taken, particularly where large volumes of oxygen are present.

Oxygen has wide industrial application for use as oxy-acetylene flame or oxy-propane flame for welding or cutting purpose apart from its medical use.

Oxidation : Oxygen has a tendency to combine with most of the elements chemically. The element is then said to have undergone oxidation. In a limited sense, oxidation means the process of direct union with oxygen. It may also mean taking away of hydrogen from a compound. Oxygen being a non-metallic element (i.e. electro-negative element), oxidation may also mean increasing the proportion of the electro-negative element or decreasing the proportion of the electro-positive element in a substance. Thus, oxidation is the process which introduces or increases the proportion of oxygen or electro-negative atoms in an element or compound, or removes or diminishes the proportion of hydrogen or electro-positive atoms from the same. Magnesium burns in oxygen to form oxide of magnesium (MgO); also ferrous chloride is oxidized to ferric chloride by the addition of chlorine, e.g. $2FeCl_2 + Cl_2 = Fe_2Cl_6$.

Reduction : Reduction is also a chemical process which in effect is opposite to oxidation, and it means addition of hydrogen or removal of oxygen or decreasing the proportion of the electro-negative element or increasing the proportion of the electro-positive element in a substance. Thus, CuO (copper oxide) is reduced to copper, when it is heated in a current of hydrogen.

AMMONIA GAS (NH_3)

Ammonia (NH_3) is a colourless gas with a strongly pungent and characteristic odour and a soapy or alkaline taste. When inhaled suddenly, it causes uneasiness and brings tears to the eyes. NH_3 is lighter than air and is highly soluble in water. 1 volume of water at the standard atmospheric pressure (760 mm of Hg) will dissolve about 1100 volumes of NH_3 at 0^0C. The solubility rapidly decreases as the temperature rises. The strongest solution obtained is known as liquor ammonia having a specific gravity of 0.88.

Ammonia is basic in reaction. It neutralizes acids forming ammonium salts. NH_3 gas and hydrochloric acid gas (HCl), react together to produce dense white fumes of NH_4Cl (ammonium chloride).

Hazards

Ammonia is neither combustible nor a supporter of combustion, but if the air is heated and if the amount of oxygen is increased, the gas will then burn with a yellowish flame, producing nitrogen, steam, and traces of ammonium nitrite and nitrate (range of flammability of ammonia is 14 to 28%).

Ammonia combines vigorously with chlorine, producing a yellowish-green flame and dense white fumes of NH_4Cl (amonium chloride). With an excess of chlorine, highly explosive nitrogen trichloride is formed.

Industrial application and hazards

The gas can be easily liquified under low temperature and pressure. Liquified ammonia is mostly used as a refrigerating agent in the cold storages for higher refrigerating effect. The critical temperature of ammonia is 132.5^{0}C and it requires a pressure of 6.9 atmosphere to liquify the gas at 15.5^{0}C. Leakage of ammonia from the chilling plants due to explosion in the ammonia compressor or from the joints in the pipes is a serious matter for any fire officer. Immediate stoppage of the leakage of the gas is important along with the segregation of the risk arca. Ammonium salts give off ammonia on being strongly heated. Salts of ammonia are extensively used as fertilizers, viz. ammonium sulphate, ammonium nitrate etc.

A fireman should never enter any building where ammonia is suspected to be leaking without donning a self-contained breathing apparatus set and protective clothing, viz. ammonia suit, as otherwise it will produce ammonia burns, leading to fatalities. Leakage of ammonia can easily be detected by its characteristic pungent and irritating smell and also by a red litmus paper which turns blue, or by a rag moistened with hydrochloric acid which gives off the heavy whitish fumes of ammonium chloride. Liquid ammonia should not be stored or passed through pipes of copper or brass, as it is likely to react with copper. Only iron or steel pipes or containers are recommended.

CARBON MONOXIDE AND DIOXIDE

Carbon forms two types of oxides, viz. (*i*) carbon monoxide (CO), and (*ii*) carbon dioxide (CO_2). During a fire, we may get both carbon monoxide and carbon dioxide in an enclosed space with restricted ventilation. During the first phase of combustion, when there is plenty of oxygen, CO_2 gas is mostly formed due to the burning of carbonaceous materials; later, due to insufficient ventilation and restricted supply of air, CO_2 gas being produced reacts with carbon and forms CO gas, e.g. $CO_2 + C = 2CO$. A fireman should be very careful about this gas which is one of the most dangerous gases. It has been estimated that an atmosphere containing only about 0.1% carbon monoxide, if inhaled for half an hour, will render about a quarter of the red blood corpuscles of the body incapable of functioning.

Carbon monoxide is also formed along with hydrogen when steam is passed over white hot coke, i.e.

$C + H_2O = CO + H_2$

This mixture of the gases, thus produced, is called Water Gas and it has got certain commercial applications due to its high calorific value.

CO_2 GAS

CO_2 gas is produced by strongly heating a bicarbonate or carbonate. Thus, when calcium carbonate is strongly heated, it produces CO_2 gas and calcium oxide: $CaCO_3 = CaO + CO_2$. Similarly, by strongly heating sodium bicarbonate, CO_2 gas may also be obtained:

$2NaHCO_3 = Na_2CO_3 + H_2O + CO_2$.

On a large scale, CO_2 gas is obtained as a by-product in the breweries during the fermentation of sugar solution or during the manufacture of lime.

COMPARATIVE STUDY OF THE PROPERTIES OF CO_2 AND CO

CO_2	CO
1. It is roughly 1.5 times heavier than air.	1. It is as heavy as air.
2. It is a colourless gas with a faint acid taste and smell.	2. It is a colourless, tasteless gas with a peculiar faint smell.
3. It is non-poisonous, but it causes suffocation and a choking effect.	3. It is highly poisonous and can cause death, even if a small quantity like 1 in 800 vol. of air is inhaled for half an hour.
4. It can be completely absorbed in lime-water or in caustic alkalies.	4. Not absorbed. It can only be absorbed by ammoniacal solution of cuprous chloride.
5. It neither burns nor supports combustion. In fact, it is used for extinguishing fire.	5. This gas is combustible and burns in air with a blue lambent flame. In fact it explodes when mixed with oxygen and ignited.
6. It is slightly soluble in water and the aqueous solution is slightly acidic.	6. It does not dissolve in water.
7. CO_2 gas, however, supports the combustion of burning magnesium, sodium and potassium with the liberation of carbon.	7. It does not do so. Being an unsaturated compound, it combines chemically with chlorine to form a poisonous substance like carbonyl chloride (phosgene gas). It also reacts with finely divided metals like cobalt, nickel and iron to form the corresponding carbonyls.

Hydrocarbons

MARSH GAS (CH_4) AND NATURAL GAS

Marsh gas is one of the main products of decomposition of vegetable matter in air. Natural gas, which mostly consists of marsh gas, is used now-a-days in the industry or for domestic purpose for illumination and it is obtained from pits during drilling for oil. It is piped under high pressure and supplied over a long distance. Natural gas is mainly marsh gas (over 80%) with small quantities of ethane, propane and butane and a very little quantity of carbon dioxide and nitrogen.

Marsh gas is, however, a colourless gas without any smell or taste. It is lighter than air and is sparingly soluble in water. It is a non-supporter of combustion, but burns with a practically non-luminous flame and also explodes violently with production of CO_2 gas when mixed with air or oxygen and fired :

$$CH_4 + 2CO_2 = CO_2 + 2H_2O.$$

Explosion in coal mines

Explosions in coal mines are due to the presence of marsh gas (which is also called fire damp) and air and their ignition takes place by contact with overheated metallic surface, sparks etc. As the coal is removed by the miners, the gas escapes from these cavities into the mine, and on mixing with the air, forms the explosive mixture which may ignite and explode on coming into contact with sparks from defective electrical appliances or any overheated machine parts. The minimum ignition energy required for marsh gas has been estimated to be 0.3 millijoules, as against 0.02 millijoules for hydrogen. The range of flammability of marsh gas is 5.3 to 14% and its ignition temperature is 538°C approximately.

ACETYLENE GAS (C_2H_2)

Acetylene is one of the important industrial gases. The manufacture and use of acetylene introduces serious fire and explosion risks.

Properties and uses

Acetylene as is used commonly, has a slight garlic smell and is lighter than air (vapour density = 0.91; air = 1), and it is an unsaturated hydrocarbon. It is also insoluble in water and is a colourless gas. Chemically pure acetylene is, however, odourless.

Hazards

Acetylene gas is liable to explode if it is compressed above 1.4 bar when it becomes very unstable, specially over 2.1 bar. It is for this reason that acetylene is dissolved in acetone in a porous filling and filled in acetylene cylinders which are maroon coloured for identification as against the black for oxygen and yellow for chlorine cylinders.

Acetylene is one of the most hazardous gases, being highly flammable and explosive. It has the widest explosive range among any of the common gases, ranging from 2.3 to 80% by volume with air and 2.3 to 93% with oxygen. Acetylene, in contact with copper or silver may form acetylides which are violently explosive and can be detonated by a slight shock or by the application of heat. Acetylene also combines explosively with chlorine.

Use and characteristics

Acetylene is used with oxygen for welding iron and steel on account of the very high temperature generated (over 2500^{0}C) and also for cutting steel plates.

Water on calcium carbide (CaC_2) produces acetylene and calcium hydroxide is obtained as a by-product:

$$CaC_2 + 2H_2O = C_2H_2 + Ca(OH)_2.$$

The gas is a non-supporter of combustion, but burns with a highly luminous and smoky flame. The smoke is due to separation of free carbon from acetylene by decomposition at high temperature. The gas burns in air with the formation of CO_2 gas and water :

$$2C_2H_2 + 5O_2 = 4CO_2 + 2H_2O.$$

The gas reacts violently with the halogens, and in particular, it reacts with chlorine with an explosive violence with the production of flame. It may also be considered as quite hazardous in contact with oxygen, compressed air or nitrous oxide. The gas is soluble in alchohol and acetone.

Acetylene cylinders are filled with a porous mass of 'Kapok' saturated with acetone. The cylinders are then filled by keeping them under brine at a low temperature. The liquid acetone absorbs 25 times its own volume of acetylene gas for each atmosphere of pressure. Therefore, at 17 atmospheres (the normal pressure for the cylinder) the acetylene capacity is about 425 times the volume of the acetone.

Storage

Acetylene cylinders should always be stored and used in an upright position, as otherwise the liquid acetone may blow through the torch during welding or cutting, resulting in dangerous and faulty operation.

Fire-fighting

The release of the burning gas from the safety valve either at the top or the bottom is not so dangerous, provided it does not affect the other cylinders. In such cases, the cylinders involved will have to be kept cool by fine spray of water, and the cylinders, which have not been heated should be removed to a safe place, making sure that the valves have been turned off first. It has been pointed out that in case of a fire involving the acetylene supply system in a factory, it will not be wise enough to extinguish the flame, unless a fuel shut-off can be effected by closing the valve. If the flames are endangering nearby combustibles, then it would be better to extinguish the flame. If the leak in the cylinder is very small and the fuse plug has not melted, it might be better to extinguish the flame and remove the cylinder from the building, before it develops into a large fire.

Precautions

If called upon to fight a fire in a building where a large number of acetylene cylinders are involved, it is not wise to get close to the cylinders to extinguish the burning jet of acetylene. Under such circumstances, it is likely that impinging jets of flame from one cylinder might be striking upon another, causing them to rupture and fly off in any direction. It would therefore be advisable to set up branches for spraying the cylinders for coolong them from a distance or from a shielded position. Every care should be taken to avoid exposure of any kind should a cylinder explode. Solid jets should not be used.

Special notes on acetylene cylinders

(*i*) The cylinders are maroon coloured with left-hand threaded valves (cylinders of all flammable gas are generally left-hand threaded);

(*ii*) The pressure in the cylinder is 15.5 bar after filling up of the gas;

(*iii*) No attempt should be made to examine and use a cylinder or tamper with its valves, after it has been involved in a fire, until the makers or suppliers have been consulted;

(*iv*) When an acetylene cylinder becomes heated, a spontaneous rise in temperature and an explosion may occur.

Cases where cylinders involved in fire are leaking

The following points are to be borne in mind while handling a leaking cylinder involved in fire : (1) cool the cylinder; (2) remove them to the open; (3) open the valves; (4) immerse them in a tank of water or sea or river; (5) when the cylinder is moved into the open, the regulator should be removed and the cylinder valve opened fully.

ETHYLENE GAS (C_2H_4)

It is a colourless gas with a sweet smell at ordinary temperature and pressure, and is an unsaturated hydrocarbon. It is almost as heavy as air, and it is slightly soluble in water, but more soluble in alcohol. The gas does not support combustion, but it is inflammable and burns with a smoky luminous flame with the formation of CO_2 and H_2O. The mixture of ethylene and oxygen or air explodes on ignition:

$$C_2H_4 + 3O_2 = 2H_2O + 2CO_2$$

Ethylene is mostly used in the preparation of alkathene or polyethylene papers, apart from its use for preserving fruits.

COAL GAS (TOWN GAS)

Coal gas is a mixture of several gases, viz. hydrogen (43 to 55%); marsh gas (26 to 35%); carbon monoxide (4 to 11%); ethylene, acetylene, benzene (2.5 to 5%); nitrogen (2 to 12%); carbon dioxide (0 to 3%); oxygen (0 to 1.5%). Thus, coal gas principally consists of a mixture of hydrogen, marsh gas, carbon monoxide and ethylene, acetylene or benzene. It is obtained by the destructive distillation of bituminous coal in 'D' shaped fire clay retorts, which are heated to a temperature of about 700 to 1000^0C by producer gas. The volatile products pass through a vertical ascension pipe, and go inside hydraulic mains, where coal gas is partially cooled and some tar and water collect, the excess of which flows into the tar well.

From the hydraulic main, the hot gases enter into a series of iron pipes, called condensers, where the gases are further cooled and more tar is condensed and run into the tar well. The liquid in the tar well separates out into two layers—the upper layer is mainly a solution of ammonia (NH_3) and ammonium salts in water and it is called Gas liquor or Ammoniacal Liquor, and the lower layer is gas tar or Coal tar.

The gas is then drawn out of the condensers by pumps and is forced up a tower filled with coke, called scrubber, for purfication. Here, it meets a spray of water which removes ll traces of ammonia and some hydrocynic acid, sulphureted hydrogen (H_2S) and carbon doixide gas.

Though it is free from ammonia, tar etc., coal gas at this stage still contains CS_2, H_2S, CO_2 and traces of HCN gases as impurities and to remove them the gas is passed through purifiers which are low rectangular iron tanks with horizontal shelves containing (*a*) slaked lime, in which mainly CO_2 as also H_2S, CS_2, HCN etc. are absorbed, and (*b*) hydrated oxide of iron which absorbs the last traces of H_2S and HCN gases.

The gas is finally collected in big gas holders (water seal type) after a final purification by passing it through a big tube, having a high voltage DC conductor (about 40,000 volt) at the centre, known as electrostatic detarrer.

The by-products obtained during manufacture of coal gas are *(i)* coal tar; *(ii)* ammonia; *(iii)* gas-lime; *(iv)* coke; *(v)* gas-carbon; *(vi)* spent oxide of iron. All these products are quite useful and have a great demand in the market.

PHOSPHINE GAS (PH_3)

This is a colourless and poisonous gas, heavier than air, possessing an offensive smell of rotten fish. The ordinary gas (i.e. not chemically pure) is spontaneously flammable in air and burns with a vortex of white smoke of phosphorous pentoxide. The gas is produced by the action of water on calcium phosphide, or by the action of dilute acids on the phosphides of Al, Fe, Zn, Sn, etc.:

$$Ca_3P_2 + 6H_2O = 3Ca(OH)_2 + 2PH_3$$

FLUORINE

Fluorine is a greenish-yellow gas, 1.3 times heavier than air. It is the most active member in the halogen family consisting of fluorine, chlorine, bromine and iodine. It is intensely poisonous and irritating and reacts with hydrogen and many organic materials with explosive violence. It is the most chemically reactive substance known. Alcohol, turpentine, ether, etc., burst into flame and are completely decomposed in contact with fluorine. Iron, zinc, tin, magnesium, nickel, aluminium and silver catch fire in fluorine when gently warmed. Metalloids such as arsenic, antimony burn in the gas, producing their fluorides. Sulphur, phosphorus, iodine, bromine, carbon and boron burn spontaneously in fluorine producing fluorides.

It also reacts explosively in contact with water vapour to form hydrofluoric acid and oxygen.

Fire-fighting

As fluorine causes severe flash burns and is a serious inhalation hazard, areas where fluorine is leaking should not be entered without self-contained B.A. sets. A solution of 5 to 10% by weight of caustic soda (NaOH) destroys fluorine gas. Water should not be used on fluorine, as it will aggravate the situation by reacting with the hydrogen in water.

CHLORINE

Chlorine is a greenish-yellow gas, with a vapour density of 2.49. In a cylinder, chlorine is stored under 5.6 bar pressure around at 38^0 C and is mostly in liquid form, which has a specific gravity of 1.47.

Chlorine is formed when hydrochloric acid is oxidized by nitric acid, or potassium permanganate, or manganese dioxide or lead nitrate. It may also be produced from bleaching powder by treating it with dilute hydrochloric or sulphuric acid.

The gas causes irritation and attacks the membrane of the throat, lungs and nose, causing immediate coughing and sneezing.

Fire hazard

Chlorine is non-flammable, but like oxygen, it is capable of supporting the combustion of certain substances and of forming highly dangerous compounds with several elemenys.

Characteristics

Chlorine supports the combustion of hydrogen, arsenic, phosphorous, lead, copper, forming their chloride. Most hydrocarbons (e.g. turpentine) react readily with the evolution of heat and light. If mixed with hydrogen, methane, ethylene, ether, or with acetylene, chlorine will explode in sunlight or in artificial light. Mixtures of chlorine and hydrogen composed of more than 5% of either component are very explosive. Paper or textile soaked in turpentine, resin, etc., will ignite spontaneously in a chlorine atmosphere. Sodium, potassium, phosphorus will burn in chlorine gas, forming their chlorides. At ordinary temperature, dry chlorine does not appreciably corrode steel or most other metals. At elevated temperatures, it may attack metals rapidly. In the presence of moisture, chlorine is very corrosive.

When involved in a fire at a temperature above 149^0 C, chlorine will react with steel cylinders, burning a hole through them.

Fire-fighting

In case of a fire, use of self-contained B.A. sets, evacuation of the workmen to the windward side or in the direction of the flank, avoiding the use of water directly on the leaky portion of the cylinder, and a thorough ventilation of the room or rooms affected are some of the things to be done first.

A leaking cylinder should preferably be submerged under the milk of lime. It may only be submerged under water when there is no other recourse, but it should be weighted so that it does not float. No effort should be made to neutralize the gas with ammonia. In case the leak cannot be stopped by the manipulation of valve on the cylinder, the best thing would be to have the gas absorbed in caustic soda solution or lime. The reaction of chlorine with lime is to produce bleaching powder.

Safe handling of compressed gases

NOTES

Oxygen: Liquifies at -183^0C.

Nitrogen: Liquifies at -196^0C.

Standard cylinders of oxygen contain 6.8m^3 (240 cu. ft.) of gas at a pressure of 136.62 bar (1980 p. s. i.) (purity 99.95%). Each cylinder weighs 76.2 kg, is 10 mm thick at the base and 8 mm thick at sides. Cylinders of oxygen should be stored in a horizontal position, not more than 1.2m high. They are painted black and the valves are right hand threaded. They may be used in horizontal position.

NOTES ON STORAGE OF GASES

Storage of gas cylinders and their fillings are subject to the gas cylinder rules of the Government of India. Cylinders of gases are to be stored in the open, under shades with all sides open. Special precautionary measures are to be taken for storage of cylinders containing gases like hydrogen, acetylene and chlorine, as also liquified petroleum gases, known as L.P.G. and the toxic and flammable gases.

CHAPTER 5

Common Organic Volatile Liquids of Hazardous Nature

Volatile liquids are those which evaporate at all temperature and pressure. These liquids are generally of organic origin and have their flash points below the ordinary temperature. Hence, they are potential fire hazards and should be stored and handled carefully in well-ventilated rooms. They may be divided under the following three categories :

(*a*) which are miscible in water and do not float, e.g. alcohol, acetone, methylated spirit etc.,

(*b*) which are not miscible in water, but lighter than water and float on it, e.g. petrol, xylene, aniline, benzene, benzine, ether, toluene etc,

(*c*) Which are not miscible in water and being heavier than water, sink, e.g. carbon disulphide, nitro-benzene etc.

Category A

ALCOHOLS

Alcohols are usually volatile and flammable. Methyl and ethyl alcohol are the two common types. The flash point varies from 12^{0}C to 38^{0}C. Ethyl alcohol (C_2H_5OH) has a flash point of 16^{0}C, whereas methyl alcohol (CH_3OH) has flash point of 18^{0}C (app.). In general, alcohols have a specific gravity of about 0.8, a vapour density of 2.5 to 3 and an explosive range of 3.5 to 18% by volume in air. The lower alcohols (like methyl, ethyl) are readily soluble in water and are used in antifreeze compounds, germicides, antiseptics and for cosmetics, etc. They burn with a faint bluish flame, which can hardly be distinguished in bright sunlight.

Hazards

Alcohols should not be mixed with silver nitrate or mercury nitrate, as explosive fulminates may be formed, nor with strong oxidizing acids like nitric, perchloric or permanganic acids, as they may explode spontaneously. They may also form powerful explosives on coming in contact with hydrogen peroxide (highly concentrated) and this can be detonated by a shock.

An alcohol–water mixture containing less than 15% alcohol will not burn continuously even if heated to its boiling point. Higher concentration must be diluted nearly to 15% before fires go out, depending upon the temperature of the liquid. Alcohol–water mixtures containing more than 20% alcohol are flammable.

Fire-fighting

An alcohol fire should not ordinarily be tackled with foam as the foam bubbles will be broken by the alcohol which absorbs water. The best recourse will be to dilute the fire with water, when it will automatically go out. Alcohol resistant foams, dry powder and carbon dioxide are suitable extinguishing agents. Fixed installations employing special water sprays are suitable for controlling fires involving tankage, drum stores and plant containing bulk quantities of alcohol.

ACETONE (CH_3–CO–CH_3)

It is a colourless, volatile and inflammable liquid, miscible in water in all proportions. It is lighter than water, with a flash point below 0^0C (-18^0C). The vapour is heavier than air (v. d.: 2.00) and forms an explosive mixture with air with explosive limit of 2.6 to 12.8% by volume in air. It is injurious if inhaled for a long time. It is generally found in concerns dealing in explosives, celluloid, cellulose paints, and gas, e.g. acetylene, manufacturers of artificial silk and as a general solvent for paints, varnish etc.

If the concentration of the vapour, which is moderately toxic, is heavy, B.A. sets are to be used and a fine water-spray for diluting the liquid is to be used. Foam, dry powder and carbon dioxide are suitable extinguishing agents for small fires or spillages. Fixed installations employing tankage, drum stores and plant containing bulk quantities of special watersprays are suitable for controlling fires involving acetone.

CLYCERINE (CH_2OH–CHOH–CH_2OH)

This is a very important article of commerce used for a variety of purposes, like manufacture of drugs, copying inks, shoepolish, toilet soaps, and lastly, for explosives etc. It is obtained as a by-product in the soap industry by hydrolyzing the fats and oils and later recovering the glycerol from the spent lye of the soap manufacturers.

Characteristics

It is a syrupy liquid, colourless, odourless with a very sweet taste, having a flash point 176^{0}C and specific gravity of 1.25. It mixes with water and boils at 290^{0}C with certain amount of decomposition, evolving flammable vapours. It is quite hazardous with an oxidizing substance, like nitric acid and a little amount of sulphuric acid when nitroglycerine, a dangerous explosive, is formed. Similarly, hot glycerine with potassium permanganate may produce a violent chemical reaction with the production of flame.

Fire-fighting

In a fire involving glycerine, water in the form of a jet may not be used, as the glycerine, on account of its high boiling point, may be at a high temperature leading to the formation of steam with explosive violence as soon as water is poured on to the fire. CO_2 or dry chemical extinguisher or dry sand should be used for extinction of the fire. Small spillages, when involved in fire, may be diluted with copious water spray and extinguished.

Category B

PETROL AND FUEL OILS

Petrol, kerosene and diesel oil are the three substances most commonly used for a variety of purposes. Unlike the aromatic hydrocarbons derived from coal-tar, the petroleum derivates, such as petrol, kerosene, light fuel oil, diesel oil or heavy fuel oil are paraffin hydrocarbons.

Classification

Petrol or gasoline, due to its very low flash point (below 24.4^{0}C) has been classified as 'Dangerous Petroleum', whereas high-speed diesel oil and kerosene have been classified as 'Non-dangerous petroleum' under the Petroleum Act on account of their higher flash point (between 24.4^{0}C and 65.5^{0}C). There are other categories of petroleum products also according to their flash point, and as per Petroleum Rules, they are categorized under Heavy Petroleum and Excluded Petroleum. Heavy Petroleum with flash point below 93.3^{0}C but not below 65.5^{0}C includes furnace oil, fuel oil, light diesel oil, whereas the Excluded Petroleum with high flash point not below 93.3^{0}C (lubricating oil) has been excluded from the purview of the Petroleum Act and the rules.

General properties

Petroleum vapours are all heavier than air and tend to collect at the ground level. Calorific value is quite high and with most petroleum fuels it is within the region 10080 to 11200 kcal/kg while for coal-tar fuels, it is below 9520 kcal/kg, as against good quality anthracite coal having calorific value of 8400 kcal/kg. The flash point, flammable limit in air in percentage volume, vapour density and ignition temperature in air of some of the petroleum products are given below:

Product	Flash point in °C, (Clased cup)	Flammable limits Lower	Uper	Ignition Tempera-ture (°C)	Vapour density (air = 1)
Petrol (gasoline Specific gravity = 0.75)	-45	1	6	246 to 257	3.0 to 4.0
Kerosene (Specific gravity = 0.82)	38 to 47	0.7	5	254 to 260	4.5
Gas oil/Disel oil (Specific gravity = 0.87)	75	6	13.5	271	
Fuel oils	110 to 190			260 to 300	
Bitumens	200 to 250			400 to 500	
Grease	95 to 315			150 to 320	
Propane	gas	2.2	9.5	468	1.56
Butane	-60	1.9	8.5	430	2.57
Natural gas	5.3 to 14	3.8	14	538 (app.)	0.55

Burning characteristics

Liquid hydrocarbons like petrol, kerosene or diesel oil burn with an orange-coloured flame with emission of dense cloud of black smoke and produce a large amount of heat. Since it is the vapour above the liquid surface which participates in the burning within the range of its flammability, there are many variables affecting the rate of flame propagation and burning which include environmental factors such as the reacting temperature, heat of combustion, vapour pressure of the liquid etc. The burning rate of gasoline is generally from 15 to 30 cm depth per hour, whereas that of kerosene is 12.5 to 20 cm depth per hour.

Boilover and slopover

When heavy fuel oils or crudes burn, a layer of hot oil is formed below the surface which extends towards the bottom of the tank at a rate depending on the type of oil involved. The temperature of this layer is of the order of 204^0C to 260^0C which is well above the boiling point of water. With distilled oils (petrol, kerosene and diesel), no expanding hot layer is formed. Thus, refined oil and products with narrow boiling range do not establish heat wave, which no doubt is influenced by the impurities and free carbon present in the crude.

Boilover : In case water is present at the bottom of a tank containing crude or heavy fuel oils, contact between water and the heated front of hot layer of oil will immediately cause a flash of the upper layer of water into steam, expanding the volume by 1700 times, and a wave of burning oil which may amount to several hundred tons, may be suddenly expelled out of the tank with a great force involving other tanks nearby and the fire-fighters.

Slopover : The slopover or spill-over is a minor boilover and takes place with wet oil containing a percentage of water burning in a tank that is full or nearly full and due to the sudden application of foam or from rain or spray from cooling branches falling upon the hot oil surface. It is for this reason that when the oil level is within 3m of the top of the tank, great care should be taken when applying foam, specially when the oil is boiling. Warning of a slopover is given by the lighter colour of the smoke at the top of the tank on the windward side owing to formation of steam, while a sizzling sound indicates wetness in oil.

Fire-fighting

Petroleum spirit has specific gravity of 0.680 to 0.760. The fuel oil and the crude, also having low specific gravity, float on water and, as such, only foam, CO_2 gas, and dry chemicals should be used for fire-fighting and water should never be used save and except for cooling down the tanks or containers.

Use of high expansion foam : For covering the spillage of petrol or oil over a large area, when involved in a fire (such as a runway for aircrafts), the application of high expansion foam (H.E. foam) or foam with light water (containing perfluoro surfactants) are the ideal agents as against ordinary protein foam. Dry chemical powders are ideal for small spillages.

XYLOL OR XYLENE ($C_6H_4(CH_3)_2$)

Xylene is a colourless, highly volatile and flammable liquid with specific gravity of 0.87, with odour like that of benzene. Its B.P. is between 137 to 142^{0}C and its flash point is 22.8^{0}C. It is fairly hazardous. The vapour density of xylene at 15^{0}C is 3.66 (air = 1). It is immiscible in water and also lighter than it and burns with a smoky flame, yellow in colour. The range of flammability in air is from 1.1 to 7.0% by volume. The spontaneous ignition temperature of xylene is 500^{0}C.

Uses

It is found in tar distillaries, as a derivative of coal-tar. It is also used in the manufacture of explosives, synthetic varnishes etc.

Fire-fighting

Foam, dry chemical, or CO_2 are the ideal fire extinguishing media. Water should not be used, as it floats on water and the fire will spread. It may be noted that the liquid can cause irritation of the skin and its vapours are toxic and B.A. sets may be necessary during fire-fighting.

Aniline ($C_6H_5NH_2$)

Aniline ($C_6H_5NH_2$) is an oily, flammable liquid which is colourless when pure, but normally of brownish colour with B.P. = 182^{0}C and specific gravity of 1.022 at 15^{0}C. It is slightly soluble in water and has its characteristic odour. The flash point is 25^{0}C (79^{0}F). It is hazardous with nitric or sulphuric acid, chlorine, bromine or with other oxidizing substances. Aniline is used for manufacture of certain dyes. Its vapour is irritant and toxic. The liquid is poisonous, if absorbed by skin or taken by the mouth.

Fire-fighting

Foam, dry powder, CO_2 are the ideal extinguishing media, but in view of its slight solubility factor, the fire can be swamped with water.

BENZOL OR BENZENE (C_6H_6)

A colourless volatile liquid, obtained from the fractional distillation of the coal-tar (9.08 litre per tonne of coal distilled); it is highly flammable. It has got its characteristic smell, with its flash point below ordinary temperature (–11.1^{0}C). Its B.P. is 80.5^{0}C. Benzene is immiscible with water and also lighter than water. It forms an explosive mixture with air. The range of flammability at N.T.P. is 1.4 to 7.5% by volume in air. It burns with a smoky flame, copiously evolving heavy soot.

Fire-fighting

Foam, CO_2, or dry chemical powders are the ideal extinguishing media. The vapour being heavy (vapour density at $15^0C = 2.69$), it tries to settle at the bottom and as such thorough ventilation is required in view of the toxic nature of the gas.

Uses

It is widely used as a solvent and for dry-cleaning and may be found in dye-manufacturing concerns as also for manufacture of certain explosives, fine chemicals, and insecticides.

SOLVENT NAPHTHA

It is a colourless liquid of specific gravity = 0.88, with a flash point of 21^0C. This is a coal-tar distillate, containing mixed hydrocarbons with small amount of benzene, toluene and a large amount of trimethyl and tetra-methyl benzol. It is highly flammable and burns with a luminous orange-coloured flame with copious amount of black smoke. It is used in rubber industries, as a solvent for rubber.

Fire-fighting

Foam, CO_2 or dry chemical powder are the ideal fire extinguishing media. Water should not be used.

BENZINE

A name given to light petroleum spirit. It is a mixture of hydrocarbons of the paraffin series with low boiling point between 50 and 65^0C. It is used for dry-cleaning and also as a solvent. It is highly flammable, requiring foam or dry chemicals for its extinction.

ETHER (DI-ETHYL ETHER) ($C_2H_5-0-C_2H_5$)

It is a colourless, mobile, highly volatile and flammable liquid. Its flash point is -40^0C and specific gravity is 0.71, but the vapour is heavier than air (vapour density = 2.55 air = 1). This heavy ether vapour, on being spilled, may travel quite a distance to a source of ignition and flash back. Containers of ether can build up considerable vapour pressure when heated and hence they should be kept in a cool location. Ether burns with a blue lambent flame which is a characteristic of its own. The range of flammability is 1.9 to 48% by volume in air. The ignition temperature in air is 185^0C.

Uses

Ether is one of the most hazardous liquids, but it is widely used as a solvent and for manufacture of certain drugs and for anaesthetic purpose in hospitals.

Special hazards

If kept for a long time in ordinary glass containers, it has been stated to form peroxide, which is responsible for its spontaneous explosion or explosion on violent shock. Storage in amber-coloured bottle in a cool place away from the source of a strong light has therefore been recommended.

Fire-fighting

Because of the wide explosive range of diethyl ether (1.9 to 48% in air) and low ignition temperature (185^{0}C), fires in di-ethyl ether are more difficult to handle than fires in gasoline and the danger of flash-back is much greater. Dry chemical, CO_2, sand, B.C.F. (Bromo-chloro-difluoro-methane) or B.T.M. (Bromo-trifluoro-methane) extinguishers are recommended for fire-fighting, but dry chemical extinguishers are the ideal for knocking out small spillage fires. Water can be effectively used to cool exposed drums and fog can provide protection for fire-fighters.

It has been recommended that fires in ether, flowing under pressure from a source, are not to be extinguished first, unless by so doing, the source of supply can be shut off immediately. Continuous vaporization of the unburnt hot liquid may create a fire and explosion hazard, much greater than the hazard of the burning ether.

ETHYL ACETATE ($CH_3COOC_2H_5$)

It is a colourless, fragrant liquid with the characteristic smell of pear drops with a flash point of -4^0C and auto-ignition temperature of 460^{0}C. It is lighter than water with a specific gravity of 0.9 and vapour pressure of 72.8 mm of Hg at 20^{0}C. The vapour density being 3.04 (air = 1), it is heavier than air. The range of flammability is 2.2 to 11.4% by volume in air.

Special hazards

Ethyl acetate is a highly inflammable liquid with explosion risk and it tends to accumulate on floor levels, in basements and in other low-lying areas, giving rise to explosion risk. It is slightly toxic, irritating to the eyes, nose and skin. The storage of a large quantity should be in metal tanks or drums in detached sheds in the open, similar to the storage of dangerous petroleum.

Uses

It is used as a solvent for coatings (paints, varnish) and plastics and also for manufacture of certain synthetic flavouring substance, pharmaceuticals, perfumes and smokeless powders.

Fire-fighting

For fire-fighting, water should not be used. Dry powder, carbon dioxide, halogenated hydrocarbon extinguishing agents and alcohol-resistant foam are recommended.

TOLUOL OR TOLUENE ($C_6H_5CH_3$)

A colourless volatile inflammable liquid with a peculiar odour like benzene, obtained from the fractional distillation of the gas oil in the coal gas manufacturing concerns. It is lighter than water (specific gravity = 0.866). Its B.P. is 110^0C and the range of flammability is from 1.27 to 7% by volume in air (more or less synchronizing with petrol). Its flash point is below the ordinary temperature (5^0C) and vapour density is 3.14 (air = 1). Most of its properties are like those of benzene.

Fire-fighting

Foam, carbon dioxide, halogenated hydrocarbon extinguishing agents like C.B.M. or B.C.F., or dry chemical powders are recommended for fire-fighting. Water must not be used.

Toluene received its name from a resin known as Tolu balsam, from which it is obtained by distillation and it is used for manufacture of explosives (T.N.T.) and in the preparation of saccharin, certain dyes and drugs.

Category C

CARBON DISULPHIDE (CS_2)

It is a heavy, colourless liquid (specific gravity = 1.29) with an offensive odour, having an ignition. It is a heavy colourless temperature so low that its vapour can be ignited from a steam pipe or a light bulb. Its low flash point (-30^0C), its wide explosive range (1 to 50%) in air, its ignition temperature of about 125^0C make it a particularly explosive and hazardous substance. It is volatile at ordinary temperature. Its vapour is heavier than air by 2.64 times and it is not miscible with water and being heavier, sinks to the bottom. It is, however, inert to most metals, ceramics and glass and it is completely stable in steel vessels.

Storage

Carbon disulphide is normally stored under water in tanks, as it is heavier than water. Carbon disulphide is insensitive to shock so long as no oxygen is present, and therefore, except when in original containers in small quantities, it should be kept blanketed with inert gas or water at all times for storage of large quantities in vessels or tanks.

Burning characteristics and fire-fighting

When burning, the flames are almost colourless and the flame temperature is relatively low. The products of combustion are SO_2 and CO_2 gases, with burning smell of sulphur and the gases evolved are both choking and irritating.

A carbon disulphide fire should be attacked with either fine water spray or dry chemical powder and the firemen must wear self-contained B.A. sets for personal protection. Small fires in containers may be extinguished by shutting off the lids and by smothering. Carbon disulphide is commercially used for manufacture of artificial silk, rubber, insecticides and fumigants, as also for vulcanizing of rubber.

NITRO-BENZENE ($C_6H_5NH_2$)

It is a yellow liquid which is heavier than water (specific gravity = 1.2) and is flammable with a boiling point of 211°C. It has the peculiar odour of benzene (bitter almonds) and it is produced as a result of nitration of benzene. The vapour is heavier than air by 4.25 times and the flash point in air is 190°C, and as such, it is not so hazardous ordinarily. It is, however, quite hazardous with nitric and sulphuric acids and other oxidizing agents. Chlorine or bromine should be kept away from it. It may decompose explosively in a fire and both the liquid and the vapours are highly toxic.

Uses

It is used in the manufacture of aniline, fine chemicals of the benzene group, dyes, explosive works, perfumary works and soaps where nitrobenzene is used as a perfume.

Fire-fighting

The fire should preferably be dealt with dry sand, dry powdered asbestos, talc or be swamped with a fine spray of water.

HYDRAZINE (N_2H_4)

Hydrazine is a colourless, corrosive, flammable liquid, which is used in jet and rocket fuels. It is also used for the production of various chemicals, and as an oxygen scavenger for removing dissolved oxygen from boiler water. It is made from NH_3. The properties of hydrazine relating to fire hazards are summarized below:

Flash point (Open cup)	Flammable limits Lower	Flammable limits Upper	Boiling point	Auto-ignition
52°C	4.7	100	113.5°C	275°C

Special hazards

Although its flash point is rather high, hydrazine possesses unusual properties which make it hazardous. There is practically no upper flammable limit and pure N_2H_4 vapour can be made to explode, with the inflammable range being very wide. It is also easily decomposed by certain contaminants, e.g. ignition occurs at 23^{0}C in the presence of ferric oxide. There is also a tendency for hydrazine to ignite spontaneously, if a large surface is exposed to air, as it happens when a porous badly-conducting material is impregnated with the liquid. Hydrazine can react explosively with many oxidizing agents, Equipments used to handle hydrazine should be made preferably of aluminium or of certain types of stainless steel. Iron, copper and steel containing molybdenum must be avoided.

Fire prevention

Intert gases should be used to blanket the surface of N_2H_4 in order to exclude oxygen from equipment or containers.

PROPYLENE OXIDE (C_3H_6O)

Propylene oxide is a highly inflammable liquid, used in the production of raw materials for plastics and solvents. Its physical properties relevant to its fire hazard are tabulated below:

F.P. (Open cup)		Flammability limits (by volume in air)		Boiling point		Density of liquids (20°C.)
°C	°F	Lower	Upper	°C	°F	
–35	–31	2.1%	21.5%	34	93	0.83

Like most of the inflammable liquids, the vapour is heavier than air and tends to accumulate near the ground. The liquid has a limited solubility in water and is toxic.

Precautionary measures

Preacautions in its handling and use should be similar to those of other flammable liquids. Areas in which propylene oxide is present should be adequately ventilated. Sources of ignition should be excluded. There is a tendency for propylene oxide to acquire an electrostatic charge by movement during its transfer through pipes, and so, all metal work in transfer equipment should be adequately bonded and earthed.

The usual commercial grade of propylene oxide contains traces of acetylene which is capable of forming explosive compounds with a number of metals viz., copper, silver, magnesium and mercury. These metals should be excluded from equipment or from areas where propylene oxide may be present. Equipment used for handling propylene oxide should preferably be constructed of steel.

Air should be excluded from equipment in which large quantities of propylene oxide are stored or transported and nitrogen, argon or some other inert gas should be used to blanket the liquid.

Fire-fighting

Spillages should be flushed away with copious quantities of water. Fire involving propylene oxide may be extinguished by dry powder, CO_2, or foam, and B.A. set should be worn during fire-fighting or rescue operation due to the toxic nature or the liquid.

CHAPTER 6

A. Characteristics of some Strong Oxidizing Agents

All peroxides, permanganates, perchlorates, perchromates are strong oxidizing agents. Ozone and fluorine (both gases at the ordinary temperature and pressure) are also strong oxidizers and will react with oxidizable substance. They should therefore never be stored with substances like charcoal, sulphur, sugar, cellulose, resin, turpentine, pigments, saw dust, alcohols etc. Since oxidizers and oxidizables react together with the production of heat, which might give rise to a fire, utmost care and precaution should be adopted in their storage.

Inorganic and organic oxidizers

Oxygen is generally released on heating the substances rich in oxygen and it is this oxygen which causes the oxidation of the combustible material (fire or explosion):

$$BaO_2 = BaO + O; \quad H_2O_2 = H_2O + O; \quad Na_2O_2 = Na_2O + O.$$

The inorganic oxidizers, such as sodium nitrate, sodium peroxide, potassium chlorate, are not of themselves combustible, but render other materials highly inflammable. Examples of other inorganic oxidizers are chlorates, chromates, perchlorates, permanganates, peroxides, nitrates and nitrites.

STORAGE

Such substances should be stored in a dry area, separated from acids and corrosive liquids with which they may react explosively and be protected from coming in contact with metallic powders, combustible solids and flammable liquids.

Organic oxidizers, such as benzoyl peroxide and acetyl peroxide are often highly flammable and being strong oxidizing agents will often explode under certain conditions. They should not only be kept away from combustible materials, but also from the inorganic oxidizing materials, in order to avoid violent reactions. We have talked about the permanganates, perchlorates, nitrates etc. Peroxides will be discussed here.

Inorganic peroxides

Inorganic peroxides liberate hydrogen peroxide (H_2O_2) with acids and decompose easily in the presence of heat or moisture to liberate oxygen. Being strong oxidizing agents, they present a serious fire and explosion risk if stored or kept with charcoal, sulphur and metallic powders.

Sodium peroxide is typical of the solid inorganic peroxides. It is a yellowish-white granular powder, which absorbs moisture from the air. In contact with organic or readily combustible material, an explosion may take place.

When wet, certain inorganic peroxides, such as those of sodium, potassium or barium will liberate heat and give off oxygen. The reactions are shown below:

$$2Na_2O_2 + 2H_2O = 4NaOH + O_2$$

$$Ba_2O_2 = 2Ba + O_2$$

STORAGE

Storage of inorganic peroxides of alkali metals should be made carefully in fire-resisting, unsprinkled construction. They should be kept sealed in tins in a dry location, away from acids or combustibles or any organic chemicals (including organic peroxides).

FIRE-FIGHTING

In case of a fire involving materials stored adjacent to alkaline inorganic peroxides, an effort should be made to avoid water or moisture coming in contact with any exposed peroxides during fire-fighting. If the substance itself is on fire, due to spillage or otherwise, it may be possible to extinguish it with dry powder extinguisher, or by covering the fire with dry sand or soda-ash. If the fire continues or the quantity involved is very large, then it may be flooded with large quantities of water from hoses at the quickest possible time.

Hydrogen peroxide (H_2O_2)

Hydrogen peroxide (H_2O_2) is another example of an inorganic peroxide most commonly used, which in certain circumstances may cause fire.

GENERAL CHARACTERISTICS

Hydrogen peroxide is a clear syrupy liquid, which in pure form is extremely unstable and releases oxygen. It is a corrosive chemical, reacting exothermally with readily oxidizable organic material.

HAZARDS

The reaction is explosive above 98^0C. It is commonly handled in water solutions ranging from 3% to 90%. The 90% hydrogen peroxide, known as H.T.P. (High test peroxide), will decompose violently if contaminated with iron, copper, chromium and other heavy metals and their salts, dirt, enzymes or rust. Combustible dusts and cellulose materials may also cause decomposition and fire. The hazard is greatly reduced in dilute solutions (3% to 30%). For solutions in water containing 27.5% or more of H_2O_2 by weight, stringent precautions should be taken with good housekeeping and cleanliness. The higher strength commercially available is usually 65%.

Hydrogen peroxide solutions are not flammable, but have pungent smell and, as strong oxidizing agents, may cause ignition of combustible materials if left in contact with such materials. In case of a fire, the container may rupture, liberating oxygen which will assist the burning of combustible materials.

STORAGE

Containers, such as drums, should be stored in isolated non-combustible buildings on concrete floor and bulk storage (of at least 99.5% purity) should be in aluminium vessels with vents to permit the escape of oxygen.

For fighting fires involving hydrogen peroxides, particularly with a higher strength, liberal quantities of water should be used to dilute and wash away escaping peroxide and to fight fires in which the peroxide may be involved.

USES

H.T.P. (High test peroxide) is used as a rocket propellant with other chemicals. It can set fire to any cellulose materials or even to green grass. Ordinary hydrogen peroxide is used as bleaching agent for textiles, wood pulp and for many other materials. It is antiseptic and is also used as a laboratory reagent.

SPECIAL POINTS

As stated before, water is the recommended extinguishing agent for fires in which H_2O_2 is present. Fire-fighters should remain alert to the possibility of rupture of drums containing hydrogen peroxide. If hydrogen peroxide drums get exposed to heat, then the contents should be poured on the ground which has been flooded with water.

Organic peroxides

Organic peroxides are mostly used in the manufacture of certain types of plastics. They are unstable chemical compounds, which can either be self-ignited or can even explode under one of the following conditions viz.: (*a*) If stored at elevated temperature; (*b*) If contaminated by a metallic, organic or acidic matter; (*c*) If subjected to an impact or friction, pressure or vacuum; (*d*) If in contact with a very hot object, spark or naked flame.

HAZARDS

Benzoyl peroxide, cyclohexanone peroxide and methyl ethyl ketone peroxide (MEKP) are the most hazardous chemical substances and are used in various industries. Benzoyl peroxide, when pure and dry, is extremely hazardous. The following figures are quoted in comparison with gun powder.

Test	Gun powder	Benzoyl peroxide
IMPACT		
Drop of 11lb. weight for non-ignition	39 in	3 in
DETONATION		
Velocity of detonation	457m /sec	830
IGNITION		
Minimum exposure to a spark for ignition	0.12 sec	0.02 sec
Maximum exposure to a spark for non-ignition	0.03 sec	0.008 sec

The danger of fire or explosion is, however, highly reduced by the addition of a carrier such as phthalate or phosphate plasticizer, saturated polyester resin, silicone fluid or a filler. The addition to benzoyl peroxide of even 25% water will reduce the danger of fire or explosion considerably. Benzoyl peroxide is supplied to the polyester resin users in the form of a paste, based on phthalate plasticizer and varying in concentration of the peroxide between 25% and 70%. Benzoyl peroxide produced in the form of 20% powder in an inert filler appears to be practically non-flammable and does not show any sensitivity towards impact.

Violent decomposition of benzoyl peroxide may also occur in contact with some chemical compounds and especially with tertiary amines and strong reducing agents.

CYCLOHEXANONE PEROXIDE

Cyclohexanone peroxide is supplied to the plastics industry either as a powder containing 5% of water, or as a paste. Cyclohexanone peroxide paste is produced in several concentrations, which vary between 25% and 85% of the peroxide. This paste is usually based on inert plasticizers such as dibutyl or dimethyl phthalate or tricresyl phosphate.

The violent decomposition of cyclohezanone peroxide, leading to self-ignition, can also be caused by various organic, acidic and metallic impurities, but the rate of decomposition depends to a very large extent on the temperature.

METHYL ETHYL KETONE PEROXIDES

Methyl ethyl ketone peroxide is obtained as a result of the reaction which takes place between hydrogen peroxide and methyl ethyl ketone.

Commercially available products develop gassing and have rather low flash points. All the commercially available MEKP are generally packed in vented containers and according to the method of production may have flash point as low as 18^0C.

A new method of production allows the commercially available products to have flash point as high as 104^0C. These products, though slightly different and known as Perex MEKP, does not develop any gassing; hence, vented containers are not required even if the product is under the influence of direct sun rays or is stored at a temperature upto 40^0C.

Hazards and burning characteristics

It may, however, be emphasized that due to the natural characteristics of MEKP, once the peroxide is ignited, it will burn vigorously and may lead to an explosion irrespective of its purity or flash point. MEKP can also undergo a very violent decomposition, if contaminated by organic, acidic or metallic impurities. The rate of decomposition depends to a very large extent on the ambient temperature. For example, if contaminated with cobalt accelerators at a temperature below 10^0C, no violent decomposition may take place for several hours. If, however, the contamination takes place above (35^0C) an instantaneous explosive reaction can occur. Sensitivity of MEKP towards iron depends on many factors and explosions of MEKP might take place when contaminated with metallic iron.

HEALTH HAZARDS

All organic peroxides are classified as strong oxidizing agents and consequently they can easily damage human tissue. Benzoyl peroxide can be considered as the least and MEKP as the most dangerous from this point of view. It is therefore imperative that if a peroxide comes in contact with the skin, the affected part must be immediately cleansed with a solvent such as acetone, benzine, methylated spirit, and then washed thoroughly with soap and warm water. A much more damaging result can be produced by peroxide entering the eyes and immediate medical attention is a must.

A small quantity of sodium ascorbate, the most effective antidote, should be kept at every works where organic peroxides are used. This product, however, is not very stable and the stock should be replenished every two or three months.

RECOMMENDATIONS FOR SAFE STORAGE AND HANDLING

For storage of large quanitities of organic peroxides, it is advisable to erect a special building for storage of these products only, and it is recommended that:

The building should be constructed in brick, concrete, or double clad asbestos-cement sheeting. Partitions, walls, floors and ceilings should be constructed from similar materials. Timber should be avoided, as far as possible, but plastic sheets and composition are acceptable.

The store should be ventilated, and windows, if any, should be arranged in such a way as not to admit direct sun rays.

It is advisable to have a water sprinkler system with thermostatically controlled valves; but in the absence of such equipment, a hosed water supply should be available in the vicinity of the store.

Electrical installation inside the store should be made from flameproof equipment and it is advisable to have switches and conduit tubes either outside the building or embedded in the walls.

On the other hand, small quantities of organic peroxides should be stored in a separate chamber and the following precautions are to be observed:

It should be a cool and dark place, far away from naked flames, sparks and other source of heat such as boilers, radiators and electric fires. Access to the storage should be restricted to skilled personnel only.

As far as possible, no other raw materials and especially accelerators should be stored in the same chamber.

EMERGENCY PROCEDURE AND FIRE-FIGHTING

Burning of organic peroxides available in the plastics industry can be divided into three stages. Immediately after ignition, peroxides burn slowly, then vigorously and eventually explosively. Timing of these stages may vary quite considerably according to the type of peroxide, its concentration and temperature of ignition. When peroxides burn they produce their own oxygen and, consequently, no blanketing method of extinguishing the fire can be used.

The main aim in extinguishing the fire should be the reduction of temperature of the peroxide. A small quantity of burning MEKP can be quickly extinguished by dry ice (solid CO_2) which would reduce the temparature of the peroxide below the flash point and consequently prevent continuation of the fire. Cold water can be quite successfully used, provided it is remembered that a stream of water, before cooling down the peroxide can carry the liquid away from the source of the flame. Wet sand can produce very satisfactory results. Carbon dioxide extinguishers are, however, not satisfactory. It must be emphasized that during the third stage of burning, a violent explosion may take place and consequently it is advisable to evacuate all personnel when peroxide is ignited. If organic peroxides are not involved in the fire, they should be kept cool by constant wetting.

B. Characteristics of some Common Oxidizable Substances

Charcoal

Charcoal can be obtained from wood or bone or from the blood from the slaughter house, by burning the substance, in a limited supply of air, in closed vessels.

Charocoal contains air in its pores. It can absorb gases and decolourize or deodourize noxious fumes or smell, and being an oxidizable substance, it readily reacts with nitrate, strong acids and other oxidizing agents. Charcoal burns in air forming carbon dioxide gas; in a limited supply of air, it forms carbon monoxide gas, e.g.

$$2C + 2O_2 = 2CO_2$$

$$2C + O_2 = 2CO.$$

RISK OF SPONTANEOUS IGNITION

Charcoal has the property of absorbing many times its volume of oxygen or other gases. It has been stated that box-wood charcoal absorbs 9 to 14 times its own volume of oxygen and upto 90 times ammonia. This capacity for absorption, surface condensation or occlusion of gases is increased by moisture present in the gases involved. The degree of spontaneous heating, to which charcoal is liable, will depend on various factors, viz. the method of manufacture, the period of exposure to air or seasoning, size of charcoal, degree of air circulation or possible contamination with fatty oils etc. The presence of grease and oils with charcoal is critical, as in the case of combustible fibres such as cotton waste or jute. Thus oils should not be stored in the proximity of charcoal.

Pyrophoric carbon

Under favourable conditions, charcoal may combine with absorbed oxygen rapidly enough to ignite. This self-ignition of freshly made charcoal is the cause of numerous fires, which occur in wood when in contact with steam pipes. The wood undergoes a slow destructive distillation until it is reduced to finely divided charcoal which ignites spontaneously. Jute, which is also a carbonaceous article containing cellulose, becomes reactive forming pyrophoric carbon at temperatures of a little over 100^0C.

Pyrophoric carbon is generally formed between 230 and 270^0C and ignites spontaneously in warm air. It may be formed due to prolonged heating of wood which may then burst into flame on exposure to air. Dried wood takes up about 30 to 90 times its own bulk of air and may ignite spontaneously where pyrophoric carbon has been formed due to external heating.

Lamp black or soot

It is manufactured by burning substances rich in carbon, e.g. turpentine, kerosene, oil, tar etc. in a limited supply of air, and passing the smoke into chambers in which coarse blankets are suspended, on which the soot or lamp black, as it is called, is collected. It has wide industrial use.

HAZARDS

Lamp black absorbs gases to a marked degree and may ignite spontaneously when freshly bagged. It has a great affinity for oily liquids and may heat up when in contact with drying oils such as linseed oil or mineral oils. The risk of dust explosion increases in the presence of unconsumed petroleum, which adheres to the carbon. In lamp black and pulverized coal, fires are more likely to result from sparks or embers than from spontaneous ignition, leading to a rapid flame spread. For fire-fighting, finely divided spray from a branch and rapidly working out of the affected stocks should be resorted to.

Sulphur

Sulphur exists in a number of allotropic forms, namely the crystalline, amorphous and colloidal forms. Ordinary sulphur is, however, a pale yellow, brittle, crystalline solid, which is insoluble in water, but soluble in carbon disulphide, benzene and turpentine. It is a non-conductor of heat and electricity and is liable to oxidation with nitrates, chlorates etc. causing explosions.

On being heated, sulphur melts into a yellow mobile liquid at 115^0C , and with a rise in temperature, the colour of the liquid darkens and its mobility decreases till at 233^0C when the liquid becomes viscous. Above 230^0C, the liquid again becomes mobile, till 444.6^0C, when it boils, giving off deep orange-red vapour.

Sulphur burns in air to produce the irritating vapour of SO_2 gas. It combines with metals to form their sulphides. When finely divided copper, iron, silver, mercury, sodium or potassium are heated with sulphur, their sulphides are formed; e.g.

$$Fe + S = FeS$$

$$2Na + S = Na_2S.$$

It also combines with carbon at red-heat, forming carbon disulphide:

$$C + 2S = CS_2.$$

Sulphur is stored in bulk in the outside yards in heavy chemical industries (e.g. for manufacture of sulphuric acid), rubber works, gas works, dyes, explosives and insecticide manufacturing concerns.

A sulphur fire is difficult to tackle on account of the very choking and irritating fumes of sulphur dioxide gas being produced. The fire should be sprayed with plenty of water, taking care to avoid scattering of sulphur powder, which might increase the intensity of fire and cause an explosion. It has been claimed by some fire officers that a fire in a sulphur stack could be smothered by sulphur powder, pouring such solids with shovels, on the burning sulphur.

Phosphorous

Ordinary phosphorus (called yellow or white phosphorus) is a translucent, waxy crystalline solid, which can be easily cut with a knife under water. Its specific gravity is 1.8, melting point is 44^0C, and boiling point is 290^0C. Phosphorus becomes volatile at ordinary temperature and gradually turns dark brown on exposure to air. It catches fire at 30^0C in moist air. It is insoluble in water, but soluble in CS_2, C_6H_6, chloroform and alcohol and is poisonous.

When exposed to moist air, phosphorus undergoes oxidation, producing white fumes of its oxides and emitting a green glow of light, visible in the dark. This is called phosphorescence. Phosphorous burns spontaneously when exposed to air and explodes in contact with oxidizing materials. In a confined volume of air, when phosphrus burns, it absorbs all the oxygen available before its extinction. Ordinary phosphorus combines with oxygen producing its oxides. It combines with metals, halogens (fluorine, chlorine, bromium and iodine) and sulphur at ordinary temperature with explosive violence. It reduces both nitric and sulphuric acid. It reacts with caustic soda or caustic potash to produce phosphorated hydrogen (PH_3) a spontaneously flammable poisonous gas.

ALLOTROPIC MODIFICATION OF PHOSPHORUS

The existence of the same chemical element in two or more different physical forms with more or less the same chemical properties, but with slightly different physical properties is known as Allotropy and the different forms are called allotropic modifications or allotropes of the element.

Yellow phosphorus or the ordinary phosphorus undergoes an allotropic modification into red phosphorus when it is heated to around 230^0 or 250^0C in a closed cast-iron pot in presence of nitrogen or CO_2. Red phosphorus is less reactive than the yellow one. Below is given a comparison of the properties of the two types

Yellow or white phosphorus	Red Phosphorus
1. Semi-transparent (wax-like solid)	Opaque, Granular—red solid
2 Specific gravity = 1.8	Sp. Gravity = 2.2
3 It is kept under water.	Kept dry

Yellow or white phosphorus	Red Phosphorus
4. Melting point – 44°C.	Melting point – 500–600°C
5. Soluble in carbon disulphide	Insoluble in carbon disulphide
6. Very poisonous	Non-poisonous
7. Ignition pòint in air = 30°C	Igntion point in air = 240°C
8. Smell – garlic	No smell
9. Reacts with caustic soda or caustic potash to produce PH_3 gas	Does not react with caustic alkalies
10. Spontaneously inflammable when exposed to air	Ignites in air at about 240°C only, and by friction
11. It glows in darkness (phosphorescence)	No phosphorescence

STORAGE

Red phosphorus can be shipped and stored without the protection of water over it, but being an oxidizable substance, it should be kept away from oxidizing agents. It is reconverted into white phosphorus on heating above 550°C in an inert atmosphere.

FIRE-FIGHTING

Phosphorus fires should always be tackled by using B.A. sets and should be deluged with copious water spray. Care should be taken to see that yellow or white phosphorus do not come in contact with air or skin as it will produce painful wounds on the skin in the latter case.

CHAPTER 7

A. General Principles of Safe Storage of some Chemical Compounds

(*i*) Organic substances are not to be stored with nitric acid, carriers of oxygen, ozone, picrates, chlorates, liquid air, fulminates, fats or oils.

(*ii*) Lamp black or carbonaceous substances are not to be stored with fats, oils, sulphur, metallic sulphides or carriers of oxygen.

(*iii*) Metals in powder form (viz. bronze powder) are not to be stored together with damp substances, dusty materials, mineral acids, ethereal or fatty oils, oil of turpentine, carriers of oxygen, ozone, flowers of sulphur.

(*iv*) Resin, turpentine, ethereal oils should not be stored with iodine, chlorine, mineral acids and carriers of oxygen.

(*v*) Carriers of oxygen, liquid oxygen and ozone must not be stored with fulminates, chlorate with organic substance. Picrates with bronze, and metallic powders, carbon, lamp black, resins, phosphorus, sulphur, hydrogen sulphide and nitric acid and dusty carbonaceous substances must not be stored together.

(*vi*) Carbides and quick-lime must not be stored with water nor damp substance with acids of any kind in the same room.

(*vii*) Strong nitric acid must not be stored with oil of turpentine, hydroiodic acid, organic substances, sulphureted hydrogen. Similarly, carriers of oxygen, carbides, metallic powder, strong sulphuric acid, picrates and chlorates should not be stored together.

(*viii*) Strong sulphuric acid must not be stored with strong nitric acid, saltpetre, metallic powders, bronzes, carbides, picrates, fulminates or chlorates.

(*ix*) Carbonates or bi-carbonates must not be stored with acids.

(*x*) Carbon disulphide must not be stored with carriers of oxygen, ozone, or liquified oxygen.

(*xi*) Fulminates, picrates or chlorates must not be stored with mineral acids, organic substances, sulphur, carriers of O_2, ozone and liquid oxygen.

(*xii*) Sulphur and metallic sulphides must not be stored with carbon, lamp black, fats, oils, chlorates or phosphate.

(*xiii*) Nitrates and substances impregnated with saltpetre must not be stored with sulphuric acid.

(*xiv*) Fats and oils, particularly vegetable oils like linseed oil, are not to be stored with organic suostances like jute or lamp black, metallic sulphides or pyrites.

(*xv*) Beeswax is not to be stored with textiles, fibres, acids, chemicals, lime, oils, paints or carbide of metals.

(*xvi*) Bleaching powder must not be stored with ether, ammonia and mineral acids.

(*xvii*) Ammonium nitrate must not be stored with acids or with carbonaceous substances like wood, cork, paper, fibres, textiles, straw, rubber or leather.

B. Chemicals upon which Water should not be Used

1.	Comphor	Colourless, crystalline solide, often wax like, m.p. 175°C, flammable and burns with a smoky flame.
2.	Carbides of calcium aluminum etc. and calcium cyanamide	Calcium carbide, greyish substance, decomposed by water to form acetylene. It is not combustible in the dry state. Calcium cyanamide is made from calcium carbide and it may contain the carbide as an impurity.
3.	Calcium oxide or quicklime	White powder or lumpe, which generate much heat on application of water. This is sufficient to ignite paper and wood under certain circumstances.
4.	Peroxides of sodium and potassium	Yellow or white powders; they give off oxygen and produce caustic soda or potash when treated with water.
5.	Metallic sodium or Potassium, rubidium or calcium	Soft, whitish metale, give off hydrogen and produces caustice alkalies on coming in contact with water.
6.	Red hot iron	Gives off hydrogen, on coming in contact with water.

7.	Coal-tar	Black viscous liquid, evolving flammable vapours which may not be easily extinguished with water and may cause a spill-over of the burning liquid.
8.	Benzene, toluol, xylene, naphtha	Distillation products of coal-tar, highly flammable and being lighter than water floats on it; water will spread the fire.
9.	Paints, resins, Varnish, turpentine, oils, fats, greases, petrol	Flammable hydrocarbons, lighter than water, and as such, fire will spread on coming in contact with water.
10.	Cellulose paint collodion	Cellulose nitrate with pigments dissolved in organic solvents like ethyl acetate, acetone, or alcohols—water will spread the fire. They may form hydrogen while on fire, on coming in contact with water.
11.	Megnesium metal, electron metal	Alloy of magnesium with a small percentage of aluminium and zinc. The burning metal is explosive in contact with water due to the formation of hydrogen.
12.	Naphthalene	A solid whitish hydrocarbon, produced during fractional distillation of coal-tar. It evolves smoky flame and melts at 79°C and the liquid on coming in contact with water will be solidified, choking all outlets.
13.	Nitrate and cyanide baths for heat treatment of metals	Used for heat treatment of various metallic parts, which are dipped in baths of molten nitrates or cyanides, raised to temperatures ranging from 449°C upwards. Water will cause violent scattering of the molten salts with explosion.

C. Molten Salt Baths (nitrate and cyanide baths)—Composition and Hazards

(*i*) In nitrate baths, the salts used are sodium nitrate, potassium nitrate or a mixture of the two. Sometimes a nitrite is added to the mixture. (*ii*) In cyanide baths, sodium cyanide and potassium cyanide are used. Heat treatment baths are usually heated by gas, oil or electricity. Electric heating, which is more common, can be done by means of elements external to the bath, either by immersion elements or by electrodes immersed in the salt.

Where nitrate or cyanide baths are used for the heat treatment of metals, stringent precautions are necessary to prevent fire, explosion and gassing. Direct firing of baths by solid fuel should not be done, owing to the risk of explosion as a result of contact between the nitrate and the fuel. The greatest danger of an accident involving a salt bath is a violent explosion and this may be caused as a result of organic dirt or dust, oil or water, or air entering the baths. As such, only dry and solid materials are to be used in the bath process and that the pots should be made of a special steel, with a low carbon content, and the temperatures are to be strictly controlled.

Location and structural precautions

Salt baths and quenching baths (the latter for immersion into water after taking out the article from the salt bath) should be housed in fire-resisting buildings, exclusively reserved for the heat treatment process. The baths should be well spaced and there should also be liberal space for working. Each salt bath should be provided with a cover, and if possible with a catch-pit, capable of containing the whole of the contents of the baths.

Combustible materials, such as wood floorings or any other combustible material of carbonaceous origin should be avoided. The fire hazards from molten salts are mainly due to any contact between them and combustible materials. This may be caused by an explosion, spillage or splashings. Accurate control of the bath temperature is essential for safety. The temperature should not be allowed to exceed 505^0C. Nitrates will react with mild steel containers at temperatures as low as 594^0C. When the bath is being heated, the heat should be applied gradually.

If aluminium alloys are under treatment, an explosion can be caused at excessive temperature by reaction between the nitrate and the alloy itself or sludge which is present, and such a reaction can be accelerated by any iron oxide present in the sludge.

Electrical safeguard

Each individual heating unit should be provided with automatic over-current protection. In the case of electrode heaters, automatic circuit breakers are preferred to fuses. Electrical heaters of the external or immersion type should be so controlled as to transmit heat at a reduced rate during the melting period. Earth leakage indication should be provided to show the existence of an earth fault in a heater.

Common safeguards for salt baths

The salts themselves, viz, the nitrates, chlorates or cyanides, as might be used in the baths, are not combustible. They create the hazard of a continuous ignition source for combustion in the vicinity if the salt spatters or otherwise escape from the bath. Water introduced in the bath in any form may turn into steam with explosive effect. Some compounds decompose violently when overheated, or if the wrong salt is added. Introduction of foreign materials may cause spattering, decomposition of the salts, or formation of interior crust in the tank, resulting in serious overheating. Nitrates, by furnishing oxygen, increase ease of ignition and intensity of burning of combustibles. Cyanides in contact with acids or moisture evolve hydrocyanic gas, which is highly toxic and flammable.

Nitrates start to decompose slowly at about 399^{0}C forming nitrites and hydroxides. Decomposition does not proceed with sufficient rapidity to prevent their use continuously at temperatures upto about 593^{0}C. Above this temperature, decomposition is increasingly rapid, until a critical temperature of about 704^{0}C is reached, when violent decomposition is likely to occur with the formation of corrosive and toxic nitrogen oxides which may also attack the steel containers and the alloy being heat treated.

Points to note

The aforesaid temperature ranges are to be borne in mind to avoid explosions in molten baths, which should be located in a building with detached and fully fire-resisting structures. The baths should preferably be constructed of chrome-nickel alloy steel, which should be placed on a concrete pad, extending at least 30 metre beyond the bath in all directions.

Cyanide baths

Cyanide baths are used mostly for producing a case-hardened surface on steel and for reheating high-carbon steel. In general, cyanide baths contain from 30% to 75% of sodium or potassium cyanide. It is highly important that the stock should be free of foreign material, particularly acids or moisture, to prevent decomposition of the cyanides and giving off poisonous hydrocyanic acid vapours.

Stringent safety precautions for personal pretection of the operators should be enforced due to extreme toxic nature of the substance. Persons working in the vicinity of bath should be protected with self-contained B.A. sets, goggles, gloves, leggings and they should not be made to work or stay for long periods.

CHAPTER 8

Common Characteristics Storage, Fire Hazard and Fire-Fighting of some Commercial Articles

Cotton

Cotton is an important article of commerce and contains cellulose. It generally consists of 90% cellulose with smaller amounts of other organic bodies. The purer the cotton, the greater the percentage of cellulose, which has been given the empirical formula $(C_6H_{10}O_5)_4$.

FIRE SUSCEPTIBILITY

Cotton is highly combustible. The combustibility is due to its fibrous nature which exposes a large surface to air. The loose mass of cotton burns freely, but when spun into textile fabric, it is still liable to catch fire. Though the fire susceptibility may not be so acute. The air space in cotton, the fine nature of the fibres, and the fact that such structure is a very bad conductor of heat render it possible for a small fire in a bale of cotton, or even in folded sheets, to spread slowly throughout the mass, smouldering its way with the help of the contained air till it reaches the outside where the air causes the fire to burn up. A very small spark or a glowing particle trapped in a bale or falling amongst bales, or possibly an oily spot giving rise to spontaneous combustion, will find sufficient air to keep it glowing, as the fine fibres readily ignite. The heat of the combustion is conserved close to the spot where the combustion is taking place. A small fire can thus be kept alive for a long time, and may find its way through the bulk, often in concentric circles, the smell of which would otherwise indicate the fire being kept in by the outer layers. Fires in cotton textiles, stacked or piled in layers, may also take place in the following way. A small fragment of oily cotton may readily ignite spontaneously, being oxidized, and start a fire in a bale. Such a fire may burn so slowly that it may smoulder for days without breaking out. Cases of spontaneous combustion in cotton bales have often been brought about by a spark falling on the cotton and starting a small path of combustion in this manner.

Cotton is readily charred when exposed to heat. Prolonged exposure to a temperature not much exceeding that of boiling water, causes incipient charring, and at 111°C to 112°C, browning takes place fairly rapidly; at 220°C to 230°C it will char completely.

STORAGE

Bales of cotton that have been soaked with water during fire-fighting present a hazard to walls owing to swelling, and also to floors owing to increased weight. Hence, such bales soaked in water should be removed from a building after a fire.

FIRE-FIGHTING

Water from sprinklers or other sources is the surest medium for extinction of cotton fires which give off dense black smoke while smouldering, often misleading a fireman about the actual size of the fire, and as such, a cotton fire requires immediate ventilation to drive off the smoke from the godown. Cotton is probably the most hazardous of all vegetable fibres, with jute coming second so far as fire is concerned.

Paper

It is fairly pure cellulose, and when loose and in sheets, it is one of the most easily ignitable of the flammable substances and burns with a black irritating smoke, converting the paper into black carbon. When paper is in rolls or tightly stacked in sheets, it is not so hazardous, because, lesser specific surface is exposed to air, as compared to its weight. The finer the paper and more the area exposed, the greater is its fire susceptibility. Carbon dioxide gas is recommended for fire-fighting, as water will spoil the paper, though fire will easily be extinguished.

Jute

Jute is an organic compound. The main constituents of the fibre are alpha cellulose (about 60%), which is the major substance cotton is composed of and hemi cellulose (about 25%), which is a powdery substance, as white as flour, and lignin (10 to 11%), a brown substance. Besides these, it contains 1% or less of fat, wax and also equal amounts of nitrogenous matter and mineral substances. So far as fire is concerned, the fat and wax, which are surface constituents are the most important.

Jute is obtained in the form of pucca and kutchha bales, compressed to 28 bar and 21 bar. The specific heat of jute is 0.324. The ignition temperature of jute is 193^{0}C. The actual flame in jute bales will not be seen till this temperature is attained, but a slow combustion may go on, with emission of plenty of black smoke.

HAZARDS

The most important property of jute in connection with the fire hazard and fire-fighting is its swelling factor when in contact with water. Jute absorbs water very rapidly and increases in volume. The total increase in volume, when jute is soaked in water, is about 45% in about 30 hours. The amount of swelling comes to about 5% in one hour when ordinary air-dried jute comes in contact with water in the form of spray. The swelling pressure in a pucca bale may be as high as 317 bar when the bale can take no more water. The swelling pressure may push out the bales, which may fall upon the fire-fighters standing below and cause loss of life. It may also push down the walls of a godown, if the bales are very near to the walls, and if there is no adequate space for the expansion while stacking the jute bales. It is therefore very important to leave a clear space of about 1m from the walls.

FIRE-FIGHTING

In jute fires, dense black smoke, which is irritating and choking, is produced in abundance and visibility inside the warehouse becomes very poor. Proper ventilation of the fire is very important and fire-fighters should ventilate the fire cautiously, and B.A. sets may be required to locate the exact position of the fire. Approach inside the godown should be made cautiously during a fire, as the bales are likely to collapse and trap a fire-fighter.

A jute fire should be handled cautiously, without haphazard use of water, which may cause a collapse of the building, as a result of abnormal increase in weight of the bales due to absorption of water. The actual seat of the fire must be located at the earliest and while entering a jute godown with a charged hose pipe, every precaution should be taken against the collapse of the bales, which might severely injure a fire-fighter or trap him inside the blazing godown. Plenty of water is required for fighting a jute fire and godowns should invariably be provided with sprinklers.

Wool

Unlike jute and cotton, which are vegetable fibres, wool is obtained from animal source. It is a nitrogenous substance, containing 16 to 17%

nitrogen without any cellulose content in it. It is also comparatively less hazardous, as compared to jute, cotton or paper, but during the processing stage, it may catch fire due to the spontaneous combustion of the oil used for softening the wool.

HAZARDS

Crude wool contains fat or oil (from about 8 per cent to about 35 per cent). This fat, however, is not of a hazardous type, its iodine value not being greater than about 27%. Rise in temperature due to oxidation may be hazardous, if the wool is tightly packed in bales of a number of layers, because heat developed cannot escape. Fluff or dust from wool is hazardous, as it is very light and can blow about in lumps that cling together and can be ignited readily by a small flame.

Wool does not char or decompose at such a low temperature as does cotton, and in this respect, it resembles certain other animal products. Badly charred wool, however, is an obnoxious material, being soaked in partly decomposed oil, and is difficult to extinguish completely or open out after proper detection. Wool does not burn so freely as cotton. During a fire, destructive distillation of the product takes place, and the gases evolved from burning wool are poisonous – hydrogen sulphide and hydrocyanic acid being among them. Water is the recommended extinguishing medium for fire-fighting.

Wood

It is one of the most important materials which is liable to catch fire and burn freely after a certain temperature is reached. Wood is a complex of many substances. Cellulose may amount to about 50% of the weight of the dry wood with ligno-cellulose and lignin. These are bodies allied to cellulose. A certain amount of starch is also present and sometimes some suger, gums, resins and esters of the higher alcohols may also be found, their nature and quantity depending on the type of wood. Some mineral matter is also present and it forms the ash when the wood is burnt. The moisture content of wood is of importance and it ranges from 50% in sap wood to 20% in air-dry timber. In green wood, water, in the form of moisture fills the cells of the wood and the interior of the tubular vessels as well. The cell walls and the walls of the vessels, which form the skeleton of the wood consist of cellulose and ligno-cellulose. As the wood dries, the water evaporates, but the wood still retains its cellular structure, with air-spaces in the interior. It is due to this reason wood does not catch fire till the water contained in it is not completely evaporated.

WOOD FIRE

When a small piece of wood is heated rapidly in air to a temperature above the the ignition point of its constituents (such as, when a match is burnt), the substance of the wood will be rapidly oxidized to carbon dioxide and water, the nitrogen from the nitrogenous matter present being liberated as gaseous nitrogen. No significant amount of smoke or smell will be produced, and only ash will be left. The oxidation is so rapid and heat is liberated so quickly that all parts of the substances are raised to the ignition point after a certain stage.

BURNING CHARACTERISTICS

Wood is not a good conductor of heat because of its cellular structure. When subjected to gradually increasing heat, the temperature of wood rises slowly and it will begin to decompose before its ignition point is reached. Up to 100°C water and small amounts of volatile esters are driven off. Further change hardly takes place till the temperature reaches about 170°C when wood begins to decompose and carbon dioxide gas is evolved. At about 200°C to 350°C, a process of destructive distillation commences and acetic acid, acetone, methyl alcohol, tar, hydrocarbons, etc. are given off. These are the principal products during dry distillation, but owing to the complex nature of the wood, a large number of other compounds are produced in small quantities also. Since volatile substances contain a smaller proportion of carbon in their molecules than do the substances originally present in the wood, carbon or charcoal is left behind. It may be borne in mind that the volatile substances may not be originally present in the wood as such, but are produced by its decomposition under the influence of heat.

If heat is further applied to the wood, the temperature rises to the ignition point of the carbon, which, if air is present, begins to oxidize and glow. The heat liberated by the oxidation is sufficient to bring about the ignition of the volatile products given off from contiguous portions of the wood. These compounds then burst into visible flame, and if the air supply is sufficient, the temperature may be raised high enough to bring about the combustion of contiguous portions of the wood as a whole. Originally in a wood fire, a vigorous combustion starts after a certain period, during which, if the fire could not be subdued, then all the three phases, i.e. (*i*) the destructive distillation of the wood, (*ii*) the ignition of the charcoal and volatile products, and (*iii*) the combustion of undecomposed wood, would take place simultaneously, and the wood closest to the seat of combustion would catch fire and the wood situated further away is destructively distilled due to the heat produced from the fire. It may be remembered that the thinner the wood and the greater the draught, the more will be the spread of fire due to increased rate of combustion. Heavy beams, except in very fierce fires, rarely burn to ash, and after a fire, may be found as carbonized masses with a layer of charcoal on the surface and undecomposed wood in the interior, and the core being intact. The crackling of a piece of wood during a fire, is due to the rupture of the wood by the boiling of the contained moisture and by the gases and vapours liberated by the decomposition.

LIBERATION OF HEAT

Between 50 to 60% of the available heat of the wood, which is about 4760 kcal/kg (8500 B.Th.U/lb) is liberated due to flames during burning, and the remainder is liberated prior to this stage from the glowing of the wood. The flaming is mainly responsible for the rapid spread of fire, but the glowing assists in maintaining the production of flame and is also the main factor contributing to the resistance of the fire to go out, due to low thermal conductivity of wood. Heat does not easily penetrate deep into the surface of wood. Flames rise vertically and consequently transmit more heat to wood above the source of flaming than below or at the side.

It may also be noted that the rate at which heat can be transmitted through timber decreases rapidly as the thickness increases and there is a minimum thickness at which combustion will take place sufficiently fast to maintain the flaming necessary to provide the external source of heat. A fully developed timber fire is difficult to extinguish and it requires plenty of water to extinguish the fire.

Rubber (C_5H_8)

Commercial rubber consists of caoutchouc, a polymerization product of isoprene, resin like substances, nitrogenous substances, inorganic matter and carbohydrates.

Natural rubber (C_5H_8) is an unsaturated hydrocarbon with heat of decomposition of approximately 9425 kcal/kg and it is chemically akin to turpentine ($C_{10}H_{16}$), though they differ in ignition temperatures – rubber burns at 285^{0}C and turpentine at 240^{0}C.

FLAMMABLITY AND BEHAVIOUR IN A FIRE

Commercial rubber melts at 220^{0}C and flammable gases are given off. Rubber softens at 160^{0}C and when the temperature reaches near about 285^{0}C, it gives off highly flammable gases, which give explosive mixtures with air, and if allowed to accumulate in confined spaces, gives off dense clouds of black smoke.

NATURAL AND SYNTHETIC RUBBER

Natural rubber is the coagulated material obtained from milky latex by making incisions on the trunks of rubber trees, and collecting the milk or latex and then subsequently processing it chemically and mixing it with other ingredients and finally vulcanizing it by heating with sulphur and accelerators.

Synthetic rubber, which is mostly butyl rubber, is obtained by polymerizing butadiene (a light petroleum gas derived from the cracking of gasoline in the final stage of refining) with styrene as the monomar, which is the principal agent in the reaction with butadiene. The product is known as Buna-S. Both the agents are toxic and highly flammable. The storage of these chemicals and their processing are subject to great fire hazard.

FIRE-FIGHTING

Like other hydrocarbons, rubber gives off dense clouds of suffocating black smoke when it burns, and as such, breathing apparatus is essential for fire-fighters. The most effective method of dealing with rubber fires is to blast out the fire with pressure-jets, say a number of 18 mm jets, at a pressure of about 5.5 bar (nozzle pressure). When rubber n bulk is involved and well alight, water sprays appear to accelerate the 'ate of combustion.

;TATIC DISCHARGE

Static electricity increases the fire risk in a rubber factory due to the parks, causing ignition of the flammable solvents used during processng of rubber products. The static spark to cause ignition must have a :ertain minimum energy and voltage. The values required are not large,)eing 200 milli ɔnth of a joule.

Naphthalene ($C_{10}H_8$)

It is a crystalline solid hydrocarbon with a characteristic smell, having a high vapour pressure at ordinary temperature. The vapour is heavier than air by 4.42 times.

PROPERTIES

Its melting point is 79^{0}C and the boiling point of the liquid is 218^{0}C. The specific gravity of the liquid is 0.97 at the temperature of the melting point of the solid. Naphthalene is insoluble in water. It is, however, soluble in most of the ordinary organic solvents, particularly in the flaky state.

FIRE CHARACTERISTICS

Naphthalene is flammable in both solid and vapour states. The range of flammability in air is from 0.9% to 5.9% by volume. A match applied to a mass of naphthalene flakes causes the substance to ignite, the heat of the match being sufficient to drive off sufficient vapour to be ignitable. Naphthalene burns with a smoky flame.

SPECIAL HAZARDS

Naphthalene would present a fire hazard because of its low melting point and its relatively low boiling point (218^{0}C) and the burning liquid might carry a fire from one part of a building to another. Due to its high molecular weight, the proportion of the vapour necessary to form an explosive mixture with air is low. Thus, from the equation $C_{10}H_8 + 12O_2 = 10CO_2 + 2H_2O$, it will be seen that for an ideal explosive mixture, 1 volume of naphthalene vapour requires 12 volumes of O_2, or approximately, 57 volumes of air.

Naphthalene, due to its high vapour pressure, possesses the property of subliming. The vapour will condense on the walls of any vessel or chamber on which the vapour can condense, and may also catch fire later and can bring about an increase in the area of the fire.

FIRE-FIGHTING

Naphthalene fires can be successfully fought by copious spray of water. It is important to ensure that the flow of the molten naphthalene due to heat is stopped first by putting sand bags or bricks to limit the spread of fire and then the spray of water should be applied.

USES

Naphthalene is used in large quantities for manufacture of certain explosives, dye stuff and in fine chemical industries, as it forms the starting point of a large number of intermediates used therein. It is also largely used in the manufacture of fire-lighters, made by dipping bundles of wood and shavings in liquid naphthalene.

COAL-TAR AND NAPHTHALENE

Naphthalene is present in coal-tar to the extent of 5 to 10% and it is obtained in fraction with a boiling point range of 175^{0}C to 230^{0}C. On cooling the distillate, the naphthalene crystallizes.

STORAGE

The storage of naphthalene presents a hazard in that if stored in a hot place, the vapour pressure might be sufficient for an inflammable mixture of air and vapour to be produced.

Drying oils

ABSORPTION OF OXYGEN AND HEAT PRODUCED

Most of the vegetable and animal oils will take up oxygen with the formation of oxidation products at the ordinary temperatures. This absorption and oxidation is accompanied by the evolution of heat. The amount of oxygen that can be absorbed varies with different oils. Of the vegetable oils, linseed oil, tung (or china-wood) oil, and hemp oil will take up most oxygen, and of the animal oils, cod liver oil and seal oil will also take up oxygen. This is due to the presence in the oil, of substances known as linolic acid which can be oxidized to produce linoxyn as a solid substance. The more linolic acid an oil contains, the more readily it will take up oxygen. The amount of linoxyn that can be produced in these oils is sufficient to cause the oil to go solid after exposure to the air for some time. Hence, they are known as Drying Oils and it is for this property of the oils that they are considered valuable, as the base for paints and varnishes.

Linseed oil is able to take up from 10 to 30% of its weight of oxygen, according to the conditions under which it is allowed to oxidize. The oil does not gain in weight by this amount as a certain proportion of the constituents of the oil is oxidized to carbon dioxide and water, which escape.

FIRE HAZARDS

This property of absorbing oxygen makes drying oils so hazardous, particularly when soaked up by fabrics, that very small amount of cotton waste soaked in linseed oil, may cause spontaneous ignition even after one hour.

The fire hazard however varies (*1*) with the nature of oil (linseed oil, particularly unboiled, is quite hazardous), (*2*) the nature of fibre, (*3*) the amount of oil that has been absorbed (an optimum quantity is required, any excess quantity in relation to a certain volume of fibre will reduce the risk owing to the air spaces in the fibres being completely filled with oil and the surface exposed to air being reduced), (*4*) the temperature of the air and the oil fibre, (*5*) the extent to which cooling can take place by conduction to the air or surrounding objects.

As the absorption of oxygen raises the temperature the rate of oxygen absorption is also increased. Once the temperature begins to rise, the processes are much accelerated, being mutually cumulative. The increased rate of oxygen absorption at higher temperature makes the storage of oily fabrics much more hazardous in warm or hot situation than where the temperature is normal. The presence of a high percentage of free unsaturated fatty acid will increase the tendency of an oil to heat, as will also the presence of metallic compounds (notably those of iron).

IODINE VALUE

Iodine value gives an indication of the amount of unsaturated acids present in fats and oil. The relative liability to spontaneous combustion of an unsaturated oil or fat can be assessed by its Iodine Value, which in short refers to the weight of iodine in gm absorbed by 100 gm of the substance. The following table shows the iodine value of some of the oils and fats:

Substance	Iodine value
Linseed oil	179 to 209.8
Cod liver oil	164 to 171
Cotton seed oil	111 to 115
Castor oil	86.6 to 88.3
Olive oil	86 to 90
Tallow	34.8 to 41.3
Butter fat	26 to 28
Coconut oil	8.4 to 8.8

STORAGE OF FATTY ACIDS, OILS ETC.

In factories where animal and vegetable oils are used, particular attention to cleanliness and tidiness is essential. Rags, cotton-waste, etc. which are used for cleaning and wiping up should never be left to lie about. They should be placed in a metal receptacle kept for the purpose. Where the oil is not recovered from the waste, it should be burnt at regular intervals, preferably daily, before the premises are closed for the night. Mixtures of vegetable (or animal) and mineral oils (as in lubricants) may be hazardous, if the fatty oil is present to a considerable extent and soaked in cotton or jute waste.

Comparative experiments in ideal conditions on the time needed for cotton waste to catch fire spontaneously, when dipped in different oils, give the following results:

Linseed oil (unboiled)	after 1.5 hours
Rape oil	after 10 hours
Castor oil	after 24 hours
Olive oil	after 6 hours
Seal oil	after 2 hours
Walrus oil	after 4 hours

Mineral oils

Crude mineral oils vary greatly in composition, but they are mixtures of hydrocarbons with small quantities of other substances containing compounds of sulphur and are flammable. Water in varying quantities may also be present with the crude.

To obtain the various products, the crude has to be cracked and subjected to fractional distillation. The mixture of hot vapours and liquid is passed to a fractionating tower, which may be 30m high with perforated steel trays set horizontally in it. The hydrocarbons with the highest boiling points condense on the bottom trays; those with the second highest boiling point, on the next trays and so on, to the top. The heaviest fraction, the so-called residue, is drawn off as a sluggish liquid from the bottom of the tower for use as heavy fuel oil or asphalt. Higher up in the column, lubricating oil condenses on the trays. At a lower temperature come the fuel oils, including gas oil and light diesel fuel. Kerosene condenses still higher up, due to its lower boiling point and gasoline (or petrol) collects at the top of the tower due to its lowest boiling point. The products derived from petroleum are many including the very large number of petrochemicals. The main distillation products from a refinery are, however, gasoline, kerosene, diesel fuel, heavy fuel oil, lubricants, greases, wax, asphalt, petroleum coke, carbon black and liquified petroleum gases, used for domestic heating and cooking. Liquid paraffin used in pharmacy as also the white oils are the petroleum products, obtained after purification and chemical treatment of the fraction after removal of the lubricating oil.

The important properties of petrol or gasoline, kerosene, diesel or gas oil have already been described under petrol and fuel oils in Chapter 5. However, a few important characteristics of each in relation to fire hazards and fire-fighting will be mentioned here.

(I) MOTOR SPIRIT OR GASOLINE

Of all the distillates from the crude and the products obtained, gasoline or motor spirit has the highest risk category on account of its very low flash point. The risks may be summarized as follows:

(*a*) The volatility of the spirit; (*b*) The relatively small percentage of vapour necessary to form an explosive mixture with air and the readiness with which the vapour can be ignited by a small flame or spark; (*c*) The heavy density of the vapour, enabling it to travel or flow considerable distances without mingling with the air and thus forming an ignitable mixture at some distance from the original source of the vapour.

(II) KEROSENE AND DIESEL OIL

Kerosene burns producing a very high temperature with a smoky orange-coloured flame and with liberation of soot. The heat of decomposition is to the extent of 11037.6 to 11138.4 kcal/kg. It is not so hazardous because its flash point is much above petrol and it is not as volatile as petrol. Diesel or gas oil has flash point above kerosene and is consequently less hazardous than the latter.

(III) DIESEL OIL/GAS OIL

This is the fraction collected after gasoline and kerosene in the fractionating column and it is used for diesel engines. The specific gravity being less than 1, it floats on water, and as such, foam is the ideal extinguishing medium backed up with CO_2 gas. Dry chemical powders, particularly with potassium base, are quite useful and may be used with foam but it should be noted that only such powders which do not break down the foam are used. Water spray projectors or mulsifyre system, ejecting very fine spray of water from fixed outlets at a high pressure, are quite useful for extinction of oil fires. For fighting fires involving light petroleum spirits, such as gasoline or aviation spirit, foam with light water, containing special surfactants with fluorocarbons, have been found to be quite effective. Such a compound of foam with light water prevents the evaporation of petrol from the surface and forms a sort of a vapour seal and causes extinction within a very short time, as have been found out by actual tests.

(IV) HEAVY FUEL OILS

Heavy fuel oils consist of crude oils from which the light motor spirit and kerosene have been removed. Such oils are naturally much less hazardous than crude oil, and present no hazard in this respect at ordinary temperature. When heated to a sufficiently high temperature, they evolve flammable vapours which can form explosive mixtures with air, and if heated to its ignition temperature and projected in a fine spray, they are ignited immediately. The production of the flammable vapour, when the oil is in contact with a hot surface, is also accelerated. If a small quantity of heavy oil is absorbed by textiles, it will readily burn when involved in a fire, though a large quantity may not do so readily.

The principal use of heavy fuel oil is for burning under boilers in specially designed burners, as also for commercial heating. These are the cheapest petroleum fuel.

Fire-fighting

All liquid hydocarbons normally burn with an orange-coloured flame and with emission of a dense cloud of black smoke and intense heat.

Precautions for use as boiler fuels : When heavy oil is used as a boiler fuel, the furnace temperature is much above the distillation or ignition point of the oil, and consequently it is necessary to guard against the risk of any oil (except that atomized for burning), coming into contact with any hot surface. The undermentioned points are important: (*1*) The oil should never run to the furnace by gravity, but should be pumped. (*2*) Pipe connections should be made at the top of the tanks to prevent oil being emitted by a fracture in a pipe. (*3*) Pumps should be so arranged and fitted that oil cannot siphon off to the burners when the pump is not working. (*4*) Means should be provided for cutting off the supply of oil to the furnace from a point at a safe distance.

No naked lights should be allowed in any furnace room or stokehold, or in the vicinity of pumps or tanks containing oil.

FIRE PROTECTION IN OIL REFINERIES

In the refining process, pertoleum products are heated to temperatures upto 510^{0}C. A refinery is a chain of units which are interdependent. The materials are piped through stills at temperatures far above that required to make them burn, if exposed to air. If a leak occurs in the system, the materials will ignite immediately.

Speed is of paramount importance in putting out fires in the refinery caused by excess pressure and leakage of the materials. In the event of pressure fires, they can be extinguished only by cutting off the fuel to isolate their burning from other units in the processing chain. Fires contained in stills, unlike pressure fires, are extinguished by cutting off the air supply and as the fuel in this case is limited and confined, there is less danger of such a fire spreading.

FIRE-FIGHTING – EQUIPMENTS AND EXTINGUISHING MEDIA REQUIRED

Each operating unit in the refinery is protected by several turret nozzles which can be positioned and aimed on a given area and left unattended, while continuing the application of a stream of water on the target for cooling down. Reels of hose with branches should be kept encased in containers with glass covers, fixed on walls, adjacent to each operating unit. Dual purpose fog nozzles (with provision for fog or jet) are generally employed. It may be remembered that fog or very fine waterspray under high pressure are the only forms in which water can be used on oil fires.

In addition to this, sufficient quantity of water, foam and dry chemical powders should also be kept in readiness for immediate use. The amount of water required depends on the size and nature of the fires and the plant to be protected. Generally, there should be a piped supply in the order of 4,546 – 45,460 litre/minute at 10 kg/cm^2 pressure. This amount should be in addition to that required for cooling purpose, e.g. by drenchers and sprinkler systems, which, if properly designed, are invaluable, as they have the great advantage of functioning when fire-fighters are withdrawn because of extreme heat and danger of possible explosions. As regards foam compound, a moderately large fire in a refinery may require 45,460 litres of compound and in view of the difficulty of handling and transporting of the requisite amount in individual foam drums to the fire ground, it has been the practice to provide foam compound mains to the higher risk areas of the plant side by side with water mains. There should also be 4500 litres capacity foam-tenders with similar capacity, water tenders, sufficient amount of rubber-lined hose stationed at strategic points within the installation along with special dry chemical tenders carrying at least 228 kg of powder with piping and discharge horns. Mobile foam monitors which can project foam from a distance are quite valuable. Emergency tenders with breathing and resuscitation apparatus and with fire-resisting clothings, such as proximity suits made of aluminized asbestos fabric with heavy felt linings must also be provided in addition to ladders of suffcient height.

As for the protection of overhead storage tanks for the products, fixed foam pourers are of doubtful value, because, they are difficult to maintain and are likely to be damaged in the explosion, which inevitably precedes a fire. Floating (pontoon) type roof for the tanks are generally considered to be safe. Fixed equipment with such type of roof can be provided for applying B.C.F. extinguishing media for the protection of the vapour seal in the peripheral space between the floating roof and the tank shell in the form of closed automatic nozzles.

Regarding the hazards for the L.P.G. (liquified petroleum gas) storage in bulk in petroleum installations, there are two important considerations, viz. prevention of spillage or serious leakage of the L.P.gas which may form a gas cloud, resulting in serious explosion and fire. The gas, being heavier than air, will tend to hang over the ground and may be carried downwind of the leakage. In such an eventuality, it will be necessary to restrict the movements of all persons and vehicles in the area, which should, as far as practicable, be evacuated. Some refineries keep a supply of gas, oil or a petroleum solvent available in the vicinity of L.P.G. storage. These can be put on a spillage to reduce the vapour formation rate and to keep the fire restricted to a small area. The main effort should be towards keeping any heat-exposed plant as cool as possible. This is best done by massive application of fine water spray/fog over the L.P.G tanks. Properly designed drenchers are invaluable here.

It is not possible to lay down all the details of the requirements. Good maintenance of the plant and good housekeeping are essential for fire prevention in any refinery or oil installation. Along with this it is also essential that the fire-fighting personnel be well acquainted with the hazards and know their job well to handle the difficult situations with confidence and team spirit. Preplanning for any eventuality is essential along with a coordinated attack on the fire, not only by fire-fighters, but also by the technical staff and plant operators who should be well conversant with fire protection of the plant.

Linoleum

Linoleum carpets are in good demand now-a-days. The finished product is not so hazardous, but the processing of the material involves great fire hazard.

PROCESSING

Grounded cork, pulverized bamboo chips and mashed leather are intimately mixed with the dough obtained by boiling linseed oil, which is finally coloured with pigments as desired. The prepared semi-solid dough is spread over dry hessian, and finally, the design is embossed over it. The finished product is kept in heating chambers for a few days for drying and then released in the market, being rolled and cut in suitable sizes.

FIRE HAZARDS

The entire processing is risky from the fire point of view. The oxidation of linseed oil is an exothermic reaction and it produces great heat. The grinding of the cork or meal is also not free from the risk of dust explosion or fire.

PRECAUTIONS

Good housekeeping and cleanliness are essential for fire prevention. Care must be taken to clear away all cork-dust deposited on hot pipes or vessels and to keep such dust away from places where fatty matters, wax, paraffin etc. or resins are being treated. All oily cork dust should be disposed of safely outside. Defective electric motors or switch-gears, which are likely to give off sparks, should be replaced and removed from the place.

In linoleum factories, solvents with low flash points such as petroleum, ether, benzol, carbon disulphide are treated with combustible substances, such as cork dusts, pulverized leather and bamboo particles under a high temperature and pressure, and the chances of fire are quite high. The fire risk is aggravated due to the static discharge, which might be caused by a variety of reasons during the manufacturing stage. All electrical appliances should have flame-proof fittings with gas-tight glands and the wirings should preferably be mineral-insulated cables.

Stringent fire-precautionary measures with fixed fire-fighting installations, such as rising mains, sprinklers etc, are essential for such occupancies and provision of plenty of water in the form of static and hydrant supply is essential.

Coal

Coal is an important article of commerce. It is liable to spontaneous combustion. If the fire is detected at a later stage, the fire takes a very long time and very strenuous effort to extinguish, with plenty of jets of water and manpower. The ignition point of coal varies with the nature of the coal – that of lignite (brown coal) being the lowest, and anthracite being the highest. In lignite, it may be as low as 250^0C and in anthracite it may be as high as 400^0C or higher.

Coal absorbs a layer of oxygen on its surface and this results in a certain amount of heat being produced. The amount of heat produced is not very great, and as found by Graham, it is about 1/20th of that evolved, when the same quantity of oxygen takes part in the actual oxidation of the coal. This adsorbed oxygen is in a reactive state, and oxidation of certain constituents of the coal takes place with further rise in temperature.

The undermentioned factors are important in deciding the probability of spontaneous ignition of coal:

1. Amount of pyrites (i.e. sulphides, FeS_2) content in coal.

2. Size of the coal stacked – with average bituminous coal, if the fragments are larger than say 3.1 to 3.8cm, the risk of spontaneous combustion, in piles of average height, is slight.

3. Moisture content in coal – percentage of moisture, which may have an accelerative effect in the heating of coal due to oxygen absorption upto a certain percentage, is important.

4. Freshness of exposed surface of coal – freshly exposed surface of coal will absorb oxygen more readily than a weatheed surface.

5. Temperature of atmosphere – higher the temperature (above 35°C) greater is the liability of spontaneous combustion. In hot climate, the risk is very high.

6. Height of pile of the coal stack – the higher a stack of coal, the more readily will it tend to heat.

7. Ventilation – natural circulation of the air, through a stack by means of channels will keep down the temperature.

8. Composition – type and chemical constitution of coal.

PRECAUTIONS TAKEN IN COAL STORAGE

Stacks should not to be more than 4.5m in height and they should be builtup slowly, i.e. one layer should be allowed to weather for some time before the next one is put upon it. At regular distance apart in the stack, tubes should be inserted in which thermometers should be placed, and readings must be taken at regular intervals of time. If the temperature is found to reach 40°C, there is considerable risk of spontaneous combustion, while if it rises to 71°C to 87°C, an outbreak is imminent. Some authorities consider that the risk, however, arises at a lower temperature. If temperatures reach danger level the stack must be broken down.

If thermometers are not available, iron rods, as suggested by Morrison, equal in length to the hight of the stack, should be inserted in the stacks at intervals of about 7.5m and tested daily by hand for heating. If heating is observed, trenching the top of the heap in various directions to depth of slightly above Im should be carried out.

SPECIAL NOTES ON FIRE PREVENTION AND PROTECTION IN COAL BUNKERS IN VESSELS

The undermentioned points are to be borne in mind in this connection:

(*i*) Prevention of the temperature going above 77°C in bunkers is quite important;

(*ii*) Mine-run coal of the size of 70 to 75 cm has a tendency to smoke;

(*iii*) Continuous movement of the stock is essential. Coal is to be drawn off systematically from the bottom;

(*iv*) Perforated pipes should be provided in the upper corner of bunker spaces for injection of steam or smothering gases;

(*v*) Steaming the bunker by closing the upper hatches, though not satisfactory in all cases, may be important in case of a fire;

(*vi*) Fires may be tackled by dry-ice, being placed 12 to 30 cm above the hot spots and closing all inlets or outlets. In practice, it was found that some 228 kg of dry-ice could successfully extinguish stubborn fires in 25933 tonne storage piles;

(*vii*) Fresh coals drawn from mines must not be mixed with coal that has been previously stored for long periods. The kind of coal that contains a large proportion of pyrites, should not be exposed long in air.

Coal-tar

This is obtained as a by-product during coal-gas manufacture. It is a black, foul-smelling, viscous liquid, containing a mixture of a large number of organic compounds (aromatic hydrocarbons). Tar is used for preservation of timber. A number of important chemicals like benzene, carbolic acid, naphthalene, creosote and anthracene are obtained from the fractional distillation of coal-tar, within different temperature ranges. Naphthalene ($C_{10}H_8$), an important article of commerce from which a number of organic compounds specially the dyes are produced, is obtained from coal-tar.

Coal-tar has specific gravity of 1.1 to 1.25 and its flash point is 45 to 65^{0}C.

FIRE-FIGHTING

Fires involving burning tar require careful handling. Foam, CO_2 or dry sand are stated to be the recommended measures for extinction of fires involving tar, but fine water spray can also be used for extinguishing such fires under certain circumstances. While tar is heavier than water, it should be borne in mind that a jet, if used, would tend to penetrate the burning surface and, in so doing, would flash to steam. The resultant expansion in volume would have disastrous consequences.

Paints, varnish, enamel, lacquer

These substances have high fire risk and hazard. Many flammable materials are used in their composition and as such, the manufacturing processes and storage present considerable risk.

PAINT

This refers to many types of decorative and protective coating and may include:

i) Oil paint, in which the base material is an oil (usually linseed oil) with some solvent which is flammable with a low flash point (32.2^{0}C);

ii) Water paint (distemper), containing dry pigment with water, with occasionally a small amount of oil;

iii) Cellulose paint, containing highly inflammable cellulose nitrate or acetate with solvents, synthetic resins and plasticizers; and *iv*) Emulsion paints, which contain water-based synthetic plastic emulsions, commonly of polyvinyl acetate or polystyrene with a plasticizer such as dibutyl phthalate and a pigment.

VARNISH

This is a solution of gum or resin in a spirit or an oil with the addition of small quantities of other materials for specific purposes. It is also highly flammable.

ENAMEL

This refers to a type of high oil paint, which is essentially a combination of paint and varnish and has quick drying properties. It is highly flammable.

LACQUER

This term usually denotes the spirit varnish. It consists essentially of a gum, such as shellac dissolved in methylated spirit. It is mainly used to provide a high gloss protective coating and its storage and processing are accompanied with high fire risk.

FIRE HAZARDS

With the exception of water paints (distemper) and the majority of plastic emulsion paints, all paints and varnishes have high fire hazards in liquid form. Spirit varnishes or lacquers are more flammable. The fire hazards of cellulose lacquers and enamels are also high, specially, those containing cellulose nitrates, where the risk is very high. The flash point of cellulose nitrate lacquers is considerably below room temperature (44^0C) and is accompanied with a severe explosion risk.

Once ignited, liquid paint burns fiercely and gives off a great deal of heavy black smoke with characteristic of an oil fire. Water is, however, not a suitable agent and foam must be used for extinction, if any substantial quantity of paint is involved. CO_2 or dry powder exstinguisher may also be used as alternative. Water may however, be used where dried paint coatings are involved.

Breathing apparatus is necessary for fighting such fires, specially indoors, because of the dense smoke and toxic fumes given off during combustion. There is also a hazard from explosion of the drums, where the tins containing the product are tightly sealed. The contents are likely to ignite instantly on exposure to air and cause severe injury to the firemen.

SPONTANEOUS IGNITION

All paints and oil varnishes are capable of self-heating when they are closely in contact with ecllusose materials and particularly fibres. Cotton waste/rags, which are impregnated with paint or oil varnish will be self-heated, if left in heaps or otherwise packed without provision for heat dissipation.

CHAPTER 9

Fire and Explosion Hazards in Plastics

Plastics

Plastic is a general name for synthetic condensation of polymerization of molecules of one or more substances. They may be defined as synthetic or semi-synthetic organic materials, capable of being moulded under heat and pressure into a given shape and of retaining that shape after heat and pressure are removed.

TYPES

Plastics fall under two varieties, viz. thermosetting and thermoplastic. Thermosetting plastic are those which require heat and pressure to mould them into shape. Once they have been subjected to heat, they become set and infusible. They cannot be softened by further heating, having undergone a specific chemical change. Thermosetting materials char at temperatures above 400^{0}C and at 700–900^{0}C, they burn sluggishly.

On the other hand, plastic materials which become soft under the influence of heat and harden when cooled are of the thermoplastic type The process of softening and hardening can be repeated indefinitely, there being no chemical reaction involved.

FIRE AND EXPLOSION HAZARDS

The fire hazards of thrmoplastic materials depend on several factors, apart from the chemical composition of the plastics. These factors are : (*i*) the form of the plastic, i.e. whether in bulk mouldings, sheet, film, fibre, liquid or powder, (*ii*) the degree of free access to air, and (*iii*) the burning material or other materials burning nearby.

Since all plastics are organic, their dusts are usually capable of forming explosive mixtures with air. Those dusts in which the plastic material contains an inert filler tend to be less hazardous than those in which a cellulosic filler, such as wood flour, has been incorporated.

The phenolic plastics are thermosetting. They are generally made from phenol or cresol, but furfural and resorcinol are also used. All these chemicals react with formaldehyde under certain conditions to give a range of resinous materials.

These resins may be used without further treatment in a solvent such as alcohol or acetone to give varnishes, adhesives and impregnating media. They are grounded and blended with fillers, pigments and other additives to give moulding powders, or used in the manufacture of laminated sheet by bonding paper or cloth.

Thermosetting moulding powders are made of urea formaldehyde and aniline formaldehyde. The latter is a glass-like material, made by the interaction of urea and formaldehyde. They are also used in the manufacture of adhesives, impregnating media and for manufacture of laminated sheet.

All urea formaldehyde resins have in general the same fire hazards as those of phenolic resins. Some coating materials in this class have sufficient resistance to heat to be suitable as stoving enamels, while others have flame-retardative properties.

USES

Aniline formaldehyde resins are mainly used for casting work and for the manufacture of laminated sheet, while melamine formaldehyde resins are used in moulding powders, for impregnating wood as adhesives and in textile finishing.

Cellulose plastics are thermoplastics. Cellulose nitrate in the form of celluloid was the original plastic material used in photographic film, moulded articles, cellulose lacquers and gun cotton.

CELLULOID AND ITS CHARACTERISTICS

Cellulose nitrate is the chemical name for celluloid. Once cellulose nitrate is ignited, it is difficult to stop the ensuing decomposition. Extinguishment can be effected by copious amounts of water, but the decomposition continues and unless the cellulose nitrate is submerged in water or the cooling is continued, reignition is likely to occur.

Cellulose acetate is less hazardous than cellulose nitrate and has replaced the nitrate in many applications. It is now being extensively used as a moulding material and in the manufacture of film and fibre.

Ethyl cellulose, though similar, is more stable than cellulose acetate and its applications are also similar.

ETHNOID PLASTICS

Ethnoid plastics are thermoplastic and form a class which includes both rigid and rubber-like products. They are formed by the polymerization of vinyl compounds and include polyvinyl chloride, polyvinyl acetate, polyvinyl alcohol, polystyrene, polmethyl methacrylate, other acrylic resins, and their esters, polythene and various co-polymers.

The fire properties of plastic within this class vary between those exhibited by polyvinyl chloride and polymethyl methacrylate.

POLYAMIDE PLASTICS

Nylon, the commonly used fabric, is the trade name for polyamide plastic. It is made by the reaction between aliphatic dicarboxylic acids and aliphatic diamines and it has extensive application in the manufacture of synthetic fibres, bristles and filaments. On the application of flame, fibres of these materials fuse and retreat from the flame rather than ignite.

TYPES UNDER BOTH THERMOPLASTIC AND THERMOSETTING MATERIALS—POLYESTERS AND CASEIN PLASTICS

Certain alkyd resins (polyesters) give rise to both thermoplastic and the thermosetting materials. They are produced by the interaction of olyhydric alcohols and polybasic acids. These materials are used as coatings for metals and fabrics and for bonding glass fabric in the manufacture of low pressure mouldings and laminated sheet with laminated applications in moulding and casting. Some polyester resins are co-polymerized with styrene or methyl methacrylate.

Casein and other protein plastics are derived from a wide variety of natural sources, such as milk or soya beans, by the reaction of formaldehyde with casein. They are used to a decreasing extent in the preparation of extruded products, sheets and mouldings. This class also includes both thermoplastic and thermosetting materials.

EPOXIDE RESINS

In the plastic industry, epoxide resins are relatively new-comers. Their applications are as adhesives, castings and coatings. They are commonly made by the reaction of epichlorohydrin and certain phenols. As heat and flame resistants, anti-corrosive varnishes and coatings, the combination of polyamide and epoxide resins are coming into use, being quite durable.

IDENTIFICATION OF PLASTICS FROM ODOUR AND FLAME

Most plastics, when involved in fire, emit toxic products of combustion in addition to carbon monoxide which will always be present in fires. The volume of carbon monoxide, which is an important point, may be so great that it may constitute major toxic hazard. The following table indicates some of the important properties of the common and basic varieties of plastics:

Chemical group	Chemical name	Thermo- (P) or thermo-setting plastics (S)	Lower explosive limit (gm/m^3 in air as a dust)	Ignition temperature (°C as a dust)	Remarks
1	2	3	4	5	6
Amino	Aniline formal-dehyde	P			Difficult to ignite. Burns with yellow flame. Black smoke and odour of aniline and formaldehyde
	Melamine formal-dehyde	S			Difficult to ignite. Odour–fishy. Self-extinguishing.
	Urea formal-dehyde	S	70	432	Difficult to ignite. Burns with blue green-edged pale yellow flame. Odour of formaldehyde or like fish. Self-extinguishing.
Cellulose	Cellulose acetate	P			Not difficult to ignite. Burns slowly with dark yellow flame. Odour of acetic acid
	Cellulose acetate (non-flammable grade)	P			Difficult to ignite. Self-extinguishing.
	Cellulose triacetate	P	35	780	Difficult to ignite. Burns with yellow flame. Odour of acetic acid.
	Cellulose acetate butyrate	P	35		Not difficult to ignite. Burns with dark yellow flame with some black smoke. Odour of butyric acid (rancid butter)
	Cellulose nitrate and celluloid	P			Extremely flammable, readily ignited. Burns with bright yellow flame. May decompose explosively; once decomposition has started cannot be stopped by water.
	Ethyl cellulose	P			Not difficult to ignite. Burns with blue-edged yellow flame.

1	2	3	4	5	6
	Epoxide	P&D			Difficult to ignite. Burns with yellow/green flame. Odourslightly sweet.

General methods and more hints for easy detection

The strip of rod of the material to be identified is held on one side of a Bunsen burner unitl it catches fire but for not more than 10 seconds. Deductions are then made form the results as mentioned below:

Thermosetting plastics: (*a*) If no flame is produced and the specimen retains its shape and the pungent odour of formaldehyde is produced, then it is a plastic material of thermosetting type falling under formaldehyde group. (*b*) Bakelite, micanite, phenol formaldehyde, which are all of the thermosetting type, will give off a strong phenolic odour, i.e. the smell of carbolic acid. (*c*) A strong fishy odour, as well as of formaldehyde, indicates a melamine formaldehyde plastic, viz. beetle or melmac. (*d*) If there is no odour other than that of formaldehyde, the plastic is a urea formaldehyde.

Thermoplastics: If a flame is produced as a result of the aforesaid test but goes out as soon as the specimen is removed from the burner, then the specimen should be held just to the edge of the flame and one of the five odours may result, viz. rubbery, bitter, sweet, milky, or vinegar. If a green zone of flame around the specimen is accompanied by a smell of burnt rubber, and if the green area is pronounced, the plastic is of the pliofilm type; but if the green area is small and enclosed in yellow, then it is a neoprene type of plastic rubber.

A green zone of flame may also occurs but if with a bitter smell only, then the specimen is of vinyl chloride resin such as Flemenol, Koroseal, Velvic; but if with a sweet smell and heavy black ash, then it indicates vinylidene chloride, resin, such as Saran. When there is no green zone but smell of burnt milk, the plastic is of the casein type.

There may be sparks from the flame of the burning plastic together with an acetic odour like vinegar, indicating cellulose acetate type of plastics sold under various trade names like Acephose, Cellulate, Kodapak, Cellomoldete. If the plastic is of the type that continues to burn after removal from the burner, the flame should be examined for colour during the very first second or so of burning. *If the specimen burns very rapidly with intense white flame and with the smell of camphor, it is celluloid and if not with camphor smell, then the plastic is known as Aceloid, Kodaloid, Xylonite, Hycoloid, or Pyralin*. When the flame is mainly blue, with perhaps a small white tip, or otherwise, as indicated in the chart below, several types of plastics might be involved:

	Smell	Exact colour of flame or its nature	Type of plastic
(i)	Very strong or sweet smell of flowers/ fruits	Blue with small white tip	Methacrylate plastics, viz., perspex, plexi-glass type, Lucite, Crysalex etc.
(ii)	Smell of fresh celery or burning plants	Entirely blue	Nylon (which can further be verified, if it dissolves in a 60% by volume of aqueous hydrochloric acid solution)
(iii)	Very slight-ly sweet odour	A weak flame	Polyvinyl formal, e.g. Formvar
(iv)	Rancid butter or cheese	(a) With sparks from the flame (b) With no sparks	Cellulose acetobutyrate Butver or some other polyvinyl butyral
(v)	Burnt rubber	Bright green mantle sur-rounding the flame.	Pliofilm.
(vi)	Acetic smell	Flame surrounded by purple mantle with sparks	Polyvinyl acetal, e.g. Alvar, Butacite or Saflex.
(vii)	Smell of butyric acid (ran-cid butter smell)	Pale yellow flame (luminous)	Cellulose acetobutyrate.
(viii)	Smell of burnt milk	do	Casein plastics.
(ix)	Sweet floral smell	Smoky flame	Polystyrene.
(x)	Burnt paper	Pale yellow colour (smoky)	Cellulose type.
(xi)	Burnt rub-ber	Weak flame, sur-rounded by green mantle with yellow	Neoprene.
(xii)	Acetic odour	Predominantly blue flame, surrounded by a yellow-green mantle, burning with difficulty and giving off sparks and the melted drops falling in water, produce foam flakes or granules	Cellulose acetate.

CHAPTER 10

A. Storage Risk

Safe and suitable storage of raw materials as also the finished products require careful consideration and planning for all safety officers from the point of view of fire risk. The storage should be so made as to eliminate the possibility of fire and the resulting damage to the extent possible. Some of the salient principles of storage for different categories of substances are enumerated below for general guidance.

Relative hazards – classification of risks

FIRE RISKS

Certain substances, called incompatible substances, may give rise to a fire or explosion when they react together by coming in contact due to breakage of containers or otherwise during storage. Examples of some such substances are given below:

(*a*) Substances reacting with each other: (*i*) acids and alkalis. (*ii*) Oxidizing agents and oxidizable substances. (*iii*) Certain mineral acids reacting with each other. (*iv*) Mineral acids with oxidizing agents. (*v*) Mineral acids with some salts of weaker acids (e.g. sulphuric acid with carbonates, sulphites, sulphides, etc). (*vi*) Substances (e.g. lime, caustic alkalis, alkali metals, sodium peroxide, and metallic powders) that react violently with water or with other substances containing their own water of crystallization. (*vii*) Caustic alkalis with certain metals, particularly if in powder form.

(*b*) Storage of substances of an unstable character.

(*c*) Storage of substances that are hazardous when subjected to heat.

(*d*) Storage of substances that evolve inflammable or toxic gases or vapours.

(*e*) Storage of substances that may give rise to spontaneous combustion.

RISKS IN RELATION TO FIRE EXTINCTION

The undermentioned points should be carefully noted:

(*a*) Substances that react violently on coming into contact during fire-fighting;

(*b*) Substances that on being heated evolve combustible or toxic gases, or gases that will support combustion;

(*c*) Soluble substances that are dangerous in contact with burning matter, being washed on to a fire;

(*d*) Explosive or readily decomposable substances;

(*e*) Substances that react with water or other extinguishing agents.

RISKS DUE TO DAMAGE RESULTING FROM FIRE

Necessary care and precautions are to be taken to avoid the following:

(*a*) Contamination of goods or chemicals by other substances in proximity, rendering them either dangerous or worthless;

(*b*) Contamination of foodstuffs (or drugs) with chemicals, rendering them objectionable or poisonous;

(*c*) Presence of substances that are hazardous when soaked with water.

B. Reaction Among Hazardous Chemicals—General Characteristics

Reaction between acids and caustic alkalis are very violent and owing to the risk of breakage of acid carboys, they should never be stored near alkalies.

ACIDS

Some mineral acids will react together, e.g. nitric and hydrochloric acids, with the evolution of nitrous fumes and chlorine, and sulphuric acid, on coming into contact with hydrochloric acid, will, by the heat of the reaction between the sulphuric acid and the water of the hydrochloric acid solution, cause hydrochloric acid gas to be evolved copiously. Hence, different acids should not be stored in close proximity.

OXIDIZING SALTS AND CARBONACEOUS SUBSTANCES

Crystalline oxidizing salts, such as permanganates and chlorates, present a hazard when stored in bags, as the crystals work their way into the bagging, and when subjected to friction, has been known to bring about an outbreak of spontaneous combustion if contaminated with organic dusts.

REACTION WITH WATER

Defective containers may also give rise to hazards from damp or leakages. Unslaked lime in particular, on coming in contact with moisture, may set fire to dry straw stored adjacently under the same roof. Other substances hazardous under such circumstances are sodium peroxide, caustic soda, carbides, phosphides and sulphides. Dampness may also cause salts such as nitrates, chlorates, etc. to dissolve and penetrate the bagging.

STORAGE OF OXIDIZING AGENTS

Bromates, chlorates, chromates, nitrates, perchlorates, permanganates, peroxides should be stored away from acids, flammable or combustible liquids or solids. Timber, sacking or paper contaminated with these salts may ignite and burn extremely rapidly under suitable circumstances. Gloves and clothing worn by operators handling the substances must be washed frequently and operators should be forbidden to smoke, even in safe condition, whilst in working apparel.

SPILLAGE OF CORROSIVE CHEMICALS

Hazards: Here, apart from skin burns or damage to structures, hydrogen may be generated in contact between damp acid salts and mineral acids (e.g. sulphuric acid, nitric acid) and most metals and between alkalis (e.g. caustic soda) and aluminium, magnesium and zinc. Nitric acid, being a strong oxidizer, spillage on dry straw or saw dust or wood shavings may give rise to flame.

HYDROFLUORIC ACID BURNS

Hydrofluoric acid (HF) is not a direct fire risk but has extreme corrosive properties. Contact with skin will produce most dangerous and painful burns. Hence, whenever it is stored, special antidotes, viz., magnesium sulphate solution for immersion and calcium fluorate for injection, should be kept handy. Qualified medical attendant should also be immediately available.

EFFECT OF HEAT

Substances hazardous when subjected to heat, form a large class. Inflammable liquids, particularly carbon disulphide, ether and acetone, and other liquids with a very low boiling point may be mentioned in this connection. In addition to such sources of heat as steam pipes, heat from insulation on metal roofs must be taken into account.

Some ammonium salts decompose at low temperatures. The carbonate, for example, breaks up at 60^{0}C, producing ammonia and carbon dioxide, which though without fire hazard, is a toxic risk.

Celluloid at a temperature considerably below 100^{0}C evolves camphor vapour. Certain solid hydrocarbons, particularly naphthalene, have a sufficiently high vapour pressure to produce ignitable mixtures with air at comparatively low temperatures. It must be borne in mind that the atmosphere in stores may remain undisturbed for considerable periods, with pockets containing hazardous air–vapour mixture. Suitable means should therefore be devised for the elimination of such pockets of explosive concentration from stores.

Toxic gases and vapours may be evolved either at temperatures little above the ordinary or under the room temperature by the action of heat. Thus cyanides of calcium, potassium, or sodium, under the action of moisture and carbon dioxide, will evolve hydrocyanic (prussic) acid; the latter, being a weak acid, can be set free from its salts such as cyanides by carbonic acid.

EFFECT OF MOISTURE

Alkali and alkaline earth sulphides evolve hydrogen sulphide under the action of moisture. Ammonium salts in contact with quicklime, or carbonate, or hydroxide of potash or soda, or with any alkaline substance, will give off ammonia. The gas is given off more readily when warm; nevertheless, it is evolved quite readily in the cold also.

Hypochlorites will evolve chlorine with dilute acids (as hypochlorous acid is a very weak acid) as also with moisture and carbon dioxide.

STORAGE IN RELATION TO FIRE EXTINCTION

As a result of the collapse of floors in a multistoreyed warehouse or walls, hazardous material which should have been well segregated, could suddenly be brought into contact. It is, therefore, difficult to eliminate such risks altogether. However, in general, it may be said that as regards storage, horizontal contiguity presents the greatest hazard (except of course, when bags or other containers of incompatibles are piled one on top of the other). As regards fire extinction, vertical proximity may not be so serious, though, in this connection, the fire-resisting properties (or their absence) of flooring and walls must be taken into account.

The risk of hazardous materials such as nitrates, chlorates, permanganates, etc. being precipitated bodily on to a fire must not be lost sight of. Not only would gases be evolved with explosive violence, but the salts themselves on coming into contact with burning matter would produce what would practically amount to an explosion.

CERTAIN PRECAUTIONARY MEASURES TO BE ADOPTED FOR STORAGE

Apart from what has been stated under Chapter 8, the following are also worth remembering:

(1) Foodstuffs, whether intended for human or animal consumption, should not be stored below drugs, chemicals, or soluble salts, alkalis, acids, etc. They should also not be stored in proximity to poisonous chemicals, and insecticides.

(2) Hazardous goods such as chlorates, perchlorates, nitrates, bichromates, permanganates, perborates, peroxides, etc. should, if possible, be stored on the lowest floors, and away from acids, and, of course, away from oxidizable matter.

(3) Ammonium salts should not be stored under or in proximity to alkalis.

(4) Packages containing poisonous substances should not, if possible, be stored on wooden flooring.

(5) Mineral acids should be stored on ground floors, which should be as far as possible impervious, and sumps should be provided into which any drainage from leaks or breakages should flow.

(6) Crates containing carboys of acids, particularly sulphuric and nitric acids, should be well packed with some inert absorbent material. Straw, paper, sawdust, shavings, etc. should never be used as packing materials for acid carboys, nor should chalk. Alkalis should not be stored in any place where acid leakage may take place; though the alkali may be in stout metal drums, these may be acted on by the acid.

(7) Lime or drums containing metal powders as also metallic sodium or potassium, caustic soda, sodium peroxide or other substances hazardous with water, should not be stored under roofing that is not in very good condition, nor should such articles be stored in any place where there would be risk of water-pipes bursting in the vicinity by frost in extreme cold climate.

(8) Volatile liquids, concentrated ammonia solutions, compressed and liquified gases, should be stored in the coolest positions available.

(9) In stores containing substances liable to evolve toxic gases, ample attention should be given to ventilation.

(10) Drying oils, varnishes, paints, etc. should not be stored in proximityto fabrics or absorbent combustible meterial, such as cotton, jute, etc. or sawdust. The flooring should preferably be non- absorbent.

CHARACTERISTICS OF CERTAIN SPONTANEOUSLY INFLAMMABLE (PYROPHORIC) CHEMICALS

In the stricter sense, pyrophoric materials are metallic powders such as iron, nickel, lead, cobalt, aluminium (usually produced in an oxygen-free or reducing atmosphere) which may glow or ignite when exposed to air. Others include potassium, and iron sulphide (FeS) which may also be pyrophoric.

PYROPHORIC CARBON

It has been claimed that wood, if heated for a long time at a temperature below its ignition point, is converted into a highly active form of charcoal which is said to ignite spontaneously in air at a comparatively low temperature. This is pyrophoric carbon.

ALKALI METALS AND COMPOUNDS

Sodium, potassium, lithium, caesium, rubidium may ignite in contact with air. They are usually kept under kerosene. They generate hydrogen violently when in contact with water. For fire extinction, dry graphite or chloride-based dry chemical powders are to be kept handy. Calcium and barium also violently react with water to produce hydrogen. Calcium carbide, calcium phosphide, calcium silicide react with water or moist air and the resulting gas may ignite or explode.

OTHER HAZARDOUS CHEMICAL SUBSTANCES

Aluminium trimethyl: Spontaneously inflammable in contact with air.

Diborane: A gas which is highly toxic and liable to ignite spontaneously in moist air.

Hydrazine: Liquid with high toxic vapours, limit of flammability 4.7 to 100%; spillage liable to ignite spontaneously.

Metallic hydrides like sodium or potassium hydride are spontaneously flammable in air. They react violently with water. For fire-fighting, dry chemicals or dolomite should be used.

Powdered metals like aluminium, powdered magnesium or powdered zinc also react with water violently as also with acids, alkalis giving out hydrogen gas, which is flammable and explosive.

Phosphorus: white phosphorus, particularly, will ignite in air spontaneously at ordinary temperature in hot climate (viz. 30^0C).

Titanium and zirconium dusts are readily ignitable – may also be self-heating, under damp conditions.

If may be remembered that for every 10^0C rise in temperature, the rate of reaction will roughly increase to double. Hence, the temperature of the storage place or the reacting substances should be kept as low as practicable.

CERTAIN FLAMMABLE LIQUIDS AND GASES

Acrolin: Toxic and highly irritant – prone to violent polymerization specially in contact with alkaline materials.

Carbon disulphide: Highly flammable liquid; vapours toxic and heavy, creeping along floor; ignition temperature slightly above 100^0C.

Ether: Another highly flammable liquid with a high vapour pressure and characteristic smell; vapour heavy with a migratory tendency; ignition temperature 180^0C; liable to shock ignition, i.e. due to sudden escape of vapour into air at a high pressure. This should be stored away from sunlight in amber-coloured bottles.

Ethylene oxide: Flammable limit 0.3–100%, i.e. this substance can burn even in absence of air. It is stored as liquified gas under nitrogen blanket as it is extremely hazardous.

Methyl Methacrylate: It is a very heavy vapour under fire exposure. It may polymerize rapidly and burst the container.

Nitromethane: It is highly explosive and may detonate under heat and shock. Extreme care should be taken for its storage which should be made in a detached shed.

Vinyl chloride: It is liable to polymerize violently if inhibitor level is not sufficient. The product of combustion includes hydrochloric acid, phosgene and carbon monoxide.

Vinyl acetate: It is a very heavy vapour. It may polymerize rapidly when involved in a fire and burst the container. Polymerization is induced by contact with peroxides.

C. Effect of Water, Heat, Acids and Alkalies on Certain Elements and Compounds

1. ACTION OF WATER ON CERTAIN METALS

Metallic element	Reaction with water
(a) Potassium (K), Sodium (Na), Rubidium (Ru), Caesium (Cs), Barium (Ba), Strontium (Sr), Calcium (Ca)	These metals are greatly reactive with water producing hydrogen. They decompose water even when the metals are cold. The hazard is maximum with potassium and sodium and the heat produced will ignite the hydrogen gas liberated.
(b) Magnesium (Mg), Aluminium (Al), Maganese (Mn), Zinc (Zn), Iron (Fe)	Burning metals docompose water or red-hot metals decompose steam. No action with cold metals.
(c) Tin (Sn), Lead (Pb), Copper (Cu)	No appreciable action on water even with burning metals.

The reactions with water for metals under (*a*) may be expressed as

$$2K + 2H_2O = H_2 + 2KOH$$

$$2Na + 2H_2O = H_2 + 2NaOH$$

$$Ca + 2H_2O = H_2 + Ca(OH)_2$$

For metals under (*b*) the chemical rea ctions may be stated as:

$$Mg + H_2O = H_2 + MgO$$

Burning magnesium also produces magnesium nitride with nitrogen of air and the water on this produces NH_3 (ammonia). Magnesium, aluminium, zinc have their relative hazards in the order stated while burning and on coming in contact with water. The chief hazard is with the splitting up of water to pro duce free hydrogen and to use the oxygen obtained from the water to augment burning.

Electron metals consist of allows of magnesium with small percentages of other metals, usually aluminium or zinc, and behave like magnesium, aluminium or zinc when involved in fire and on coming in contact with water. So is the case with Duralumin used for the construction of the body of aircraft.

Read hot iron reacts with water with e xplosive violence.

$$3Fe + 4H_2O = 4H_2 + Fe_3O_4$$

A vigorous reaction takes places when red hot zinc is attacked by steam, and hydrogen is liberated.

$$Zn + H_2O = ZnO + H_2$$

Burning aluminium with water or boiling water with aluminium powder will have the following reaction:

$$2Al + 6H_2O = 2Al(OH)_3 + 3H_2$$

A few other substances that react with water are described below:

(*i*) The reaction of quicklime with water (called slaking of lime) is to produce slaked lime with evolution of great heat, e.g.

$CaO + H_2O = Ca(OH)_2$ (slaked lime).

(*ii*) Calcium carbide reacts with water immediately to produce acetylene gas and a large quantity of heat is also produced, viz. $CaC_2 + H_2O = C_2H_2 + CaO$ and with more water, the calcium oxide formed with heat will become slaked lime and the final action may be expressed as, $CaC_2 + 2H_2O = C_2H_2 + Ca(OH)_2$.

(*iii*) Calcium phosphide with water will produce the spontaneously flammable gas phosphine (PH_3), e.g.

$Ca_3P_2 + 6H_2O = 3Ca(OH)_3 + 2PH_3$.

(*iv*) Sodium and potassium peroxides react with water to produce oxygen, e.g. $2Na_2O_2 + 2H_2O = 4NaOH + O_2$. The reaction produces large amount of heat.

(*v*) Aluminium sulphide (Al_2S_3), a greyish-black solid, reacts with water to produce H_2S, viz. $Al_2S_3 + 3H_2O = Al_2O_3 + 3H_2S$. The compound is decomposed in the same manner by atmospheric moisture when exposed to air.

(*vi*) Metallic hydrides, viz. sodium hydride (NaH) or calcium hydride (CaH_2) react with water to produce hydrogen, which may catch fire and explode when present in suitable concentration.

Solubility in water

All nitrates are soluble in water; so also are the ammonium salts. Most of the chlorates and permanganates of potassium which are strong agents are soluble in water.

2. ACTION OF HEAT ON CERTAIN CHEMICAL SUBSTANCES

(*i*) Nitrates of potassium, sodium and barium, when strongly heated, are decomposed to form oxygen and the corresponding nitrite, viz.

$$2KNO_3 = 2KNO_2 + O_2$$

(*ii*) Nitrates of strontium, calcium, magnesium, aluminium and copper, on being strongly heated, are decomposed to form oxygen, nitrogen peroxide and oxide of the metal:

$$2Ca(NO_3)_2 = 2CaO + 2N_2O_4 + O_2$$

$$2Sr(NO_3)_2 = 2SrO + 2N_2O_4 + O_2$$

$$2Ba(NO_3)_2 = 2BaO + 2N_2O_4 + O_2$$

(*iii*) Also, nitrates of silver on being strongly heated are decomposed to form oxygen, nitrogen peroxide and metal:

$2AgNO_3 = 2Ag + 2NO_2 + O_2$.

(silver nitrate, first of all, is reduced to silver nitrite).

(*iv*) Lead nitrate on being strongly heated evolves oxygen, e.g

$2Pb(NO_3)_2 = 2PbO + 2N_2O_4 + O_2$.

(*v*) Ammonium nitrate on being strongly heated does not evolve oxygen. The reaction at about 250^{0}C is very violent with explosion. This may be written as $NH_4NO_3 = N_2O + 2H_2O$. The nitrous oxide (N_2O) supports combustion just like free oxygen.

(*vi*) Potassium chlorate gives off oxygen on being strongly heated, e.g. $2KClO_3 = 3O_2 + 2KCl$.

(*vii*) Potassium permanganate on being strongly heated, similarly, gives off oxygen, viz. $2KMnO_4 = O_2 + K_2MnO_4 + MnO_2$.

(*viii*) Calcium carbonates, on being heated at a high temperature, or when involved in a fire, evolve carbon dioxide gas, viz. $CaCO_3 = CaO + CO_2$.

(*ix*) Most of the ammonium salts dissociate at high temperature giving off ammonia gas, viz. ammonium chloride, ammonium carbonate (e.g. $NH_4Cl = NH_3 + HCl$).

(*x*) Certain peroxides (of barium and hydrogen) give off oxygen on being strongly heated, e.g.

$$2BaO_2 = 2BaO + O_2 \text{ (bright red heat at } 800^0\text{C)}$$

$$2H_2O_2 = 2H_2O + O_2$$

(*xi*) Potassium permanganate, an oxidizing agent, when strongly heated, breaks up and evolves oxygen: $2KMnO_4 = O_2 + K_2MnO_4 + MnO_2$.

3. CHEMICAL REACTIONS BETWEEN OXIDIZING AGENTS AND OXIDIZABLE SUBSTANCES

(*i*) When potassium permanganate is rubbed with sulphur or phosphorus, an explosion may occur. Similarly, the reaction of a strong oxidizer with any organic substance, such as alcohol, sugar, charcoal, shellac etc. is accompanied with fire and explosion. The reaction of potassium permanganate with hot glycerine $C_3H_5(OH)_3$ is quite violent, leading to a fire.

(ii) Reactions between sulphur and chlorate of potash or sugar and chlorate of potash or shellac with chlorate of potash in presence of heat or percussion is accompanied with disastrous consequences resulting in severe explosion or fire.

(iii) Nitrates react violently with charcoal, when heated or subjected to friction or percussion. In fact, the composition of gun powder is potassium nitrate, sulphur and charcoal.

(iv) Strong and concentrated nitric acid with straw or paper may lead to a fire.

(v) The reaction of gaseous chlorine with metallic powders or with an organic substance like turpentine or with an oxidizable substance like phosphorus is invariably accompained with fire.

(vi) Hydrogen peroxide (concentrated to the extent of about 90%) called H.T.P. (High Test Peroxide) is most dangerous with any organic substance. Even green vegetation will catch fire, in contact with it, due to accidental spillage.

4. REACTION WITH MINERAL ACIDS

(a) Sulphuric acid (H_2SO_4)

(i) Strong sulphuric acid reacts with crystals of permanganates and manganese heptoxide (Mn_2O_7) which may decompose violently into manganese dioxide (MnO_2) and free oxygen (O_2).

(ii) Sulphuric acid has a great affinity for water. If a small quantity of water is added to a large volume of concentrated acid, the acid will mix with water with the evolution of considerable heat and the water will be converted to steam and the temperature may rise as high as 120^0C. Hence, it is dangerous for a fireman to use water for fires involving strong and concentrated sulphuric acid in chemical plants or laboratoties or in factories. This may lead to explosion.

(iii) Strong and concentrated sulphuric acid will char paper, sugar, alcohol, starch by extracting the element of water from it, viz. $C_{12}H_{22}O_{11}$ (sugar) + H_2SO_4 = 12C + ($11H_2O$ + H_2SO_4). The burning action of concentrated sulphuric acid with charring of cloth or paper is due to the powerful dehydrating action on the cellulose $C_6H_{10}O_5$.

(iv) Cold concentrated acid (H_2SO_4) does not react with metals but if the acid is dilute it attacks metals like zinc, iron, lead, tin, magnesium

etc. to produce hydrogen, with a large quantity of heat, which might explode, if the gas produced comes in contact with electric sparks or naked flames under certain circumstances.

(b) Nitric acid (HNO_3)

(*i*) Nitric acid contains a high proportion of oxygen and is a powerful oxidizing agent.

(*ii*) When concentrated nitric acid, which is warm, comes in contact with warm powdered charcoal or sawdust or with glowing charcoal or with glowing chips of wood, a violent reaction resulting in fire takes place.

(*iii*) The reaction of nitric acid with some organic compound may be explosive as in the case of the concentrated acid coming in contact with alcohol specially at a higher temperature. On the other hand, dangerous substances may be produced when glycerine is treated with concentrated nitric acid with a proportion of sulphuric acid to act as a drying agent to abstract the water, viz. $C_3H_3(OH)_5 + 3HNO_3 = C_3H_5(NO_3)_3 + 3H_2O$.

(c) Hydrochloric acid (HCl)

Cold hydrochloric acid will attack most metals to form a chloride of the metal and evolve free hydrogen. The acid reacts with strong oxidizing agents to produce free chlorine.

All acids tend to react with alkalies or bases dangerously with explosive violence depending upon the degree of concentration and the quantity involved. There are two practical methods of dealing with spilled mineral acids, viz. (*i*) dilution with profuse quantity of water, and (*ii*) neutralization. The correct action to be taken will depend on the circumstances present and the technique of handling the situation.

5. ALKALIES

Alkalies like caustic soda or potash produce hydrogen when in contact with aluminium or zinc and may cause hydrogen explosion when present in suitable concentration in the vicinity of a naked flame, viz. $2Al + 2KOH + 2H_2O = 2KAlO_2 + 3H_2$. Like acids, dilution and neutralization are the two ways of dealing with them on the fire ground.

Potassium carbonate and charcoal, when very strongly heated, produce potassium carbonyl, which leads to explosion, unless the product is cooled very rapidly.

6. OTHER IMPORTANT CHEMICAL REACTIONS

Thermite reactions: Metallic aluminium powder shows a great affinity for oxygen. If a mixture of aluminium with oxides of heavy metals such as iron oxide (Fe_2O_3) is heated, a violent chemical reaction starts. The oxide of iron is reduced to iron in a molten stage and aluminium is converted to aluminium oxide, e.g., $2Al + Fe_2O_3 = Al_2O_3 + 2Fe$.

It has been estimated that 1kg of thermite liberates 868 k cal, which, though much smaller than the heat liberated by the corresponding quantity of coal, is not readily dissipated and is retained within the mass with the result that the temperature rises to 2700^0C together with the production of brilliant light. The process has technical application sometimes in the welding of broken iron rails, parts of a ship etc.

7. REACTION BETWEEN ZINC DUST AND CARBON TETRACHLORIDE (BERGER'S PROCESS)

A mixture or zinc dust and carbon tetrachloride in a proporation of one to two with zinc oxide and diatomite (kieselguhr) is known as 'Berger mixture'. A vigorous chemical reaction takes place, resulting in the formation of zinc chloride, which is volatilized by the heat of the reaction and tends to form smoke. These volatile hygroscopic chlorides have been widely employed as smoke producing agents. Mixtures resulting in the production of zinc chloride smokes are most widely used. They are termed as 'H.C. smoke'. Berger was a French army officer in the First World War. He carried out experiments with metal powders and their use as weapons.

Reaction of chlorine with hydrogen and metals

Chlorine has a affinity for hydrogen and metals and the resulting reaction may be violent. A number of incidents ending in fatalities have occurred.

(*i*) Aluminium powder and C.T.C. (carbon tetrachloride) may result in severe explosion.

(*ii*) Trichloroethylene may also react with aluminium powder similarly, but may not be so severe in effect.

(*iii*) Aluminium chloride may act as a catalyst to produce hydrogen chloride. Trichloroethylene has the ability to react with hydrogen chloride to form acetylene. Such an auto-catalytic reaction occurred some years ago in U.K. and it resulted in an explosion in which several firemen were killed.

CHAPTER 11

Liquefied Petroleum Gas—Handling and Storage

Liquefied petroleum gases, better known as L.P.G., are produced during the refining of the crude oil. They are mostly butane (C_4H_{10}) and propane (C_3H_8), and are stored in the cylinders in the form of liquids. The vapour pressure of these gases are quite high. Commercial butane has a vapour pressure of 2.5 bar and propane exerts 13.2 bar pressure at 37.8^{0}C. A mixture of 60% butane and 40% propane gas exerts a pressure of 7.8 bar at 37.8^{0}C. The boiling point of propane is about –42^{0}C and the same for butane is –5^{0}C. The latter is marketed under different trade names e.g. Bursane, Indane, Cal-gas etc. with a small percentage of butylene in it. The weight per gallon of the liquid 15.6^{0}C at 2.2 kg. is for butane and 1.9 kg. for propane. The flash points of propane and butane gases are –104^{0}C and –60^{0}C respectively. The vapour density (air = 1) of butane at 15.6^{0}C and at normal atmospheric pressure (1 bar) of Hg is 2.07 and that of propane is 1.55.

Uses

Butane is generally used for domestic purposes in cylinders painted red and is sold under various trade names. It exerts a pressure of about 2 bar (app.) in the container, which may vary according to temperature. Propane, on the other hand, exerts a pressure of about 7 bar (app.) under the same condition. It is mostly used as industrial fuel as also for cutting metals, viz. for 'oxy-propane flame'.

General characteristics and fire hazards

The characteristics of these gases are that they are heavy as compared to air and they do not readily disperse off in air if there is leakage from the distribution system. In the liquid stage the hazard is somewhat greater than that of gasoline because of the pressure under which they are stored. They tend to hang about on the floor and collect in pits and this is one of the possible sources of danger and flash back. The range of flammability of butane is from 1.5 to 9% by volume in air and 2 to 10% in the case of propane.

The gases are non-toxic but will not support life. They burn with a blue flame when mixed with correct proportion of air and if the air supply is insufficient the flame turns yellow at the edges and no smoke is produced during burning. Smell is deliberately added if the content is insufficient to provide a distinctive smell.

The other interesting characteristics of L.P.G. are their high calorific values as compared to town gas, e.g. the calorific value of commercial butane is about 28492 kcal/m^3 and that of propane is about 22,260kcal/m^3.

Emergency procedures and safety requirements

In case of the gas igniting from the outlet or from other place due to leakage, there is practically no hazard so long as the gas burns; but if there is no fire and the gas continues to come out through the valve assembly on the cylinder or due to leakage from pipes, a hazardous condition is created and immediate action is to be taken to shut down the valve and a thorough ventilation of the room is essential. The electrical switches near about must not be operated for any purpose and all sources of fire/flame of any kind to be immediately removed from the vicinity. The area is to be cordoned off and no person to be allowed to stay near about. It will be advisable to remove the cylinder to a safe place outside the building in the open and watch carefully with a charged line of hose till the gas is entirely released.

APPENDIX 1

Problems on Gas Equation, Diffusion of Gases, Molecular Weights and Volumes, and Normality of Chemical Solutions

a) Gas equation

When the pressure and volume of a given mass of any gas change simultaneously with temperature, the relation between them becomes

$$PV = RT \tag{A1.1}$$

where R is universal gas constant and T is absolute temperature, i.e. where $T = t + 273$, where $t =$ temperature in ^{0}C. It also follows from the relation (11.1) that, if P_1 and P_2 are the pressures at the absolute temperatures T_1 and T_2 respectively,

when volume changes from V_1 to V_2 then,

$$\frac{P_1V_1}{T_1} = \frac{P_2V_2}{T_2} \tag{A1.2}$$

When the pressure P remains constant, then, as per Charles' law,

$$\frac{V}{T} = \text{Constant} \tag{A1.3}$$

where V and T stand for volume and absolute temperature respectively. When the temperature remains constant, then, by Boyle's law,

$$PV = \text{Constant} \tag{A1.4}$$

where P and V stand for pressure and volume respectively.

b) Combined effect of temperature and pressure on the density of a gas

If D_1 be the density of a certain mass of a gas at temperature T_1 absolute and at pressure P_1, and also, if D_2 becomes the density of the same mass of gas at temperature T_2 absolute and at pressure P_2 then by Boyles' and Charles' law,

$$\frac{D_1T_1}{P_1}=\frac{D_2T_2}{P_2} \tag{A1.5}$$

c) Gaseous diffusion

Graham's law states that the relative velocities of diffusion of the gases, at constant pressure, are inversely proportional to the square root of their densities.

If v_1 and v_2 are velocities of diffusion of two gases, whose densities are D_1 and D_2 respectively, then,

$$\frac{v_1}{v_2}=\frac{\sqrt{D_2}}{\sqrt{D_1}}$$

or

$$v_1\sqrt{D_1}=v_2\sqrt{D_2} \tag{A1.6}$$

By the velocity of diffusion of a gas, it is meant the volume of the gas coming out through a porous pot, per unit time. If *a* cc of the gas diffuses out in *t* ses, then the velocity of diffusion of the gas is given by

$$v=\frac{a}{t}\ \text{cc per sec.} \tag{A1.7}$$

Example (1): A gas occupies 200 cc at N.T.P. What will be its volume, when the temperature and presure become 27^0 C and 190 mm of mercury respectively?

Formula: $\frac{P_1V_1}{T_1}=\frac{P_2V_2}{T_2}$ (equation A1.2)

Given: $P_1=760$ mm $P_2=190$ mm

$V_1=200$cc $V_2=?$

$T_1=(273+0)=273$ abs $T_2=(273+27)=300$ abs

Now,

$$\frac{760\times200}{273}\ \frac{190\times V_2}{300}$$

or

$$V_2 = \frac{760 \times 200 \times 300}{273 \times 190} \quad 879.12 \text{ cc}$$

Example (2) : What volume would a litre of a gas, measured at 27^0 C occupy, if heated to 127^0 C, pressure remaining constant?

Formula: $\frac{V}{T}$ = constant = $\frac{V_1}{T_1}$ (equation A1.3)

Given : V = 1 litre $V_1 = ?$

$T = (273+27) = 300^0$ abs $T_1 = 273+127 = 400^0$abs

$$\frac{1}{300} = \frac{V_1}{400}$$

$$\therefore V_1 = \frac{400}{300} = 1.333 \text{ litre}$$

Example (3): At what temperature would 750cc of a gas measured at 27^0 C will occupy one-third of the volume?

Formula: $\frac{V}{T}$ = constant = $\frac{V_1}{T_1}$ (equation A1.3)

$T = t + 273$ (equation A1.5)

Given V = 750 cc $V_1 = \frac{750}{3} = 250$ cc

$T = (273+27) = 300^0$ C

We have, from equation A1.3,

$$\frac{750}{300} = \frac{250}{T_1}$$

or

$$T_1 = \frac{250 \times 300}{750} \quad 100^0 \text{ abs}$$

Now

$$t = T_1 - 273 = 100 - 273 = -173^0\text{C}$$

Example(4): One litre of a gas under 720mm pressure is compressed to 250 cc. Find the new pressure, if the temperature remains constant.

Formula : PV = constant = P_1V_1 (equation A1.4)

Given : P = 720 mm $P_1 = ?$

V = 1 litre = 1000cc V_1 = 250cc

To find P_1, we apply equation A1.4

i.e. $720 \times 1000 = P_1 \times 250$

$\therefore P_1 \; \frac{720\times1000}{250} \; 2880$ mm of mercury.

Example (5): The density of a gas is 14 at 27^0C and 760 mm. What will be its density at 7^0C and 740 mm?

Formula: $\frac{D_1T_1}{P_1}=\frac{D_2T_2}{P_2}$ (equation A1.5)

Given: $D_1=14$ $D_2=?$

$T_1=(273+27)=300$ abs. $T_2=(273+7)=280$ abs

$P_1=760$ mm. $P_2=740$ mm

To find D_2, we may write

$$\frac{14\times300}{760} \; \frac{D_2\times280}{740}$$

or

$$D_2=\frac{14\times300\times740}{280\times760}-14\ 61$$

Example (6): The density of hydrogen is unity and that of oxygen is 16. Find the ratio of their velocities of diffusion.

Formula: $\frac{V_1}{V_2}=\frac{\sqrt{D_2}}{\sqrt{D_1}}$ (equation A1.6)

Given V_1 = velocity of diffusion of hydrogen, V_2 = velocity of diffusion of oxygen.

$D_1=1 \quad D_2=16$

we may write $\frac{V_2}{V_1}=\frac{\sqrt{D_1}}{\sqrt{D_2}}=\frac{1}{\sqrt{16}}=\frac{1}{4}$

i.e. velocity of diffusion of hydrogen is four times that of oxygen

Example (7): If 16 cc of hydrogen diffuse in 100 seconds, what volume of sulphur dioxide will diffuse in the same time under the same conditions? Given that the density of SO_2 is 32 and that of hydrogen is 1.

Formula: $V=\frac{a}{t}$ (equation A1.7) and $\frac{V_1}{V_2}=\frac{\sqrt{D_2}}{\sqrt{D_1}}$ (equation A1.6)

Given: $D_1=1$ (for H_2) $D_2=32$ (for SO_2)

$V_1=\frac{16}{100}$ $V_2=\frac{V_{SO_2}}{100}$

To find out v_{SO_2},

$$\frac{\frac{16}{100}}{V_{SO_2}}=\frac{\sqrt{32}}{1}=\sqrt{32}$$

or

$$\frac{16}{V_{SO_2}}=\sqrt{32}$$

$$V_{SO_2}=\frac{16}{\sqrt{32}}=\frac{16}{4\sqrt{2}}=2\sqrt{2}=2.83 \text{cc per sec.}$$

d) Relation by weight and volume between reactants and the products.

The relation by weight and volumes or by volumes only, as the case may be, between reactants and the products of a chemical reaction can be easily known from the following basic considerations:

(*a*) The chemical equation is taken to express the reaction at N.T.P. (i.e. at 0^0 C and 760 mm of Hg). Hence, the volume of any gas evolved or taking part in ther eaction is understood to have taken place at N.T.P.

(*b*) One gm-molecular weight of any gas occupies 22.4 litre at N.T.P.

(*c*) One molecule of a gas occupies 2 volumes.

(*d*) One litre of hydrogen at N.T.P. weighs 0.089 gm.

(*e*) The molecular weight of a gas is twice its density.

Example 8: What weight of carbon must be burnt in air so as to yield 10 litre of CO_2 at N.T.P.?

$$C + O_2 = CO_2$$

i.e. 12 gm of carbon is required for producing 22.4 litre CO_2 at N.T.P., since atomic weight of C = 12.

Thus, it is seen that 22.4 litre of CO_2 will be obtained by burning 12 gm of carbon.

1 litre will be produced from 12/22.4 gm of carbon.

$\therefore$ 10 litre will be produced from $\frac{12}{22.4} \times 10 = 5.36$ gm

Example (9): How much zinc is required to produce 2240 litre of hydrogen at N.T.P. by the action of sulphuric acid upon it?

$$Zn + H_2SO_4 = ZnSO_4 + H_2$$

65 gm of zinc is required for 22.4 litre of hydrogen at N.T.P., since atomic weight of Zn = 65.

Thus, it is seen that 22.4 litre of hydrogen will be obtained by the action of 65 gm of Zn.

$\therefore$ 1 litre of H_2 will be obtained from 65/22.4 gm of zinc.

or 2240 litre will be produced by $\frac{65}{22.4} \times 2240$ gm = 6500 gm of zinc.

Example (10): 160 gm of marsh gas are burnt with oxygen. What volume of carbon dioxide will be produced at N.T.P.?

$$CH_4 + 2O_2 = CO_2 + 2H_2O$$

Atomic weight of C = 12 and H = 1.
(16 gm of CH_4 produce 22.4 litre of CO_2 gas).

Thus, it is seen that 16 gm of CH_4 are burnt to produce 22.4 litres of CO_2 at N.T.P.

$\therefore$ 1 gm. of CH_4 will produce 22.4/16 litre of CO_2

160 gm of CH_4 will produce $\frac{160 \times 22.4}{16}$ litre of CO_2 gas

= 224 litre of CO_2.

Example (11): What volume of SO_2 you would get at 15°C and 740 mm pressure by burning H_2S obtained from 11 gm of sulphide of iron?

We know $FeS + H_2SO_4 = FeSO_4 + H_2S$

i.e. 88 gm of FeS will yield 22.4 litre of H_2S at N.T.P.

or 11 gm of FeS will yield $\frac{11 \times 22.4}{88}$ litre at N.T.P.

Consider the equation $2H_2S + 3O_2 = 2H_2O + 2SO_2$.

From the above equation we find that when H_2S burns in air it gives its own volume of SO_2, i.e. 2 × 22.4 litres of H_2S will give 2 × 22.4 litre of SO_2.

Hence, $\frac{11 \times 22.4}{88}$ litres of H_2S at N.T.P will yield $\frac{11 \times 22.4}{88} = 2.8$ litre of SO_2 at N.T.P..

Let 2.8 litre of SO_2 at N.T.P. occupy V litre at 15°C and 740 mm pressure.

Now applying the formula

$$\frac{PV}{T} = \frac{P_1 V_1}{T_1},$$

we have

$$\frac{2.8 \times 760}{273} \frac{V \times 740}{15 + 273}$$

or

$$V = \frac{2.8 \times 760 \times 288}{740 \times 273} 3.03 \text{ litre.}$$

Example (12): 100 cc of liquid carbon disulphide (specific gravity 2.6) is burnt in oxygen. Find the volume of the resulting gases at N.T.P.

100 cc of CS_2 will weigh 100 × 2.6 = 260 gm (since specific gravity of liquid carbon disulphide is 2.6)

Also, $CS_2 + 3O_2 = CO_2 + 2SO_2$

(76 gm) 22.4l + (2 × 22.4l at N.T.P.)

The volume of the resulting gases is

22.4 + 2×22.4 = 67.2 litre of $CO_2 + SO_2$ at N.T.P.

Hence, 100cc or 260 gm of CS_2 will yield $\frac{260 \times 67.2}{76}$ 229.89 litre of CO_2 and SO_2 at N.T.P.

e) Acidimetry and alkalimetry: definition of standard and normal solutions

The determination of total quantity of an acid present in a solution is known as acidimetry and the determination of the total quantity of an alkali present in a solution is known as alkalimetry. The determination is made by neutralizing the acid or alkali in presence of an indicator with an alkali or acid of known strength.

The *standard* solution of a substance is the solution which contains a known weight of the substance dissolved in a known volume of it. A *normal* solution of a substance is a substance in a solution which contains one gram-equivalent of the substance per litre of the solution. Mentiond below are the different ways of expressing strengths of chemical solutions:

(a) Percentage strength: 5% sulphuric acid means 5 gm present in 100cc 10% nitric acid means 10gm contained in 100cc. of solution.

(b) Strength in terms of normality: As stated above, this means the number of gm-equivalent of solute present in 1 litre of the solution. Thus N (HCl) means one litre of it (1000 cc), which contains 1 gm-equivalent of hydrochloric acid.

(c) Strength in terms of gm/litre: N(H_2SO_4) means 49 gm of sulphuric acid present in a litre of the solution and (N/10) HCl means 3.65 gm of hydrochloric acid present in a litre of the solution, taking into consideration the molecular weight of the acids.

APPENDIX 2

Table A2.1 (a) FLASH POINT IN DE GREES CENTIGRADE IN CLOSED-CUP TEST

Materials	Class of hazard	Ignition temperature in °C	Flash point in °C
Acetone (Di-methyl ketone)	EH	538	–18
Allyl alcohol	H	378.5	21.1
Amyl acetate	EH	382.1	25.0
Benzene	EH	587.0	–11.1
Benzine	EH	287.8	–18
Butane	EH	430	–60
Butyl alcohol	H	365 to 478	11.1 to 29
Butyl acetate	EH	423	17.8 to 31.0
Butadiene	EH	429	–17.8
Carbon disulphide	EH	100	–30
Camphor	H	448	65.6
Coal-tar	H		22.8 to 32.2
Coconut oil			215.5
Di-ethyl ether	EH	185	–40
Ethyl acetate	EH	460	–4
Ethyl alcohol	EH	423	16
Ethyl chloride	EH	519	–50
Glycerine	H		176
Kerosene	H	254 to 260	38 to 47
Lubricating oil (Motor oil)	H	371	232
Methyl alcohol	EH	464	18
Naphthalene	H	526	80

Materials	Class of hazard	Ignition temperature in °C	Flash point in °C
Oil of turpentine	EH		35
Paraffin	H		158 to 195
Petrol (Gasolene)	EH	246 to 257	–45
Petroleum ether	EH	287.8	–18
Phenol	H	715	79.4
Tallow	H		265
Toluene	EH		5
Turpentine	H		35
White spirit	EH		26 to 65
Xylene	EH	464 to 529	18.3 to 25

Note: 'EH' signifies Extra Hazardous and 'H' signifies Hazardous, when the materials mentioned are present in appreciable quantities in a building. The list by no means is exhaustive and is only illustrative.

Table A2.1 (b) SPECIFIC GRAVITY AND VAPOUR DENSITY OF CERTAIN FLAMMABLE LIQUIDS WITH THEIR CHEMICAL FORMULA

Name	Specific gravity	Vapour density	Chemical formula
1. Methyl alcohol	0.8	1.1	CH_3OH
2. Ethyl alcohol	0.8	1.6	C_2H_5OH
3. Acetone	0.8	2.0	CH_3COCH_3
4. Amyl acetate	0.9	4.5	$C_5H_{11}OCOCH_3$
5. Carbon disulphdie	1.3	2.6	CS_2
6. Pentane	0.6	2.5	C_5H_{12}
7. Octane	0.7	3.9	C_8H_{18}

Table A2.2 CALORIFIC VALUE OF CERTAIN COMMONMATERIALS

	Substance	Calorific value kcal/kg	Moisture content (%)
1.	*Coal, coke and charcoal*		
	Coal (Anthracite)	7011–7745	2.3–2.2
	Coal (Bitumen)	5611–8103	14.2–1.6
	Coal (Lignite)	291–2296	90.3–54.7
	Coal (Peat)	6496–7174	0.2–0.1
	Coke or charcoal	7235	3.2

	Substance	Calorific value kcal/kg	Moisture content (%)
2.	*Wood and straw*		
	Ash	4749	Dry
	Beach	4206	13
	Oak	4021	13
	Pine (softwood resinous)	4665	10.4
	Straw	2795	Dry
3.	*Petrol and oil*		
	Crude fuel oil	10422–11037	
	Gasoline	11088–11491	
	Kerosene	11038–11138	
	Coal-tar oil	11138–11304	
	Gas oil	10786–10965	
4.	*Asphalt*		
	Pure asphalt	9610	
	Pure bitumen	8478	
	Paraffin	10058–11262	
	Pitch	8467	
5.	*Gases* (kcal/m^3)		
	Coal gas	4006 – 5966	
	Producer gas (kcal/m^3)	890 – 1603	
	Water gas	3536–5966	
6.	*Textiles*		
	Cotton	4010	
	Silk (fibre)	5169	
	Wool	5482	
7.	*Paper/starch/explosives*		
	Paper, cellulose	4239	
	Starch	4262	
	Gun cotton	1064	
	Dynamite	1299	
8.	*Fats and tallow*		
	Animal fat	9576	
	Butter fat	9391–9436	
	Lard	9677	
	Tallow	9576	
9.	*Miscellaneous chemicals*		
	Carbon disulphide	3433	
	Ethyl ether	12320	

Substance	Calorific value kcal/kg	Moisture content (%)
Linseed oil	9442	
Paraffin wax	11256	
Phosphorus	5925	
Camphor	9363	
Napthalene	9682	
Ethyl alcohol	7143	
Benzene	10072	
Methyl alcohol	5459	
Butane (liquid)	12034	
Hydrogen	34136	
Methane	13362	
Rubber	9425	

Table A2.3 SELF-IGNITION TEMPERATURE OF CERTAIN SOLIDS

Materials	°F	°C	State of materials
Wood			
Pine	442–446	228–232	Shavings
Douglas fir	500	260	Shavings
Pine (white)	507	264	Shavings
Paper and textiles			
Paper (newsprint)	446	230	Cuts
Paper (filter)	450	232.2	Cuts
Cotton (absorbent)	511	265	Roll
Woollen (blanket)	401	205	Roll
Nylon (parachute)	536	280	Roll
Silk)	1058	570	Roll
Fibre board and rubber			
Wood fibre board	421–444	216–230	Piece
Synthetic rubber (G.R.S.)	590	310	Coagulen
Metals			
Aluminium paint fibres	959	515	Fine powder
Tin	842	450	Fine powder
Magnesium	883	471	Fine powder
Mangsnese	1004	538	Cuts
Zinc	1202	649	Fine powder

Materials	°F	°C	State of materials
Miscellaneous			
Nitrocellulose fibre	279	137	Roll
Matches	325	162	Heads
Carbon soot	366	186	
Shellac	810	432	Scales
Paint Film (oxidized linseed oil varnish)	864	462	Powder

Table A2.4 APPROXIMATE FLAME TEMPERATURE

Colour of flame	Temperature range °C
incipient red heat	500 to 550
Dark red heat	650 to 750
Bright red heat	850 to 950
Yellowish red heat	1050 to 1150
Incipient white heat	1250 to 1350
White heat	1450 to 1550

Table A2.5 TEMPERATURE OF OXY-GAS FLAMES

Clour of flame	Temperature range °C
Bunsen flame (coal gas with full air supply)	1871
Hydrogen flame	1900
Acetylene flame	2548
Oxy-coal gas blowpipe flame	2200
Oxy-hydrogen flame	2420
Oxy-carbon monoxide flame	2600
Oxy-acetylene flame	3100 to 3315
Atomic hydrogen flame	3400

Table A2.6 FUSION POINTS OF COMMON ELEMENTS AND SUBSTANCES

	Fusion points °C
Aluminium	658
Antimony	630
Bismuth	268
Borax	75
Brass (85% Cu and 15% Zn)	1030
Bronze (67% Cu and 33% Zn)	745
Calcium	842
Calcium carbide	3000
Camphor ($C_{10}H_{16}O$)	175
Caustic soda	318
Copper	1083
Ferro nickel (60% nickel, 33% Cu and 6.5% Fe)	1360
Glaubersalt (Na_2SO_4, $10H_2O$)	900
Gold	1064
Gun metel (90% Cu and 10% Zn)	1000
Iron (pure)	1530
(a) Cast (pig iron)	1150
(b) Steel	1430
(c) Stainless steel (90 to 92% Fe, 8% Cr, 0.4% Mn and less than 0.12% C)	1450
(d) Wrought iron	1510
Lead	327
Magnesium	651
Manganese	1900
Manganese steel (86% Fe, 13% Mn and 1% C)	1510
Magnesia	3000
Nickel	1435
Picric acid	122
Platinum	1755
Potassium chlorate	359
Potassium iodide	625
Quicklime	2500
Silver	961
Silver nitrate	208
Sodium nitrate	333
Sugar	160
Tin	232
Tungsten	1700
Zinc	419

Table A2.7 ULTIMATE AVERAGE STRENGTH OF SOME COMMON MATERIALS

Material	Compression strength (bar)	Tensile stress (bar)
Bricks (best hard)	828	27.6
Bricks (light red)	69	2.76
Brickwork (common)	69	3.45
Cement Portland (1 month old)	276	27.6
Concrete (Portland cement)	138	13.8
Pine (white)	379.5	483
White oak	483	690

Table A2.8 COEFFICIENT OF EXPANSION AND SPECIFIC HEAT OF CERTAIN COMMON MATERIALS

Substances	Coefficient of linear expansion per °C	Specific heat
Aluminium	0.0000255	0.21
Brass	0.0000188	0.089
Brick	0.000009	
Cement and concrete	0.000010 to 0.000014	0.20
Copper	0.0000167	0.094
Glass (common)	0.000009	0.16
Glass (pyrex)	0.000003	0.19
Gun metal	0.000018	0.0862
Iron (cast)	0.0000102	0.11
Iron (Wrought)	0.0000119	0.11
Stainless steel	0.000011	
Sand	0.000009	0.21
Steel	0.000012	0.11

APPENDIX 3

(A) PEAK FLAMMABILITY VALUES OF HALOGEN COMPOUNDS FOR COMBUSTION OF N-HEXANE IN AIR

(percentage of vapour by volume required to inhibit combustion of n-hexane in air)

Compound	Formula	% by volume
Carbon tetrachloride	CCl_4	9.9
Methyl bromide	CH_3Br	7.1
Chloro-bromo-methane (C.B.M or C.B.)	CH_2ClBr	6.4
Bromo-chloro-difluoro-methane (B.C.F. or Halon 1211)	$CBrClF_2$	5.2
Bromo-tri-fluoro-methane (B.T.M. or Halon 1301)	$CBrF_3$	4.9
Dibromo-difluoro-methane	CBr_2F_2	3.6

Note 1 : The inhibitory factor might change for different types of fuel but the values will be considerably less than 28% of the volume of the space required for inerting the atmosphere for fire extinction.

Note 2 : Vaporizing liquids stated above as halogenated hydrocarbons act as negative catalysts in the combustion process. They slow down and finally stop the reaction, while themselves remaining unchanged. Considerable ionization takes place within the flames. In a fire involving hydrocarbons, the OH^- radical plays a very important part in the chain reactions. With a halogenated hydrocarbon compound with Br, it is considered that the OH^- radical reacts with HBr released as follows : $OH^- + HBr \rightarrow H_2O + Br^-$. The OH^- is thus removed from the process, but HBr can be regenerated by the removal of a hydrogen atom from any radical that is less reactive than OH^-, e.g. $Br^- + HR \rightarrow HBr + R$. Similar reactions may occur with other halogens, but bromine is more effective than either chlorine or fluorine. Hence, the superiority of bromine-containing agents is recognized. B.C.F. is superior to B.T.M. for deep-seated fires only; but in general, B.C.F. is about 18 to 20% less effective than B.T.M. against most fires.

(B) IMPORTANT PHYSICAL PROPERTIES OF THE LATEST TYPE OF THE VAPORIZING EXTINGUISHING MEDIA WITH LOW INHIBITORY FACTOR

Name	Boiling point °C	Vapour density (gas) (air = 1.0)	Specific gravity (liquid)
Chloro-bromo-methane (C.B.M.)	68	4.5	1.95
Bromo-chloro-difluoro-methane (B.C.F.)	–4	5.7	1.83
Bromo-triflouro-methane (B.T.M.)	–58	5.2	1.58

Note: The lower boiling point of B.C.F. indicates that it will be vaporized more quickly than CBM and will react with the flames more rapidly. On the other hand the higher boiling point of B.C.F. as compared to BTM shows that B.C.F. is more likely to reach the surface of a petrol (hydrocarbon) fire than BTM in droplets rather than in vapour form, suppressing further formation of flammable vapours from the burning liquid. The BTM, having the lower boiling point, is likely to be converted entirely to the vapour phase after being expelled from the extinguisher.

(C) TOXIC HAZARDS OF VAPORIZING EXTINGUISHING MEDIA

Carbon tetrachloride (C.T.C.) and methyl bromide (MBr) have threshold limit values of 25 and 20 parts per million (ppm) respectively. Their use in fire service has been abandoned due to their toxicity, causing a permanent damaging effect on the liver.

B.C.F has been extensively tested on rats and guinea pigs and death only occurs after exposure to a concentration of 32% or more for 15 minutes. The inhalation of 4–5% for one minute is the maximum that can be tolerated, but any effect on dizziness, etc. rapidly wears off on exposure to fresh air. The use of hand extinguishers or local application system is unlikely to involve health hazard but in total flooding system the design concentration is generally within the range of 5 to 8% B.C.F. by volume.

During fire extinction, the halogenated hydrocarbons with Br break down to release HBr. The pyrolysis products, mainly the hydrogen halides and possibly some free halogens, are usually present in low concentrations after a fire. Due to their extreme irritating effect, specially above a concentration of 20 ppm, they themselves give their own warning to leave the confined space, which must be thoroughly ventilated before re-entry without breathing apparatus is attempted. It may be added that any halogenated hydrocarbon extinguishing media with fluorin will produce HF (hydrofluoric acid) as a pyrolysis product which is quite hazardous.

(D) TOXICITY OF PLASTICS–RESULTS OF RESEARCH WORK IN UK BY J.F.R.O.

P.V.C. plastics are less toxic, except for the liberation of HCl gas when involved in fire and they are more fire-resisting than styrene or alkathene.

Polyurethane foam, as used for upholstry work is dangerous, as at 700 to 800^0 C it produces sufficient quantity of hydrocyanic acid gas, which might be fatal to a fireman unless protected by B.A. set. The toxicity factor of P.V.C. as analyzed in the laboratory are as follows :

Substance	Toxicity factor
Hydrocyanicacid (HCN)	1.6×10^{-1}
Benzene	3.7×10^{-4}
Toluene	7.1×10^{-5}
Total xylene	3.8×10^{-5}
Naphthalene	1.6×10^{-3}
Phsgene	Not recorded

This shows that PVC when involved in fire, is much less toxic as against other types of plastics.

CHAPTER 12

Part 2: Electricity in Relation to Fire Hazards: Preliminaries

Electricity is a form of energy which we utilize daily either for obtaining light or heat or we use it as power for driving fans, motors etc.

Conductors and insulators

Flow of negatively charged electrons is known as flow of current, and materials which allow the flow of electric current are called conductors. On the other hand, certain materials which set up a high resistance to the flow and do not allow the current to pass through them are called insulators. For the current to flow along a conductor in a circuit, there must be a difference in potential (i.e. the electric pressure) between the two conductors. This is called the supply voltage.

Flow of current

Flow of electricity and flow of water have the following similarities: (*i*) Electric current depends on potential difference, as flow of water depends on the difference of level of water. (*ii*) Flow of water increases with the difference of level in the two vessels, the strength of current increases with the increase in the differnce of potential. (*iii*) For the flow of water, it is necessary to join the two vessels by a pipe, so also for the flow of electricity, where it is necessary to complete the circuit between the positive and the negative conductor. (*iv*) Wider the pipe more, water flows through it; so also, thicker the wire the more current will pass through it.

Ohm's Law

The relation between current, resistance and electric pressure, i.e. the voltage, is expressed by Ohm's Law, which states that current flowing in an electrical circuit is directly proportional to the voltage and inversely proportional to the resistance of the circuit, i.e.

$$I = \frac{E}{R}$$

where I represents current in amperes, E represents voltage or potential difference in volts and R is the resistance in ohms.

If the resistance of the circuit (i.e. the path through which current flows) is low, then for the same voltage there will be greater flow of current. It is for this reason that the insulation resistance of the conducting wires is so important. Excessive pressure on the line, over-heating, age and condition of the wiring, dampness or mechanical damage will cause the insulation to break and permit leakage of the current.

Specific resistance

A few examples of conductors and insulators are given below. The resistance of a centimetre cube of the substance (i.e. the resistance of one centimetre length of wire having one square centimetre of cross-section) is known as specific resistance. The resistivity of the insulators is in the order of millions of ohms (1 million ohm = 1,000,000 ohms, also 1 microohm or millionth of an ohm = 10^{-6} ohm).

Table 12.1

Conductors	Specific resistance in microhms per cm^3
Silver (annealed)	1.56
Copper (annealed)	1.696
Copper (hard drawn)	1.731
Gold	2.2
Aluminium	2.91
Lead	10.4
Iron (soft)	10.7
Iron (cast)	70
Mercury	95
Graphite	3000

Conductors	Specific resistance in microhms per cm
Insulators	*Resistance*
Porcelain	
Silk	
India rubber	
Shellac	Resistance very high; of the order of several millions of ohm. Hence no current will pass.
Mica	
Glass	
Vulcanite	
Polyvinylchloride	
Nylon	
Terylene	

Effect of temperature on conductors and insulators

The resistance of a substance varies with the change in temperature and as a result the increase in temperature in a conductor causes an increase in resistance. One exception to this is carbon, in which a rise in temperature causes a decrease in resistance.

In the case of insulators, however, a rise in temperature causes the resistance to decrease. This is a very important point, as the value of insulation can be seriously impaired if subjected to high temperature, causing current to flow such as in rubber, mica, shellac etc.

Recently, a number of insulating materials has, however, been found which can withstand temperatures of 200^0C and higher and they are mostly silicone groups of varnishes and bonding materials used for winding of motors or transformer coils.

Heating effect of current

When current flows through a conductor it generates heat. This depends on the square of the value of current, the resistance of the circuit and the time. This is expressed as $H \alpha\ C^2RT$, where H stands for heat, C for current strength in amperes, R = resistance in ohms and T = time in seconds. Also, the work done due to the current flowing through a conductor is expressed as $W = C^2RT \times 10^7$ ergs, and the heat produced is

$$H = \frac{W}{J}$$

where J is the mechanical equivalent of heat $=4.2\times10^7$ erg/calories. Hence,

$$H=\frac{C^2RT\times10^7}{4.2\times10^7}\text{ calories}=0.24\times C^2RT\text{ calories}$$

since the work from one calorie of heat $=4.2\times10^7$ ergs.

HEAT DEVELOPED DUE TO SHORT CIRCUIT–FIRE RISK

From the above, it follows that if the flow of current through a conductor is exceeding its capacity due to overload on the circuit, as a result of high wattage lamps or heavy duty motors or domestic heaters being used, the cable will be hot. The heat factor will gradually increase depending upon the time and the resistance of the circuit. If the current is twice its normal load, the heat developed will be four times. Similarly, if it is three times the normal load, the heat will increase to nine times. In case of a short circuit, i.e. due to the accidental contact between the current wire and the neutral or the earth, the full current will rush to the earth point, resulting in a heavy arc at the earth connection and very high temperature, which may set fire to the insulation or to the materials stored nearby. In other words, when current passes through a much shorter path to the earth, than what it is normally designed for, without encountering any resistance, it is known as Short Circuit and the heavy arcing, which results, will melt the conductor with the formation of beads near the earth contact. The temperature of the arc is of the order of 2500^0C.

Over-current protection—thermal fuse

For protection against short circuit and the resulting fire, a thermal fuse is normally inserted near the main supply in the circuit and it is through this wire that the main supply current flows in the circuit. The fuse is a short wire of an alloy of tin and lead. it has a melting point of about 155^0C and is connected in 'series' with the circuit. It melts due to over-current and disconnects the circuit immediately.

Opinions vary as to the proper overload at which the fuse should function; normal practice favouring an overload current to be disconnected is from 50 to 75% for motor circuits, 30 to 40% for main lighting, and 50 to 100% for lighting sub-circuit.

When a fuse blows off suddenly, the cause should be investigated first before replacing it again with the correct one which is important. The fuse is the weakest link in the circuit and it is like a safety valve in a boiler. A blown off fuse is to be replaced by another of the correct rating. If the fuse is of too high a rating or the earth path is not of sufficiently low resistance, the fuse may fail to blow off and the over-current keeps flowing in the circuit and an arc may occur at the point of fault.

As against the porcelain fuse carrier with a fuse wire connected between two terminals, now-a-days cartridge fuses are used which consists of a fuse in a sealed tube. This is to contain the arc, when the fuse blows off.

Sparks, arcs and overheated wires

Fire starts with heat and there are a number of ways in which electricity can give rise to heating. Apart from excess current passing through a circuit, loose connections or small breaks in wiring can lead to a sucession of sparks or continuous arcing. A spark may be enough to set fire to flammable gases, vapours or dusts, while an electric arc, if it persists long enough, can ignite solid combustible materials.

Importance of good earthing connection

An unsatisfactory earthing system can be more dangerous than none at all, since it can carry an earth-fault current to a potentially more dangerous area. This might mean, for example, that the fault current made its way to earth through a pipe carrying an inflammable liquid or gas and the arc at the contact point on the pipe where the cable is connected might be of sufficient intensity to burn a hole in it and ignite the vapour or gas. If conduit is used as the earth return path, it must afford continuity to a good earth. An electrical fault is most likely to lead to fire when it is allowed to persist. The importance of providing a good earth to enable fuses and circuit breakers to operate cannot be over-emphasized. In the case of residential premises a 2 metre pipe buried in earth with charcoal and salt on alternate layers may be good enough.

It is, however, obligatory under Rule 61 (2) of the Indian Electricity Rules, 1956, that the frame of every generator, stationary motor and as far as practicable, portable motors and the metallic parts (not intended as conductor) of all transformers and any other apparatus used for regulating or controlling energy and all medium voltage energy-causing apparatus, shall be earthed by the owner by two separate and distinct connections with earth.

The earth resistance should be the lowest and the data given below give an idea of the minimum requirement.

Large sub-station including the power station	1 ohm.
Small sub-station	2.5 ohm.
Residential houses	10 ohm.

However, the minimum of 1 ohm earth resistance in all cases should be aimed at for fire safety.

CHAPTER 13

Electric Wiring and Types of Cables

Safety in an electrical installation depends on good wiring, proper earthing and the use of correct type of cable. Types of cables commonly available are given below:

(*i*) V.I.R. cable (i.e. vulcanized India rubber cable);

(*ii*) P.V.C. (i.e. plastic cable);

(*iii*) Flexible rubber cable;

(*iv*) Workshop cable (i.e. C.T.S. (the cab tyred sheath), or T.R.C. (tough rubber cable);

(*v*) Lead sheathed cable; and

(*vi*) Mineral insulated cable (i.e. a cable in which a highly compressed refractory mineral insulating material, such as magnesia, is contained in a solid drawn copper sheath).

Out of the above, the V.I.R. cable and the plastic cables introduced into the market have found wider applications. P.V.C. or plastic cables have good mechanical and electrical qualities. Being a thermoplastic material, it melts at about 100^0C. It is resistant to corrosion and oxidization. It may, however, give HCl (hydrochloric acid) vapours during a fire in considerable quantity.

V.I.R. cables are quite strong and durable for all permanent wirings. Different types of wirings with aforesaid types of cables are in vogue and the following may be noted. They are: (*i*) cleat wiring; (*ii*) capping and casing system; (*iii*) conduit wiring; (*iv*) concealed wiring (i.e. where the cables in conduit pipes are embedded in walls inside the mortar or plasters); and lastly (*v*) the pyrotanex system, i.e. wiring with mineral insulated cables. Of all the types, the wiring with mineral insulated cables or in M.S. screwed conduit pipes, as continuously bonded to earth, is the best. Exposed wiring such as cleat wiring supported on porcelain or other materials like wooden battens etc. with clips to support, are undersirable. In conduit wiring, the cables are well protected and the chance of damage to the conductors is very little and consequent dangers due to short circuit and the formation of arcs are also minimized due to earth continuity with the 1.9 cm steel conduit pipes whereasin the exposed types there is every chance of the conductor getting damaged due to deterioration of outside insulation as a result of atmospheric humidity, temperature, dirt or dust reacting on the insulation.

In the conduit system, the insulated conductors carrying the current also get protection from the mechanical damage apart from the circuit being rendered dead should any trouble develop in the wirings due to earthing effect. The wooden capping and casing system also protects the wirings likewise but it may not safely dissipate the fault current to earth in case of leakage between the conductors.

Protection of cables against fire or explosion

If cables are installed in a situation where flammable or explosive dust, vapour or gas are likely to be present, or where explosive materials are handled or stored, the cables must be enclosed in screwed solid-drawn steel conduit or must be metal-sheathed and armoured or mineral-insulated and copper-sheathed. If a conduit containing cables passes from a hazardous area to a safe area, a flameproof sealing-box must be inserted where the conduit enters the safe area.

Mineral-insulated copper sheathed cables can be used with advantage where fire hazards are the greatest. It is particularly useful in petrol installations and in places where flammable gases are encountered. It can also be employed in places where relatively high temperatures are encountered.

Flameproof switch

When current is flowing through a circuit which is suddenly broken, a momentary arc or flash takes place at the point of the break in the circuit. The intensity of the arc in such cases depends, amongst other things, on the voltage of the circuit and the ampereage. This is of great practical importance as even in the ordinary low voltage domestic type switch-gears, a momentary arc is produced whenever the current is turned off from the switch.

It is therefore of importance that ordinary switches or lamp holders must not be used in hazardous occupancies or locations, where there might be considerable accumulation of flammable vapour. Electrical switch-gear or appliances to be used in such positions must be of the flameproof type with gas-tight glands so that any sparking or arcing occurring inside any switch or appliance might not come in contact with the flammable vapour–air mixture outside, causing fire or explosion. Flameproof switch-gears with gas-tight glands, are extensively employed in the underground mines and particularly in such locations as petrol refineries, gas undertakings etc.

Distribution

From the main switch the current is carried throughout the premises in a series of circuits each brought to a distribution box and protected by a fuse. A separate switch is employed for each appliance to turn it on or off including the plug points. Although the wiring on the appliance side of the switch should be dead, when it is off, it should be appreciated that the distribution wiring in the premises, irrespective of its size, will always be alive and to avoid it, the main switch is placed in the live conductor and the circuit becomes disconnected when it is opened as shown in Fig.5.

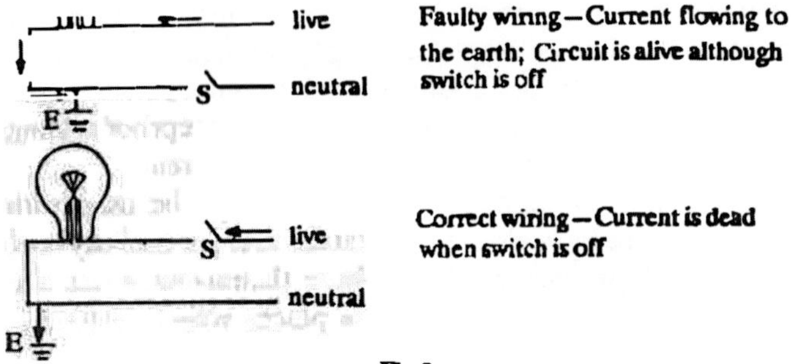

Fig.5

The circuits are terminated either in a fixed electricity-consuming device, e.g. a lamp, a fan, or in a socket outlet, from which connections can be taken for temporarily working any light, fan, radio or heaters by means of flexible wiring. The most common type of flexible wiring may be two separate conductors with one or two layers of insulations finished off with a silk or cotton braiding twisted together.

Flexible wiring and associated hazards

Flexible wiring is meant for a variety of purposes, but it is subject to misuse to a great extent. Connections from a plug socket to a table lamp, electric iron, call bell etc. are normally made by means of flexible wiring. The wiring may be laid under the carpet on the floor, and being daily trampled on, the insulation on the cable may be chafed or damaged and a short circuit, resulting in the formation of an arc, is not uncommon. This arc may give rise to a fire. Besides, the frequent movement of a table lamp or the iron may also weaken the conductor and the insulation may not be sufficiently strong (particularly with rubber-insulated flexible cables) and this may also cause a short circuit or electric arc.

Size of cable in relation to current strength

The conductor wire in the case of flexible wiring is made of a few strands of copper. The number of the strands and the thickness depend upon the capacity of the conductor to withstand the load. An idea of the size of the wire in relation to the current flowing may be had from the following table:

Table 13.1

Strands	Wire size (mm)
5 amp	3 × 0.800
15 amp	7 × 0.800
25 amp	7 × 1
40/50 amp	7 ×1.12

As per I.S.S. diameters of wire in mm.

CHAPTER 14

Use of Electricity for Lighting

The most common use of electricity is for illumination besides small domestic power. Illumination may be had by use of the following: (*i*) incandescent lamps; (*ii*) arc lamps; (*iii*) vapour lamps; (*iv*) luminous discharge tubes.

Incandescent lamp

This is the most common type of lamp used. The current passes through a coiled wire of high resistance with a high melting point, called the filament, placed in a glass globe which may either be filled with an inert vapour like argon or it may be in a stage of high vacuum as per Fig.6.

Gas – filled lamp

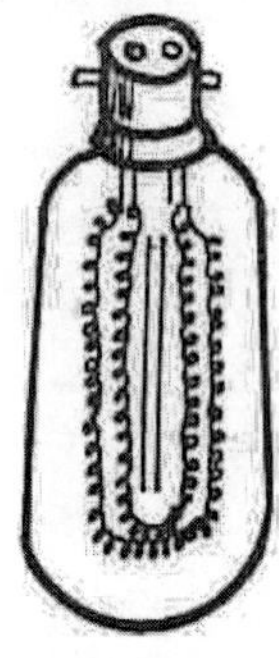

Vacuum lamp

Fig.6

Due to the passage of the current, the filament (which is normally an alloy of wolfram and osmium with a melting point of about 3500°C) becomes white hot and emits the light. The operating voltages are not normally above 220 volt.

Electric lamps are safer than any other source of light but with high wattage lamps, the glass may become hot enough to ignite inflammable materials which might be in contact with it. Celluloid is particularly dangerous; paper or textile lamp shades and curtains etc. should not be allowed to touch the lamps. The temperatures of gas-filled lamps (75 to 150 watt) vary from 118^0 to 170^0C while those of the vacuum type (60 to 180 watt) vary from 67^0 to 69^0C, depending upon the length of time the lamp has been glowing. The efficiency of gas-filled lamps, which is given by watt per candle power, is about double that of an ordinary evacuated lamp. A gas-filled lamp consumes about 1.6 watt per candle power.

Arc lamp

These are generally used in ships or in connection with photographic works or in cinematograph machines. The voltage never exceeds 80 volt and the current employed is D.C. Intense bluish-white light is emitted by an arc struck between the tips of two carbon rods at a temperature of nearly 3000^0C. A crater is formed due to the sublimation of carbon particles at the end of the positive carbon electrode which is generally twice the diameter of the negative electrode, which becomes pointed as a result. It is from this crater in the positive electrode that most of the light is emitted. Fire hazards arise because of the very high temperature of the arc and, as the carbon rods burn away, fragments of incandescent carbon are liable to drop and set fire to the combustible articles near about.

Vapour lamp

This is mostly used now-a-days in railway stations and in public thoroughfares where a strong illumination is required. A small quantity of mercury or sodium is contained in a gas-filled quartz tube enclosed in an evacuated glass bulb.

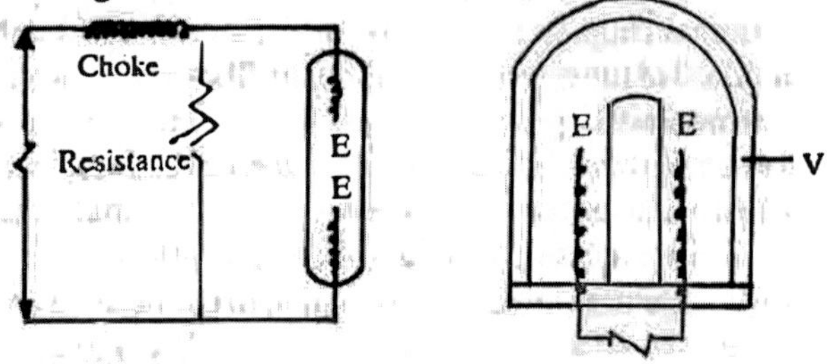

Circuit of a medium pressure mercury lamp

A.C. sodium vapour lamp

Fig.7

When the current is turned on, the mercury is heated and vapourized and the current passing through the vapour causes it to glow. The colour of the light emitted depends on the material used, mercury giving a bluish-green light and sodium an orange-yellow light. Normal voltage, not exceeding 250 volt, can be employed for these lamps but each must be fitted with a choke and a condenser to limit the current passing. Of the different types of lamps which are in this group, one starts the discharge through a rare gas from alkaline eletrodes which are heated by a filament at a high temperature through sodium vapour; the other starts the discharge at normal temperature through a rare gas until a little mercury contained in the tube is sufficiently heated to produce vapour through which the discharge is maintained as long as the lamp is working. The two types are shown in Fig.7.

HEATING EFFECTS

Unlike the comparatively cold glow which is produced in the cathode sign tube (such as neon signs), the glow in a vapour discharge lamp requires a high temperature (500–600^{0}C). For this, the inner globe is surrounded by vacuum or oxygen contained in an outer globe so as to conserve the heat and maintain the temperature. Neverthless, a certain amount of heat reaches the outer globe, the temperature of which is likely to be about 350^{0}C – a figure in excess of the hottest part of the tungsten filament gas-filled incandescent lamp.

FLUORESCENT TUBE

In the fluorescent tube, which is a modified form of vapour lamp, the light emitted by the mercury vapour strikes a thin layer of the flourescent material deposited on the inside of the tube and causes it to emit visible light.

It usually consists of a glass bulb in the shape of a tube 25 to 38 mm in diameter and with lengths varying from 46 to 122 cm. The tube is usually fixed with terminal rings to a board behind. At each end of the tube, there is a small coil of tungsten wire, called the filament, which is coated with an electron-emitting material and the terminals of the coil are brought outside. Within the bulb there is argon gas at a moderately low pressure (a few millimeters of mercury) and a very small quantity of mercury. The inside surface of the tube is coated with zinc silicate, cadmium silicate or calcium tungstate, according to the desired colour.

The terminals from the mains supply (A.C. or D.C.) are connected to the tube through a bayonet lamp cap at the two ends. If the effective voltage of the mains is higher than the voltage necessary to run the lamp a resistance is connected in a series to drop the voltage to the required extent (for D.C.) or a large coil of wire wound on soft iron core, called the ballast choke, is connected in series (for A.C. supply). The two heating coils at the two ends of the tube situated inside, are connected with a push button switch as shown in Fig.8.

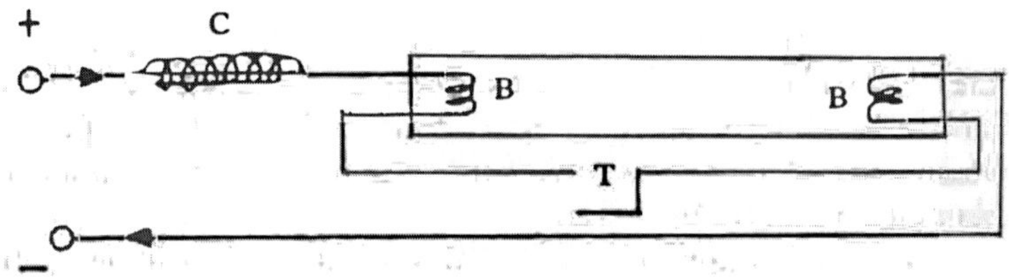

Fig.8 Circuit diagram of fluorescent lamp
C = ballast choke; T = push-button switch

On pressing the switch current is established through the choke and the two coils at the ends and the switch. The current heats the filaments and electrons are emitted. These electrons make the passage through the tube partially conducting. Now on releasing the switch, the current in the circuit tends to fall to zero value and the self-induction of the choke creates a momentary high voltage impulse to start the discharge within the tube. Once discharge starts, the electrons move with a high speed from lower to a higher potential every now and then, colliding with argon atoms and giving out the characteristic colour of argon. In a short time, mercury also vaporizes due to heat and the luminous radiation inside the tube is due to a combination of argon and mercury.

Radiation from argon and mercury is mainly confined to blue, violet and ultraviolet. The ultraviolet radiation is injurious to eyes and tissues. For this reason the coating of fluoresecnt material is inside the tube. The coating absorbs the ultraviolet or violet radiation and re-emits the bluish-green radiation. The usual life of such a lamp is 1000 hrs. It is also interesting to note that more than 50% of the electrical energy is converted into light energy is a fluorescent lamp, while about 20% of the energy in an ordinary electric lamp is converted into light. The actual tube attains a temperature of about 40^0C or a little above that of the surrounding air when working and as such it is safer than an ordinary electric bulb.

Luminous discharge tube

When a high voltage current passes through a gas contained inside a glass tube at a very low pressure, the gas becomes luminous and emits a colour depending on the gas in use, e.g. neon produces pink, CO_2 gas produces white and hydrogen produces green. High electrical pressure is required, viz. 150 to 200 volt per 30 cm run, though more than double the working voltage is required in most cases to produce the first initial glow of the gas. The voltages employed are 300 volt or more, depending on the length of the tubes which can be moulded into any shape. In view of the high voltage required, transformers are invariably employed, which are generally 30 to 38 cm sq. in size of 5, 12 or 15 kV output and are mounted close to discharge tubes in considerable numbers, depending on the number of tubes.

As transformers cannot be operated with D.C., A.C. will invariably be required and to get the same from the D.C. supply, the current has to be converted by means of a converter.

PRECAUTIONERY MEASURES

All such installations are provided with a main switch controlling the entry of the current into the system by means of a separate switch called the 'fireman's switch', which is mounted on the fascia of the building, out of reach of the public, but accessible to the fire service. The switch cuts the current to the transformer and renders the whole of the installation dead. From the point of view of safety, before the commencement of any work the circuit is to be rendered dead by operating the fireman's switch. In the case of D.C. voltage, this switch cuts the current to the rotary converter producing A.C. voltage and renders the whole circuit dead. The transformers stated above should be placed in well-ventilated positions and locked up in fire-resisting enclosure with 'danger' mark. The high tension leads from such transformers have produced trouble due to improper care. The standard practice is now to use, for the main parts of the leads, vulcanized-rubber-insulated cable with close-fitting lead or other metallic sheathing (armoured if necessary), which should be earthed. The absence of contained air-spaces thus prevents any brush discharge and the evolution of ozone with its deleterious effects on the insulation.

There is the risk of arc formation from the bare ends of the connections to the two ends and special protection is to be taken for proper insulation of the connecting wires, which may exceed 45 cm. It should be enclosed within glass tube. The framework of the sign should be an incombustible element, e.g. though teak, oak or other hard wood, not less than 19 mm thick or plywood encased in metal may be permitted.

Heating effect and common hazards regarding lighting equipments

Incandescent filament lamps become hot enough to ignite fluff and dust and such flammable materials as cellulose nitrate if stored nearby. Lamps should be so placed, guarded or enclosed, as to prevent contact with flammable materials. With the pendant type of lighting, heat from the lamps may in time damage the insulation of the flexible cords connected to them. Fittings which obstruct the flow of air over the lamps may increase the temperature, and deposits of fluff or 'fly' on the cords and fittings substantially increase the fire risk.

Stem pendants (i.e. pendants formed of conduit) are preferable to flexible cords for suspending lighting fittings and should be regarded as essential where there is exposure to combustible deposits. With insulated wiring system, insulated conduit may be used.

Use of twin flexible cords for pendant lighting should be avoided. Tough-rubber-sheathed and P.V.C. sheathed cords are both less liable to be ignited by an internal short circuit or conductor breakage than twin flexible cords.

Discharge lamps should be switched off if a fault becomes apparent by flickering or failure to light, as otherwise the starting gear may overheat. The chokes associated with the various types of discharge lamps or tubes may cause fire due to faults leading to intense local heating, without operating the fuse protection. Chokes should be installed in fire-resisting surroundings. Thermal cut-outs are available, which, if installed in contact with the windings, tend to lessen the risk.

CHAPTER 15

Generation of Electricity

Electricity is generated either by mechanical means or chemically with the help of cells or accumulators.

Accumulators

The cells or the accumulators provide electrical energy from the chemical energy produced by the reacting chemicals. The voltage obtained from the cells or the accumulators is quite small – from 2 volt for each cell to 24 volt for the latter – and the current, unlike A.C., is continuous and uninterrupted and is generally utilized intermittently and not for a continuous and prolonged period, unlike current produced by generators run by mechanical means, which may supply current at a voltage of 220 or above.

Series and parallel connections

A cell is one unit and a battery consists of a number of such cells connected together. If the cells are connected in series, the total voltage of the battery will be the sum total of the voltage of each cell. Thus, to obtain 12 volt, 6 cells of 2 volt each may be connected in series. To increase the capacity of a battery (i.e. the current strength), the cells are connected in parallel in which case the voltage, of course, does not change. Chapter 17 may be referred to for further details.

Lead-acid cells

A simple lead acid-cell is made up of two lead plates suspended in dilute sulphuric acid. In this type, both the positive and negative plates are made of lead having the structure of a grid or net work. The interspaces in the grid are filled with a paste of red lead (Pb_3O_4) and sulphuric acid of specific gravity 1.20. Before charging (i.e. during discharge), a chemical action takes place forming PbO_2 and $PbSO_4$ in both the plates: $Pb_3O_4 + H_2SO_4 = PbO_2 + 2PbSO_4 + 2H_2O$. After charging, $PbSO_4$ of the positive plate is converted to PbO_2 while both $PbSO_4$ and PbO_2 of the negative plate are converted to spongy lead.

The cell, after having current passed through it for a period, is capable of giving out electrical energy, as a consequence of the chemical reactions between the lead of negative plate, the dilute sulphuric acid (specific gravity = 1.20 to 1.28) and the lead peroxide of the positive plate and due to release of hydrogen ions during the electrolysis of the acidulated water. The dilute acid is known as the electrolyte.

The current passed through the cell during charging must be in the correct direction, and if not, serious damage to the plates will result. The charging current should not exceed that recommended by the makers. If it does, the paste will be loosened from the plates, which will buckle and sulphate will be formed on them. Similar effect can be brought about by too heavy discharges and by overcharging.

The capacity is expressed in ampere-hours. Thus, if the capacity of the cell is 45 ampere-hours, then a steady current of 3 ampere can safely be drawn for 15 hours.

Nickel–iron cell

This type of cell consists of nickel and iron as electrodes with an alkaline (generally 20% caustic potash) solution as the electrolyte. The negative plate is iron and the positive plate is nickel oxide. This type of cell is far more robust than lead-acid type and is capable of being charged and discharged at much higher rates without damage. Its main disadvantage is that its E.M.F. is only about 1.55 volt when fully charged, and this voltage gradually drops during discharge. The voltage of lead-acid cell is about 2.5 volt, when fully charged, and remains at 2 volt for most of the time it is discharging.

A battery of given voltage, when made up of nickel-iron cells, is considerably heavier and more bulky than one of similar capacity composed of lead-acid cells.

Characteristics of the cells of the lead-acid and alkaline batteries

In a lead-acid cell, during discharge, the specific gravity of the electrolyte may fall upto 1.15, and when charged, the specific gravity is restored to its former value. The correct value when fully charged is always specified by the makers. The state of charge can be determined from the value of the specific gravity whch can be measured by the use of a suitable hydrometer. Special attention is needed during the charging of the cells due to the release of hydrogen gas and the likelihood of sparks from the electrodes. Charging of accumulators from 220 volt D.C. main is quite risky as there is enough power to wreck any number of batteries and set fire to their surroundings if the full supply voltage is inadvertently applied directly to the battery terminals.

During use, the level of the electrolyte will become lower and this should always be maintained to cover the plates. The level must always be restored by the addition of distilled water and never with acid.

The state of charge of a nickel-iron cell cannot be determined by the specific gravity of the electrolyte. The only indication is the voltage, which is a reasonable guide due to the falling characteristic of the voltage in this type of cell. Voltage, on the other hand, is no guide in the case of the lead-acid cell, as it is not related to the state of charge. The electrolyte in a nickel-iron cell should also be 'topped up' with distilled water.

Alternating current and direct current

The current from an oridnary cell or an accumulator, known as D.C., flows continuously in one direction so long as the external circuit is closed. But, if the current does not flow in this way and reverses its direction periodically, flowing for one time in one direction and then reverse flowing for another equal time in opposite direction in the same manner, then the current in the external circuit is called an alternating current.

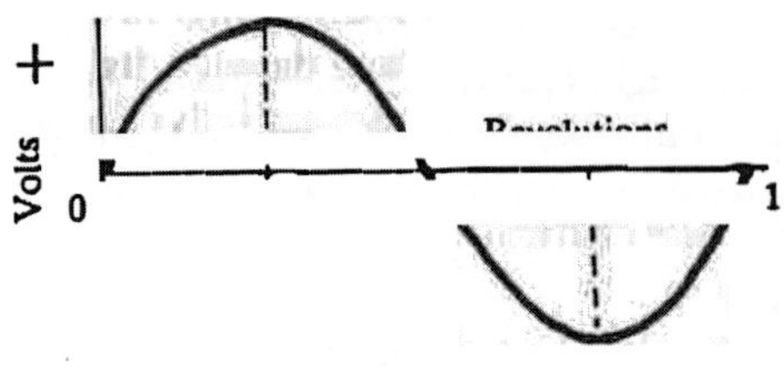

Fig.9

If a coil be rotated in a uniform magnetic field, the E.M.F. (voltage) and the current in the coil alternately flows in the opposite direction and the intensity varies from maximum to zero and vice versa. Such a current as stated above, is alternating current. If a graph of the volatage is plotted against revolutions of the coil, it will be as shown in Fig.9.

RELATIVE ADVANTAGE OF A.C. AND D.C. SUPPLY SYSTEMS

(a) The advantage of using D.C. are the following: *(i)* It is the D.C. only which can be used for charging of accumulators and for electroplating, and electrotyping. Some appliances like traction system

and elevators work more efficiently with D.C. (*ii*) It is less dangerous to use D.C. than A.C. of the same voltage if there is faulty insulation. (*iii*) D.C. requires a single thick wire to transmit, but for transmission of A.C., a stranded wire is required (skin effect).

(*b*) The advantages of using A.C. on the other hand are: (*i*) One of the most important advantage of using A.C. over D.C. or continuous current is the extreme ease with which the transformation from a low to a high voltage or vice versa can be accomplished. (*ii*) Since thinner conductors can be used for transmission of power on A.C., it is more economical to transmit over long distances, and high voltages can be used for its transmission with small line loss. (*iii*) It can be easily converted into D.C. by means of rectifiers. (*iv*) The strength of an alternating current can be reduced by a choke or a condenser and the waste of energy in doing so is almost negligible. For reducing the strenght of D.C. in a circuit an ohmic resistance is used, resulting in a good deal of loss of electrical energy in the form of heat. (*v*) A.C. motors and other appliances are more simple to construct and are mechanically more robust and require less attention.

Single phase, two phase and three phase current

The generator producing a single alternating E.M.F. is called single phase generator. If, however, instead of a single coil being placed in a uniform magnetic field, two coils are placed at right angles to each other, each connected to its own pair of slip rings, it will be seen that current in one coil will be maximum, when the current in the other coil is minimum and vice-versa. Such an alternating current is called a two phase alternating current and the generator is known as a two phase alternating current generator.

If instead of two coils at right angle to each other, three coils are placed, inclined at 120^0 to each other, each connected to its own pair of slip rings, the current thus produced is called a three phase current and the generator is known as a three phase generator.

A poly-phase alternating current can thus be produced also by using a number of separate coils with their respective slip rings. In actual practice, two types of genetators are normally used to produce alternating current: (*1*) those where the field magnets are stationary and the armature rotates, (*2*) those where the armature is stationary and the field magnet rotates. The rotating part is known as rotor and the stationary part is known as stator.

Characteristics of alternating current – frequency and cycles/ sec

In A.C. circuit the number of times the current attains a maximum value in each second is called the number of cycles and the number of such cycles in one second is known as frequency. The strength of the current in an alternating circuit does not depend on the E.M.F. and the resistance does not also follow Ohm's law. As the current is variable, the electromotive force arises in the circuit on account of its self-induction and capacity. For the same reason the current and E.M.F. are not in the same phase, i.e. the current is not maximum when the E.M.F. is maximum.

R.M.S. value

In an alternating current circuit, the current attains maximum value in course of its positive or negative swing. The main value of the current is called the 'peak value of the current'. The average current or the mean current does not express the strength of steady current. The strength of the constant current = $1/\sqrt{2} \times$ maximum current. This is known as root mean square current (R.M.S. current). The effective voltage of an A.C. supply is, similarly, $1/\sqrt{2} \times$ maximum volt = $0.7 \times$ maximum volt.

Generation of current by mechanical means – alternators and dynamos

The principle of generation of electricity, either A.C. or D.C., is the same, viz. rotation of a coil within a magnetic field. The alternating E.M.F. or current can be made unidirectional by a device called the 'commutator'. In case of an alternator, there are slip rings in place of the commutator and the ends of the armature coil are attached to the slip rings, which are rigidly attached to the armature shaft and are insulated from it. In an alternator, an armature having a coil of wire wound over a soft iron cylinder with the sliprings, and two metallic brushes lightly pressing against the slip rings to collect the charges, rotates within a magnetic field which may be a permanent magnet as shown in Fig.10.

In a dynamo a number of coils are wound upon a cylindrical piece of iron called armature at equal inclination. The coils are connected in series on the armature shaft and the ends of each are connected to two metallic strips of copper, insulated from each other by mica in what is known as commutator. The armature, with the commutator fitted on it, rotates within the field magnet and it is known as direct current dynamo. The commutator changes the A.C. produced to D.C. and the current thus produced is collected by means of hard carbon brushes, pressed on the commutator. A D.C. dynamo does not normally produce a current in excess of 650 volt.

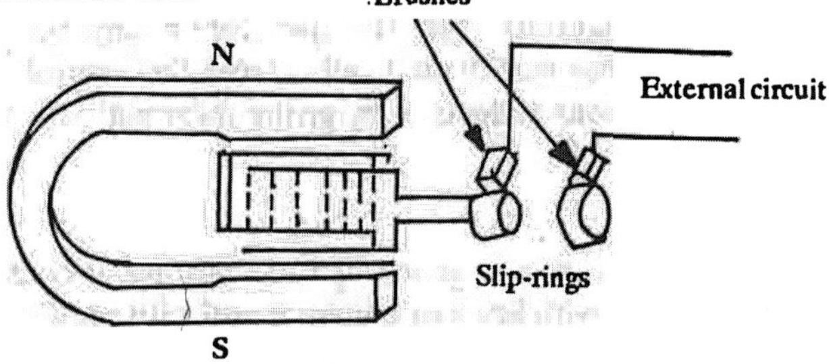

Fig.10 Alternator

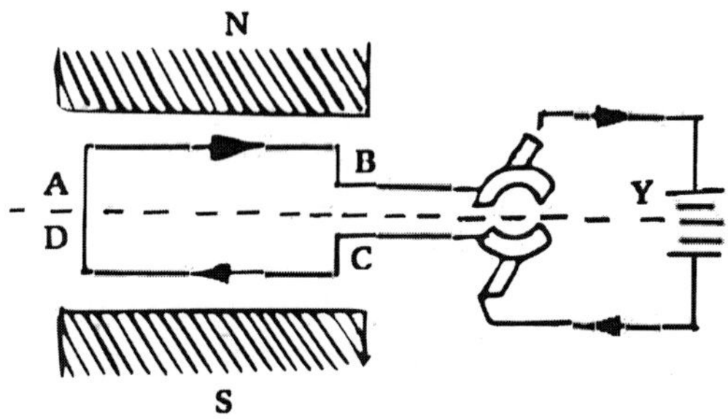

Fig.11 Dynamo

In a large or medium sized generating station, the generator may be rotated either by thermal power or hydropower, or by a diesel engine (for a small station). Generally, thermal power stations are more common in our country though hydroelectricity is slowly taking its place, followed by nuclear generating stations.

Thermal power station

In a big thermal power station, huge boilers are installed to drive turbines with the help of superheated steam in a separate turbine room where the turbines are used to drive the alternators. In fact, both are situated and coupled together and is known as the turbo-alternator fitted with a tank with about 13620–18160 litre of lubricating oil (depending upon the size), which circulates through the machine. The flash point of the turbine oil is about 205^{0}C and the ignition temperature is 371^{0}C. There is also a switch-room through which the supplies to the different transformers are effected and a control room which watches and controls the functions of the different machines. The control room gets indications on its panels by means of visual and audible signals of various defects developed in the trans formers or the switch-gears before it goes to a dangerous stage. The operator on duty, according to the situation, can either rectify the trouble from the control room by manipulating the various gadgets or by giving information to the shift engineer about the trouble.

FIRE RISK

A modern power station is generally fire-resisting. It consists of a steel framed building with brick or concrete and with reinforced concrete panel walls with separate fire-resisting cubicles for its transformers and switch-gears. In the generating stations the main fire risk is due to oil and the high voltage fault current which may either electrocute a man or cause a fire due to the formation of an arc and igniting the bitumen, rubber, textile covering on the conductors or the insulating oil or other materials used on the electrical equipments and a large quantity of lubricating oil circulating through oil pipes for lubrication of the turbines and alternators.

In a generating station, the turbo-alternator, rotating with high speed and producing a high voltage current, introduces in some respects, serious fire hazards. If there is any leakage of oil through fractured oil pipes and if the oil comes in contact with hot turbine or superheated steam pipe, it will immediately ignite and with the aid of forced draught for cooling the generator and with forced oil circulation, a veritable inferno may develop in a few seconds, resulting in serious fire and fatalities. The superheated steam has a temperature of about 440^0C and is released at a pressure of 44 kg/cm^2, which by itself is a potential fire risk.

FIRE-FIGHTING

Fires in generators are usually dealt with by the use of CO_2 equipment and the burning oil by the water spray projectors; but the main difficulty is the inacessibility to the burning materials within the generator and the fact that the machine takes about 20 minutes to run down and become stationary. A fire officer should be acquainted with these hazards and the fire risks relating to the defective transformers, oil filled cables and switch-gear and the fuel stores.

TRANSMISSION LINES

The current generated is transmitted through special type of heavy duty cables in view of the output from power station alternators ranging from 10,000 kilowatt to 70,000 kilowatt. In a big city, there may be more than one generating station depending upon the consumption of electricity. The generating stations are linked together and to the main centres of consumption by a network of high voltage conductors called the 'grid', which may be upto 132,000 volt or even 4,00,000 volt. The transmissions may be through underground cables or overhead wiring of stout aluminium wire fixed on iron pillars, being well secured and insulated from the pillars or the neighbouring wires used for other purpose, like telephone or telegraph. In the case of underground cables, a very good insulation of the wiring is required. Underground cables are in general, insulated with oil or wax-impregnated paper and are lead sheathed along with jute or coarse textile covering.

INSULATION OF HIGH VOLTAGE WIRING

Cables are usually made in the form of a number of strands of copper wire twisted together in the form of a conducting core and then covered with the requisite number of layers of insulation and lead sheathing to prevent the access of moisture and armouring to provide the mechanical strength. For a conductor carrying 33,000 volt, the general arrangement for insulation of a three-core cable is (from outside) jute wrapping then wire-armouring, paper covering, lead covering and finally the cores of inner wire are insulated from each other by means of paper covering. Hence, in a fire involving these cables, dense black smoke with the burning of waxy substances and bitumen would be evolved. In view of the nature of the insulated coverings, such a fire is difficult to extinguish once it gets a good hold over the substance.

DISTRIBUTION SYSTEM—GRID

From the generating stations, current is fed by means of the 'grid' to the sub-stations, where, by means of transformers, the voltage is increased to cope with the requirements of the area concerned. Such sub-stations might be situated far away from the main generating station and hence a voltage drop results. Sometimes, from the main grid, a wayside factory may also tap the current by means of suitable step-down transformers. For domestic installations, current is tapped from the feeder cables, which are supplied with current from the respective sub-stations. Generally, the transmission lines are supplied with 1,32,000 volt and sometimes even with 2,75,000 or 4,00,000 volt. The need for the employment of high voltage is that it allows greater power to be transmitted over long distances. The minimum size of conductor and the transmission loss are proportional to the current, and for a given power, the higher voltage allows smaller-size conductors to be used and also reduces the losses.

Sub-station

Although it is necessary to employ high voltages to move the large quantities of power from one part of the country to another, a conversion to lower voltage has to take place before the power can be used. This is performed in several stages by means of transformers in a substation.

The voltage has first to be reduced from 1,32,000 volt to 33,000 volt. This is achieved by connecting transformers to the 1,32,000 volt transmission line through switches so that they can be switched on or off as necessary. The transformer steps the voltage down to 33,000 volt being fed through switches, to another network, somewhat similar to the grid, but covering a much smaller area.

From the 33,000 volt network, transformers are once again connected as before, but this time reducing the voltage to 11,000 volt.

The final stage of transformation is from 11,000 volts to the usable voltage of 415 to 440 volt, 3 phase or 240 volt, single phase A.C. supply.

Transformers

Transformer is an important device with the aid of which electrical transmission is effected involving alternating current supply only.

There are two coils in a transformer, the primary and the secondary, both of which are very carefully insulated from each other. The coils connected to the input are called the primary and the other, from which a supply is taken, is called the secondary. If the transformer is small, the coils are simply kept apart from each other and cooling is achieved by air circulation, whereas, if the transformer is a big one, oil is used for cooling and insulation. The important points to check in a transformer are whether adequate arrangement exists for cooling of the heat generated during transmission; also, whether the transformer has been mounted and fixed properly with a good earthing. The location of the transformer, condition of the oil used both for insulation and cooling, overheating due to arcing between transformer coil windings as a result of insulation failure, and lastly, the fire-fighting arrangements existing at the site are important points for consideration.

FUNCTION OF A TRANSFORMER AND THE PRINCIPLES INVOLVED

It should be noted that the object of a transformer is either to step-up or step-down the voltage depending upon the requirements. In other words, in the case of a step-up transformer, the voltage will be increased in proportion to the ratio of the number of turns of the coils between the primary and the secondary, i.e. the more the number of turns on the secondary, the more will be the voltage increase. If there are 100 turns on the primary and 1000 turns on the secondary, the voltage increase will be 10 times; whereas in a 'step-down' transformer, opposite is the case. That means that the number of turns on the secondary is less than that on the primary, (say 1000 turns on the primary and 100 turns on the secondary). It should be borne in mind that the voltage in the secondary, which is tapped for use, is dependent on ratio of the number of turns of the windings between the primary and the secondary.

This effect is due to the laws of electro-magnetic induction. If the strength of current through a coil of wire is altered regularly in a periodic cycle – such as in an alternating current, which changes its direction and its value with a definite number of cycles per second (what is called 'frequency') – an alternating current will be induced in another coil, situated adjacent to the first one. The current thus produced is called the 'induced current' and it is produced in the secondary coil, which is situated quite close to the primary coil, through which an A.C. supply is flowing. Transformers are built on this principle of induced current. and follows the law of Electromagnetic Induction.

It may be noted that in a circuit, power remaining the same, increasing the voltage results in decreasing the current since power = current × voltage. Hence, for high voltage transformers of step-up type, the secondary coil is comparatively thinner than the primary coil.

RISKS IN THE TRANSFORMER

The presence of sufficiently thin mineral oil with a flash point of about 149^{0}C in large quantity and high voltage current are the two main risks in a heavy duty transformer as generally met within an electrical sub-station or generating station. To avoid fire hazards due to oil, air cooled transformers or transformers having non-flammable liquid coolants, viz. silicone-based plastic emulsion (Askarel insulation) are being used in place of ordinary oil-filled transformers.

OIL AS COOLING MEDIUM

To a fire officer, the oil in the transformer or the switch-gear is the main source of the hazard. A very rough estimate of the amount of oil involved in the construction of the transformer (not very large) may be gained from the working standard of roughly 2.3 litres per kVA or so, and to achieve the necessary cooling effect, large quantities of oil have to be used. Some examples are given below:

Transformer capacity	Minimum requirement of oil (lit)
500 kVA	818
15 MVA, as used at 33,000 volts. (1 MVA = 1,000 kVA; MVA stands for mega volt-ampere).	15456

COOLING OF TRANSFORMERS

There are radiating fins on the body of the high voltage transformers upto 33,000 volt. They also improve the dissipation of the heat in addition to the general cooling effect produced by the circulation of oil. The working temperature of a transformer should not exceed 40 to 50^0C.

In oil-filled switch-gears or transformers, volatilization of the oil by arcing (due to faults having developed) and the consequent rupture of the tank (due to internal explosion) with flaming oil and oil vapours flooding the compartment are the most serious features of the fire and a good structural protection by sectionalizing the transformer chamber or chambers from the rest of the premises is essential. The fire will otherwise inevitably spread and will be difficult to extinguish. For this reason, all transformer chambers, switch-gears etc. are mounted in separate buildings or in chambers opening to the outdoor air, and sealed up from the inner side.

TRANSFORMER MOUNTING

Oil-cooled transformers should be surrounded by dwarf walls and a trench under the transformers should be provided through which the oil contained in the transformer finds its way out to a concrete pit (sufficient to hold the entire qnantity of oil). Under the transformer, there should be granite chippings which are about 45 cm deep. The granite chippings are to be placed on iron gratings under the pit.

In case of a fire the blazing oil, while passing through the granite chippings, gets cooled and the clear oil may be filtered and allowed to be drained away to a safe place outside, where it is automatically extinguished due to the cooling effect of the granite, and in case any fire is found still blazing, this may be attacked with a foam branch of suitable size. However, now-a-days, the tendency is to provide a dwarf-wall round the transformer, normally 25 to 38 cm high which will contain the entire amount of the oil contained inside the transformer.

FIRE PROTECTION OF TRANSFORMERS

Transformers are protected by the waterspray projector system (High Velocity Sprinkler system), which not only extinguishes the fire but also cools the transformer. In addition to this, CO_2 extinguishers, buckets of sand and sufficient amount of foam should be available to meet with any situation. Generating stations, in addition to the H.T. transformers, have oil-filled switch-gears or circuit breakers which may also rupture and explode by formation of an arc inside and the blazing oil may thus be thrown all around.

General fire precautions in generating stations

There may also be fires in the outside yard where coal or oil is stored. In an oil-fired furnace there is danger of an oil fire. In the turbine room the oil in the governor mechanism or in the gears may get cracked into lighter fractions on coming in contact with heated surface of the turbo-jets or steam pipes and may catch fire. Apart from these risks, in a generating station, there may be considerable amount of other flammable materials such as paint on steel work and insulation on cables. Burning insulation and, in particular, the bitumen used for sealing joints gives off dense clouds of smoke. It is, therefore, necessary for fire-fighters to use B.A. sets when entry has to be made inside. It should also be borne in mind that H.T. cables do not generally run near the ground level. They are generally placed about 2.5 metre high from the floor level inside the room or in underground cable ducts. Under no circumstances, during fire-fighting, should any such parts or machinery or cables be touched by a fireman standing on earth without clear instructions from the shift engineer-in-charge that it is safe to do so.

CHAPTER 16

Motors and Starters

From the generating station current is transmitted through the sub-stations. An industrial concern will tap the current from the common grid and will step it down according to the requirement. It will have a small sub-station with switch-gears and control room.

In industrial undertakings fires are more frequent in motors. The causes may be the short-circuits and break-down of the insulation of the coils due to overheating or overloading and the damage caused by damp or dust or contamination of the windings with oil. Undue heat, dirt, dust and constant dampness are all inimical to a motor which must be suitably designed and protected when used under adverse condition. It must be borne in mind that all electrical plant and equipment should be suited to the duty it has to perform, both in regard to location and loadings.

How a motor works — general principles

A motor works due to the effect of a magnetic field on a conductor carrying current. The strength of the magnetic field around a conductor is proportional to the strength of the current carried by the conductor. The Fig.12 will explain how a torque is produced in a motor:

If a conductor A without any current in it is placed between the poles N and S of a magnet, the magnetic field between the poles of the magnet NS will remain undisturbed. But when a current is passed through the conductor within the magnetic field, between the poles of the magnet, as shown in the Fig.13, the current will produce a field round the conductor which will interact with the field between the two poles of the magnet.

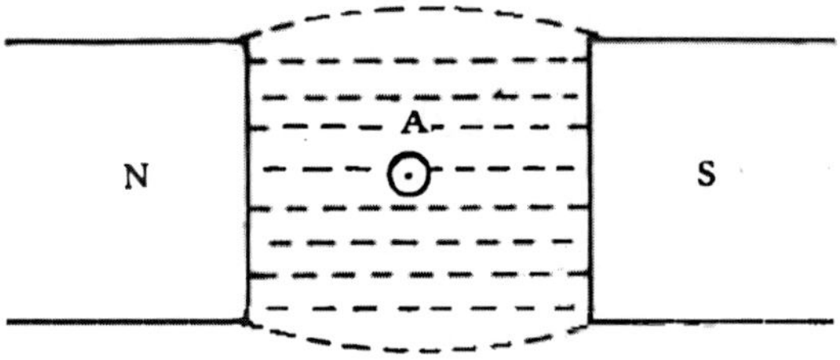

Fig.12 Magnetic field between poles of a magnet

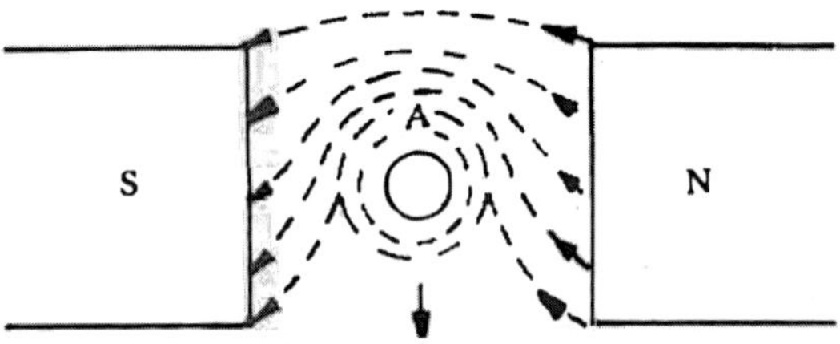

Fig.13 Effect of current on conductor in a magnetic field resulting in torque

The tendency for the field will be to take up the position, as shown in the Fig.13, resulting in a clockwise force round the conductor and a force north to south between the magnets. On the other hand, if the current in the conductor is reversed, the effect will be to move the conductor out of the field in the opposite direction, as shown in the Fig.14.

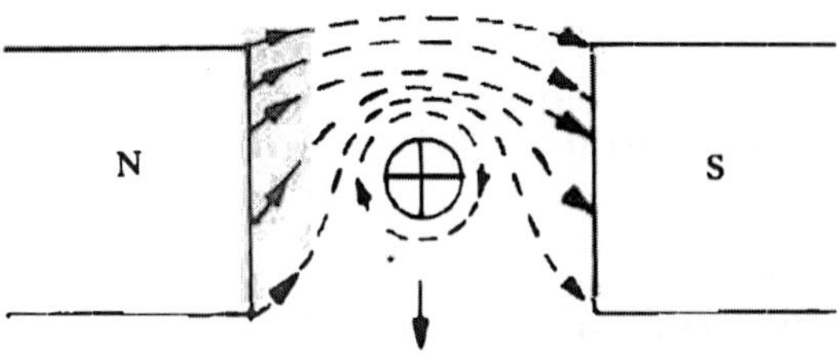

Fig.14 Change in the direction of force in armature (conductor) due to change of direction in the magnetic field

If the direction of the current or the polarity of the magnetic field is changed it will result in a change of direction of the conductor, i.e. to produce a turning motion (a torque) in the conductor. Hence to maintain the direction of rotation, it is necessary to arrange for the current in the loop of the coil (conductor) to be reversed after the two sides have passed out of the magnetic field. This is achieved in a motor by the use of a rotary switch, known as 'commutator'. The magnitude of the torque is determined by the field strength and the strength of the armature current.

Function of electric motors and types in common use

The function of a motor is to provide the motive power at the expense of electrical power. A motor should not be run on a continuous overload and circuit breakers should be installed in such a way that it operates whenever there is an overload. A motor, either A.C. or D.C., is generally designed to run at a full load for a stated time at a stated maximum increase of temperature (often for 6 hrs at a temperature of 21^0C above that of the surroundings). Both D.C and A.C motorss are available. D.C motors consist basically of a number of conductors, carrying current, which are free to rotate under the influence of a magnetic field. A.C. motor are normally of two types, viz. squirrel-cage and slip-ring types.

SQUIRREL-CAGE TYPE

Squirrel-cage induction motor (viz. A.C. electric fans) are the most straight-forward and simple in design. They are therefore relatively cheap and robust. The squirrel-cage motor is suitable for driving pumps, fans, lifting hoists and textile machinery and it is of advantage when the precise horse-power required can be specified. The rotor in this type has no external electrical connections but consists of bars placed longitudinally around a drum (very similar to the armature of a D.C. machine). At each end bars are connected together forming a cylindrical cage. The stator contains a system of coils which are supplied from the A.C. supply. The speed of the motor itself cannot be varied but where variable speeds are required it can be used in conjunction with variable speed.

SLIP-RING TYPE

Slip-ring induction motors work in the same manner as the squirrel-cage type but are more elaborate in their construction. The rotor, instead of consisting of solid bars, has coils similar to D.C. armature. Ends of the coils are brought out and connected to slip-rings which run under brushes. In this way, an external resistance can be connected in the rotor circuit.

Adding resistance in the rotor winding at starting has three desirable effects : (*a*) it increases the starting torque, (*b*) it reduces the starting current, and (*c*) it improves the power factor on starting.

When the machine has completed its run-up, the rotor resistance is cut out by connecting the slip-rings together by means of a switch. A variable resistance can be used in the rotor circuit and this has the effect of giving some speed regulation, though this method also causes a loss of effciency.

SINGLE-PHASE AND THREE-PHASE MOTORS

Single-phase motors are used only for light work where not more than about 1.5 to 2.2 kW is required and somewhat complex arrangements have to be made in their design to make them self-starting. It is, however, much more staight-forward and economical to use three-phase motors.

D.C. motors must not be run below the rated voltage, as on a full load, it is likely to cause serious overheating of the coils and excessive sparks at the commutator which might lead to a fire. On the other hand, running at a voltage too high is also likely to cause excessive sparking and overheating of the coils. As stated before, a motor is generally designed to run at full load for a stated time at a stated maximum increase of temperature, often for 6 hours at a temperature of approximately 21^0 C above that of the surroundings.

Overheating of motors

Armature and rotor clearance should be regularly checked. Due to wear in bearings, the armature may rub on pole pieces or the rotor may come into contact with the stator and may result in the overheating of the conductors by distortion of the magnetic flux and friction of the rotating parts against the stator and finally fouling and possibly burning out. It is, therefore, very important that there should be adequate lubrication and attention on the bearings. A.C. motor (induction motors) has, as a rule, the smallest clearance between the rotor and the stator (possibly only 0.158 cm as against 0.635 cm in D.C.). In addition to the causes of overheating, the risk of single phasing of a multiphase A.C. motor due to the other phases being blown off, and the consequent overheating of the motor coils, resulting in fire, is also to be properly guarded against and taken care of.

Care and maintenance

Daily inspection of commutators, brushes, bearings etc., particularly for D.C. motors, by a competent electrician is desirable. In a fluffy atmosphere the sparks from the commutator of a D.C. motor may give rise to a fire. In D.C. motors general defect arises due to faults in commutators and/or brushes, resulting in severe sparking and consequent fires from short-circuiting of the segments. Sparking will also occur due to 'proud mica', which, protruding beyond the commutator segments, tend to make the brush jump instead of remaining smoothly in contact during the whole revolution. Fires are also caused by friction and the consequent heating of bearings following faulty or insufficient lubrication.

It is sometimes argued that the objection to the use of motors in industry or in other explosive atmosphere applies mainly to D.C. motors and to a less extent to slip-ring A.C. motors and not at all to induction motors of the squirrel-cage type, in which the current does not traverse any sliding contacts at all. While the liability to sparking is certainly in diminishing ratio in the cases mentioned, it can scarcely be claimed that the danger is entirely absent under all circumstances in induction motors, and distinctions in their favour would seem to be best avoided. However, it is a safe practice to use pipe-ventilated type motors in very hot atmospheres, with insufficient ventilation or in dangerous atmospheres provided the intake of the air is at a safe distance and it is well covered by fine wire mesh.

Motors should be wiped down periodically with a suitable non-fluffy material and all cotton or jute fibres, carbon dust etc. should be carefully removed from the commutator and brush gears. The location of the motor close to a combustible material is prohibited because sparks might give rise to trouble. A motor should be placed on rigid platform in a well-ventilated room and should preferably be covered by a removeable, very fine wire mesh cage when it is to be used in a fluffy or dusty atmosphere.

Eddy currents

Eddy currents are the electric currents induced in a conducting medium subjected to a varying magnetic field. In accordance with Lenz's law which states that in all cases of electromagnetic induction, the direction of the induced current is such that it always tends to oppose the very cause to which the induced current is due, the eddy currents circulate in such a direction as to tend to prevent variation of the magnetic field.

Eddy current plays an important role in the conducting medium. For example, eddy current loss in both magnetic field and electric circuits of inductors, transformers and A.C. machines reduce their overall efficiency, imposing at times a limit on their permissible output or electric rating. The effects can, however, be minimized by subdividing the electric circuit into conductors of small cross-sectional area and magnetic circuit into their laminations with an insulating coating on each conductor or lamination. Eddy current effects can also be applied usefully in the induction type furnaces where the charge is a conducting material which needs induction heating for work-piece forging and the surface hardening of steels.

Self-inductance and mutual inductance

Inductance is the property of an electrical circuit, giving rise to the phenomenon of electromagnetic induction. If the inductive effects are due to linkages between the circuit and the magnetic field of the current flowing in it, the circuit is then said to have self-inductance which can be defined as the back e.m.f. induced in a circuit per unit rate of change of current in that circuit.

If the effects are due to linkages between the circuit and the magnetic field of a current flowing in some other circuit, the pair of circuits constitute a mutual inductance which is defined as the e.m.f. induced in the secondary circuit when the current in the primary is changing at a unit rate. The linkage depends on the size and the shape of the coils, the number of turns and the material occupying the surrounding sphere and is the product of flux through the coil by the number of turns.

Starters for D.C. motor

Back e.m.f.: When an electric motor is running at speed, it is endeavouring to generate a current in the reverse direction to the applied e.m.f. The reverse pressure developed due to the rotation of the armature in the field is known as the 'back' or 'counter' e.m.f.

This back e.m.f. is proportional to the speed of the motor and the power obtainable from the motor is the product of back e.m.f. and the current through the armature. When the motor is running at full speed, equivalent to a very considerable resistance, the current flowing through the motor is greatly reduced by it. On the other hand, when the motor is at rest, this back e.m.f. is absent as there is no rotation of conductors in the field. If at that stage the full supply pressure were applied to the armature, a current would flow through the windings which would be much in excess of the current that would flow when the motor is on full speed. This heavy current may be thirty to forty times the full-load current. Hence, if the full pressure were applied to the motor while it was at a stand-still, the heavy current would cause excessive heating of the armature coils, possibly resulting in the ignition of the insulation and the burning out of the motor. To provide against this, all but the smallest motors must be furnished with a starting resistance or starter in series with the armature.

Starters for three-phase A.C. motors

The small induction motor may be switched straight on to the supply without the intervention of a starting resistance. In the larger types the excessive current taken at starting resistance should be inserted into the rotor circuit. An induction motor at rest is very similar to a transformer which is short-circuited with a resistance inserted in the secondary by taking the ends of the coils to slip-rings and thence through brushes to a separate resistance somewhat similar to that used for starting D.C. motors. Only exception here is that a resistance is required for each winding, i.e. in the case of three-phase, three separate resistance coils with three separate sets of contact studs upon which three arms of a hand-operated triple starter make contact.

In the case of squirrel-cage type of motor, where there is no electrical connection to the rotor and where slip-rings are eliminated, the fire hazard is definitely less though the possiblity of over-heating of the coils and their burn-out are not entirely absent and the same could be caused by overloading the motor or allowing its ventilation to be impeded by accumulation of dust or dirt in the air vents, or by running it in an unsuitably high temperature.

Hazards with D.C. motor starters

The starters of D.C. motors are more hazardous than the motor itself and, as a matter of safety, they should always be located away from combustible materials. The staters are mostly resistance coils (though enclosed in a cast-iron case) which produce heat and should therefore be ventilated. The ventilation opening should be on the sides of the case and not on the top or bottom so that dirt cannot fall directly into the casing, and hot molten metal or smouldering fluff fall from it to the floor. In jute or saw mills it is sometimes quite common to find the oily saw dust or fluff round the pivot or the contact arm of the starter and a quantity of charred material inside the resistance box on the coils themselves and between the contacts. It is recommended that the starter, from fire prevention point of view, should not be placed on a combustible base, viz. wooden lining or a timber partition or wall and that such material should be at 60 cm distance from it vertically above, 30 cm below and 15 cm horizontally at the sides. Combustible bases to be avoided, but in case it cannot be done, it must be protected by a sheet of asbestos or asbestos cement composition.

Fire prevention and protection

Any extinguisher of the vaporizing media type, e.g. extinguishers with Bromo-choloro-fluoro methane (B.C.F.) or Choloro-bromo-methane (C.B.M.) may be used. Carbon dioxide extinguishers are, however, the best in circumstances, resulting in fires in motors or electrical appliances.

Most of the electrical motors rely on air-circulation round the casing to keep them cool, and if the air vents become blocked or the casing becomes covered with fine wood shavings, the motor will overheat, setting fire to insulation. Both mechanical and electrical overloading will cause overheating of the motors leading to a fire and these two point require frequent attention and checking.

Arcing and overheating are the two factors which start electric fires. Arcs can occur at switch contacts, through undue wear and tear, at loose connections at any point and at breaks in the insulations where the current may subsequently are to an earth conductor or the neutral conductor. Overloading of a circuit beyond its capacity will give rise to overheating, which is most likely to occur at high resistance sections such as loose connections or frayed wires. Breakdown of insulation in an electrical appliance may cause a partial short circuit, which can also overload supply wiring.

An unsatisfactory earthing system can be more dangerous than no earthing at all since it can carry an earth fault current to a potentially more dangerous area. Good earthing arrangements and effective circuit protection in general will reduce the chances of a fire. Over-current protection as magnetic circuit breakers or thermal fuses of the correct rating is quite important.

In atmospheres where flammable concentration of vapour or gas may occur, only the appropriate flameproof or intrinsically safe electrical apparatus and installations should be used. Equipments for use in damp or corrosive atmospheres should be designed for the particular condition. Please refer to Chapter 20 for details on flameproof fittings or on intrinsically safe electrical apparatus.

CHAPTER 17

Application of Ohm's Law—Series and Parallel Circuits

Ohm's law states that $I = E/R$ where I = current in amp, E = volt and R the resistance of the circuit in ohm. If the potential difference between two points a and b is $E_a - E_b$, then the equation is

$$I = \frac{E_a - E_b}{R}$$

or

$$IR = E_a - E_b.$$

If the plates of a cell are connected externally through a resistance of R ohm, the electromotive force E drives electricity both inside and outside the cell, so that it goes through both external resistance R in the wire and internal resistance r in the cell. Hence, $I = E/R$ can be expressed as

$$I = \frac{E}{R+r} = \frac{E}{\text{total resistance}}$$

or

$$E = IR + Ir$$

but

$$IR = E_a - E_b$$

Problem 17.1: If an incandescent lamp of 200 ohm resistance takes a current of 1.25 amp, what voltage is required to work it?

Here R = 200 ohm, C = 1.25 amp

$\therefore \frac{E}{200}=1.25$ (since $C=\frac{E}{R}$)

$\therefore E = 200 \times 1.25 = 250$ volt.

Problem 17.2: A cell having an e.m.f. of 2 volt has a P.D. of only 1.8 volt. When a current of 5 amp is drawn from it, what is the internal resistance of the cell?

Here $I=\frac{E}{R+r}$, i.e. $E = IR + Ir$

Also we know

$IR = E_a - E_b = 1.8$ volt.

Substituting, we get

$2 = 1.8 + Ir$

Since $I = 5$ amp, we get

$2 = 1.8 + 5r$.

or $5r = 2-1.8$

i.e. $r = \frac{0.2}{5} = 0.04$ ohm

Problem 17.3: If an incandescent lamp of 80 ohm resistance takes a current of 0.75 amp, what voltage is required to work it?

Since $I=\frac{E}{R}$

or $E = I \times R$,

substituing the values,

$E = 0.75 \times 80 = 60$ volt.

Problem 17.4: The poles of a cell having e.m.f. of 1.08 volt and internal resistance of 0.2 ohm are joined by a wire having resistance of 5.2 ohm. Find the strength of the current.

$E = 1.08$ volt, $r = 0.2$ ohm, $R = 5.2$ ohm

Substituting the values in

$I=\frac{E}{R}$

we have

$I = \frac{1.08}{0.2+5.2} = \frac{1.08}{5.4} = 0.2$ amp.

Series and parallel connections: resistances in series and parallel

SERIES CONNECTION

When the resistances are joined end to end so that the same current flows through each in turn, they are said to be connected in series (Fig.15.) The total effective resistance R of the circuit will be $R = r_1 + r_2 + r_3$ (sum of individual resistances).

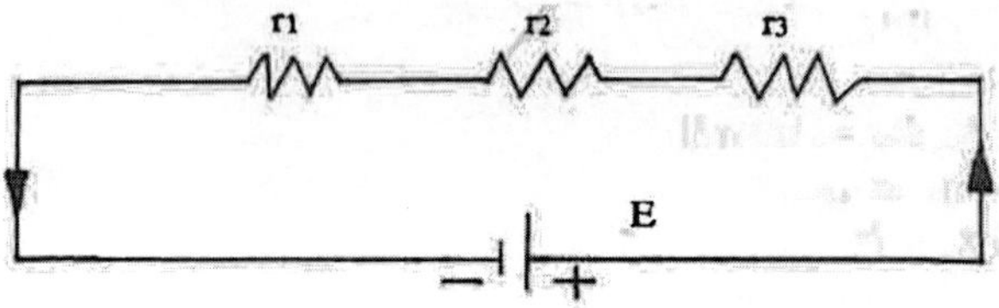

Fig.15 Series connection

PARALLEL CONNECTION

When several resistances say r_1, r_2, r_3 etc. are joined between two point a and b, as shown in Fig.16, so that the current (I) divides between them, they are said to be in parallel. The total current I, entering at a, divides into three parts i_1, i_2 and i_3 which unite again at b. Each component, however, has the same voltage across it. The total current flowing will be the sum of individual current across each component. Thus

$$I = i_1 = i_2 + i_3$$

Here, the amount of current passing through each of the resistance r_1, r_2 and r_3 connected in parallel, may be calculated as,

$$i_1 = \frac{E_a - E_b}{r_1}$$

$$i_2 = \frac{E_a - E_b}{r_2}$$

and

$$i_3 = \frac{E_a - E_b}{r_3}$$

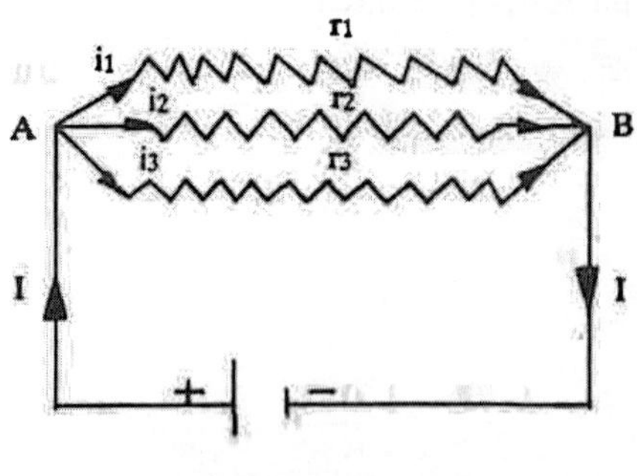

Fig.16 Parallel connection

In the case of resistances connected in parallel, the total effective resistance, R, may be calculated as

$$\frac{1}{R} = \frac{1}{r_1} + \frac{1}{r_2} + \frac{1}{r_3}$$

It may be noted that when battery current is weak for self-starters, two batteries are connected in parallel to provide the requisite current to the self-starters.

Problem 17.5: A circuit consists of two resistances, in series, of 30 ohm and 80 ohm and the voltage applied across them is 220 volt. Calculate the current passing through the circuit.

Here, the total resistance of the circuit = 30 + 80 = 110 ohm

Since $R = r_1 + r_2$, hence, according to Ohm's law, $I = E/R$.

$$\text{the current} = \frac{220}{110} = 2\,amp.$$

If the same resistances of 30 ohm and 80 ohm are conneceted in parallel, the resistance

$$\frac{1}{R} = \frac{1}{30} + \frac{1}{80} = \frac{8+3}{240} = \frac{11}{240}$$

whence

$$R = \frac{240}{11} = 21.8 \text{ ohm(app.)}$$

Hence, when connected in parallel, the total effective resistance is much less than that when connected in series.

Problem 17.6: Two resistances of 20 ohm and 40 ohm are connected in parallel. If the supply voltage is 100 volt, find out the current flowing through the individual resistances and also the total current flowing through the circuit. Calculate also the power consumed.

Here, applying Ohm's law, we get the current flowing through the individual 20 ohm and 40 ohm resistances as i_1 and i_2 respectively.

$$i_1 = \frac{\text{voltage difference between a and b}}{20} = \frac{100}{20} = 5 \text{ amp.}$$

$$i_2 = \frac{\text{voltage difference between a and b}}{40} = \frac{100}{40} = 2.5 \text{ amp.}$$

Since power consumed in a circuit, in watt, is measured as the product of voltage and current flowing through it, we get the total power consumed as voltage × total current flowing in the circuit. The total current = 5 + 2.5 = 7.5 amp. Hence power = 100 × 7.5 = 750 watt.

Calculation of voltage drop

as the voltage applied to a circuit is the difference in potential from one end of the circuit to the other, it follows that this must drop in value from point to point round the circuit. The voltage drop is determined by the product of current and the resistance faced (i.e. $I \times R$) and the drop from point to point is always equal to the total applied voltage.

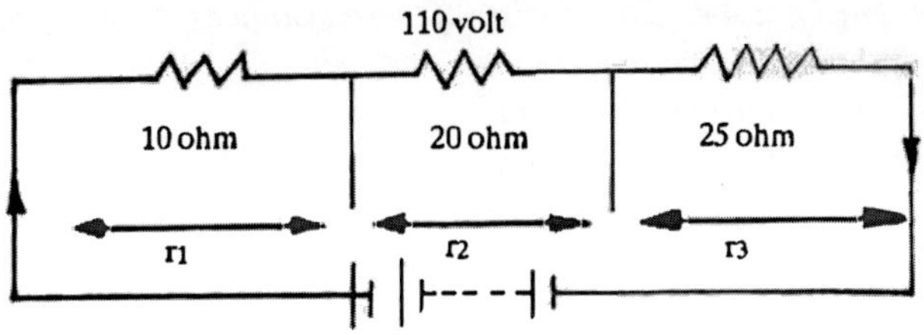

Fig.17 Calculation of voltage drop

The total resistance of the circuit given in Fig. 17 = 10 + 20 + 25 = 55 ohm.

Hence, total current I = 110/55 = 2 amp.

Here, by applying the aforesaid rule, the voltage drop across the

10 ohm resistance (r_1) $= I \times r_1 = 2 \times 10$ ohm = 20 volt.

20 ohm resistance (r_2) $= I \times r_2 = 2 \times 20$ ohm = 40 volt.

25 ohm resistance (r_3) $= I \times r_3 = 2 \times 25$ ohm = 50 volt.

∴ The total voltage drop $= I\,(r_1 + r_2 + r_3) = 20 + 40 + 50 = 110$ volt.

The power used in each resistance, when added up equals total power used by the circuit, viz. power utilized in r_1 = current × voltage drop = 2 × 20 = 40 watt. Similarly, across r_2 and r_3, it will be 2 × 40 = 80 watt and 2 × 50 = 100 watt respectively.

∴ The total power consumed = 40 + 80 + 100 = 220 watt.

Connection of cells in series and parallel and their effects

SERIES

The cells are connected in series, when the positive terminal of one is connected to the negative of the next and so on.

If the cells are grouped in series, as in Fig.18, having an e.m.f. of E volt each and internal resistance r ohm, and if there are n number of cells and

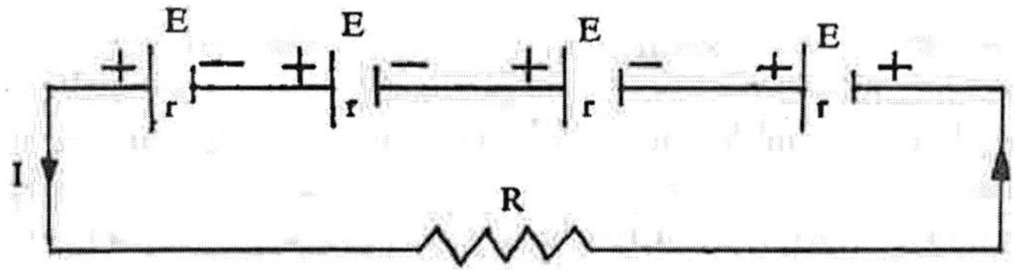

Fig.18 Grouping of cells in series

the circuit is externally connected by resistance of R ohm, then by Ohm's law, the current I in the circuit flowing through each cell is given by

$$I=\frac{nE}{R+nr}$$

If R, the external resistance, is very large compared to nr, then, $I=nE/R$, i.e. the current is practically n times that due to a single cell but when r, the internal resistance, is very great as compared to R, then the parallel current will be advantageous and the current is equivalent to that of a single cell and the combination has no advangage; in the latter case, $I=nE/nR=E/R$.

PARALLEL

When the cells (say n numbers) are connected with one another in such a way that all the positive poles are joined at one point a and all the negative poles are connected together at another point b, then the combination is in parallel, as shown in Fig. 19.

Here, the voltage of the systems is that of a single cell and the total internal resistance is 1/n of the resistance of the single cell,

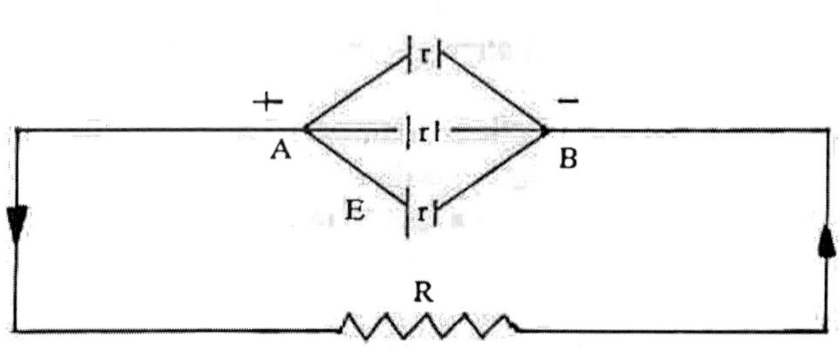

Fig.19 Grouping of cells in parallel

i.e. $I=\frac{E}{R+r}=\frac{nE}{nR+r}$

If R, the external resistance, is very small compared to r then $I=nE/r$, i.e. the current is n times that due to one cell. Thus, if two batteries of 6 volt each are available and 12 volt are required for the starter motor, then batteries are connected in series; on the other hand, if more current is required out of two weak batteries to give the initial starting torque to the self-start motor, the batteries are connected in parallel.

Problem 17.7: A battery of 10 cells joined in series yields a current of 1 amp when the external resistance is 10 ohm, and a current of 0.6 amp when the external resistance is 20 ohm. Find the e.m.f. and the internal resistance of the cells.

Let r = the internal resistance and E = e.m.f. of each cell.

Here n = 10.

In the first case, R = 10 ohm.

$\therefore I=\frac{10E}{10r+10}$

or $10E-10r=10$

or $E-R=1$ (A)

In the second case, $0.6=\frac{10E}{10r+20}$

or $10E=6r+12$

$\therefore\ 5E-3r=6$ (B)

From (A) and (B), we get

E = *1.5* volt, r = *0.5* ohm.

Problem 17.8: Three wires, each of 30 ohm resistance, are arranged in parallel and connected to a battery of 10 Leclanche's cells, each having an e.m.f. of 1.5 volt and internal resistance of 3 ohm. Calculate the P.D. (i.e. the voltage drop) across the battery terminals, the current in each wire, and also that in the battery.

Here, in the battery, 10 cells are connected in series. The total e.m.f. of the combination $=1.5\times10=15$ volt.

Total internal resistance $=3\times10=30$ ohm.

Since, the resistance are in parallel,

$\frac{1}{R}=\frac{1}{30}+\frac{1}{30}+\frac{1}{30}=\frac{1}{10}$

$\therefore R=10$ ohm.

Hence the current in the battery

$$I=\frac{15}{30+10}= 3/8 \text{ amp} = 0.375 \text{ amp.}$$

Also, the current in each wire $=\frac{\text{total current}}{3}=0.125$ amp

The P.D. between the terminals of battery = current × resistance = 0.125 × 30 = 3.75 volt

Problem 17.9: One cell has e.m.f. of 2 volt and internal resistance of 0.7 ohm. How much resistance is to be added to get current strength of 5 amp?

If the required resistance is R ohm, then the total resistance of the circuit = R + 0.07 ohm.

$$\therefore \quad C=\frac{E}{R+r}$$

or

$$5=\frac{2}{R+0.07}$$

Hence $R = 0.33$ ohm.

Problem 17.10: How many 40 watt lamps may be used on a 220 volt circuit without blowing out the 10 ampere fuse?

Here power consumed = 40 watt for each lamp.

Also, the supply voltage = 220.

∴ Current consumed by each lamp = power/voltage. Hence, current consumed = 40/220 = 2/11 amp by each lamp.

Since in a domestic circuit the lamps are connected in parallel, the requisite number of lamps for a 10 amp fuse will be

$$10 \div 2/11 = 10 \times 11/2 = 55 \text{ lamps.}$$

Problem 17.11: The lighting circuit of a house is wired in parallel. The main supply is 240 volts. The bulbs in the circuit are 5 of 100, 5 of 60, and 10 of 40 watt. (a) What amperage would pass through the fuse wire if all the bulbs are switched on together? (b) What would be the effective resistance of all the bulbs?

(*a*) Total wattage = 5 × 100 = 500 W

5 × 100	= 500 W
5 × 60	= 300 W
10 × 100	= 400 W
Total	= 1200 W

Also watts (W) = $V \times A$ (i.e. voltage × amperage)

Hence, ampere (A) $= \frac{W}{V} = \frac{1200}{240} = 5$ amp.

(b) $V = A \times R$ (Where V = voltage, A the amperage and R the resistance (from Ohm's law)

$$\therefore \; R = \frac{V}{A} = \frac{240}{5} = 48 \text{ohm}.$$

Problem 17.12: The cable of an electric motor has a resistance of 0.35 ohm in each conductor. The normal current is 25 amp and the voltage at the supply end of the cable is 220 V. (a) calculate (i) the voltage across the motor terminals; (ii) The power loss in the cable. (b) If the motor is stalled and the current rises to 120 amp, calculate (i) the voltage across the terminals, (ii) the percentage rise and the power loss in the cable.

(*a*) (*i*) Voltage drop $V = IR$ (I = current and R = resistance) = $25 \times 0.35 = 8.75$ volt.

This is in one conductor; therefore, the total drop = $8.75 \times 2 = 17.50$ volt.

Initial voltage = 220V and loss = 17.5V.

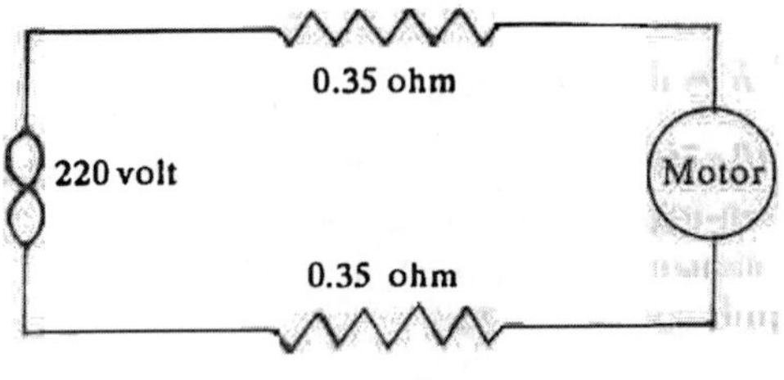

Fig.20

Hence, voltage across motor = 202.5 V.

(*ii*) Power drop $W = I^2R = 25 \times 25 \times .35$ per cable = 218.75 W per cable.

Hence, for two cables, total power drop = $218.75 \times 2 = 437.50$ W.

(*b*) (*i*) $V = I \times R = 120 \times 0.35 = 42$ V per cable.

Total voltage drop = $2 \times 42 = 82$ V

$\therefore$ stalled voltage across motor = $220 - 84 = 136$ V

(*ii*) Power drop $W = I^2R = 120 \times 120 \times 0.35 = 504$ 0W per cable.

$\therefore$ Power drop in both cables = $5040 \times 2 = 10080$W

Hence, percentage of power loss in cables

$$= \frac{\text{new power}}{\text{old power}} \times 100 = \frac{10080}{437.5} \times 100 = 2304\%.$$

Problem 17.13: Two 15 W indicator lamps of 110 volt are connected in series across a 220 V supply. One lamp fails and it is replaced by a 25 W lamp of 110 V. Calculate (i) the voltage across each lamp; and (ii) the power dissipated in each lamp. *(Graduateship Exam., 1988)*

Since $R = \frac{V^2}{W}$,

Resistance of 15 W lamp $= \frac{110^2}{15} = 807$ ohm.

Similarly, resistance of 25 W lamp $= \frac{110^2}{25} = 484$ohm.

Total resistance = 807 + 484 = 1291 ohm.

As per Ohm's law, $I = \frac{V}{R} = \frac{220}{1291} = 0.17$ amp.

(*i*) Voltage across 15W lamp ($V = I \times R$) = 0.17 × 807 = 137 V
Also voltage across 25 W lamp = 0.17 × 484 = 83 V
(*ii*) Power dissipated in 15 W lamp ($W = I \times V$) = 137×0.17 = 23.3 W.
Power dissipated in 25 W lamp = 83 × 0.17 = 14.1 W.

Problem 17.14: The power circuit of a house supplied at 250 V had the following items in use: 1000 W iron for half an hour, 2000 W kettle for 0.25 hour and 3000 W fire for 1 hour. If the charge per unit (kilowatt-hour) is 90p, what was the total bill for electricity consumed? What was the resistance of each item, and the total effective resistance of the circuit?

(*a*) Total electric consumption per circuit :

for 0.5 hour, $\frac{1000}{2} = 500$ W = 0.5 kW/h (for the iron).

For 0.25 hour, $\frac{2000}{4} = 500$ W = 0.5 kW/h (for the kettle).

For 1 hour, $\frac{3000}{1} = 3000$ W = 3 kW/h (for the fire).

Total units consumed = 4 k W/h

Cost @ 90p per kW/h = 0.90 × 4 = Rs 3.60.

(b) To find out the resistance we have to get the amperage consumed by each appliance from the formula

$R = V/A$ and also from $W = V \times A$ or $A = W/V$

Hence, amperage for the first appliance $= \frac{1000}{250} = 4$ amp.

Similarly, for the other two appliances, the amperage will be

$$\frac{2000}{250}=8 \text{ amp and } \frac{3000}{250}=12 \text{ amp.}$$

Therefore, resistance for each appliance (from the formula $R = V/A$ are 250/4, 250/8 and 250/12, or 62.5 ohm, 31.25 ohm and 20.8 ohm respectively.

(c) The total effective resistance can be found out from the formula

$$\frac{1}{R}=\frac{1}{r_1}+\frac{1}{r_2}+\frac{1}{r_3}$$

or

$$\frac{1}{R}=\frac{4}{250}+\frac{8}{250}+\frac{12}{250}=\frac{24}{250}$$

or

$$R=\frac{250}{24}=10.4 \text{ ohm.}$$

Problem 17.15 : From the circuit shown below, calculate (i) the current flowing from the sources, (ii) the voltage drop across ab *in the circuit, (iii) the current in the 24 ohm resistor, (iv) the power dissipated in the 24 ohm resistor.* *(Graduateship Exam., 1974)*

The question concerns Ohm's law and the series and parallel circuit.

The supply voltage is 240. The total resistance is to be found out first.

First, the effective resistance of the circuit bc to be found out and since the two resistances of 24 ohm and 8 ohm are in parallel connection, we have

$$\frac{1}{R}=\frac{1}{r_1}+\frac{1}{r_2} \quad \text{i.e.} \quad \frac{1}{R}=\frac{1}{24}+\frac{1}{8}=\frac{4}{24} \quad \text{or } R = 6 \text{ ohm.}$$

We have to consider now the whole circuit, in series, with bc as 6 ohm.

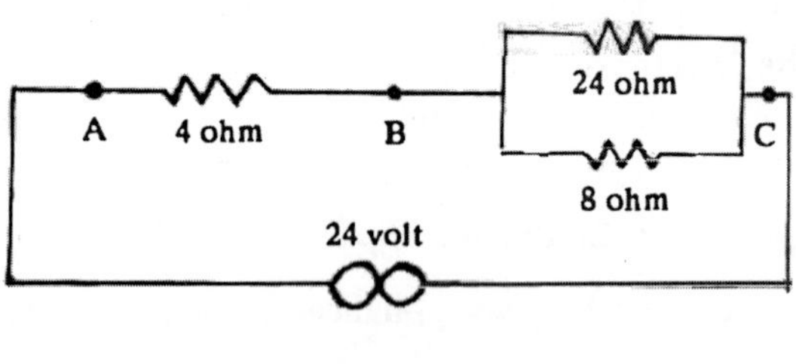

Fig.21

Hence, the total effective resistance $R_t = r_1 + r_2$
or $R_t = 4 + 6 = 10$ ohm.

Nowwe can findout the current, after having obtained the resistance and voltage.

(*a*) Since $I = \frac{E}{R}$ (Ohm's law), we have $I = \frac{240}{10} = 24$ amp.

(*b*) Also, the voltage drop acrossABmay be found out as $E = IR = 24 \times 4 = 96$ V.

(*c*) 96 volt have been used for forcing the current throughABHence, voltage across BC = 240 − 96 = 144 V and the current in the circuit = 144/24 = 6 amp.

Therefore, power dissipated
$W = I^2R = 6^2 \times 24 = 864$ W.

CHAPTER 18

Heating Effect of Current: Application of Joule's ,Law

We have noted earlier that the amount of heat produced in a circuit depends on the magnitude of resistance, current strength, and the time, i.e. $H \alpha C^2 Rt$. If a current of C ampere flows through R ohm resistance for t seconds, then heat produced

$$H = 0.24 \times C^2 RT$$

The above relation is obtained from

$H = C^2 Rt / J$ where J, the Joule's equivalent of heat, is equal to 4.2×10^7 erg/calorie.

or

$$H - \frac{C^2 Rt \times 10^7}{4.2 \times 10^7} \quad (W = \text{work} = C^2 Rt \times 10^7 \text{ erg}).$$

$$= 0.24 \ C^2 Rt \text{ calorie}$$

Also,

$$H = \frac{W}{J} = \frac{ECt}{J} = \frac{C^2 Rt}{J}$$

since $E = C \times R$, where $=$ the resistance of the wire.

Problem 18.1 : A coil of resistance 2 ohm is immersed in a kilogram of water and is connected to the terminals of the battery of internal resistance 4 ohm and e.m.f. 6 volt for 3 minutes. Find the rise in temperature of water where $J = 4.2 \times 10^7$ erg/calorie.

Let $T\,^0$C be the rise of temperature of water. the strength of current flowing through the wire is viven by

$$I=\frac{E}{R+r}=\frac{6}{2+4}=1\,\text{amp}$$

Heat developed in the coil

$$=\frac{C^2Rt\times10^7}{J}$$

$$=\frac{1\times2\times3\times60\times10^7}{4.2\times10^7}$$

$$=\frac{6\times60}{4.2}\ \text{cal}$$

Heat absorbed by water $=1000\times T$ cal.

$\therefore\ 1000\times T=\frac{6\times60}{4.2}\qquad\therefore\ T=\frac{6\times60}{4.2\times1000}=0.085^0$ C nearly.

(This problem can also be solved by applying the formula $H=0.24C^2Rt$).

Problem 18.2: A current of 1.2 amp passes for one minute through a wire, whose resistance is 25 ohm. Find the amount of heat developed and the potential difference between the ends of the wire.

Since

$$C=\frac{E}{R}\ \text{(Ohm's law)}$$

$$E=C\times R$$

i.e.voltage difference between the ends of the wire $=1.2\times25=30$ volt.

Also, heat developed

$$=0.24\ C^2Rt=0.24\times(1.2)^2\times25\times60$$

$$=0.24\times1.2\times1.2\times25\times60$$

$$=518.4\ \text{cal.}$$

Problem 18.3 : A 10 ohm coil of wire is used to heat 1000 gm of water from 15°C to 100°C in 20 minutes. How much current must be used? What is the amount of power consumed?

Heat required for 1000 gm of water to be heated from 15°C to 100°C $=1000\times1\times(100-15)=85{,}000$ calories (specific heat of water $=1$)

This is equal to $=0.24\times C^2\times 10\times 20\times 60$

$$\therefore \quad C^2=\frac{85,000}{0.24\times 10\times 20\times 60}=\frac{85,000}{48\times 60}$$

$$=29.51 \quad \therefore \quad C=5.43 \text{ amp.}$$

Since power consumed $=C^2\times R$, (power $=C\times E$, i.e. current×voltage and $E=C\times R$).

Hence, power consumed = $29.51\times 10=295.1$ watt.

Problem 18.4 : An electric blanket is rated at 240 volt, 80 watt. Owing to a short circuit, it becomes over-heated. Examination shows that half of the heating element has been cut out of circuit. What has been the effect on (a) the current, and (b) the wattage? *(I.F.E., 1969)*

Here, the voltage = 240 volt

and the current $=\frac{\text{watt}}{\text{voltage}}=\frac{80}{240}=\frac{1}{3}$ amp.

Also, the resistance of the heating element, a factor due to which heat is produced, can be found out by Ohm's law from the above two factors by dividing the voltage by current, i.e.

$$240\div\frac{1}{3}=720 \text{ ohm.}$$

In view of the fault developed, the resistance left is only $720\div 2=360$ ohm.

$\therefore$ The current $\frac{240}{360}=\frac{2}{3}$amp

i.e. current is doubled due to the fault. Also, since the voltage remains the same, the wattage will be

$$240\times\frac{2}{3} \text{ (since wattage } C\times E) = 160 \text{ watt.}$$

Problem 18.5: An electric heater for a 200 litre tank is rated at 3 kWh with an efficiency of 90%. The water is heated from 20^0C to 50^0C. Given that one litre of water weighs 1 kg and 1 kW provides 240 calorie/sec, how long would it take for the tank to reach 50^0C?

(Graduateship Examination. 1982)

The weight of 200 litre of water = 200 kg $=200\times 1000$ gm. Since 1 calorie of heat is required to raise 1 gm of water through 1^0C, the total heat required to raise the temperature of 2,00,000 gm of water to $30^0C=200{,}000\times 30$ calories.

Also, the heater is rated at 3 kWh with 90 per cent efficiency and as such, it will provide $3\times240\times90\%$ or 648 calorie/sec. (Since 1 kW provides 240 calorie/sec).

Hence, the time taken to reach 50^0C

$$=\frac{200{,}000\times 30}{648}\ \text{second}$$

or 2 hr 34 min.

Problem 18.6 : A current of 1.6 amp flows for 5 min through a wire of 3.4 ohm resistance, immersed in 50 gm of water in a container of weight 50 gm with specific heat of 0.2. Calculate the rise in temperature.

Here the heat given out by the wire

$$=0.24\times1.6\times1.6\times3.4\times5\times60\ \text{calorie.}$$

Also, the heat gained by the water and the container

$=50\times t\,^0C+50\times0.2\times t\,^0C$, where $t\,^0C$ is the rise in temperature.

$$50t^0+10t^0=60\ \ t^0C.$$

Hence

$$60t\ =\ 0.24\times1.6\times1.6\times3.4\times300=626.69\ \text{calorie.}$$

$$\therefore\qquad t\ =\ 10.44^0C$$

Problem 18.7 : Calculate the time required to boil 2 litre of water at 25.4^0C by an electric heater supplying energy at the rate of one horsepower (1 calorie $=4.2\times10^7$ erg).

Here the rise in temperature $=100–25.4^0C=74.6^0C$.

The heat required for the water to boil $=2\times1000\times74.6$ calorie.

Also the heat given out by the heater

$$=\frac{ECT}{J}=\frac{746t\times10^7}{4.2\times10^7}\quad[IHP=E\times C=746\ \text{watt}]$$

Hence,

$$\frac{746t}{4.2}=2\times1000\times74.6$$

$$\therefore\qquad t=\frac{2000\times4.2}{60\times10}=\frac{42}{3}=14\ \text{min.}$$

Problem 18.8: An electric heater having a resistance of 12 ohm is being operated from 220 volt power line. If no heat escapes from it, how much time is required to raise the temperature of 4 kg of water from 15^{0}C to 80^{0}C?

(Graduateship Examination, 1983)

Resistance = 12 ohm and voltage = 220 volt.

Therefore, current = $\frac{220}{12}$ amp (Since $C = \frac{E}{R}$ by Ohm's Law)

Heat produced H (joule) = C^2RT

or $$H = \frac{C^2Rt}{4.2} \quad (J = 4.2 \text{ Joule/cal}).$$

or, $$H = \frac{220}{12} \times \frac{220}{12} \times 12 \times \frac{t}{4.2} \quad (t = \text{time in seconds})$$

Since heat lost by one body = heat gained by another body = mst, where m = mass, s = specific heat and t = the difference in temperature, substituting the values we have:

$$\text{(heat lost)} \frac{220}{12} \times \frac{220}{12} \times 12 \times \frac{t}{4.2} = 4 \times 1000 \times 1 \times 65 \text{ (heat gained)}$$

since m = 4× 1000 gm, s for water = 1, and 65^0 C is the difference in temperature,

Therefore,

$$t = \frac{4.2 \times 4 \times 1000 \times 65 \times 12 \times 12}{220 \times 220 \times 12} = \frac{32760}{121} \text{ sec} = 4.51 \text{ min.}$$

CHAPTER 19

Static Electricity

Static electricity is produced as a result of friction between two non-conducting substances. When a glass rod is rubbed with a piece of silk cloth, the rod acquires a charge of static electricity which, unlike dynamic electricity, is not mobile. It remains static on the body of the substance and unless safely conducted to earth, will produce a spark, depending upon the accumulation of charge, by accidental contact with earth.

Lightning is a good example of the formation of static electricity. The lightning flash is caused as a result of the discharge of the static charges between the clouds. In industry, the running of beltings over pulleys is a frequent cause of static accumulation. The beltings are usually of some non-conducting material such as canvas (now-a-days nylon) and build up a charge, sometimes of considerable strength, as it rotates over the pulleys. Where there is no possible fire risk, charges might be allowed to dissipate to earth by sparking, but in a flammable atmosphere, precautions are to be adopted so that there might not be any static discharge which may cause a fire. Either a series of rollers running on the beltings or copper brushes connected to earth are commonly employed to discharge the static. Stout metallic chains firmly embedded to earth, of which one end is soldered to a fixed part of the machine, are also employed to dissipate the static charges produced in various operations in industrial undertakings.

Generation of static due to various Industrial processes

Static electricity is also produced when a non-conducting liquid (like petrol, benzol, naphtha etc.) passes through pipes or tubes which are not properly earthed. The voltage produced will depend on the rate of the flow of the solvent through the pipe. Dolczalek, the Russian physicist, stated that a rate of flow of 1 meter/sec is liable to produce a potential of 1000 volt, while ignition by spark can be effected at an electric pressure of only 300 volt. To dissipate the static generated, arrangements are made when petrol is being pumped in underground tanks from tanker wagons by connecting the metal portion of the discharge faucet of the petrol pipe delivering petrol (specially of high octane value) to tanks by means of pipes with braiding of stout metallic spiral wire. In the case of the tanker (where static might be generated due to jerking and jolting of the vehicle containing petrol in the tanker) dissipation is effected by means of stout metallic iron chains trailing behind the tanker vehicle touching the earth. Static generation in such vehicles or trolleys can also be dissipated by wheels fitted with 'conducting rubber' (i.e. a kind of rubber in which the percentage of sulphur is less to make it conducting).

HOSPITALS

In hospitals, operation theatres are the places where static charges might be generated, resulting in a fire from the tiny spark either between the surgeons' gloves and the body of the patient while being transferred from the stretcher or the trolley to the operating table, or between the trolley itself and the anaesthetist's hand. The patient while being removed to the theatre on the trolley in the lying position builds up the static due to the friction between his body and the rubber sheet which is ordinarily an insulator. Here, the static charge cannot dissipate to earth of its own because the trolley wheels, being made of rubber, are non-conducting. It is here that the 'conducting rubber' has been found to be useful and the static charge produced is dissipated to earth safely through the trolley wheels made of conducting rubber. Garments of silk or fur are also liable to generate static charge while being rinsed in petrol or benzene.

STATIC ELIMINATION

It has been claimed that in the case of non-conducting liquids such as petrol, benzol etc., the use of metallic soap will eliminate such hazards (e.g. addition of 0.05% of magnesium oleate). This increases the electrical conductivity of petrol or the solvent used for the dry-cleaning of silk goods. Metallic soaps, viz. a solution of magnesium oleate in petroleum ether is added to the organic solvents employed for such purpose. Static electricity is also dissipated if the relative humidity of the atmosphere is not allowed to fall below 60%.

STATIC ELIMINATORS

Static generated in industrial operation can also be eliminated by either of the undermentioned four processes, viz. (*1*) bonding and earthing of the machinery which are likely to produce static, (*2*) humidification, (*3*) ionization of atmosphere, (*4*) application of high voltage D.C. potential in the field.

Characteristices of static charges and reduction of hazards

Considerable charges may be developed on polythene, certain types of rubber and P.V.C. by rubbing with another material. As they are poor conductors, the charge on some parts might be retained for a long time even though other parts are in contact with earth. Earthing a non-conductor, it may be noted, is of little value because the flow to earth is impeded. The safeguard then is to prevent the accumulation of charge and there are two methods of doing this. One is to introduce a filler material such as carbon black in rubber which is more conducting or make the surface more conducting by coating it. The second is to make the surrounding atmosphere more conducting by means of radioactive source. The hazard of introducing such a source has to be weighed against the hazard from the static electrical discharge.

All metal parts of plants handling flammable liquids or ignitable dusts must be connected to earth by a definite stable and low-resistance path. The earthing system of such a plant should ensure that the resistance to earth of structural steelwork, fixed and movable plant items remain at less than 10 ohm throughout the life of the plant. To ensure this, the earthing system has to be checked and replaced after plant maintenance and plant modification. The checking of the complete earthing system must he a scheduled item of plant maintenance.

Static electricity is produced by the movement of surfaces. Whenever plant operators move, the surfaces of their clothing move against one another and on wool, plastic sheeting and some other synthetic fibres, large electrostatic charges might be produced. When ordinary boots or shoes are worn and the atmosphere is dry, the charges produced might be sufficient to raise the potential of a person to a voltage sufficient to cause shock when earthen objects are touched and incendiary sparks might occur.

When a liquid flows through a pipeline there is a separation of charge at the interface between liquid and pipe. Any turbulence increases the area of contact of the liquid with pipe. The charging rate for a liquid depends on its linear flow velocity—the rate at which it moves along the pipe. This velocity is increased by constriction, orifice plates, valves and sharp bend which might also increase the turbulence.

Excessive charging due to constriction, bends or orifices could be dangerous if it occurs immediately before the entry of the liquid into the tank. This could be overcome by inserting an earthed section of pipe between the constriction and the tank which must allow enough time for the charge to leak away. The rate at which the charge leaks away depends on the electrical resistivity of the liquid and is usually expressed as the time for half the charge to leak away – a half-value time. It has been recommended that the time for the liquid to flow through the earthed section of pipe should be three to four times this half-value time.

If more than one liquid phase is involved, i.e. where there are two or more immiscible liquids, the charging rate might be considerably increased as a result of a very intimate contact between the globules of the liquids. Of interest is the effect of water, as solvents do, in some processes, contain water. It has been found that pumping gasolne might produce a maximum field strength of 4–5kilo volt per metre. The addition of 6% of water to the mixture raised this value by a factor varying between 2 and 50 times at the same pumping speed.

It is not true that earthing makes for absolute safety and fire and explosion caused by static electricity are not necessarily attributable to an earth fault. If a product has a high electrical resistivity, any charge accumulated on it will discharge to earth only slowly so that charge might build up on a product even though a plant is effectively earthed.

The only way to overcome this is by the use of an antistatic additive. Oil-handling operations may be carried out safely by ensuring that the resistivity of liquids should be less than 10^{11} ohm per cm. This in turn ensures that less than one minute after generation, the static charge is reduced by a factor of 1,000,000. This means, the charges on such liquids are not hazardous providing there is a direct path to earth allowing the charge to dissipate. This is important because if the electrical resistivity of a liquid is decreased and it is contained in an electrically insulated vessel (made of rubber, glass or plastic) conditions could be produced that increase the possibility of spark discharge from the surface of the liquid. The fitting of an earthed metal plug into the bottom of such a vessel will overcome this.

The rate of flow of a liquid through a pipeline is also important. As the velocity of flow is reduced, the rate of generating charge is reduced also, and for hydrocarbon–water mixtures, a linear velocity of one metre per second is reckoned to be safe. At this rate the splashing and stirring up of the water layer at the bottom of a tank is not great, nor is the emulsification of the water. But at rates lower than one metre per second, a hazard might arise because water pockets might accumulate at low points in the line and later entrained when pumping speeds are increased.

CHAPTER 20

Fires due to Electricity

Sometimes the cause of a fire due to electricity is wrongly ascribed. Phenomena like short circuit, blowing of the fuse are quite common, but they are wrongly described as the cause of fires. The real causes of a fire from electricity are the following: (*a*) lightning, (*b*)electrostatic sparks, (*c*) electric arcs and (*d*) overheating of wires and cables by excessive currents.

Lightning

Whenever clouds carrying opposite static charges come in contact witth each other, the static is discharged in the form of a lightning flash within a fraction of a second. It has been estimated that the potential reached in a thunder cloud before the flash is of the order of one thousand million volt and the discharge current is of the order of 100,000 ampere. We can easily imagine the fate of the structure through which such a heavy current will discharge even if it is for a very short duration. This invariably results in a fire and collapse of the structure.

None can forecast with accuracy that a particular building will never be struck with lightning. But it has been calculated that the most violent electrical discharge which is likely to occur might be safely dissipated by a copper conductor with a cross section of 0.5 sq.cm or by an iron conductor of 1.3 sq.cm. It is very essential that this conductor should have no bad joints or bad earth, as even a resistance of 1 ohm due to bad earth connection might raise the potential of the conductor to 100,000 volt with disastrous results.

Electrostatic sparks

Though the exact voltage of the electrostatic sparks which may cause fire in a flammable vapour–air mixture or in an atmosphere laden with flammable dust has not yet been fully ascertained, the fact remains that a stout spark between electrodes may set fire to an inflammable mixture. This is closely akin to that of the ignition of the 'fire damp' in mines.

Electric arcs

An electric arc is a powerful flame and can very easily set fire to a combustible substance near about. Dangerous situations are encountered when a direct current circuit is used to operate electromagnetic appliances, e.g. electric alarm, signalling circuits etc. Such arcs, due to breakage of the wire or due to short circuit between the positive and the negative wires because of deterioration of the insulation, constitute one of the most dangerous kinds of electrical effect in so far as fire is concerned.

Overheating of cables due to excess current

Deterioration of the insulation due to overage, inexpert handling and corrosion of the insulation due to electrolysis might cause a heavy drainage of the current and overheating of the installation. Substitution of the fuse by a wire heavier than the conductor which it is supposed to protect will no doubt cause excessive current to flow along the conductors and subsequently lead to a fire.

Fires in electrical machinery

In fires involving electrical gears, there will invariably be some oil or greasy substance which become overheated due to the formation of an arc or a heavy discharge of current to the earth through the body of the machine. As a result, the oil becomes hot, expands and ruptures the vessel with the resultant spillage all around the floor. Common examples are H.T. switch-gear, transformer etc.

Though foam is generally used for such fires, carbon dioxide gas in cylinders is very useful for fighting such fires as it is most non-damaging and clean in action. A concentration of this gas above 15% in atmosphere is required to inhibit combustion.

Effects of alternating current on steel conduits

It will also be interesting to note here the effect of the passage of A.C. through cables laid in steel conduit. If in an A.C. circuit of simple design, only one cable passes through a short length of steel tube, and in another case, both cables together pass through another short piece of steel tube, it is found that the steel tube through which only one cable passes is heated to such an extent that it is impossible to touch it with bare hands a few minutes after switching on the current. The steel tube through which two cables pass remain cooler. This is due to the formation of eddy current in the steel tube which at the normal frequency and voltage used for domestic occupancies produces the heating effect. If the two cables of a two-phase system are laid together in the same tube, the current in the two cable are flowing in opposite directions and consequently neutralize each other's effect.

Safety factors concerning use of electricity

All electrical apparatus, machines, wirings, transformers and switch-gears are designed to operate at a given current, which, if exceeded, will overheat the equipment and may cause fire. Short circuits and earth faults are amongst the most common causes of overloaded circuits. The overloading of motors on account of mechanical faults such as the seizing of bearings, has also given rise to a number of fires.

Most of the electrical apparatus require some degree of cooling or ventilation for safe operation and the absence of it will cause the apparatus to overheat and may cause fire. Electrical equipment installed in dirty and untidy surrounding is more prone to fire than equipment in clean and tidy premises. Therefore, steps should be taken to eliminate, as far as possible, dust, dirt, waste material, packing material, oily rags, overalls and other combustible deposits on or near any equipment.

Moisture being a conductor of electricity can cause earth faults and short circuits. It may cause deterioration of insulation and damage conduit and other protective metal work, thereby shortening the safe life of an installation. Therefore, in damp situations, equipments should be resistant to the effects of moisture.

A number of serious fires are caused by electrical apparatus which has been left switched on and unattended. All such apparatus should be designed with the possibility of excessive temperature rise in mind and be provided with adequate protective gear of the thermal type. Such apparatus should receive regular and thorough maintenance.

Change of layout may give rise to unsuspected dangers. Lights, heaters, motors, switch-gears, cables, portable equipments or any equipment which originally might have been correctly and safely installed might become dangerous if changes take place in their use or surroundings. Such changes may expose the equipment to accumulation of combustible material, conditions of excessive heat or restricted ventilation, or to the flammable atmospheres of dust or vapour where none existed before. This might also lead to overloading. Unskilled interference or tampering, though done with the best of intentions, might also create potential hazards.

Cables and wirings should be of the correct rating and size for the current requirements of the apparatus. They should be securely installed, properly supported and protected against mechanical damage, heat, vibration and against the ingress of moisture and corrosive substances. They should not be run in any position where they or their metal enclosures might accidentally come into contact with any other services especially gas piping. Heavy gauge screwed conduit or armoured cable is suitable where mechanical damage is liable to result from the installation. P.V.C. sheathed cable is appropriate where there is possiblity of attack from chemicals and mineral oils. Aluminium cables might require additional protection when exposed to mechanical damage. Mineral-insulated metal sheathed cables are advisable where there might be exposure to heat but these cables also require additional attention.

Motors and their control gears should be of the appropriate rating for the load they have to carry. They should not be used in ambient temperatures in excess of which they have been disigned unless allowance has been made in their ratings, or unless special cooling facilities are arranged. They should, where possible, be so installed as to be free from contact with combustible materials, and so situated that there is no obstruction to natural ventilation, unless provision is made for forced ventilation (pipe). Where motors are exposed to dusts or deposit-forming vapour, overheating is likely to occur unless attention is frequently given. The installation of fan motors within ducting should be avoided since access for maintenance is usually difficult. The motors, together with the machinery driven, should be maintained in good condition to prevent fires caused by faulty brush gear, failure of automatic short-circuiting devices, seized bearings and belts. Each starter should incorporate protection for the motor against overloads and single-phasing and unless back up protection for the circuit is provided, it should be capable of breaking satisfactorily the maximum possible short-circuit current.

Fuses cannot provide close protection against overloading and in the case of such motors as small direct-on-line start machines, where the starters are not fitted with overload trips, severe heating may occur without blowing the fuses. For motors not under direct supervision, inbuilt thermal overload trips provide a safeguard measure against sustained overheating. This is more useful than mere fuse protection.

Safety devices in flammable atmosphere for electrical fittings, switches

It may be impracticable to exclude electrical fitting in a flammable atmosphere. There are, however, safety devices to exclude the possibility of a fire due to sparking or arcing. Where flammable gases or vapours are liable to be present, certified flameproof apparatus should be used.

Flameproof fitting

The term flameproof here means that if any flammable gas enters and is ignited inside the enclosure of the fitting, the flame will not be communicated to the external atmosphere. This is achieved by making the enclosure strong enough to withstand any explosion inside and by limiting the gaps between joints of the case and of clearances for shafts. It may also be mentioned that an apparatus which is flameproof in one gas may not necessarily be flameproof in another. There are, however, two alternatives, which may be applied in appropriate circumstances.

PRESSURIZED APPARATUS

An inert gas is maintained here at a higher pressure within the case of the apparatus than the atmosphere outside so that it is not possible for gases or vapours to enter the enclosure. The higher pressure is maintained by fitting gas-tight glands.

INTRINSICALLY SAFE EQUIPMENT

This is used in equipments like telephone and instrument control circuits. The equipment is designed to limit the energy in the circuit that enters the area of possible danger so that any spark that could be produced would be too weak to ignite the gas or vapour for which the equipment has been certified.

CHAPTER 21

Protective Devices and Safety Requirements

Protection against mechanical damage

Improperly made joints in cables may produce hot spots to which the protective device may not be responsive. All joints should be either soldered or made with porecelain connectors containing mechanical clamps. It is better to dispense with joints in circuit wiring by using a looping in system. Use of flexible cords and cables should be avoided except where absolutely necessary.

Safety devices

Every separate circuit should be protected against excessive current by switch or fuse-gear of adequate breaking capacity and suitable to the supply conditions. All switch and fuse-gear should be of the correct design and rating. No addition to the circuit should be made without first determining that the switch and fuse-gear are capable of operating satisfactorily under the additional load and of protecting the complete circuit against faults.

Protective gear is designed to interrupt the supply when current flows in excess of the safe circuit rating, and protection can be applied against earth faults, short circuits and overloads.

EARTH FAULTS

Earth faults are a common cause of fire, and it is therefore desirable that such faults should be cleared as promptly as possible so as to prevent destructive heating. The resistance of the earth circuit should be low enough to pass sufficient current to actuate the protective gear before the temperature exceeds a safe limit. It is also important to ensure that the thermal capacity of the earth circuit is adequate under fault conditions to carry fault currents without undue temperature rise.

LIGHTING EQUIPMENT AND SAFETY REQUIREMENTS

Incandescent filament lamps of 100 watt and above become hot enough to ignite fluff and combustible dust as also materials like cellulose nitrate. Lamps should be so placed, guarded or enclosed, as to prevent contact with combustible material. Stem pendants (i.e. pendants formed of conduit) are preferable to flexible cords for the suspension of lighting fittings and should be regarded as essential where there is exposure to combustible deposits.

The use of twin flexible cords for pendant lighting should be avoided. Tough rubber sheathed and P.V.C. sheathed cords are less liable to be ignited by an internal short circuit or conductor breakage than twin flexible cords.

Fluorescent lamps should be switched off, if a fault becomes apparent by flickering or failure to light, as otherwise the starting gear might overheat. The chokes associated with discharge lamps may cause fires through faults leading to intense local heating without operating the fuse protection. Thermal cut-outs are available which, installed in contact with the windings, tend to lessen the risk.

HEATING EQUIPMENTS USED IN INDUSTRY

There had been a number of fires due to defective or bad construction of the heating equipments. Infra-red heating equipment for drying painted, dipped or sprayed articles should be constructed of non-combustible materials. The insulation should be of heat-resisting type and the lamps or elements and their reflectors should be mounted in such a way as to prevent the deposit of any residue upon them. Since, it is usually impracticable to use flameproof heaters, it is necessary to provide ventilation which is adequate to prevent the formation of flammable concentration of vapour. The fans for effecting this should be interlocked with the supply of heaters which in turn should be interlocked with any conveyor used for the carriage of the article past the heaters. Thus when the fans or conveyors stop, the heaters are switched off.

THERMAL PROTECTION–THERMOSTATS

Heating apparatus such as ovens and baths should never be left in operation unattended unless some form of reliable thermal protection is provided. Thermostats should be duplicated on apparatus associated with unattended processes and be frequently tested to ensure satisfactory operation. Protection against fires caused by immersion heaters in tanks, containing inflammable materials, such as oil, bitumen, creosote or tar is best afforded by level indicators and thermostats associated with the heating elements.

Thermostats are more liable to fail than normal switches. If not properly maintained they may (*i*) fail in their function or even catch fire on being covered with fluff or filled with dust, (*ii*) oxidize or melt at the contacts through repeated heating and deteriorate generally due to the same cause, (*iii*) melt and stick in the closed position, specially when working on heavy loads, or (*iv*) suffer damage from arcing.

TEMPORARY INSTALLATIONS

It has been found that temporary installations in a factory or in a domestic occupancy are sometimes allowed to remain for a long time in the open, contiguous to gas pipes, water mains, or the building face, and as a result, deteriorate and develop earth fault with consequent disastrous results.

A temporary installation should, as far as possible, comply with requirements for permanent work and should not be continued to be in use longer than three months unless it either complies with the requirements in every detail or is completely overhauled at three-monthly intervals.

Adequate protection is to be provided against excess currents and means of isolation, in case of a fault, should be provided in all parts of a temporary installation. Where earthing is necessary, its efficiency (i.e. earth resistance) should be proved by test. Where a temporary installation is to be supplied with current from a permanent installation, the current ratings of the parts of the permanent installations affected should be adequate for the extra load to be imposed upon them.

Tough rubber sheathed or P.V.C. sheathed cables are to be used, which should be held in position by porcelain cleats. If steel-armoured cable is used it should be adequately secured. Flexible cords and cables should be used only where essential. If the installation is exposed to the risk of mechanical damage, it should be tough-rubber sheathed or P.V.C. sheathed.

Finally, every temporary installation in an industrial undertaking should be under the charge of a competent person who should accept the responsibility of the installation and its use and for any alteration or extension. It is advisable to have the name and designation of such a person prominently displayed close to the main switch or circuit breaker.

Extensions to installations and recommendations

The rating and loading of existing circuits to which extensions are connected should be checked to ensure that they will not be overloaded. Where all the 'ways' of existing fuse-boards are occupied, extension circuits should be connected to additional fuse-boards which should be independently supplied if looping them to existing fuse-boards overloads the mains or sub-mains. Care should be taken not to disturb the insulation on existing conductors when drawing new cables into conduit which are already occupied by cable.

CHAPTER 22

Portable Equipments and Safety Requirements

Portable equipments sometimes cause trouble. The use of low voltage through a transformer (usually 110 volt or lower) as a safeguard against shock is, to an extent, effective against fire risk. Every piece of portable apparatus should be fed from a separate socket outlet, preferably non-reversible, and supplied from a properly protected circuit. When not in use, portable equipment should be disconnected from the supply by withdrawing the plug.

Portable apparatus should be connected by tough rubber-sheathed flexible cable or cord. P.V.C. sheathed cable should be used where the cable or the cord is likely to come in contact with mineral oil.

Damaged flexible cable should be replaced entirely or repaired by vulcanizing. Taped joints or repairs by taping should be avoided. Pilot lamps should be provided when portable non-luminous heating appliances such as electric irons are in operattion.

Permanent installations — inspection

An installation should be periodically inspected and tested and report be obtained on its condition as prescribed under the regulations. Inspection should take place at intervals of not more than three years. It is advisable that complete tests of insulation and earthing, as referred to below, should be carried out at least every year:

(*i*) Polarity of single-pole circuit switches;

(*ii*) Insulation (i.e. the value of the insulation resistance to earth);

(*iii*) Earthing (the value of the earth fault loop impedence in its bearing on the efficiency of protective gear);

(*iv*) The condition of the flexible cords and cables, switches, fuses, plugs, socket outlets, motors, heating elements, lamps and any other electric equipment;

(*v*) Overloading of conductors, motors and accessories;

(*vi*) Checking the motors for conditions of bearings and clearance of rotors etc.

A permanent record should be kept of all test reports and action to be taken to remedy the faults.

Importance of proper insulation

Insulation is liable to deteriorate with age. Signs of deterioration may sometimes be not detected by the insulation test alone and the protective covering may keep its insulating properties for some time. The danger is that a breakdown may occur suddenly without warning, perhaps due to crumbling of the insulation when disturbed, or due to the presence of moisture. Many old installations may be in wood casing and slip socket conduit which give no protection against moisture. Hence, with old cables particularly, visual inspection should supplement the insulation tests. Equipments are now available for carrying out ionization test by which deterioration and other defects of the insulation may be found out.

Maintenance

Maintenance consists of detecting and eliminating overloading, ascertaining whether any illicit tampering with the settings of protective gear has occurred, and replacing faulty or damaged equipment and also tightening of loose terminals and connections. It also includes replacing sections of wiring whose insulation has perished or damaged, especially flexible cords and cables; correction of sparking at brushes on motors, preservation of earth connections, checking fuses and pilot lamps, maintaining good ventilation of motors and other equipments, and lastly, checking of the integrity and gaps of flameproof equipment are also part of maintenance.

Recommended first-aid fire-fighting equipments

Water and foam are not normally suitable for use on fires involving live electric equipment as they may conduct electricity. When it is possible to cut off the current before attempting to extinguish the fire, the most general extinguishing agent is water which would also be effective for dealing with fires in ordinary combustible materials in the vicinity. If, oil or other flammable liquids are involved, foam should be used. In the case of electrical fires where it is not possibnle to cut off the current, and for minor fires, where it is desired to avoid water damage, carbon dioxide or one of the other gaseous extinguishers using halogenated hydrocarbon should be used. Dry powder or dry sand may also be useful on small fires, but use of sand on machinery is inadvisable.

Suitable equipment for dealing with fires in electric wiring and apparatus, which do not contain oil, is shown below:

1.	If the current is cut off and the circuit is dead	Soda-acid extinguisher, portable pumps,	water (gas pressure) extinguisher, water buckets, hose reels
2.	For minor fires and where it is not possible to cut off the current	CO_2 extinguisher; B.C.F. exterguishers;	C.B.M., dry powder (gas pressure) extinguisher

Foam extinguisher should be provided for switch-gears and other equipments containing oil but it should be ensured that the equipment is dead before the foam is used. The extinguishers listed against (2) are also suitable for use on fires in oil-filled apparatus. However, the choice of the exact extinguishing media would depend on particular circumstances and the risk involved.

CHAPTER 23

Electrical Accidents and their Causes

Alternating current at 220 volt is *more dangerous* than direct current at 220 volt. Although A.C. registers 220 virtual volt, it really fluctuates between ± 311 volt.

The resistance of human body, when the skin is slightly wet, has been found to be as low as 300 ohm and as such it acts as a good conductor. The effect of electricity on the human body varies greatly with different persons. Experiments show that A.C. at a frequency of 50 Hz and greater than around 30 volt may produce a severe shock for most people if good contact is made. According to most of the authorities, A.C. with frequencies of 20 to 70 Hz and with currents in excess of 22 milliamp are most dangerous, while D.C. has less severe effect. The immediate effect of an alternating current is to cause the muscles to contract involuntarily and, as such if an A.C. conductor is inadvertently touched, it is impossible to leave it. It is, however, not necessary to touch one of the conductors of a circuit to receive a shock. Any conducting material which is electrified through contact with a live circuit will suffice.

The principal dangers to firemen lie in touching a conductor in the dark or smoke and especially if it has been displaced by the fire or if it has electrified other conducting material, and in directing a jet of water of foam on to live electrical equipment. When a fireman is wet or standing in water, the danger of receiving a fatal shock is greatly increased even when he is wearing a non-conducting helmet. Damp and perspiration under the helmet, combined with its wet exterior tend to provide a path for the current through the body.

In buildings damaged by fire, where the electric wiring has been exposed or dislodged, it is unwise to attempt to touch any wire until it is certain that the circuit has been rendered dead, and without the use of appropriate rubber gloves or without the fireman's axe with insulated handle. If it is absolutely necessary to touch a conductor in a building, the back of the hand shall be employed. If it is live, the shock will then jerk the hand clear and will not cause it to grasp the wire.

Rescuing a person from live electric wiring

If a person has been caught by live electric wire, his body forms a part of the circuit and any effort to touch him is equivalent to touching the circuit. Where high voltages are involved the only solution lies in isolating the current. At lower voltages (3,300 volt and below) rubber gloves, a celing hook or a length of dry hose, preferably rubber lined, may be used to pull the victim clear of the wiring. Even several thickness of sheets of dry newspaper, a woolen coat, or silken cloth may be employed for this purpose in normal households.

In case of D.C. when a person is pulled clear of the circuit, severe burns may result from arcing. For this reason it is always advisable to switch off the current, whenever possible, and that too, speedily. In a person thus rescued, even though the signs of life may appear to be absent, artificial respiration with or without the use of resuscitation apparatus should be resorted to immediately till the person revives or a doctor pronounces the victim dead.

Overhead transmission lines

It is extremely dangerous to climb a standard tower carrying high voltage lines and specially towers on which transformers, switch-gears or boosters are mounted. As a general rule, no tower should be climbed without authorization from the electricity board officials forewarning one of the dangers and of the distance necessary for safety. No rescue of persons on live voltage conductors should be attempted until full clearance is received. Use of metal or metal-reinforced ladders or their manoeuvring in the vicinity of transmission towers or under transmission lines is strictly prohibited, unless carried out under conditions closely controlled by a competent board official.

A particular work may, however, be necessary where overhead transmission lines have fallen on to vehicles or where the vehicle is in contact with them. Any vehicle when in contact with the line, is to be treated as 'live'. Generally, the persons within a vehicle are quite safe from electrocution and the hazard is due to fire arcing through tyres. Electrocution freqently takes place due to panic of the person inside the vehicle. If the person is able to jump out clear of the vehicle without touching any part of the vehicle and the ground at the same time, he will be safe. If the person is unable to jump or is trapped in the vehicle he should be left there until the vehicle can either be pulled safely clear of the line or the line is confirmed to be dead or earthed properly.

Power lines found lying on the ground – even those apparently intended for low voltage – should in no circumstances be moved. In some cases transmission lines can continue to operate with one conductor on the ground and full voltage would automatically be restored immediately it is lifted from the ground. In other cases, it is possible for a line to be re-energized whilst the conductors are being moved.

Safe voltage for general adoption

From the point of view of general safety, 110 volt derived from a single-phase double-wound transformer with the centre point of the secondary winding earthed is considered to be safe. This restriction limits the maximum shock voltage between line and earth to 55 volt rather than 67 volt which will be the app-roximate figure if three phase step-down transformers were used.

Electrical accidents on building sites

Sometimes electrical accidents do take place on building sites, where construction work is going on, due to defective installations and damp conditions. It is desirable to use 110 volt in all such cases particularly for general lighting of the site or within building under construction. The lamps should be of weather-proof construction and firmly mounted on poles. Cables should preferably be of the armoured or screened type including an earthen core to which the metal-work of the lamps or supporting structures of metal should be bonded.

Portable flood lights could also be operated at 110 volt and the cables for feeding the lights should be multi-strand flexible cord pattern with properly and firmly secured fitting in the supporting stand. Plugs for the connection of portable apparatus should be of good metal-clad construction of 30 amp capacity and made of tough rubber or other robust insulation material.

It may be mentioned that in the U.K. and in the United States, the whole range of portable tools suitable for operation at 110 volt are easily available. In India the use of 110 volt system has so far not been introduced except in underground mines.

CHAPTER 24

Fire Risk at Generating Stations—Hints on Safety

The recommendations in this regard are as follows:

Switch-gear

(*1*) Switch-gear should be divided into suitable sections interconnected by circuit breakers. Each section should be separated from adjacent sections by fire-resisting partitions. In major installations, it may be desirable to house the sections in separate buildings.

(*2*) Individual sections of switch-gear should not be normally used for controlling, generating or transforming plant having an aggregate rating of more than 60,000 kVA together with a corresponding amount of feeder supply.

(*3*) Feeder circuits should be connected to the various sections in such a manner as to ensure the maintenance of all essential supplies even with any one section out of commission.

(*4*) The current loading per circuit breaker or busbar should not normally exceed a limit of 2000 amp. When loading individual circuits approach this limit, consideration should be given to the adoption of higher busbar voltage.

(*5*) Separate vent pipes from each phase switch tank or tank group to the outside of the building should be provided where ever possible. These pipes should be reasonably straight, free from sharp bend and projecting in an upward direction so as to ensure the free dispersion of any gases which may be given off from the oil in the switches under normal operating conditions.

(*6*) The primary circuits of voltage transformers should be provided, in addition to protection by suitable fuses, with a sensitive form of automatic protective device such as that for the bus zone, feeder or power transformer circuits. Current-limiting resistances should be employed in series with primary fuses, the carrying capacity being proportional to the time/current rating of the fuses. Secondary circuits should always be protected by suitable fuses installed as near to the voltage (potential) transformer as is safe and practicable.

(*7*) Control or operating busbars, when run near electrically operated switches, should be protected from the effects of fire or short circuit either by screening or by effective separation. Fuses for branch circuits to individual switches should be in the screened or protected area and not near the switches themselves since damage at the fuses may bring about a fault on the control busbars.

Cables

(*8*) Where cables pass through a switch-room floor into a basement or cable tunnel, adequate precautions should be taken to prevent (a) the draining of oil from the switch-room into the basement or tunnel, (b) the slipping of the cables (if burnt away from their dividing boxes) into the basement or tunnel.

(*9*) In addition to the usual cable clamps above the floor level, cables should also be clamped immediately below floor level and in addition to the usual kerb round the cable at floor level each cable or group of cables should, where possible, be protected by a pipe or a form of heat-resisting material rising to a height of at least 45 cm above floor level or terminating just below the cable gland, sealed at the bottom and filled with sand or small pebbles.

(*10*) Alternately, where it is impracticable to use this method of protection, a tight asbestos floor seal should be made and the cable between floor level and dividing box should be wrapped with asbestos webbing. The webbing should not be less than 0.3 cm in thickness and two layers would halflap (i.e. four thickness) and should be put on each cable. To render it non-absorbent to oils, this webbing should be painted with a fire-resisting paint and further protection may be given by providing one wrapping of thin steel tape and wound half lap from the bottom up.

(*11*) Jute serving should be removed from all cables in switch-room basements and tunnels; where this is impracticable, individual cables should be protected by a 10 to 1 mixture of clean, sharp sand and cement applied direct on the jute to a thickness of 5 to 7.5 cm.

(*12*) Main cables connected to any one section of the busbars should be separated from the main cables connected to any other sections by fire-resisting partitions wherever possible.

(*13*) Where existing cables rest on the floor of tunnels or basements, they should be separated into groups of vertical barriers of tiles, brick, concrete, and the trenches so formed should be filled with small pebbles (not sand).

(*14*) Control cables should be divided in the same way as main cables and should follow an entirely different route where control cables are necessarily run in the same basement or tunnel as main cables. Special precautions (such as asbestos lagging, moulded asbestos barriers etc.) should be taken to prevent fire spreading from one set of cables to the other.

Building

(*15*) Buildings should be of fire-resisting construction and any part of the steel framework, which is liable to distortion by fire, should be protected with brickwork concrete or asbestos. Roof trusses may be protected with substantial asbestos shields or moulds to delay the effect of fire.

(*16*) Apparatus other than switch-gear involving special risk of fire or explosion should be segregated into separated sections or in separated buildings. Where such apparatus has to be located in the main building, it should be segregated by fire-resisting partitions into a separate chamber with entrance from the outside of the building.

(*17*) Roof lights should be of wired glass. Other windows should preferably be of plain glass.

(*18*) The type of building construction should be such that relief of the pressure is afforded in the event of an explosion resulting from a failure of switch-gear or other apparatus. Such relief may be provided to varying extents by window glazing, light doors or other means. It is suggested that the combined area of the doors and windows in the outside walls should be of the order of one-third of the total area of the walls.

(*19*) Every switch-room, transformer room or fire-resisting section—unless such room or section is of small size—should be provided with two doors preferabaly at opposite ends. Any emergency door in outer walls should preferably open outwards.

(*20*) Doors between sections should be fire-resisting and self-closing. A sill or other means should be provided at any opening, including ventilation openings, to prevent the flow of oil from one section to the other. The sill should be capable of holding all the oil in each section and should be of a minimum height of 15 cm where two or more transformers are located in one room and where it is not practicable to have barrier walls of full height. Each transformer should be surrounded by a sill to prevent any leakage of oil from one flowing under another.

(*21*) The floors of switch and transformer rooms containing oil-filled apparatus should be provided with suitable drainage so that oil may flow away freely. The drains should pass to soakaways situated outside the buildings and away from exits or entrances—the soakaways consisting of pits, filled with pebbles graded from 2.5 to 5 cm.

(*22*) The floor of each switch-gear cubice should be dished and have an individual drain pipe to the soakaway. Where more than one transformer is located in a room, this practice should be adopted in respect of each separate transformer.

(*23*) The floors of switch-gear cubicles, switch-rooms, transformer rooms should have a minimum slope of 1 in 100 to the drainage pipe, but a slope of 1 in 30 or 1 in 40 should be adopted where possible.

(*24*) Adequate heating and ventilation of switch-rooms to prevent condensation of moisture are essential.

(*25*) Where fire-resisting partitions are of brick, they should not be less than 25 cm in thickness and preferably reinforced. In the case of existing unsectioned switch-houses, such partitions or suitable barriers constructed of asbestos-covered steel, stone or reinforced concrete should be added.

Maintenance of equipments

(*26*) As most fires having an electrical origin are due primarily to failures of insulation, it is important that the insulation of all electrical equipment should get frequent attention and be systematically inspected at regular intervals.

(*27*) All parts of switch-gear and transformers to be examined frequently and carefully for signs of overheating, cracking or for any other indication of incipient failure of insulation.

(*28*) main and auxiliary contacts and protective gear should be inspected and subjected to operation test and test of the oil used in switches and transformers should also be made at regular intervals.

Routine testing of switch-gear

(*29*) Periodical testing of the insulation of such parts under skilled supervision is desirable and the test should be carried out at intervals of about six months. Normally, the tests are only against insulation and over-voltage and the latter should be carried our with an A.C. voltage having a value of not less than 1.6 times the normal (R.M.S.) voltage across the insulations under test.

(*30*) Over-voltage tests should be preceded by a careful inspection of the switch-gear and it is advisable to make measurement of the power loss (watt loss) and current during the test. All records of tests are to be maintained.

Special steps to be taken in an emergency

(*31*) If a fault develops and fails to clear itself automatically owing to the faulty equipment being outside the protected zone, or due to the protective gear failing to operate, the faulty section should be isolated by hand as quickly as possible even though this may involve an interruption of supply. Where a fire results from such a fault and persists after the supply has been cut off, any adjacent sections of the installation, which is likely to be affected by the fire, should also be made dead as soon as possible. This applies particularly where an oil fire has started.

(*32*) It is important that in the event of a fire the local fire brigade should be called immediately, either from a street fire alarm or from a direct telephone line or exchange telephone and the staff concerned should be familiar with them. The telephone number of the local fire brigade should be prominently displayed with requisite instructions on a Fire Notice Board.

Fire prevention and fire-fighting equipments

(*33*) Cooperation with the local fire brigade is essential and from time to time opportunities should be given to the officers of the brigade to make themselves familiar with the layout of the generating station, switch-gear, transformer and with the location of the local fire-fighting appliances provided especially where any alteration or extension have been made. A framed plan showing the position of water supplies, hydrants, means of access and special danger zone and other useful information should be displayed at suitable points.

(*34*) Neither the self-contained breathing apparatus nor the respiratory devices should be used except by men trained in their use and in this connection the local fire brigade should be consulted.

(*35*) Hand fire-fighting appliances should be provided in adequate numbers and so placed that they are readily available to attack any fire in its initial stage on any part of the installation. There should also be an ample supply of dry sand in bins with suitable scoops or shovels.

(*36*) With regard to places such as unattended switch-rooms, where the occurrence of a fire may prevent access, it is essential that a sufficient number of portable fire-fighting appliances be provided outside the place, adjecent to the entrance, e.g. in lobbies or on staircases.

(*37*) For fighting oil fires, following equipments are recommended:

(*a*) Switch-room, indoor transformer and underground sub-station may be protected by : (*i*) Emulsion-forming waterspray projector; (*ii*) CO_2 apparatus, provided risks of re-ignition is adequately covered. These are of fixed installation type. In addition, portable appliances such as (*iii*) hand appliances and sand, and (*iv*) hose and foam equipment to enable foam or watersprays to be produced and applied manually after rendering the circuit dead are also used.

(*b*) Outdoor transformers may be protected by (*i*) fixed apparatus such as emulsion-forming nozzles and (*ii*) portable apparatus using dry chemical powder or foam under certain conditions.

(*38*) Cable basements and cable tunnels of limited cubic capacity may be protected by carbon dioxide apparatus where effective sealing from the outside atmosphere can be ensured and in other cases by ordinary water sprinklers.

Special notes

(*i*)Local fire brigade to be consulted for installing fire hydrants;

(*ii*) It is important that all members of the staff of the electricity undertaking should be familiar with the handling of the fire-fighting appliances installed so that when the occasion for use arises, no time is lost;

(*iii*) All fire appliances and equipments should be properly maintained by trained personnel and kept in a state of readiness, fit for emergency use;

(*iv*) Automatic fire alarms are to be installed at vulnerable places and to be maintained properly;

(*v*) 'Fire Notices' indicating the telephone number of the nearest fire station and actions to be taken in any emergency to be displayed at all places, especially near the hazardous locations;

(*vi*) Mock fire practices, and fire drills to be conducted at regular intervals in which all members of the staff should participate.

(*vii*) The layout of the building with the location of the transformers, switch-gears, underground cable ducts, water supply and fire-fighting equipments installed should be displayed near the main entrance to facilitate the fire-fighting operation.

CHAPTER 25

Part 3: Hydraulics and Water Suppplies for Firemen: A. Introduction

Water is the life blood for the fire service. No amount of appliances or equipment would be of much use if sufficient water is not available at the fire ground. A fireman must be conversant with at least the elementary hydraulics and with the ways in which he could get his requirement of water for fire-fighting from the limited sources available under the most difficult circumstances.

For the purpose of fire-fighting, water in the form of a jet or spray at suitable pressure is required and it is conveyed to the seat of the fire by means of delivery hose and branch pipe. The requisite pressure for producing a good jet or spray is produced by the pump.

Cubical content and weight: Pascal's law of transmission of pressure

Water is virtually incompressible and will readily take the shape of the container. According to Pascal's law, pressure applied anywhere to an enclosed body of fluid is transmitted equally in all directions. Water exerts equal pressure in all directions at the same height from the surface.

If cubical container of 1 m height with the same length and breadth is filled with water completely, it will exert a pressure of $H\rho g$ N/m^2 in all directions at any point at this height, where H = height in metre, ρ = density of water (1000 kg/m^3) and g = 9.81 m/sec^2.

Head and pressure

The downward pressure of a liquid in an open vessel is proportional to its depth or the height of the surface above the point at which the pressure is measured. A cubical container having each side of 1 m length, when filled with water, will be having a mass of water of 1000 kg since the density of water is 1000 kg/m^3.

The force due to gravity on this mass of water is 1000×9.81N and this force is acting on the base of the cube of area of 1 m^2.

If instead of a container with a volume of 1 cu.m, we consider a column of water H metre high but with a square base having each side as 1 m, then the total mass of water will be $H\times1000$ kg and the force exerted by it upon the base will be H×1000×9.81 newton (N). Thus the pressure exerted on 1 sq. m of floor area will be

$$P = 9810\times H \text{ sq m} \tag{25.1}$$

Since N/m^2 (= 1 pascal) is a very small unit, even for measuring the atmospheric pressure, a larger unit of pressure, namely bar, which is equal to 100000 N/m^2 is used. Taking the bar as a unit of pressure, the equation (i) will be

$$P = 0.0981\times H \text{ bar} \tag{25.2}$$

$$\text{or } H = \frac{P}{0.0981}$$

$$\text{or } H = 10.19\times P \text{ meters} \tag{25.3}$$

Atmospheric pressure and suction lift

Nature abhors vacuum—there is air everywhere. It is this atmospheric air which exerts a pressure equally on all sides like the pressure of a column of water. The pressure exerted by this column of 1m square is 101325 N/m^2 (1.013 bar) or approximately 1 bar. This is the atmospheric pressure. When a length of suction hose is connected to the intake of the pump and is lowered into water, there is atmospheric air both inside the suction column, pump casing, and on the outside near the strainer on the water. The result is that the pressure is balanced; if the pump can manage to drive off the air from its casing and the suction hoses connecting it, the pressure inside and the outside will immediately be unbalanced and, the air pressure outside being higher, will immediately push the water through the strainer to the suction column and the pump casing will be filled up with water. The rapidity with which this is done depends on how quickly air is driven off the pump casing and the suction hoses. In other words, this depends on the vacuum produced and the negative pressure (as opposite to the positive pressure with which water is delivered from the pump through the deliveries) available for the suction of water.

When an absolute vacuum is formed in the suction side, i.e. when air is completely driven off from the pump casing and the suction inlet (only theoretically possible), water may be lifted upto a height of 10.35 m (34 ft) only. This lift of water is equivalent to the pressure of $0.0981 \times H = 0.981 \times 10.35 = 1$ bar (app), i.e. the atmospheric pressure.

The atmospheric pressure available has to perform the following tasks:

(*i*) Raising the water from its existing level to the level of the intake of the pump;

(*ii*) Overcoming frictional resistance to the water both on entering and on passing through strainer and suction hose ;

(*iii*) Overcoming the resistance due to the change of direction as the water enters the pump impeller (known as pump entry loss);

(*iv*) A certain proportion of the available atmospheric pressure is used in creating flow in the water.

In view of the factors under items (*ii*) and (*iii*), it is not possible to obtain the full 10.35 m suction lift. There will definitely be some diminution in the static lift and though 8.5m are sometimes obtained under very good conditions, 7.5m can be considered the approximate practical maximum.

Suction lift and output

It may be remembered that greater the suction lift the less will be the output of water as the total potential power available to do the work of

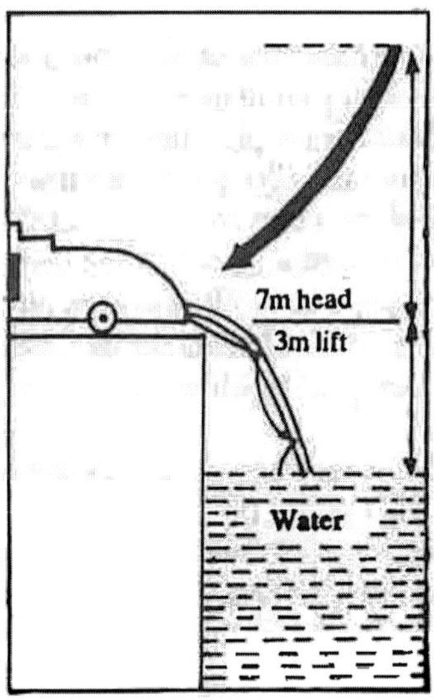

Fig.22 Suction lift and head

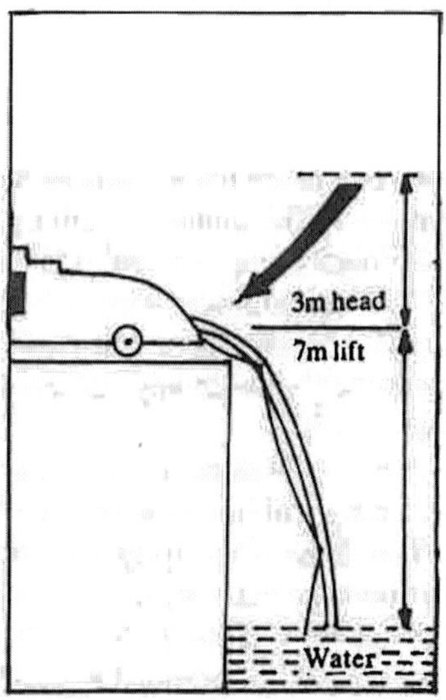

Fig.23 Suction lift and head

raising the water to the pump is 10.35 m, and the net power available can be found out after deducting the static head from this. Thus a pump working from open water with a static lift of 3m will require 3m pressure head for raising the water. This subtracted from 10.35 m will have a pressure equivalent to 7m (app.) to do the rest of the work of overcoming all the resistances and creating flow. Thus, with a static suction lift of 3m (including loss at the pump entry and in the strainers) less the head necessary to create flow; water can be forced through the suction hose to the pump as shown in Fig. 22. Similarly, with a suction lift of 8 m, a pressure equivalent of 10–8m or 2m of water would be left to do the rest of the work, as illustrated in Fig. 23. Hence, it is imperative that the suction lift should be as small as possible and pump should be taken as near as possible to the source of water. The number of suction hoses used should also be minimum, as more number of hoses than what are required will unnecessarily produce friction loss.

Characteristics of centrifugal pump used by the services

Of the different types of pumps available, centrifugal pumps are used everywhere by the fire service on account of their efficiency and light weight. The function of the pump is to impart to the water the necessary energy to create an efficient jet for fire-fighting.

With any centrifugal fire pump working at any given engine speed, the pressure and quantity delivered vary inversely. The pump will give either a high pressure at a low quantity, or a high quantity at a low pressure. The result is that the pump can run at any point between an open discharge and large quantity full throttle with a low pressure, or against a closed valve at full throttle with no quantity and high-pressure without damage to the pump. Flexibility is one of the main advantages of the centrifugal pump; it enables the man on the discharge side of the pump to vary his conditions with safety. Where hand-controlled branch pipe is used, it is possible for the man on the branch pipe to shut off his nozzle completely without any damage to the pump, even when working at a high speed.

It must, of course, be remembered that in such a case the pressure in the pump will immediately rise, probably beyond the strength of the delivery hose. A pump operator knowing his job will immediately retard his throttle when the pressure rises beyond say 7.1kg/sq.cm (110 p.s.i.).

Fig.24 is a typical illustration of the characteristic curve of any centrifugal fire pump. The figures relate to no specific unit but are used simply for purpose of illustration. The curve has been drawn with the vertical scale showing the pump pressure in bar and

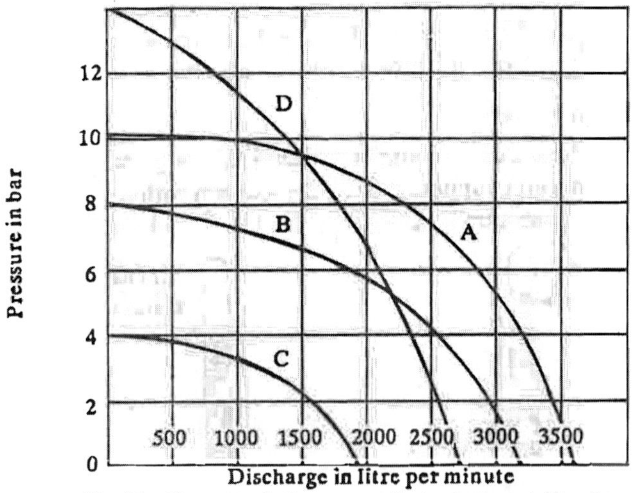

Fig.24 Characteristic curves of a typical centrifugal pump

the horizontal scale showing the quantity of water in litre per minute. The curves A, B and C are pressure–quantity curves at three different constant speeds. With a pump driven by an internal combustion engine with a constant throttle setting, it is impossible to maintain a constant speed when altering the pressure and quantity conditions, as the speed varies with the load on the engine.

Pump entry loss

Apart from loss of pressure available for lifting the water due to friction in the suction column, there is loss of pressure also due to the water entering the pump impeller and changing its directions. This is known as pump entry loss. This is mostly due to the design of the pump and it has been seen that two pumps with same suction lift and same length and diameter of suction hose give different outputs. It is only the best design of the pump and the inlet and the position of the vanes or guide rings that can minimize this loss.

Effect of high altitude

As stated before, the atmospheric pressure is 1 bar or 10.35m (say 10m) head at the sea level. As we go higher up on a mountain or down below a shaft or mine, we will have less or more pressure respectively. This is on an average of 30 cm for every 300m elevation above mean sea level. The output also will decrease four per cent for every 300 m elevation above sea level. Thus a pump working at Simla will not be able to draw water from the same lift at the same engine speed as it would have at the plains. It would also not be able to achieve the maximum of lift 7.5m that is expected out of a good pump at sea level.

Suction lift with hot water

In the case of hot water the suction column and the pump casing become filled with water vapour, thereby the vacuum within the pump is broken and this considerably affects the lift. Fig.25 shows the effect of

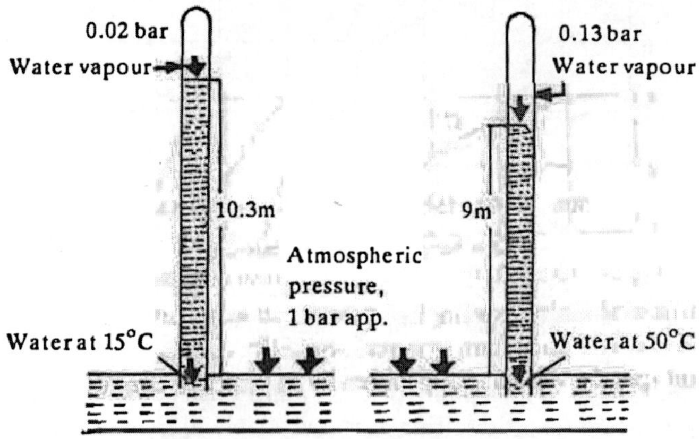

Fig.25 Diagram showing how vapour from hot water fills the space above the liquid in the tube due to evaporation. The higher the temperature, the more will be the space occupied by vapour over liquid with higher vapour pressure.

temperature and water vapour. It may be remembered that the maximum theoretical suction lift is at a comparatively low temperature – in the region of 16^{0}C. The higher the temperature of water, the lower the lift, e.g. at 52^{0}C, the lift will be about 7m whereas at 79^{0}C, it will hardly exceed 2.4m and at about 94^{0}C, the lift will be nil. As per I.S. specification for pumps, the suction lift will decrease one per cent for every 2.8^{0}C rise in water temperature as shown in Fig. 26.

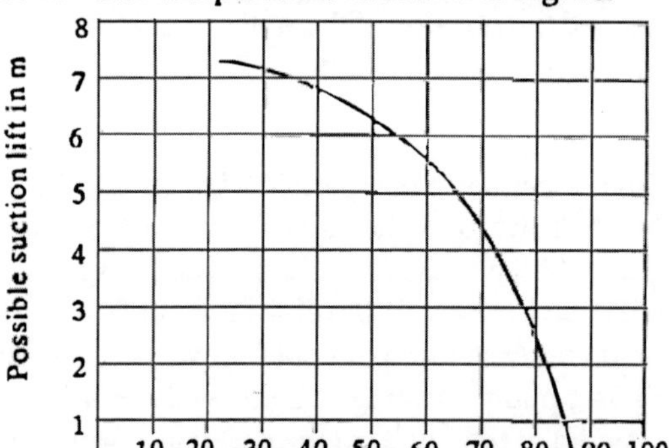

Fig.26 Approximate maximum suction lifts at different temperatures

B. Flow of Water through Pipes

Water flows in a pipe because of the difference of pressure at the two ends. If two tanks of identical capacity are filled to the same level with water and connected by a pipe, there will be no movement of water; but if the level of water in one of the tanks is higher than that in the other, water will always flow from the higher to the lower one. The rate of flow of water moving per second is called the velocity and it is generally expressed in metre per second. The amount of water a pipe can carry depends on its size and on the speed with which water is moving in it.

Capacity per metre run – calculation of velocity and flow

It can be stated that the capacity of 1m of hose of d mm diametre, i.e. the volume of liquid in litres contained in 1 m of hose is equal to

$$\frac{d^2 \times 0.7854 \times 1000}{1000 \times 1000} = \frac{d^2 \times 7.854}{10000} = \frac{8d^2}{10000} \text{ litre app}$$

Thus, if we know the total quantity of water coming out of the pipe line in one minute and divide this figure by the amount of water contained in one metre, we get the velocity in metres per minute, and dividing this figure by 60, we get the velocity in metres/second(m/s).

To calculate the quantity of water passing through a hose or pipe, the following relationship should be used:

$$Q = v \times A$$

where Q = quantity of water in cu.m/sec, v = velocity in m/s and A is the cross-section of the pipe in sq.m.

Now, to find out the discharge from the pipe in litre/min, where the diameter of the hose is in mm, we have to convert Q in cu m/sec to litre/min using the relation

$$Q = \frac{L}{60 \times 1000}$$

(L in litre/min and as 1 cu m = 1000 litre)

Also A, the cross-section of the pipe in sq.m $= d^2 \times 0.7854$

$$= \left(\frac{d}{1000}\right)^2 \times 0.7854,$$

where d is in mm.

Substituting in $Q = v \times A$, we have

$$\frac{L}{1000 \times 60} = v \times \frac{0.7854\,d^2}{1000^2}$$

or $L = vd^2/21.2 = vd^2/20$ (app), i.e. $v = 20L/d^2$

Here, if we know the velocity and the size of the pipe line, we can find out the quantity of water discharged in litre/min by multiplying the velocity in m/sec and the litres contained per metre of the pipe line.

Friction factor and loss

Before proceeding further it will be better to understand the friction factor which indicates the factor of resistance of the flow of water during its passage through any pipe or the hose. It varies according to the type of hose. The aim is to keep this factor very low by suitable design of the hose so that better output of water might be obtained. Loss of pressure due to friction loss depends, amongst other things, upon the friction factor of the pipe. The laws governing the friction loss are the following:

(*i*) It varies directly with the length of the pipe;

(*ii*) For the same velocity, it decreases directly with increase in diameter;

(*iii*) It increases, approximately, as the square of the velocity or rate of flow;

(*iv*) It increases with the roughness of the interior of the pipe;

(*v*) It is, for all practical purpose, independent of pressure.

It may be noted that where large quantities of water are to be pumped through a hose, the reduction of velocity of flow, either by twinning hose lines or by employing hose of larger diameter such as 90 mm is of the greatest importance in reducing friction loss and hence the pressure required at the pump. The reduction of the velocity is also of practical importance. In relay pumping, where water has to be pumped over a long distance, generally two or three lines are provided in parallel. Addition of each line reduces the velocity. Thus in the case of two deliveries, the velocity is reduced to half and the friction factor would be reduced to one-fourth. In the case of three deliveries, the friction factor will be reduced to one-third and the benefit derived will be that water can be pumped to nine times the distance than what would have been possible to get with only one length of delivery.

Velocity and pressure

To force water through a hose, it is evident that sufficient pressure must be available at the pump to overcome all these factors and provide a margin which will yield either an efficient jet in the case of a plain nozzle, or sufficient energy in the case of a spray or diffuser branch to break up the water stream and project the spray efficiently. The pressure required for this purpose varies with the different types of hose in use. The pressure is expressed in terms of the kg/cm^2 or bar required to force a given quantity of water/minute through 25m of the hose. Thus, water leaving the pump and entering the hose does so at a certain pressure and it also travels at a certain velocity. It has both pressure and velocity energy associated with it, as shown in Fig. 27.

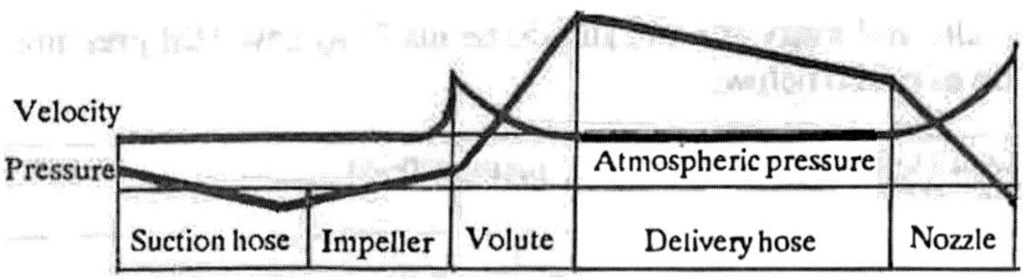

Fig.27 Effect of velocity and pressure at different stages

The nozzle substituted at the end of a line of hose converts the pressure energy to velocity energy. By substituting smaller sizes of nozzles, the velocity of water issuing out of the nozzles is merely increased; as the same quantity of water will have to pass through the reduced orifice the velocity of the outgoing water would increase in proportion. Thus a 25 mm nozzle substituted in place of 70 mm diameter hose (open ended) will increase the speed by 4900/625 = 7.84 times.

Water hammer

Water moving through a pipe has both mass or weight and velocity. If the flow is suddenly stopped, the kinetic energy possessed by the moving water is instantaneously converted into pressure energy which is absorbed by the pipe and its fittings and the sudden shock may rupture the hose.

The kinetic energy may be measured by the formula $1/2\,mv^2$ (where m = mass of water and v = the velocity).

If 1500 litre/min of water is passing through 200m of 70 mm hose (at a velocity of 6m/sec) and the flow is suddenly checked, the kinetic energy, which is a measure of the amount of water hammer, will be ½ × 1500 × 6^2 (app). The total mass of the moving water in this case is 100 (litre per 25 m length of hose) × 8 (number of length) × 1kg (mass of water/per litre) = 800 kg and this is moving at 6 m/sec or nearly 22 km/h. Thus, suddenly stopping the flow of water in the hose would be analogous to driving a motor car of equivalent weight at 22 km/hour into a brick wall.

It may be noted here that total water hammer depends either on the mass of the water moving or on its velocity. Hence, smaller mains of 150 mm or less in diameter are more liable to water hammer than the bigger one.

Discharge through nozzle

For every nozzle there is an optimum pressure at which it will give the best results and every attempt should be made to have that pressure. They are as stated below:

Size of nozzle (mm) Best operation	pressure (bar)
12.5	2.5
15	3.5
20.0	5.0
25.0	7.0

The discharge from a nozzle can be calculated from the formula

$$L=\frac{2}{3}\ d^2\ \sqrt{p}$$

where d = diameter of the nozzle in mm and p is the pressure at the nozzle in bar. Thus the discharge in litre/min, using a 20 mm nozzle at 4 bar pressure

$$=\frac{2}{3}\times 400\times\sqrt{4}=530\ \text{litre/min.}$$

If water is coming down by gravity with a velocity of vm/sec from a tank placed above ground level through a pipe, then $v=g\times t$ where g is the acceleration due to gravity and t is the time taken to describe the space above the ground level. Now dividing both sides by g, we have $v/g=t$. It is also known that the space described by a moving body in t seconds is

$$S\ =\frac{gt^{\ 2}}{2}$$

Substituting v/g for t, we get

$$S\ =\ \frac{1}{2}\times g\times\frac{v}{g}\times\frac{v}{g}$$

i.e. $$S=\frac{v \times v}{2g}=\frac{v^2}{2g}$$

Now, this space may be called the head or height of water (h), i.e. $S=h$. Hence

$$h=\frac{v^2}{2g}$$

or

$$v^2=2gh$$

or

$$v=\sqrt{2gh}$$

The relation $h=v^2/2g$ is called the velocity head.

Loss of head and pressure

When water is flowing through a pipe or hose of a certain diameter with a certain velocity, the loss of head due to friction is dependent upon the velocity of water passing through the delivery hose or pipe and it may be remembered that this loss is uniform throughout as the velocity of water and the diameter of the hose are constant. But if the diameter of the hose is larger the flow will be less. The loss of head or pressure due to friction will also depend on the length of the hose or pipe and its internal construction. In case of delivery hose it will vary depending upon the type of hose, i.e. whether it is unlined canvas, rough rubber-lined or smooth rubber-lined or plastic-lined, and for each type of hose or pipe, there is a constant factor called friction factor (f) which varies according to the type of the hose or pipe and has to be taken into consideration for calculating the friction loss.

Taking into account the laws of friction loss due to the flow of a fluid in a pipe, the formula for calculation of friction loss or loss of head for turbulent flow has been derived as.

$$h_f \text{ (head lost in friction)} = \frac{2flv^2}{Dg}$$

(all measures in metres only)

The loss of pressure in bars (p_f) from the above may also be calculated and written as

$$p_f=\frac{20flv^2}{d}$$

(all measurements in metres except diameter d, which is in mm, l = length in meatare, v = velocity in m/sec).

Where the velocity is not given but the diameter of the hose is given in mm as also l in litre/min, then lossa of pressure (p_f) is

$$p_f = \frac{90000 \times f \times l \times l^2}{d^5} \text{ in bar.}$$

Thus, if we know the quantity of fluid flowing per minute, the length of the hose, diameter of the hose and the friction factor, which may vary from 0.01 to 0.005 according to the type of hose and smoothness of the internal surface of the pipe, we can find out the loss of head or the pressure due to friction loss.

Friction factor

Tests carried out with hose and piping of various sizes suggest that for all practical purposes, the friction (f) for fire service hose of all diameter can, on an average, be reckoned as

Type of hose	Friction factor
Non-percolating hose (90 mm diameter with standard instantaneous coupling)	0.007
All other hose	0.005
Percolating hose (Excluding 90 mm hose)	0.010

PRACTICAL CONSIDERATIONS

Factors affecting loss of pressure due to friction during pumping water over distances in course of fire-fighting is important. Friction factor depends upon the velocity of water which again determines the flow per minute. Hence it can be said that more the output the greater will be the friction. It can also be stated that friction varies as the square of the velocity. These two generalizations are very important.

Knowing the pressure at the branch and the nozzle size, the discharge is easily calculated by the formula

$$l = \frac{2}{3} d^2 \sqrt{p}$$

where d = diameter of the nozzle in mm and p is the branch pressure in bars. After finding out the discharge (l) in litre/min, we may also find out the velocity (v) from the relationship

$$v = \frac{20l}{d^2}$$

From the above, the loss of pressure due to friction can be calculated from the formula

$$p_f = \frac{20\,flv^2}{d}$$

For example, with a 25 mm nozzle at the end of 150m of 70 mm non-percolating hose with a branch pressure of 4 bar and friction factor for the hose as 0.005, both the discharge (l) and the velocity may be calculated first from the aforesaid formula, which come to 830 litre/min and 3.4m/s respectively. Applying the value of v, the velocity, in the formula,

$$p_f = \frac{20\,flv^2}{d}$$

We have

$$p_f = \frac{20\times0.005\times150\times3.4\times3.4}{70} = 2.48 \text{ bar(app)}.$$

To maintain a branch pressure of 4 bar, a pump pressure of 2.48 + 4 = 6.48 bar will therefore be necessary. If twin lines of hose are used from the pump, the total flow of 830 litre/min is divided equally and with the branch pressure of 4 bar, only 415 litre/min will be flowing in each line of hose and the velocity will be 1.7 m/sec. As the velocity is halved, the friction loss is reduced to one quarter, i.e. 0.62 bar and the pump pressure required to maintain a branch pressure of 4 bar will be 0.62 + 4 = 4.62 bar. Thus halving the velocity has reduced the pressure difference between the two ends of the hose line to one quarter. Thus when considerable quantities of water are required to be passed through hose, the reduction of velocity of flow, either by doubling the hose lines or by employing hose of larger diameter has a distinctive advantage in reducing friction loss and the pressure required at the pump.

It is important to remember that at any given flow, friction loss is inversely proportional to the fifth power of the diameter. For instance, comparing 45 mm and 70 mm hoses, it is interesting to note that

$$\left(\frac{70}{45}\right)^5 = 1.56^5 = 9.2$$

Thus, a single length of 45 mm hose will offer the same hydraulic resistance to flow as 9 lengths of 70 mm hose.

PRESSURE LOSS FOR VARYING TYPES OF HOSE

As already stated, sufficient pressure must be available to pump water through hose for varying distances to overcome the friction loss. Depending upon the different sizes of hose, the loss of pressure will vary as per the discharge from the hose. This has been shown in a graphical form in Fig. 28

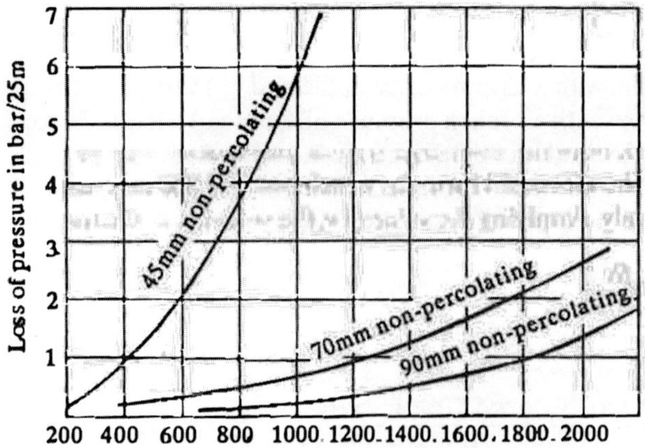

Fig. 28 Pressure loss per 25m for various types of delivery hose

It may be seen from the Fig. 25 that for different rates of discharge, the pressure loss is maximum for 45 mm hose as against 70 or 90 mm hose. In fact, for a 90 mm hose the loss of pressure per 25 m is quite small.

RANGE OF FIRE STREAM AND HEIGHT OF EFFECTIVE JETS

The function of a nozzle is to convert pressure energy into kinetic energy in order to provide a good jet performance. The maximum height to be reached by the water before breaking up depends on two factors, viz. (*i*) sufficient velocity to send the water to the required height, and (*ii*) The correct mass of water for the size of the nozzle. The theoretical height to which water will rise, when projected vertically from a nozzle, is proportional to the square of the velocity as per the formula

$$H=\frac{v^2}{2g}$$

where H = height in metres and v the velocity in m/sec.

The theoretical height for the water is equivalent to the pressure (metre head) at the nozzle, but this height is practically never reached due to various factors. The effective height of an efficient fire-fighting jet is considerably less than the theoretical height.

After comprehensive tests by water engineers, finally a formula has been given by John R. Freeman. After conversion into metric units, this relation is given by

$$H_d = H - \frac{0.43H^2}{d}$$

H_d is the height of the highest drop in metres, H is the metre head of pressure and d, the nozzle diametre in mm. When using this formula, it is accepted that the effective height of a good fire-fighting jet is only about two-third of the height of the highest drop. The formula then becomes:

$$H_e = \frac{2}{3}\left(H - 0.113\frac{H^2}{d}\right)$$

where H_e = the effective height of a jet of water.

Jet reaction

When water is projected from a nozzle, a reaction equal and opposite to the force of the jet takes place at nozzle and the nozzle tends to recoil in the direction opposite to the flow. Hence, people holding the branch must exert sufficient effort towards the jet to overcome this reaction. The whole of the reaction takes place as the water leaves the nozzle and, whether or not it strikes any object, has no effect on the reaction.

The jet reaction in newton can approximately be calculated from the formula

$$R \quad \frac{2\times p\times a}{10}$$

where R = reaction in newton, p = pressure in bar at the nozzle and a = cross-sectional area of the nozzle in sq. mm.

By substituting $0.7854\times d^2$ for a, the formula becomes

$$R \quad \frac{1.57\times p\times d^2}{10}$$

where d = diameter in mm.

Problem: What is the difference between the reaction of the water leaving a 25 mm nozzle as compared with a 12.5 mm nozzle if the pressure in both cases is 7 bar?

Since $R \; \frac{1.57 \times p \times d^2}{10}$

(*a*) For 25 mm nozzle,

$$R \; \frac{1.57 \times 7 \times 25^2}{10} = 687 \text{ newton (app)}$$

(*b*) For a 12.5 mm nozzle,

$$R \; \frac{1.57 \times 7 \times 12.5^2}{10} \approx 172 \text{ newton (app)}$$

Back pressure

If a line of hose is taken up by means of a ladder or otherwise, there will be a back pressure on the pump which is equal to the weight of the column of water of vertical height of the outlet on the hose above the pump.

Thus, if a charged hose is extended up a fire escape so that the vertical height of the outlet is 20m, then the back pressure on the pump is equal to the weight of the 20m column of water, i.e. $0.0981 \times 20 = 1.962$ bar.

This back pressure acts on the pump in a direction opposite to the flow of water so that if 6 bar be the pressure at the pump, the available pump pressure for working purpose will be $6–1.962 = 4.038$ bar, or 4 bar.

In addition to this there will be further reduction of the available pressure for producing the jet due to the friction loss depending upon the quantity of water pumped. Thus, if 1 bar be the loss due to friction in the delivery hose, then only (4–1) or 3 bar will be available for use.

CHAPTER 26

Water Horsepower and Efficiency of Pumps

Power and work

Power is the rate of doing work and work is the product of the force acting against a body in moving its position to a distance in a unit time. Thus work = force × distance.

The rate at which work is performed is measured in watts (W). One watt is the power expended when a resistance of 1 newton is overcome through a distance of 1 metre in 1 second, i.e. 1 Nm of power is defined as work per second.

$$\text{power} = \frac{\text{force(newton)} \times \text{distance(metre)}}{\text{time (second)}}$$

and is expressed in watt.

Water power

This is the power required to deliver a given quantity of water against a given head or pressure in a given time. If flow in litres/ min (*l*) and pump pressure in bars are known, the water power can be determined by multiplying the flow in litre/sec (*l*/60), the head in metres (pump pressure in bars × 10.19) and the force required to raise the water (9.81 newton per litre), i.e.

$$\text{water power } (WP) \qquad 9.81\times\frac{L}{60}\times 10.19\times P$$

or

$$WP = \frac{100\times L\times P}{60} \text{ watt.}$$

Brake power or brake horsepower

This is the effective or useful power developed by a prime mover or electric motor. This usually takes the form of a brake applied to the driving shaft and this effective power is consequently referred to as brake power (BP). The power developed depends on the cubic capacity and the number of cylinders in the engine and varies with the speed of revolutions of the engine.

Pump efficiency

The efficiency of a machine is found by comparing the useful power developed with the total power. It is the ratio of the water power output to the brake power input. No fire pump is 100 per cent efficient and the manufacturers design pumps to give a definite output at a certain percentage of efficiency. If the efficiency of the pump is known, the brake power required to deliver that output can be calculated from the formula

$$BP = \frac{WP}{\text{efficiency}}$$

Water horsepower and pump characteristics

The rating of a pump gives an idea of its performance. Thus in the case of a centrifugal pump of 3500 litre/min capacity running at a high speed and delivering water through lines of delivery hose to hand-controlled branches, if the branches are shut off with the pump running at high speed, it will generate a high pressure without any discharge with the pressure rising to about 10 bar.

If the branches are then opened sufficiently to allow the presure to drop to 8 bar, the output will then fall to 2200 litre/min. Opening the branches further will allow the pressure to drop to 6 bar with the output increasing to about 2850 litre/min. If the brances are now removed completely, allowing the pump to discharge through open ended hose near to its full capacity, there will be no pressure recorded in the gauge.

Thus it is seen that at a fixed opening of the engine throttle, flow increases as pressure is reduced, i.e.

flow × pressure = constant,

or

$F \times P = C.$

But we also know that

$$F \times P \times \frac{5}{3} = \text{water power},$$

where F = flow in litre/min and P is the pressure in bar.

Thus water horsepower depends on the flow and the pressure at which water comes out. In other words, water power depends on the amount of the throttle opening. If this is increased then either or both of F or P will be increased. If water power remains unaltered and the value of P is increased, the value of F must be reduced and vice versa.

It may be stated finally that there is a maximum output for any type of pump when it is working at any particular pressure; if a pump is working at this maximum, no further output can be obtained at that pressure irrespective of the means adopted. The only method of obtaining an increased output at a constant throttle setting is by reducing the pressure against which the pump is working. But such a reduction will only result in an increase of flow, depending on the characteristic curve of the pump, which is graphically represented in Fig. 24. The graph shows the pumps at A, B, C and D running at various speeds with different flow against varying pressure. Curve A shows a nil discharge at 10 bar and maximum quantity (3400 litre/min) at 1 bar.

CHAPTER 27

Water Relay

Water is not always available readily from any source near the fire ground. Water has to be transmitted sometimes over a long distance from the available source by means of pumps and delivery hose to the fire ground by what is known as relay technique. Every fireman should be familiar with certain basic principles of water relay.

The principles of water relay

It has been stated earlier that frictional resistance varies as the square of the velocity of the water passing through the hose. Hence, for a successful relay, this velocity is to be reduced to a minimum by using hose of a large diameter or alternatively by using twin or multiple lines. As a result, when water is being delivered through twin lines of hose, the velocity of water in it is halved and the friction is also reduced to quarter of what would have happened had a single line of delivery hose of the same size been used.

The standard practice in water relay is to pump water at a pressure of 7 bar. Any gain in flow achieved by operating at a higher pressure than 7 bar is likely to be only minimal. Pressures in excess of 7 bar, therefore, should not normally be used unless any specific situation requires it. If a relay is not producing sufficient water within the capabilities of the pump and the pressure is already more than 7 bar, the output can only be improved by increasing the size of the hose or by shortening the distance between the pumps.

If a single line of 70 mm hose can convey 1125 litre/min of water to a distance of 225m, then the same quantity of water can be delivered to four times the original distance, i.e. 900 m, by using twin lines of the same size of hose. The same quantity could be pumped through single 90 mm hose for a distance of 500m or to about 2075m using twin 90 mm hose.

With large capacity pumps in use, however, an output of 4500 litre/min could be pumped through 50m of twin 70 mm hose or through 125 m of twin 90 mm hose. By resorting to larger sized hose the same quantity could be pumped through 325 m of twin 100 mm hose or through 625 m of single 150 mm hose. The hydraulic advantage of using large diameter hose are, therefore, apparent particularly where large quantities of water are involved. More water can be pumped over a given distance or fewer pumps and ancillary equipment used to perform a given task than would be the case when using hose of smaller diameter.

For a long distance relay, increase in pressure of the pump will not solve the problem as after a certain stage, it will reduce the output and addition of longer lengths of hose would also reduce the quantity of water to be delivered. Besides, the strength of the hose will also have to be examined to get more output by increasing the pump pressure. The characteristic curve for a centrifugal pump will show the different output for various pressure and how the output is reduced for pressure in excess of 7 bar.

Considering all these factors, a standard relay practice has to be adopted. This involves the use of a base pump at 7 bar pressure designed to give a minimum of 1600 litre/min with a static lift of 3 m. Pumps should, therefore, be placed into the hose line at such intervals that friction loss or losses due to static heads or gains due to the same in view of an uneven terrain, will just be sufficient to absorb 7 bar pressure.

Adjustment of distance due to variation of level of ground

As a result of the variation in the level of the surface, the pump pressure remaining the same, the distance between the pumps will only has to be adjusted. The procedure is to calculate the difference in height between the two pumps in metres and divide this by 10 to give the static head requirement in bars. This figure should then be divided again by the operating pressure of the relay and the distance between the pumps to be reduced by the resulting fraction.

Difference in the level of less than 10 m may be normally disregarded as that will only amount to a variation of flow by about 7 per cent at the recommended relay pressure of 7 bar.

Thus in a relay operation, if a section of a relay intended to deliver 2250 litre/min using twin lines of 90mm hose has to be laid up a hill of such a gradient that the difference in level over a distance of 20 lengths (the standard relay spacing over level ground with this size of hose) is estimated at 20 m, then dividing this by 10 will give a pressure reduction of 2 bar. This is 2/7, of the recommended relay pressure (7 bar) and the standard relay distance of 20 hose lengths (500 m) should therefore be reduced by 2/7, i.e. to about 14 lengths (350 m).

Alternately, if the relay has to be laid down hill on a similar gradient, the distance between the pumps should be increased by 2/7, i.e. to about 26 lengths of hose (650 m).

Relay pump indicators

To assess the pump positions correctly over varying gradients while pumping water over a long distance, an instrument has been designed to indicate where pumps should be placed. This instrument is known as Relay Pump Indicator and is constructed on the same principle as that for altimeter being sensitive to small changes of altitude. The dial is calibrated in lengths of hose and both friction loss and gradient variation are integrated into the calibration. Existing relay pump indicators are calibrated for 150 mm hose but it can also be calibrated for any other chosen diameter of hose and to incorporate a dial accordingly.

Standard distance

This will depend on the discharge characteristics of the different types and the size of the hose against the flow required at the normal operating pressure of the relay which is 7 bar. The graphs showing the distance in metres as against the flow in litre/min for the various sizes of hose has been plotted in Fig. 29a and Fig 29b. However, it will be useful to remember the following chart relating to the distance between the pumps for delivery of 1125, 2250 and 3500 litre/min of water at 7 bar pressure – the normal pump pressure for relay work. The chart shows the number of 25 lengths of non-percolating hose for different flow.

Types of hose	Nominal flow (litre/min)		
	1125	2250	3500
70 mm single line	9		
70 mm twin lines	36	9	4
90 mm single line	20	5	
90 mm twin line		20	9

Placing of pumps

Pumps should be placed in a relay operation at the distance stated above. Speed is essential in laying the hose and placing the pumps. All

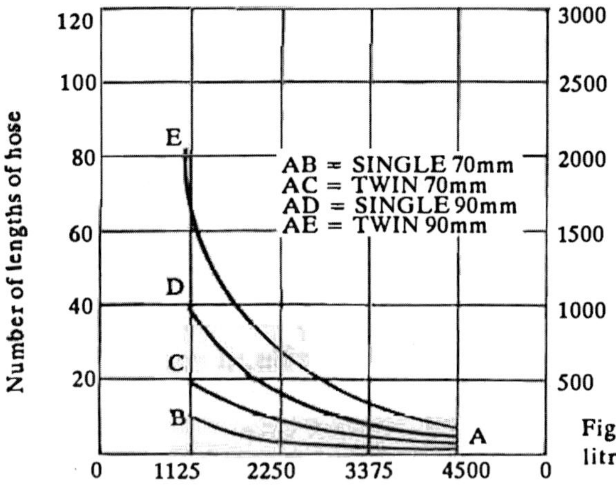

Fig.29a Flow in litre per minute

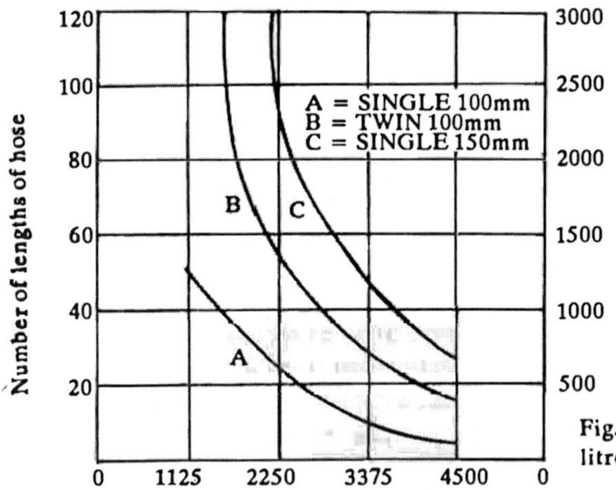

Fig.29b Flow in litre per minute

personnel should see that at least a single line from the nearside delivery is completed first and water is pumped into this line before completing the other line for immediate attack on the fire. The pumps in a relay should all be of the same type designed to give the requisite amount of water. In the standard relay technique, large pumps of a minimum of 1800 litre/min capacity should be used as it is essential to have a minimum flow of 1600 litre/min, when the relay is operating at 7 bar.

There will, however, be no advantage by inserting heavy pumps in a relay composed mainly of the large (1800 litre/min) pumps since the limited capacity of the large pumps will restrict the flow and thus prevent advantage being taken of the larger capacity of the heavy pumps. It should be remembered that the capacity of a relay is governed by the capacity of the smallest or least efficient pump. The supply pump (base pump) in the case of static supply may, however, be of larger capacity. A pump of a higher capacity can compensate for the lift by supplying the same quantity of water at higher engine speed. Small size pumps with small output should never be used in a relay to avoid any bottleneck.

Relay technique

The success of a relay depends not only on the correct spacing of the pumps but on each pump operator having sufficient knowledge to operate his pump correctly with correct interpretation of the gauge reading. The supply pump should be working at the full speed, ensuring that the maximum output is obtained. The pressure at the pump outlet will depend on the quantity being delivered and the friction loss in the delivery hose between the pump and the first intermediate pump. It is rather on the efficiency of the pump operator that the success of the relay depends.

The intermediate pump operator is to keep a constant watch on the compound gauge and the engine throttle should be so regulated as to make the compound gauge needle remain as near zero as possible (i.e. a very slight pressure reading). While operating the relay, if the operator of the first intermediate pump notices that a pressure reading has appeared on the compound gauge, he should immediately conclude that the supply pump has for some reason increased its output and his pump is not running at sufficient speed to take away this quantity of water but is throttling the supply. The pump operator should, therefore, increase the speed of his pump until the compound gauge needle returns to zero showing that he is discharging the maximum amount of water which the supply pump can provide.

On the other hand, if the operator notices that his compound gauge needle has gone over to the vacuum side, it should be obvious to him that his pump is running at too high a speed for the amount of water the supply pump is passing on to him and he is tending to create a vacuum in the delivery hose at the entry to his pump, thereby collapsing the delivery hose and restricting the flow. In such cases the speed of his pump is to be reduced until the needle returns to zero. Any change in the output of the supply pump will be recorded on the gauges of the first intermediate pump and any variation made to the speed of the intermediate pump will be recorded on the compound gauge of the second intermediate pump and so on with all subsequent pumps so that each pump operator by watching these indications is able to keep the relay in balance.

USEFULNESS AND GENERAL UTILITY

In cases of shortage of water supply or the source of water supply being at a distance during any emergency, relay pumping plays a very important part in fire-fighting. It is, however, possible to obtain from a well-organized relay, irrespective of the distance, as large an output of water as could be obtained from one pump working directly from an open water supply on to a nearby fire. For this, the distances between the pumps should be ideal as also the size of the hoses and their layout.

TYPES OF RELAY

Relay pumping: The term relay pumping is used when water is being relayed from one point to another. In this system the supply or base pump after pumping water over a distance (say 0.8 km) discharges the water into a dam. The next pump lifts water from the dam and pumps it over a further distance (which should be equal to the first section) into a second dam. Pump number three, lifts the water from dam number two and pumps it over a further distance and so on as shown in Fig.30.

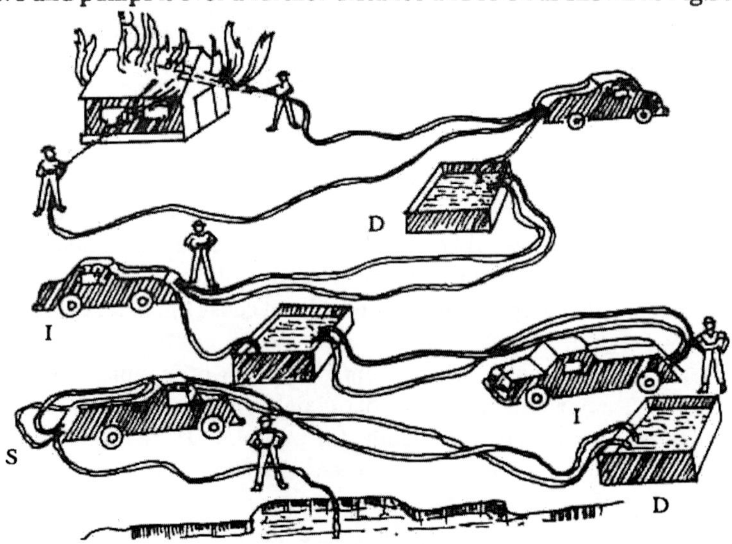

Fig.30 Relay pumping

Series pumping: In the series pumping, (i.e. where the pump No. 1 is called the 'lifting pump') water being pumped over a certain distance is delivered into the collector box or breeching of a second pump called an 'intermediate pump'. This intermediate pump in turn pumps the water over a further distance, which should be the same as the first section into the collector box or breeching of a second intermediate pump. Thus from each pump, the water is finally discharged into the fire being received into the collector box or breeching of the last pump. This is

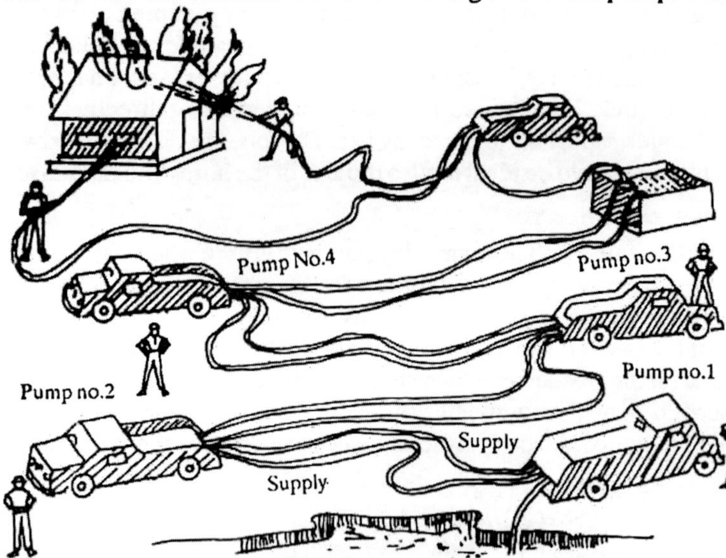

Fig.31 Series pumping

shown in Fig. 31.

It appears that in series pumping, if any one of the pumps used becomes out of order or does not work satisfactorily the whole relay is affected and no water would reach the fire; whereas in relay pumping, so long as there is water in the dam, any temporary defects for a short while in any one of the intermediate pumps will not cause the water to be completely stopped.

Collector pumping: Apart from these two procedures for relay pumping, there is a third process of obtaining a good supply of water in an emergency. This is called collector pumping. Here the fire pump receives water from two or more sources. A supply pump, working from one source of water, pumps into the collector box of the fire pump while a second supply pump, pumping from a second source of water, also pumps water into the collector box of the fire pump. This process is very important in cases where the quantity and pressure of the water at a fire ground from the nearby hydrant is inadequate. The idea is to have one good jet for fighting the fire instead of having too many weak jets.

General considerations : equipments required

Before starting the relay, there are two factors for primary consideration. They are: (*i*) whether there is sufficient length of hose to cover the required distance, and (*ii*) if there are sufficient number of pumps to maintain the necessary pressure after covering the distance. Every relay operation should begin after the answer to these questions are satisfactory.

As for laying the hose, there are two processes—either by means of hose-laying lorries, or by means of hand. As the latter process is unsuitable for a long distance, hose-laying lorries are used. The most suitable speed for hose laying lorries is 32 kmph and the hoses laid should be such as to avoid any traffic obstruction. Sharp bends in the hose should be avoided and there should always be sufficient slack hose to make the bends to the pump as easy as possible. While laying hose for relay (or otherwise), great care must be taken to avoid dragging the hose, especially if there is glass or other debris on the road surface. It is always advisable to have one or more lengths of spare hose of the same type available at each pump for replacing the burst or damaged lengths in the section of the relay for which the pump is responsible. Burst or damaged lengths should only be replaced, as a last resort by hose of lesser diameter (i.e. 90mm hose should not be replaced by 70 mm). Since the capacity of the relay is governed by the smallest diameter of hose employed, even one length of 70 mm diameter hose in a 90 mm relay will restrict the flow to a very considerable extent.

Regarding the pumps, drivers should see that the water cooling system on all pumps is functioning properly. The conical strainers in the suction inlets of intermediate pumps should be removed and connection to the pump made by means of suction adaptor instead of through the collecting heads, and spare pumps should always be readily available to replace the defective ones without any delay during operation.

CHAPTER28

Calculation of Area, Volume and Capacity of Different Types of Containers

(i) The area of a rectangular tank = length × breadth, and its volume = length × breadth × height.

If the dimensions are expressed in metre it will give the result in cu. m. If the result is then multiplied by 1000 (i.e. the number of litres in 1 cu.m.) the total capacity of the tank in litres is obtained. Thus, volume of a rectangular tank $= l \times b \times h$ in cu.m and the litres contained $= l \times b \times h \times 1000$ litre.

(ii) Rectangular tank with a sloping bottom: The volume of such a tank will be length × breadth × average depth. The average depth can beobtained by adding the minimum and the maximum depths at the shallow and deep ends of the tank and dividing by 2. The capacity in litres of this tank will be length × breadth × average depth × 1000 (all units are to be taken in m.)

(iii) Circular tanks and ponds : The volume of a circular tank depends on its area multiplied by its depth, and its water capacity in litres is obtained from this figure (in cu.m) being multiplied by 1000. The area of any circular tank is of course πr^2, where $\pi = 22/7$ and r is the radius of the tank. It may also be represented by the formula $d^2 \times 0.7854$, where d = the diameter of the tank. A quick method of obtaining the approximate capacity in litres of a circular tank of diameter D is $800 \times D^2 \times h$ where D = diameter and h = depth, both in metres.

On the other hand, if for any reason it is impossible to measure the diameter but the circumference is known, the capacity in litres may be obtained approximately by use of the formula $80\,c^2h$ where c = circumference and h = the depth of the tank, both in metres.

(iv) Capacity of irregular shaped tanks: In most cases, the depth of such tanks or lakes is not uniform. The capacity of such ponds or lakes in cubic metres is calculated conservatively by finding out the surface area in square metres and multiplying it by average depth in metres and by two-third of the same, i.e.

$$\text{Capacity} = \frac{2}{3} \times (\text{surface area} \times \text{average depth}) \text{ cu.m}$$

A very approximate estimate of the capacity of such a pond or lake will be 700 × (surface area in sq.m × average depth in m) litre.

Triangular, pyramidal, hexagonal or other geometrical shaped tanks— areas and volumes

(i) Triangle: Area of a triangle = 1/2 base × altitude (altitude is the perpendicular distance from an angle to the base on the opposite side).

If a, b, c represent the length of the sides of the triangle, then the area of the triangle $= \sqrt{s(s-a)(s-b)(s-c)}$.

Here $2s = a + b + c$

or $s = (a + b + c)/2$,

The area multiplied by the depth of the tank will give the volume.

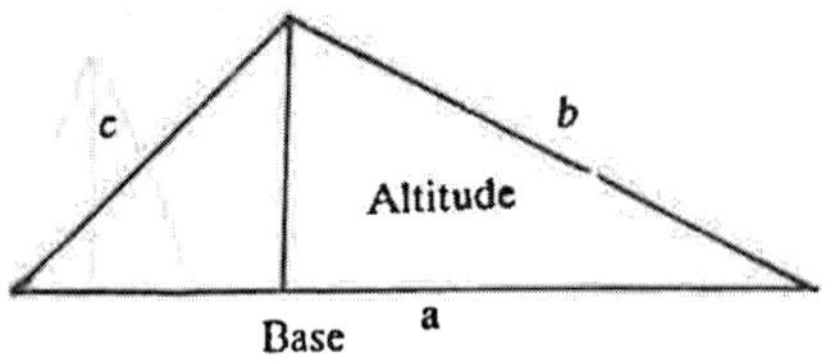

Fig.32

(ii) Parallelogram: Area of a parallelogram $= h \times b$. Here, h = height of the perpendicular distance on the base from the opposite side, b = length of base. The area multiplied by the depth of the container will give the volume.

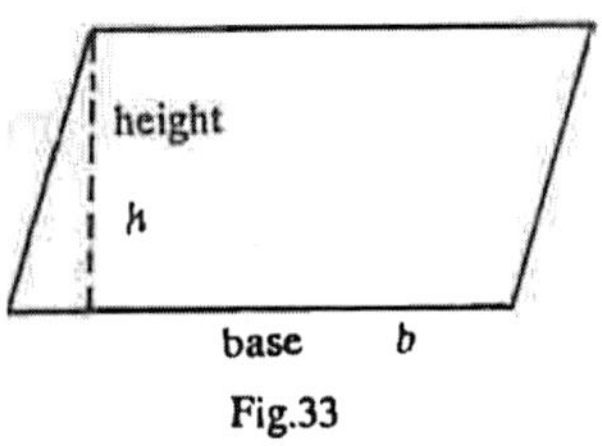

Fig.33

(iii) Trapezoid: Area of a trapezoid $= (a + b)h/2$. The volume will be area × depth of the container. Here, a and b are lengths of the two parallel sides, and h = height.

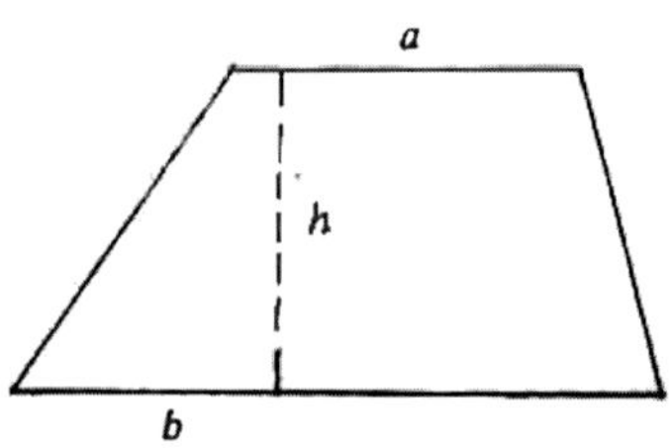

Fig.34

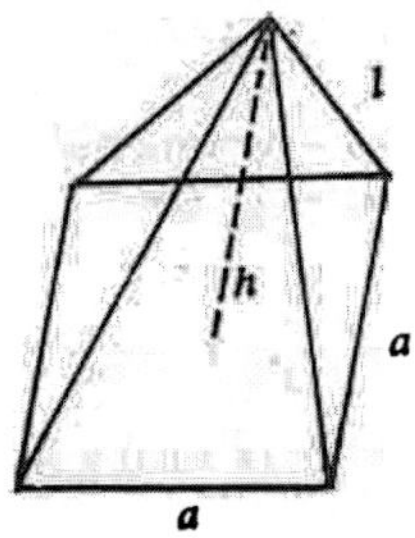

Fig.35

(iv) *Pyramid with regular base:* Lateral area $= 0.5 \times h \times a \times l$, volume $= 1/3\, h \times$ rea of the base.

Here, n = length of side of the base, a = length of each side of the base, h = perpendicular height from vertex to the base, l = slant height.

(v) *Cone*: Area of the curved surface of a cone $= \pi r^2 \sqrt{(r^2 + h^2)}$

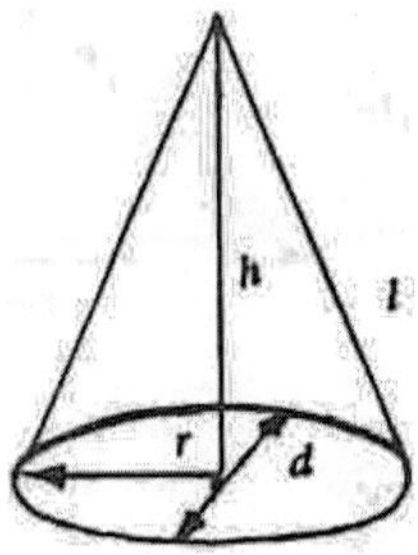

Fig.36

$$\text{Volume} = \frac{\pi \times d^2 \times h}{12}$$

Here r = radius, d = diameter of the base, h = height, l = slant height.

(vi) *Cylinder*: Area of curved surface $= 2\pi r h$

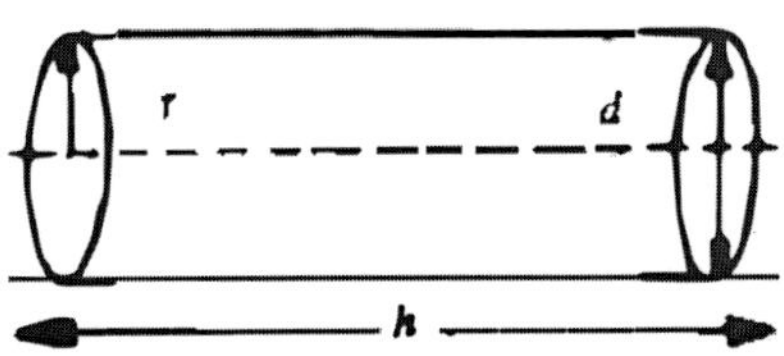

Fig.37

$$\text{Volume} = \frac{\pi \times d^2 \times h}{4}$$

$$= \pi r^2 h$$

Here r = radius, d = diameter, h = height.

CHAPTER 29

Problems Relating to Moving Bodies, Force etc.

Notes

Velocity = distance/time
Power = force$\times$velocity
Impulse = force$\times$time in seconds $= f\times t = mv - mu$
where m = mass of the body, v = final velocity, and u = the initial volecity.
1 watt = 1 joule/sec and the unit of work is joule.
Momentum = mass$\times$velocity $= m\times v$.

Problem 29.1 : 10.8 mega joule of energy are used every hour to drive a generator producing an output of 2 kW of electricity. What is the efficiency of the generator ?

Here 10.8 MJ produce 2 kW of electricity.

Hence, input to the system = 10.8 MJ of energy = 10.8×10^6J

Output from the system = $2\times10^3\times60\times60$ per hour (since 1W = 1 J/sec)

Therefore,

$$\text{efficiency } (E) = \frac{\text{Output}}{\text{Input}}\times100 \quad \frac{2\times10^3\times60\times60\times100}{10.8\times10^6} \quad 66.6\%$$

Problem 29.2 : A bullet leaves a rifle muzzle at 1000 m/sec aimed at a man 500m away. How long will it take to reach the man?

$$v = \frac{d}{t}$$

where d = distance, t = time and v = the velecity.
Therefore

$$t = \frac{d}{v} = \frac{500}{1000} = 0.5 \text{ sec.}$$

Problem 29.3 : A man has to be lowered down a vertical shaft for rescue work. In order to ascertain the length of the rope required, a small stone is dropped down the shaft. It takes 3 seconds to clatter on the bottom. How deep is the shaft?

Since $s = ut + \frac{1}{2}gt^2$

where s = the distance, u the initial velocity, t the time in sec and g = the acceleration due to gravity = 9.81m/sec^2, substituting the values,

$$s = 0 \times t \times \frac{1}{2} \times 9.81 \times 3 \times 3 \quad = \frac{1}{2} \times 9.81 \times 9$$

$$= 44.10 \text{ m.}$$

Problem 29.4: A ball weighs 0.2 kg. It is struck by a bat with a force of 800N. What is the velocity of the ball if the force is applied for (a) 0.2 second and (b) 0.5 second ?

Since $ft = mv - mu$

where f = the force applied, m = mass, v = the final velocity and u = the initial velocity, we have, for (a), from the above formula,

$800 \times 0.2 = 0.2 \times v$

or

$$v = \frac{800 \times 0.2}{0.2} = 8 \text{ m/sec.}$$

Similarly for (b),

$800 \times 0.3 = 0.2v - 0,$

or

$$v = \frac{800 \times 0.3}{0.2} = 12 \text{ m/sec}$$

(The initial velocity in both cases is 0)

Problem 29.5: A fire appliance has a mass of 8 tonnes and is sliding with brakes locked at 5m/sec. If the coefficient of friction is 0.12, how much power (in watt) is being developed?

$$\text{Power} = \frac{\text{work done}}{\text{time taken}} = \frac{\text{force} \times \text{distance}}{\text{time taken}}$$

Also force = mass × acceleration

Frictional force = mass × acceleration × coefficient of friction

= 8 × 1000 × 10 × 0.12 = 9600

Also, velocity $= \frac{\text{distance}}{\text{time}}$

Hence, power = force×velocity = 9600×5 m/sec = 48000 watt.

Problem29.6: A diesel-engine-driven pump has an output at the engine shaft of 63 kW at full power. The fuel consumption at full power is 0.6 litre/min. If the specific gravity of the fuel is 0.75 and calorific value 42,000 kJ/kg, calculate the efficiency of the engine.

(Graduateship Exam – 1984)

Since power is the rate of doing work and one watt is the work equivalent to one joule in one second, output of 63 kW has to be converted into joules.

Work done in one minute = 63×1000×60J (out put)

Fuel consumed = 0.6 litre/min

Mass of fuel consumed per minute = 0.6×0.75 kg

Each kg of fuel has a calorific value of 42,000 kJ

Therefore, the energy available = $0.6 \times 0.75 \times 42000 \times 10^3$J

Also, efficiency of the engine

$$= \frac{\text{output}}{\text{input}} \times 100$$

$$= \frac{\text{work done}}{\text{energy available}} \times 100$$

$$= \frac{63 \times 1000 \times 60}{4.2 \times 10^3 \times 450} \times 100 = 20\%$$

Problem29.7: Two ladders resting on horizontal surface have their heads touching, thus forming an angle of 105^0. One is 6m long and is pitched at an angle of 45^0. Find the length of the second ladder.

(Graduateship Exam – 1982)

This question can be solved by utilizing some trigonometrical functions. Refer to the triangle drawn below.

Let AB and AC represent the two ladders, of which ladder AB is 6m, pitched at an angle of 45^0.

Now, if a perpendicular AD is dropped on BC, we get a right angled triangle ABD. From the trigonometrical relations, we have

$$\frac{AD}{AB} = \text{Sin}45 = \frac{1}{\sqrt{2}}$$

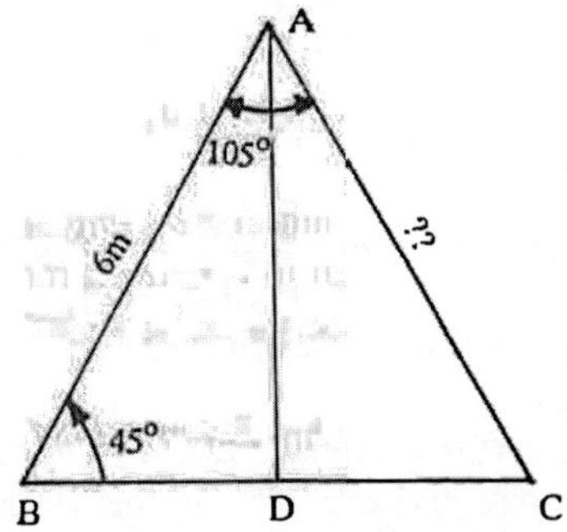

Fig.38

i.e.

$$\frac{AD}{6}=\frac{1}{\sqrt{2}}$$

or

$$Ad=\frac{6}{\sqrt{2}}=4.242 \text{ m}$$

Since $<ABC = 45^0$ and $<BAC = 105^0$

$\therefore <ACB = 30^0$. Also

$$\text{Sin } 30 = \frac{AD}{AC}$$

or

$$\frac{1}{2}=\frac{AD}{AC}$$

whence, AC = 2AD = 2×4.242 = 8.484 m

Problem 29.8: (a) A monitor fixed on a platform 5m above the ground level, when operated at an angle θ, gave a throw of 65 m striking the roof of a building. If the tangent θ is of the order of 4/3, determine the height of the building.

(b) An airfield crash tender, after attaining a velocity of 80km /hour was suddenly brought to rest within a distance of 25m. Calculate the value of the retardation applied and the time taken to stop the vehicle.

(Graduateship Exam – 1986)

(*a*) Let P be the height of the building and Q the position of the moniter and PQ the throw of the jet as shown in the right angled triangle OPQ; OP and OQ are in the ratio of 4:3.

From pythagorus theorem, we have

$$PQ^2 = OQ^2 + OP^2.$$

Substituting the values, we have

$$PQ^2 = 3^2 + 4^2 = 25$$

or

$$PQ = 5.$$

That is PQ = 5. when OP = 4.

Now applying unitary method, if PQ = 65, then

$$OP = \frac{4}{5}\times 65 = 52 \text{ metres.}$$

Hence height of the building is 52 + 5 = 57 metres since the monitor is placed 5m above the ground level.

(*b*) Velocity of the vehicle = 80 km/hour, i.e.

$$\frac{80\times1000}{60\times60}=\frac{200}{9} \text{ m/s}$$

The vechicle was brought to rest in 25 metre. Now, we have to apply the formula

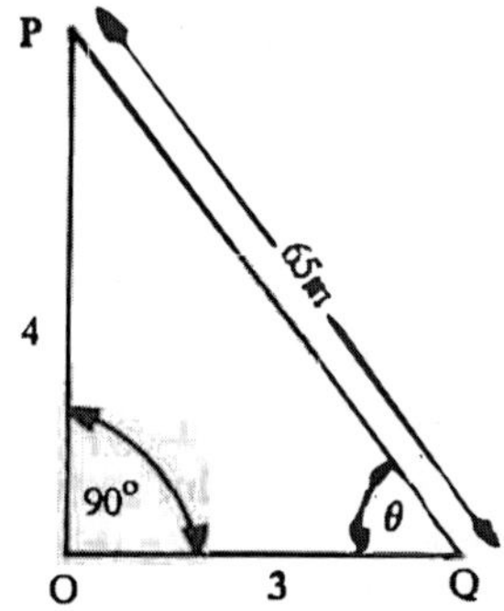

Fig.39

$$v^2 = u^2 - 2fs$$

(since this is a case of retardation).

As the vehicle was suddenly brought to rest, the final velocity $v = 0$ and the initial velocity $= u$

$$u^2 = 2fs \text{ (where } f = \text{ the retardation)}$$

Substituing the avaluesa, we have.

or,

$$\left(\frac{200}{9}\right)^2 = 2\times25\times f \; (s = 25\text{m}). \text{ Hence } f = -9.8746 \text{ m/sec}^2.$$

Also to find out the time taken to stop the vehicle, we have to apply the formula $s = 0.5\,vt$ ($u =$ the initial velocity = 0)

Substituing the values, we have

$$25 = \frac{1}{2}\times\frac{200}{9}\times t$$

or

$$100t = 225$$

or

$$t = 2.25 \text{ second}$$

Problems on Thermal Expansion, Specific Heat and Thermal Capacity

Notes

i) The final length of a body due to expansion from heat can be calculated from the formula $l_t = l_0 (1 + \alpha t)$. Here l_0 = the original length, l_t = the final length due to expansion; α = the coefficient of linear expansion and t = the rise in temperature.

ii) Coefficient of superficial expansion = $\beta = 2\alpha$

iii) Coefficient of cubical expansion = $\gamma = 3\alpha$

iv) The specific heat capacity of a body is the number of joules required to raise 1 kg of the substance through 1^0C = mass × specific heat.

v) Heat lost by a body = heat gained by another body,

or $m_1 \times s_1 \times t_1 = m_2 \times s_2 \times t_2$,

here, m_1 = mass in gm; s_1 = specific heat, t_1 = difference in temperature of one body and m_2 = mass of another body, s_2 = its specific heat, and t_2 the difference in temperature.

Problem 29.9 : A brick having a mass of 2 kg has a temperature of 200°C. It is allowed to cool to 20°C. How much heat has been released ? (Specific heat of brick = 1.2 J/kg).

1 kg of mass raised through 1^0C gives out 1.2 J of heat. Hence 2 kg raised to $(200–20)^0$C = 180^0C will release $180 \times 1.2 \times 2 = 432$ joule of heat.

Problem 29.10 : A 8m long steel girder is built into the brick supporting pillars of a roof. Due to fire, the temperature of the girder increases by 400^0C. What is the final length of the beam at this temperature? (Coefficient of linear expansion of steel = 0.000015).

By applying the formula,

$l_t = l_0 (1 + \alpha t)$ where α = coefficient of linear expansion, we have

$l_t = 8(1 + 0.000015 \times 400)$

$= 8 + 8 \times 0.000015 \times 400$

$= 8 + 0.048 = 8.048$m.

Problem29.11: At 20^0C, a sphere of tin has a radius of 100 mm. It is heated to 80^0C. What is the increase in volume ? (Coefficient of linear expansion of tin = 0.00002).

The coefficient of cubical expansion = 3 × coefficient of linear expansion. In this case, the coefficient of cubical expansion (volumetric expansion) = 3×0.00002 = 0.00006.

The original volume of the sphere $=\frac{4}{3}\times\pi r^3$

$=\frac{4}{3}\times\pi\times100^3$

Hence the increase in volume

$=\frac{4}{3}\times\pi\times100^3\times0.00006\times60$

$=4\times100\times6\times2\times\pi$

$=4800\pi$

$=15085 \text{ mm}^3$

(given by original volume × coefficient of volumetric expansion × rise in temperature).

Problem29.12: A bulk oil storage tank is a cylinder – 7.5 m in diameter and 6m high. It is constructed of steel and filled with heavy fuel oil at 20^0C. If as a result of fire, both tank and the contents are raised to 300^0C, how much oil will be forced out ? (Coefficient of linear expansion of steel is 11.4×10^{-6} and coeffieient of cubical expansion of oil is 900×10^{-6}).

The coefficient of superficial expansion (which refers to area) is twice that of the linear expansion, and the coefficient of cubical expansion (which refers to volume) is thrice that of the linear expansion.

The volume of the tank at 20^0C $=\frac{\pi}{4}d^2h=\frac{\pi}{4}\times7.5^2\times6$

$= 265 \text{ m}^3.$

Increase in volume of the tank at 300^0C

$=265\times3\times11.4\times10^{-6}\times280$

$= 2.54 \text{ m}^3$ (rise in temperature = 280^0C).

Also, increase in the volume of oil

$=265\times900\times10^{-6}\times280 = 66.78\text{m}^3$

Therefore, spillage = increase in volume of oil–increase in volume of tank = 66.78–2.54 = 64.24 m^3.

Problem 29.13: The density of mercury at 0^0C is 13.6 and at 200^0C it is 13.1. Calculate the cubical expansion of mercury.

$$\text{Density} = \frac{\text{mass}}{\text{volume}}$$

Volume of a given mass of mercury at $0^0C = \frac{m}{13.6}$

and volume of the same mass of mercury at $200^0C = \frac{m}{13.1}$

Hence, increase in volume $= \frac{m}{13.1} - \frac{m}{13.6}$

We know that the increase in volume = original volume × coefficient of cubic expansion × rise in temperature

Hence, coefficient of cubical expansion

$$= \frac{\text{increase in volume}}{\text{original volume} \times \text{temperature rise}}$$

Substitutng the values, we have the required cubical expansion

$$= \frac{\frac{m}{13.1} - \frac{m}{13.6}}{\frac{m}{13.6} \times 200} = \frac{m(13.6-13.1)}{13.1 \times 13.6} \times \frac{13.6}{200m}$$

$$= \frac{0.5}{178.16} \times \frac{13.6}{200} = \frac{6.8}{35632}$$

Now, log 6.8 = 0.83251

and log 35632 = 4.55184

Subtracting, we have

$0.83251 - 4.5518 = \bar{3}.71933$

Antilog $\bar{3}.71933 = 0.0001980 = 0.19 \times 10^{-3}$

which is the required cubical expansion of mercury.

Problem 29.14: 15 kg of alcohol at 15^0C is placed in a copper container of mass 75 kg which is at a temperature of 200^0C.

(a) What will be the temperature of alcohol and copper when both have come to the same temperature? Assume that no heat is lost to the surrounding.

(b) What quantity of alcohol will boil off?

Given the specific heat capacity of copper = 400 J/kg^{0}C

Specific heat capacity of alcohol = 2400 J/kg^{0}C

Latent heat of vaporization of alcohol = 8,60,000J/kg
Boiling point of alcohol = 78^0C

(*a*) Heat lost or gained by a body may be calculated from the formula $m \times s \times t$ as stated before. Hence, heat capacity of the copper container = $75 \times 400 \times (200-15)^0$C = 5,550,000 J

Also, heat required to vaporize all alcohol at boiling point

$$= 15 \times 8,60,000 = 12,9000,000 \text{ J}$$

Since there is insufficient heat to vaporize all the material, there will be some alcohol left at boiling point.

Common temperature will therefore be 78^0C.

(*b*) Available heat energy of copper container at 78^0C

$$= 400 \times 75 \times (200-78)^0 \text{ C} = 3,660,000 \text{ J}$$

Energy needed to raise alcohol to boiling point

$$= 2400 \times 15 \times (78 - 15^0) = 2,268,000 \text{ J}$$

Balance of energy available to vaporize alcohol = 1,392,000 J

Hence, alcohol boiled off $= \dfrac{1,392,000}{860000} = 1.62$kg

(Since latent heat of vaporization of alcohol is given as 860,000 J/kg)

Probleam 29.15: Steel components are being hardened by quenching in an oil bath. The component is heated to 760^{0}C and immersed in a bath of oil which is initially at 80^{0}C. Each component causes 15gm of the oil to boil off as it is put into the oil. If each component has a mass of 2.5 kg and there is 100 kg of oil in the bath, what will be the temperature of the oil after 10 components have been quenched? (Membership Exam – 1977)

Given : the latent heat of vaporization of oil = 300 kJ/kg
specific heat capacity of oil = 2100 J/kg^{0}C
specific heat capacity of steel = 460 J/kg^{0}C

Heat lost due to vaporization of oil = $10 \times 0.015 \times 300 = 45$ J (since 15 gm = 0.015 kg).

Total heat content of components = $10 \times 2.5 \times 460 \times 760 \times 10^{-3}$
= 8740 kJ.

Total Heat content of oil at start

$$= 100 \times 2100 \times 80 \times 10^{-3} = 16800 \text{ kJ}$$

Total heat content of bath and components

$$= 16,800 + 8740 - 45 = 25,495 \text{ kJ}$$

Eventually all the components and the oil will come to the same temperature (t) at which they will have 25, 495 kJ of heat.

Therefore,

$$(10\times2.5\times460\times10^{-3}\times t) + (100\times2100\times10^{-3}t)=25{,}495 \text{ J}$$

(Since heat gained $= m \times s \times t$)

$$\therefore t=\frac{25{,}495}{(10\times2.5\times0.46)+(100\times2.1)} = 115^0 \text{C}$$

Problem 29.16: In a petrol engine the piston is made of aluminium and the cylinder liner is of steel. At full load, the temperature in the cylinder is 5200C and, at this temperature, there must be 0.1 mm gap between the piston and the cylinder. The bore is 120mm. What must be the clearance when the engine is cold (20^0 C)? *(Membership Exam – 1977)*

Coefficient of linear expansion of Aluminium $= 25 \times 10^{-6}/^0$C

Coefficient of linear expansion of steal $= 11 \times 10^{-6}/^0$C

At the initial stage, the decrease in diameter of the piston

$$= 119.9\times25\times10^{-6}\times500=1.50 \text{ m.m}$$

Also, the decrease in diameter of the cylinder

$$= 120\times11\times10^{-6}\times500=0.66 \text{ mm}$$

Difference $= 1.50 - 0.66 = 0.84$ mm

Hence, at 20^0C the gap will be $0.84 + 0.1 = 0.94$ mm

Problem 29.17: (a) An electric pan of steel having a 2 kW element, weighing 700 gm and containing 2.5 kg of water at 20^0C is switched on. If no heat is lost to the surroundings, how long it will take to boil off the water to steam ? (Specific heat of steel = 460 J/kg; specific heat of water = 4200 J/kg and latent heat of vaporization of water = 226000 J/kg).

(b) What will be the effect on the rate of heat production when an electric hot plate rated at 1 kW, designed to operate on 440 volt, is connected to 220 volt mains ? *(Graduateship Exam – 1985)*

(a) Heat lost $= E\times C\times t$, = power $\times T$ (in seconds)

Power = 2 kW. Hence, heat lost $= 2000\times t$.

Heat gained by electric pan is $m \times s \times t$ (where m = mass in gm, s = specific heat and t = the difference in temperature).

(i) Hence, heat gained by the pan $= \dfrac{700\times460\times80}{1000} = 25{,}760$ J

(Since 80^0C is the difference in temperature; the weight of the pan to be converted to kg.)

(*ii*) Similarly, heat gained by 2.5 kg of water

$$= 2.5 \times 4200 \times 80 = 84,0000 \text{ J}$$

(*iii*) Heat required for conversion to steam at 100^0C

$$= 2.5 \times 22,60,000 = 56,50,000 \text{ J}$$

Hence, total heat gained,

$$= 25760 + 840000 + 5650000 = 65,15,760 \text{ J}.$$

Since heat lost by one body = heat gained by the other,
heat lost by 2 kg element = total heat gained

or

$$2000 \times T \text{(seconds)} = 65,15,760$$

or

$$T = 65,15,760/(2000 \times 60) = 54.298 \text{ minutes.}$$

(b) Power = $C \times$ voltage;

Hence

$$C = \frac{\text{power}}{\text{voltage}}$$

or

$$C = \frac{1000}{440} = \frac{25}{11} \text{ amp, at 440 volt}$$

Similarly, for 220 volt,

$$C = \frac{1000}{220} = \frac{50}{11} \text{ amp}$$

We also know that $H = 0.24\ C^2Rt$ cal, where H = heat produced, C = current amp, R = resistance is ohm, t = time in second.

Hence, when the hot plate is connected to 220 volt mains,

$$\text{the heat produced} = 0.24 \times \frac{50}{11} \times \frac{50}{11} \times \frac{220 \times 11}{50} \times t = 218t$$

$$\left(\text{since } R = \frac{E}{C} = \frac{220 \times 11}{50} \text{ for 220 volt}\right)$$

When it is connected to 440 volt main, the heat produced will be

$$0.24 \times \frac{25}{11} \times \frac{25}{11} \times \frac{440 \times 11}{25} \times t = 240\ t$$

Hence for a given length of time, when the hot plate is connected to 220 volt, the current flow will be double, but the heat produced will be the same

Problem 29.18: *A cylindrical storage tank made of mild steel plates, measures 10m in diameter and 5.6m in height and is filled with heavy oil at 20^0C. Calculate the quantity of oil spilling out of the tank if the temperature of the tank and the contents are raised to 27^0C as a result of overheating. (Coefficient of the linear expansion of mild steel is 0.000012, and the coefficient of cubical expansion of oil is 0.0009)*

(Graduateship Exam – 1985)

Diameter of the tank = 10m and height of the tank = 5.6 m

Hence, the volume of the tank

$$= \frac{22}{7} \times \frac{10}{2} \times \frac{10}{2} \times 5.6 \text{ cu m.}$$

$$= 440 \text{ cu.m.}$$

Initial temperature = 20^0C

Final temperature = 27^0C

Hence, rise in temperature = 7^0C

Since the coefficient of linear expansion of mild steel = 0.000012, and that for cubical expansion of mild steel = 3× 0.000012, the expansion of the tank, therefore, will be $440 \times 0.000012 \times 3 \times 7 = 0.110$ cu.m.

Similarly, volumetric expansion of the oil

$$= 440 \times 0.0009 \times 7 = 2.772 \text{ cum}$$

Therefore, the quantity of the oil spilling over

$$= 2.772 - 0.110 = 2.662 \text{ cum.}$$

Problems Relating to Expansion of Gases

Notes

By combining Boyle's and Charles' law for gases, we get

$$\frac{P_1 V_1}{T_1} = \frac{P_2 V_2}{T_2} \quad \text{where}$$

P_1 = original pressure, P_2 = increased pressure, V_1 = original volume, V_2 = increased volume, T_1 = original temperature, T_2 = increased temperature

(T_1 and T_2 are in ^{0}K, i.e. -273^0C = 0^0K absolute temperature)

Problem 29.19: A cylinder charged to 200 bar has a volume of 24,000 mm^3 at 27^0C. It is involved in a fire and reaches a temperature of 327^0C; its volume increases to 30,000 mm^3. What will be the pressure in the cylinder?

Since

$$\frac{P_1 V_1}{T_1} = \frac{P_2 V_2}{T_2}$$

Hence,

the increased pressure, $P_2 = \frac{P_1 V_1 \times T_2}{T_1 \times V_2}$

$$P_2 = \frac{200 \times 24000 \times 600}{300 \times 30,000} = 320 \text{ bar.}$$

Problem29.20: A cylinder at −230C contains gas at a pressure of 10 bar. If the bursting pressure = 50 bar, at what temperature does failure take place?

By applying the formula

$$\frac{P_1 V_1}{T_1} = \frac{P_2 V_2}{T_2}$$

and also considering that $V_1 = V_2$, we have

$$\frac{P_1}{T_1} = \frac{P_2}{T_2}$$

So that

$$T_2 = \frac{P_2 T_1}{P_1}$$

or

$$T_2 = \frac{50}{10} \times 250 = 1250\ ^0K = 1250 - 273 = 977\ ^0C$$

Problems Relating to Density and Specific Gravity

Notes

$$\text{Density} = \frac{\text{mass}}{\text{volume}}$$

Density of water = 1000 kg/m^3

Also, weight of 1 litre of water = 1 kg and 1000 kg of water occupy 1 m^3.

Problem 29.21: A stone weighing 6 kg is lowered into a vessel full of water. The overflow amounts to 2.5 kg. What is the density of stone and upthrust on it ?

i) 2.5 kg of water has a volume of 2.5 litre

Therefore, the volume of stone = 2.5 litre = 0.0025 m^3 (1 m^3 = 1000 litres).

$$\text{Density } \frac{\text{mass}}{\text{volume}} \quad \frac{6}{0.0025} \quad 2400 \text{ kg/m}^3$$

ii) Upthrust of the fluid displaced = 2.5 kg×g = 2.5×9.81 = 24.525 N.

Problem 29.22: A tank has a length of 2m and breadth of 1 m and is 1 m deep and has a mass of 50 kg. It is floating in water (density = 1000 kg/m^3). What height of the tank is above water ?

The mass of the tank is 50 kg.

Hence, mass of water displaced = 50 kg

Now 1000 kg of water occupy 1 m^3

Therefore 50 kg would occupy $\frac{1}{1000} \times 50 = 0.05 \text{ m}^3$

Area of the tank = 2m^2

Therefore, height of tank below water = $\frac{0.05}{2} = 0.025$ m

Total height = 1m

Height of tank above water (1–0.025) m = 0.975 m.

Praoblem 29.23: A tanker is loaded with 50,000 m^3 of fuel oil of density 800 kg/m^3. After unloading, 5% of the mass discharged must be loaded as water ballast. What mass of water is required ?

$$\text{Density } \frac{\text{mass}}{\text{volume}}$$

Hence, mass = density×volume

$= 800 \times 50{,}000$ kg

$= \frac{800 \times 50{,}000}{1000}$ 40,000 tonne

Also, water ballast = 5% of the mass

$= 40{,}000 \times \frac{5}{100} = 2{,}000$ tonne

Problem 29.24: A road tanker falls into a river and gets submerged with 1m water above it. The tanker is carrying 12,000 litre of naphtha and the weight of the tanker is 13.6 tonne. As a fire officer called out to extricate the submerged tanker from the water, work out what capacity of crane you will order for

a) lifting the tanker to surface; and

b) lifting the tanker 1m above water.

(Specific gravity of petroleum product = 0.75 and the tanker is made of steel and the specific density of steel = 8.5, ignoring tyres etc).

(Graduateship Exam – 1986)

Weight of the empty tank = 13.6 tonne

Weight of naphtha = 12,000 × 0.75 (specific gravity)

= 9,000 kg = 9 tonne

(since 1 litre weighs 1 kg and 1000 kg = 1 tonnes)

Hence, total weight of tank (including naphtha)

= 13.6 + 9 = 22.6 tonne

a) Therefore, the theoretical capacity to lift the tanker out of 1m of water will be 22.6 tonnes.

b) Also, the theoretical capacity for lifting the tanker just to the surface of water, should be equal the total weight of the tanker with naphtha, less the weight of the water displaced by the tanker, (i.e. the volume of the tanker) = 22.6–13.6 = 9 tonne.

Problem 29.25: Bell metal is composed of 4 parts of copper to 1 part of tin by weight. If the density of copper and tin is 8900 kg/m^3 and 7300 kg/m^3 respectively, calculate the density of bell metal.

(Graduateship Exam – 1986)

Let M be the mass of tin in the alloy. Then mass of copper = $4M$

Therefore mass of alloy = $M + 4M = 5M$

Also, total volume of the alloy = volume of copper + volume of tin.

Since

$$D=\frac{M}{V}$$

and

$$V=\frac{M}{D},$$

the volume of alloy

$$=\frac{4M}{8900}+\frac{M}{7300}$$

$$\frac{(4\times7300)\ M+8900\ M}{8900\ \times7300}\quad\frac{M\,[(4\times7300)+8900\ ]}{8900\ \times7300}$$

$$\text{Density of bell metal} = \frac{5\,M\,(8900 \times 7300)}{M\,[(4 \times 7300) + 8900]} = 8526.24\ \text{kg/m}^3$$

Problem 29.26: a) A fully covered, mild steel water tank measures 3m×2m×2m height. The tank is made of 4mm thick m.s. plates and the bottom plate is 5 mm thick. It is mounted on the terrace of a 22 m high building on four supporting pillars, each 50 cm×50 cm and 1 m high. If the specific gravity of mild steel is taken as 7.462 times that of water, calculate the load that will be borne on each sq. cm of the pillars when the tank is full. Ignore filling manhole and other connections or the sagging effect of the tank.

b) If the base of the tank is connected to a downcomer pipe, what will be the static pressure at the lower hydrant 1m above the ground?

(Graduateship Exam – 1987)

a) Volume of the bottom plate = $3 \times 2 \times 0.005$ m = $0.03\ \text{m}^3$

Volume of the remaining plates including the top and the sides = $(3 \times 2 \times 3) \times 0.004 + (2 \times 2 \times 2) \times 0.004 = 0.104\ \text{m}^3$

Hence, the total volume of the steel plates of the water tank = 0.03 + 0.104 = $0.134\ \text{m}^3$

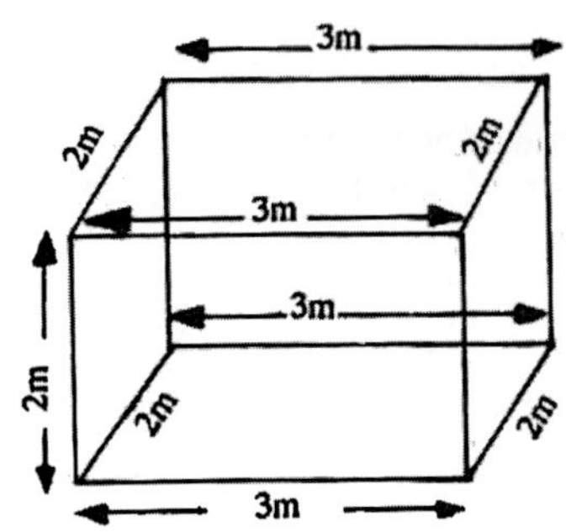

Fig.40

Therefore, the mass of the steel
$= 0.134 \times 7.462 \times 1000$kg
= 999.908kg
(since specific gravity of steel = 7.462)

Mass of water contained in the tank
$= 3 \times 2 \times 2 \times 1000$
= 12,000 kg
(since 1 m^3 of water weighs 1000 kg)

Therefore, total mass on 4 pillars
= 999.908 + 12,000 = 12,999.9 kg.

Hence, mass on each pillar of surface area of

$$50\text{cm} \times 50\ \text{cm} = \frac{12999.9}{4} = 3249.975\ \text{kg} \text{ or, say } 3250\ \text{kg}$$

Therefore, load on each cm^2 of the pillar

$$= \frac{3250}{50 \times 50}$$

$= 1.3$ kg per cm^2

b) Static pressure $p = 0.0981 \times h$ bar

Total height of the building = 22 m
Height of the pillar = 1m
Hence, total height = 23m
Also, as the lowest hydrant is 1m above ground floor, the effective height = 23–1 = 22m

Therefore p = 0.0981×22 = 2.158 bar.

Problem 29.27: A 4m by 3m internally oblong tank contains 100 litre of salt solution (specific gravity = 1.15) and the same weight of oil (specific gravity = 0.95) floating on it without mixing. Find the height of the upper oil surface, above the base of the tank.

(Associate Membership Exam – 1957)

Weight of salt solution = weight of oil
Weight of 100 litre of salt solution = 100×1.15 kg (since weight of 1 litre of fresh water = 1 kg)

Weight of oil = 4×3×x×0.95 kg (where x = the height of oil in metres)
Hence,

$$x = \frac{100 \times 1.15}{4 \times 3 \times 0.95} = \frac{115}{11.4} = 10.08 \text{ m}$$

Also, weight of 100 litre salt solution = 100×1.15 kg

If y be the height of salt solution, with 4m by 3m measurement, then this volume of salt solution will exert a weight of y×4×3×1.15 kg. This is equal to 100×1.15kg.

$$\text{Hence, } y = \frac{100 \times 1.15}{4 \times 3 \times 1.15} = 8.33 \text{ m}$$

Therefore the total height = 10.08 + 8.33 = 18.41 m

Problem 29.28: A pipe with 200 mm internal diameter and 4 m length with 25mm thick walls is filled with water. Calculate the total weight of the pipe and its contents if the material forming the walls of the pipe has a specific gravity of 3.6. (Associate membership Exam — 1960)

Weight of water in 200 mm pipe (4m long)

$$= \frac{8d^2}{10{,}000} \times 4\text{kg} = \frac{8 \times 200 \times 200}{10000} \times 4\text{kg} = 128 \text{ kg}$$

(since capacity of a pipe in litres/ metre = $8d^2/1000$ and 1 litre of water weighs 1 kg).

External diamater of the pipe with 25mm thickness all around = 200 + 25 + 25 = 250 mm.

Weight of water contained in 250 mm pipe of 4 m length

$$= \frac{8\times250\times250}{10000}\times4=50\times4=200\text{ kg}$$

Weight of metal in 250 mm pipe with specific gravity of 3.6 = (200–128)×3.6 = 72×3.6 kg.
Hence total weight of metal and water

$$= (72\times3.6) + 128\text{ kg } = 259.2 + 128 = 387.2\text{ kg}$$

Problem 29.29: Pump capacities are sometimes rated at tonne per hour. How many litre/ min of salt water with a density of 1.027 would equal an output of 60 tonne per hour?

60 tonne per hour = 1 tonne/minute = 1000 litre/min. Since salt water is heavier than ordinary water by 1.027 times, the requisite flow rate of salt water

$$\frac{1\times1000}{1.02} = 980.39\text{ litre/min.}$$

Hydraulics and Water Supply for Firemen

All fire officers should have basic knowledge about hydraulics and the problems relating to the availability of water on the fire ground for fire fighting. The subject has been dealt with in the relevant chapter in this book.

Some typical problems have been solved here in the C.G.S. system (in S.I. units). For the various formulae used in solving the problems and the related other information, Appendix 2 may be referred to.

Problem 29.30: A stand pipe is fitted to a hydrant on a 100 mm water mains. A gauge is fitted and the hydrant turned on. The gauge reads 5 bar. With a nozzle fitted and water flowing at 1500 litre per minute, the guage reads 3.75 bar. What is the maximum output from the hydrant ?

Maximum ouput from a hydrant may be calculated from the formula

$$\text{Output} = L\times\sqrt{\frac{S.P.}{S.P.-R.P.}}$$

where *S.P.* = static pressure
R.P. = running pressure
L = flow of water in litre/ min
Substituting the values, we have the maximum output

$$= 1500 \times \sqrt{\frac{5}{5-3.75}} \quad 1500 \times \sqrt{\frac{5}{1.25}}$$

$$= 1500 \times \sqrt{4} = 1500 \times 2 = 3000 \text{ litre.}$$

Problem 29.31: A water tender working at a pressure of 7 bar, pumps water through a line of hose 70 mm in diameter and 84 metre in length, delivering 735 litre of water per minute through the nozzle attached with the hose. If 30% is the loss of pressure due to friction when water reaches the nozzle, detennine the friction factor of the hose.

(Graduateship Exam — 1985)

Loss of pressure due to friction = 30% of the original pressure

$$= \frac{30 \times 7}{100} = 2.1 \text{ bar}$$

Also, velocity of water $\frac{21.2 \times 735}{70 \times 70} = 318$

(from the formula $v = \frac{21.2\,L}{d^2}$)

Also, loss of pressure due to friction

$$P_f = \frac{20\,flv^2}{d}$$

Substituting, we have

$$P_f = \frac{20 \times f \times 84 \times 3.18 \times 3.18}{70}$$

or

$$2.1 = \frac{20 \times f \times 84 \times \times 3.18 \times 3.18}{70}$$

or

$$f \text{ (friction factor)} \quad \frac{2.1 \times 70}{20 \times 84 \times 3.18 \times 3.18} = 0.00864$$

Problem 29.32: A pipe, 120 m long and 10 cm in diameter, is the outlet from a reservoir. The coefficient of friction is 0.002 and the pipe descends at a gradient of 1 in 12. If the issuing water shows no loss of head during its flow, detennine the velocity of water.

(Associate Membership Exam — 1951)

Since the gradient of the pipe is 1 in 12, the loss of head due to gravity = 120/12

By applying the formula for the loss of head, we have

$$h_f = \frac{2flv^2}{Dg}$$

or

$$10\text{ (loss of head)} = \frac{2\times 0.002\times 120\times v^2}{\frac{1}{10}\times 9.81} = \frac{2\times 0.0021\times 120\times v^2}{0.981}$$

or

$$v^2 = \frac{10\times 0.981}{2\times 0.002\times 120} = \frac{9.81}{0.04\times 12} = 20.43$$

or

$$v = 4.5\ \text{m}.$$

Problem 29.33: (a) A pipe with an internal diameter of 15 cm slopes uniformly from a reservoir which is 500 m away and is 300 m above the outlet of the pipe. What will be the pressure caused by the difference in height.

(b) How much pressure will be lost by friction when water flows through the pipe at 3 m/sec (coefficient of friction to be taken as 0.0025).

(a) The pressure caused by the difference in height

$P = 0.0981 \times H$ bar $= 0.0981 \times 300 = 29.43$ bar

(b) Pressure lost due to friction because of water flowing along 500 m with a velocity of 3 m/sec is given by the formula

$$P_f = \frac{20\,flv^2}{d}$$

Substituting the values, we have

$$P_f = \frac{20\times 0.0025\times 500\times 9}{15} = 20\times 0.0025\times 100\times 3 = 15\ \text{bar}$$

Problem 29.34: A closed channel is in the shape of an equilateral triangle with a perimeter of 3 m. Water is flowing continuously through it at 1 m/sec. What will be the diameter of a cylindrical pipe which will carry the same total volume but at 10 m/sec.

Since the area of an equilateral triangle $= 0.433\times\text{side}^2$, the area of the closed channel $= 0.433\times 1^2 = 0.433$ sq metre.

Discharge per minute through this closed channel may be determined by the formula

$Q = Av$ (see Appendix 2)

or

$Q = 0.433\times 1\times 60\times 1000 = 433\times 60$ l/min (since 1 m^3 contains 1000 litre of water)

Also, $L = \frac{vd^2}{20}$ (see Appendix 2)

Substituting the values for the velocity through the cylindrical pipe, we have

$$L=\frac{10\,d^2}{20}$$

or

$$\frac{1}{2}d^2=L$$

or

$$\frac{1}{2}d^2=433\times 60$$

or

$$d^2=433\times 60\times 2$$

or

$d=227.94$ mm or say 228 mm.

Problem 29.35: A 100 mm diameter pipeline, 800 metres long and having a coefficient of friction of 0.02, is laid down a steady slope. The velocity of the water in the pipe line is 2m/sec. The water pressure in the inlet and outlet is 4 bar each. Calculate the gradient of the pipe.

(Graduateship Exam – 1970)

Loss of pressure in the pipe line $P_f=\frac{20\,flv\,2}{d}$

Substituting the values, we have,

$$\frac{20\times 0.02\times 800\times 2^2}{100}=2\times 0.2\times 32=12.8\ \text{bar}$$

Also,

$$H=10.19\times P=10.19\times 12.8=130.4\ \text{m.}$$

The pressure lost at the inlet and outlet = 4 bar, i.e. the pressure lost due to the friction is overcome by the pressure gained due to gravity in the gradient of 800 metre of the pipe line. Hence the requisite gradient

$$1\text{ in }\frac{800}{130.4}$$

or

1 in 6.13m or say 1 in 6.

Problem 29.36: A pipe, 120m long and 150mm in diameter, is the outlet for a reservoir. The coefficient of friction is 0.02 and the pipe descends at a gradient of 1 in 12. If the issuing water shows no loss of head during its flow, determine its velocity in m/sec.

(Associate Membership Exam — 1951)

Here, as the water coming out of the pipe along the gradient shows no loss of head, the loss of metre head due to friction in 100 m of the pipe is made good due to the effect of gravity caused by the gradient of the pipe (1 in 12).

The loss of head due to gravity $= \frac{120}{12} = 10$

Since $P = 0.0981 \times H$ bar, we have, after substitution for H,

$$P = 0.0981 \times 10 = 0.981 \text{ bar}$$

Also, the loss of pressure $= \frac{20flv^2}{d} = 0.981$ bar

or

$$0.981 = \frac{20 \times 0.02 \times 120 \times v^2}{150}$$

or

$$0.981 \times 150 = 20 \times 0.02 \times 120 v^2$$

or

$$v^2 = \frac{150 \times 0.981}{2 \times 2 \times 12} \quad 3\ 07$$

or

$$v = 1.75 \text{ m/sec}$$

Problem 29.37: Find the specific speed of a centrifugal pump delivering 0.75 m^3/sec against a net head of 15m when running at 725 r.p.m.

Here $Q = 0.75\ m^3$/sec and $H = 15$ m and $N = 725$ r.p.m.

Specific speed $N_s = \frac{N \times \sqrt{Q}}{H^{3/4}}$

Substituting the values, the specific speed $= \frac{725 \times \sqrt{0.75}}{15^{0.75}}$

$= 82.4$ units.

Problem 29.38: A solid cube of 12 cm side is made of a material which is melted and cast in the form of an upright regular square pyramid standing on a square base of 18 cm side. Assuming that 10% of the material is lost in the process, determine the height of the resulting pyramid and volume of water in litre such a pyramid will hold.

(Grad, I.Fire.E Exam — 1960)

Volume of 12 cm side cube = $12\times12\times12=1728$cc

Volume of pyramid at 10% less volume = $\frac{1728\times9}{10}=1555.2$ cc

Area of base of pyramid = $18\times18 = 324$sq. cm

Also, volume of pyramid = $\frac{\text{area of base}\times\text{ height}}{3}$

Therefore,

height = $\frac{3\times\text{volume of pyramid}}{\text{area of base}}=\frac{1555.2\times3}{324}=14.4$ cm.

Volume of pyramid = 1555.2 cc = 0.0015552 cu.m

Therefore, water contained = $1000\times0.001552=1.55$ litre.

Problem 29.39: A totally enclosed rectangular tank with external dimensions of 3m by 1m with 1m depth, contains 1.5 tonne of water. Find (a) the depth of water if the tank stands on one of its two square faces.

(b) The total area of internal surface wet by water when the tank rests on one of its other four faces. (Associate Membership Exam – 1948)

(*a*) The tank contains 1.5 tonne of water or 1500 litre of water or 1.5 m^3 of water.

When the tank stands on 1×1 metre ends, the area of the base = 1sq.m.

Hence, the depth of water = $\frac{1.5}{1}=1.5$ metre

(*b*) When the tank stands on 3×1 m base, the area = 3sq.m

Hence the depth of watein this case will be $\frac{1.5}{3}=0.5$ m.

The total area of internal surface wet will therefore be

$3\times1 + (3\times0.5\times2) + (1\times0.5\times2)$

$= 3 + 3 + 1 = 7$sq.m.

Problem 29.40: How many square centimetres of exterior surface are there in a square pyramid block of stone 40 cm high and with a base area of 3600 sq. cm? If submerged in a tank, how many litres of water will it displace?

Convex area of a pyramid = $\frac{\text{perimeter of the base}\times\text{slant height}}{2}$

Since the base area is 3600 sq. cm

∴ the length of each side = $\sqrt{3600}=60$m

Hence, the perimeter of the base = 60×4 = 240 cm

The slant height = $\sqrt{40^2+30^2}=50$ c.m.

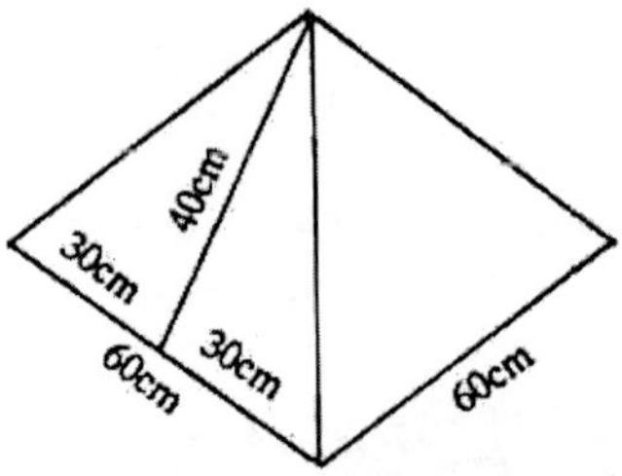

Fig.41

$\therefore$ convex area $= \frac{240 \times 50}{2} = 6000$ sq. cm

Hence the total exterior surface of the pyramid

= area of base + convex area of pyramid

= 3600 + 6000

= 9600 sq. cm

Voume of pyramid = $\frac{\text{area of base} \times \text{vertical height}}{3}$

Since area of base = 3600 sq. cm = 0.36 sq. m
and height = 40 cm = 0.40 m,

Volume of pyramid $= \frac{0.36 \times 0.40}{3} = 0.048\ m^3$

Since 1 m^3 of water occupies 1000 litre, 0.048 m^3 would displace $0.048 \times 1000 =$ 48 litre of water.

Problem 29.41: A sphere is 2/3 the volume of a cylinder of the same diameter and height. If the internal diameter of a cylinder is 75 cm containing water which is 5 cm below the top rim, how many iron spheres of 7.5 cm, in diameter will have to be submerged in the cylinder to cause the water to overflow? (Graduateship Exam – 1950)

Since volume of sphere = 2/3 the volume of cylinder of the same height and diameter,

$\therefore$ volume of 7.5 cm diameter sphere with the same height

$= 7.5^2 \times 0.7854 \times 7.5 \times \frac{2}{3}$ (since volume of acylindar $= 0.7854 \times D^2 \times h$

$= 7.5^2 \times 0.7854 \times 5$

Volume of empty space with 5 cm from top in 75 cm diametre cylinder $= 75^2 \times 0.7854 \times 5$

$\therefore$ Number of spheres required to fill the volume of

$$75^2 \times 0.7854 \times 5 = \frac{75^2 \times 0.7854 \times 5}{7.5^2 \times 0.7854 \times 5} = 100 \text{ spheres}$$

Hence, the number of spheres required to cause the water to overflow = 100 + 1 = 101 spheres.

Problem 29.42: A rigid container in the form of a truncated cone has a circular base of 4m internal diameter and a circular open top of 1m diameter. When filled with water, the vertical depth of it is 2m. How many litres of water it contains and what will be the diameter of the surface of the remaining water, if sufficient water was removed to reduce its depth to 1m?

Volume of the frustrum of a cone $= \frac{H}{3}(A+a+\sqrt{A\times a})$

Substituting the values, we have the volume

$$=\frac{2}{3}\left[(4^2\times 0.7854+1^2\times 0.7854)+\sqrt{4^2\times 0.7854\times 1^2\times 0.7854}\right]$$

$$=\frac{2}{3}\left[16\times 0.7854+0.7854+\sqrt{16\times 0.7854\times 0.7857}\right]$$

$$=\frac{2}{3}\times 16.4934 = 10.9956 \text{ cu. m}$$

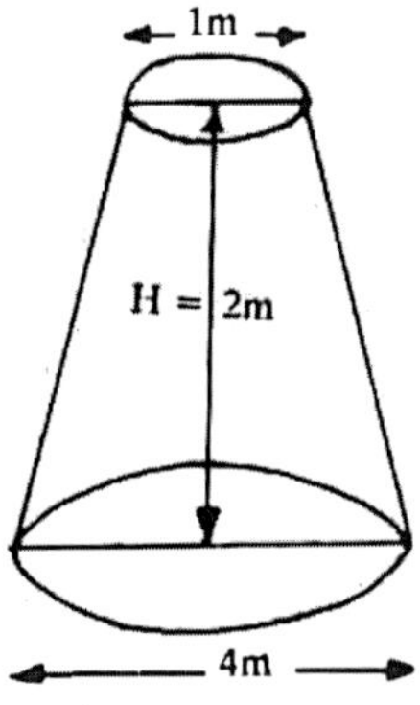

Fig.42

Since 1^3 contains 1000 litre of water, the water contained in the truncated cone= 10.9956×1000 litre= 10,995 litre.

Here the diameter decreases from 4m to 1m for 2m vertical height.

Therefore, decrease per metre rise is 3/2. Hence, increase in diameter, as per above ratio, when depth is lowered to 1 metre = 1.5m

∴ Diameter at depth of 1 metre = 1 metre + 1.5m = 2.5 metre.

Problem 29.43: A rectangular swimming pool, measuring 10m×6m with a uniform sloping bottom is being filled from a hydrant on a 100 mm main. The velocity of the water in the main is 2 m/sec. After 2.5 hour, the depth of the water at one end of the pool is 1 m. Calculate the depth at the other end. (Graduateship Exam – 1970)

The discharge per minute in litres from the pipe $= \frac{vd^2}{20}$

Substituting the values, we have, the discharge from the pipe

$$=\frac{2\times 100\times 100}{20}=1000 \text{ l/min}$$

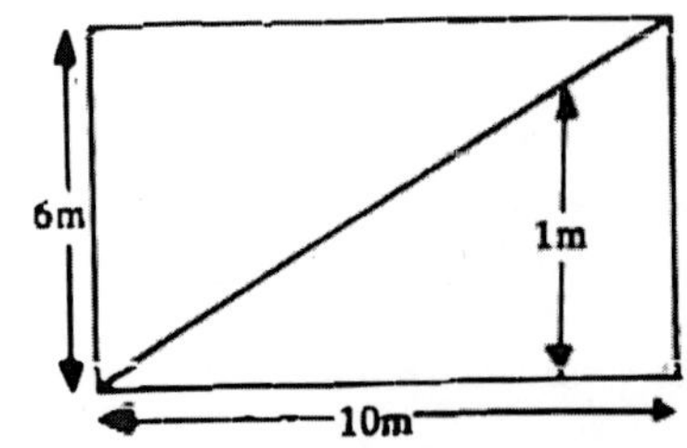

Fig.43

∴ in 2.5 hour (150 min) the discharge will be 1000×150 = 1,50,000 litre.

Since 1 m^3 contains 1000 litre of water, therefore, 1,50,000 litre will occupy 150 m^3.

Since the area of the swimming pool = 10m×6m, the average depth of the tank

$$= \frac{150}{10 \times 6} = 2.5 \text{ m.}$$

As the pool has a uniform slope and the depth at one end is 1 metre, hence the average depth = 0.5m ∴ the depth at the other end must be 0.5 metre more than the average depth, i.e. 2.5 + 0.5 = 3 m.

Problem 29.44: Calculate the number of sq. m of material (no overlap) required to construct a square pyramid (two faces) with a square hose of 8 m side and a vertical height of 3m. How many litre of water will such a pyramid contain? How long will it take to pump out one-fourth of the contents using two 25 mm nozzles at a nozzle pressure of 6.25 bar?

Surface area of pyramid including the base (5 faces)

$$= \frac{\text{perimeter} \times \text{slant height}}{2} + \text{area of base}$$

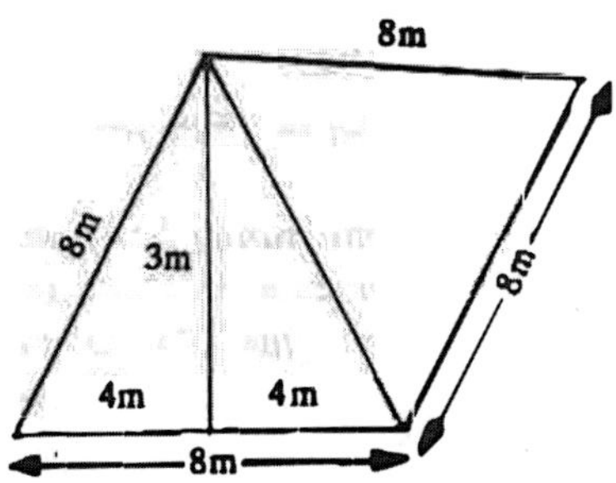

Fig.44

Now the slant height may be calculated by drawing a perpendicular from the apex of the pyramid over the base, with the help of Pythagorus's, theorem.

Slant height = $\sqrt{4^2+3^2} = \sqrt{25}$ = 5m

(Since half the base = 4m and the height of the triangle = 3m)

Also the perimeter, with 8m side = 4×8 = 32m and the area of the base = 8×8 = 64 sq. m.

Substituting the values, the total surface area of the pyramid

$=32\times\frac{5}{2}+64=80+64=144$ sqm.

Litres contained in the pyramid = volume of the pyramid in cu.m $\times 1000$.

The volume of the pyramid

$$=\frac{\text{area of base} \times \text{vertical height}}{3}$$

$$=\frac{64\times 3}{3}=64$$

Litres of water contained = 64×1000 = 64,000 litre

One-fourth this quantity = 16,000 litre

Two 25mm nozzle, at a nozzle pressure of 6.25 bar, will discharge

$2\times\frac{2}{3}\times 25\times 25\times\sqrt{6.25}$ = 2083.2 litre/min.

(since output from one nozzle = $\frac{2}{3}\times d^2\sqrt{p}$)

Hence, time taken to pump out one-fourth of the contents

$$=\frac{16{,}000\text{ litre of water}}{2083.3}=7.68\text{ minute.}$$

Problem 29.45: A circular static water tank of uniform cross section having a diameter of 10m is to be filled up with water up to a level of 3.5 by two different sources. One source discharges water through a hose pipe of 70 mm diametre in which water flows with a velocity of 4.24 m/sec. The second source is a pump with a brake power of 30 kW working at a pressure of 7 bar when the pump efficiency is rated at 70%. Calculate the time taken to fill the tank. *(Graduateship Exam — 1983)*

Capacity of a circular tank $=\pi r^2\times h\times 1000$ litre

Substituting the values, we have the capacity of the tank

$$=\frac{22}{7}\times\frac{10}{2}\times\frac{10}{2}\times\frac{35}{10}\times 1000=275000\text{ litre}$$

Also, quantity of water discharged per minute through hose pipe

$$=\frac{vd^2}{21.2}=\frac{4.24\times 70\times 70}{21.2}=980\text{ litre/min.}$$

As for the discharge from the pump with 70% efficiency and with brake power of 30 kW, we have to calculate first W.H.P. of the pump, where

$$\text{W.H.P.} = \frac{E \times \text{B.H.P.}}{100} = \frac{70 \times 30}{100} = 21 \text{ kW} = 21{,}000 \text{ watt}$$

Also,

$$\text{W.H.P.} = \frac{100 \times L \times P}{60}$$

or

$$21{,}000 = \frac{100 \times L \times P}{60} = \frac{100 \times L \times 7}{60}$$

or

$$L = \frac{21000 \times 60}{100 \times 7} = 1800 \text{ litre/min}$$

Therefore, the total quantity of water received in the tank per minute = 980 + 1800 = 2780 litre.

Hence, the time taken to fill the tank $= \frac{275000}{2780} = 98.9$ min.

Problem 29.46: A pump with a brake power of 17.5 kW is engaged to operate a branch with a nozzle of 21 mm diameter, fitted at the end of non-percolating hose 70mm in diameter and 140 m in length, at the fifth floor of a building 17.25m above pump level, discharging 735 litre of water/min. Calculate the efficiency rating of the pump if the friction factor of the hose is 0.005. (1 metre head = 0.1 bar) . (Graduateship Exam – 1984)

Since L (output) $= \frac{2}{3} d^2 \sqrt{P}$

Substituting the values, we have $735 = \frac{2}{3} \times 21 \times 21 \times \sqrt{P}$

or

$$\sqrt{P} = \frac{5}{2}$$

or

$P = 6.25$ bar

Also, loss of pressure due to friction is calculated from the formula

$$P_f = \frac{9000 \times f \times l \times L^2}{d^5}$$

Substituting the values, we have

$$P_f = \frac{9000 \times 0.005 \times 140 \times 735 \times 735}{70 \times 70 \times 70 \times 70 \times 70} = 2.025$$

The height at which the branch is being operated = 17.25m

Hence, pressure loss due to head of water $= \frac{17.25}{10} = 1.725$ bar

The pressure required by the pump for working

$$= 6.25 + 2.025 + 1.725 = 10 \text{ bar}$$

Also, W.H.P. of the pump

$$= \frac{100 \times L \times P}{60} = \frac{100 \times 735 \times 10}{60} = 12{,}250 = 12.25 \text{ kW}$$

$$\text{Efficiency of the pump} = \frac{\text{W.H.P}}{\text{B.H.P}} \times 100 = \frac{12.25}{17.5} \times 100 = 70\%$$

Problem 29.47: Water is pumped into a storage tank of dimension 4m×4m×3m. The tank is 60m above the pump. The pumping system is 70% efficient. If the power input to the pump is 15kW, find the time taken to fill the tank. (Take g= 10m/sec²).

$$\text{Efficiency} = \frac{\text{W.H.P}}{\text{B.H.P}} \times 100$$

$$\therefore \quad \text{W.H.P.} = \frac{\text{B.H.P} \times \text{efficiency}}{100} = 15000 \times 0.7 = 10{,}500 \text{ W}$$

$$\text{Water head} = 60 \text{ m and } P = \frac{\text{head}}{g} = \frac{60}{10} = 6 \text{ bar}$$

$$\text{Also W.H.P.} \frac{100 \times L \times P}{60} = 10{,}500 \text{ W}$$

Substituting the values we have

$$10{,}500 = \frac{100 \times L \times 6}{60} = 10L$$

$\therefore \quad L = 1050$ litre/min

Capacity of the tank $= 4 \times 4 \times 3 \times 10^3 = 48{,}000$ litre

$$\text{Time taken to fill the tank} = \frac{48{,}000}{1050} = 45.7 \text{ min.}$$

Problem 29.48: A fire pump is 75% efficient and is driven by a motor of 40 kW brake power.

a) What water power is the pump capable of delivering?

b) When 2250 litre of water per minute is being taken from the pump, show that the pump will be operating at 8 bar pressure.

c) The pump is delivering 2250 litre of water per minute at 8 bar pressure through two lines of 70 mm diameter hose of 5 lengths each, terminating in branches with identical nozzle. What nozzle size will be required at each branch to deliver this quantity of water? (Assume that the hose is laid over level ground and the friction loss in each hose line is 0.2 bar per length).

(Graduateship Exam – 1977)

a) Efficiency $= \frac{\text{W.H.P}}{\text{B.H.P}} \times 100$

or

$$\frac{75}{100} = \frac{\text{W.H.P.}}{40}$$

Hence W.H.P = 30 kW = 30,000 W

b) We know that

$$\text{W.H.P.} = \frac{100 \times L \times P}{60}$$

or

$$60 \ \text{W.H.P.} = 100 \times L \times p.$$

or

$$P = \frac{60 \times \text{W.H.P}}{100 \times 2} = 8 \text{bar}$$

c) Friction loss per length = 0.2 bar

∴ friction loss for 5 lengths = 5 × 0.2 = 1 bar

Also nozzle pressure

= pump pressure – friction loss

= 8 – 1 = 7 bar

Pump output = 2250 litre/minute

∴ each nozzle output $\frac{2250}{2}$ = 1125 litre/min

Also, output (in litre/min) $L = \frac{2}{3} d^2 \sqrt{P}$

or

$$2d^2\sqrt{P} = 3 \times \text{output}$$

or

$$d^2 = \frac{3 \times \text{Output}}{2\sqrt{P}} = \frac{3 \times 1125}{2 \times 2.65} = 636.79 \text{mm}$$

Hence

$$d = 25 \text{mm (app.)}$$

Problem 29.49: A pump with brake power of 30 kW and with an efficiency of 80% discharges 2400 litre of water/min at a pressure which is 0.9 bar higher than the pressure of the 1600 litres/min discharged by a second pump having an efficiency of 65%. What is the brake horse power of the second pump? *(Membership Exam — 1978)*

For the first pump $E = \frac{W.H.P}{B.H.P} \times 100$

or

$$E \times B.H.P = W.H.P \times 100$$

or

$$80 \times 30 = W.H.P \times 100$$

or

$$W.H.P. = \frac{80 \times 30}{100} = 24 \text{ kW} = 24000 W.$$

Also, $W.H.P. = \frac{100 \times L \times P}{60}$ (W.H.P. in watt)

$$\therefore \quad P = \frac{60 \times W.H.P}{100 \times L} = \frac{60 \times 24000}{100 \times 2400} = 6 \text{ bar}$$

For the second pump, the pump pressure = 6–0.9 = 5.1 bar.

$$W.H.P. = \frac{100 \times L \times p}{60} = \frac{100 \times 1600 \times 5.1}{60} = 13{,}600 \text{ W} = 13.6 \text{ kW}$$

Again, efficiency $= \frac{W.H.P}{B.H.P} \times 100$

or

$$65 = \frac{13.6 \times 100}{B.H.P}$$

Hence, $B.H.P = \frac{13.6 \times 100}{65} = 20.92$ kW.

Problem 29.50: A 45mm diameter hose is accidentally connected to a 70mm diameter hose on the fire ground. Calculate the pressure loss due to this enlargement when the quantity of water flowing is 1.6 m³/min. *(Graduateship Exam — 1982)*

We know, $v = \frac{20\,L}{d^2}$

For 45 mm hose, $v_1 = \frac{20 \times 1600}{45 \times 45}$ ($1.6 m^3$/min = 1600 litre/min)

$= 15.8$ m/sec

For 70mm hose $v_2 = \dfrac{20\times1600}{70\times70} = 6.5$ m/sec

Now as H (pressure head) $= \dfrac{v^2}{2g}$

Hence the difference in pressure head $= \dfrac{v_1^2}{2g} - \dfrac{v_2^2}{2g}$

$$= \frac{v_1^2-v_2^2}{2g} = \frac{(15.8)^2-(6.5)^2}{2\times9.81} = \frac{207.4}{19.62} = 10.57\text{m (head loss)}$$

Also, $p = \dfrac{H}{10.19} = \dfrac{10.57}{10.19} = 1.04$ bar, pressure loss.

Problem 29.51: A dam 8m by 3m by 1m is filled by 2 pumps in 6 minutes. The pumps are working at a pressure of 9 bar and are both drawn by engines of 40 kW brake power. Given that the first pump is delivering 2100 litre/min. Calculate the efficiency of both the pumps.

(Graduateship Exam – 1976)

Capacity of the dam $= l\times b\times h = 8\times3\times1 = 24\text{m}^3 = 24000$ litre.
As the dam is filled in 6 minutes, the rate of flow

$$= \frac{24,000}{6} = 4,000 \text{ litre/min.}$$

Since the first pump delivers 2100 litre/min,
$\therefore$ the second pump will deliver 4000–2100 = 1900 litre/minute

Also, W.H.P. $= \dfrac{100\times L\times p}{60}$

Hence, W.H.P. for the first pump

$$= \frac{100\times2100\times9}{60} = 31,500 = 31.5\text{ kW}$$

Efficiency for the first pump

$$= \frac{\text{W.H.P}}{\text{B.H.P}}\times100 = \frac{31.5}{40}\times100 = 78.75\%$$

For the second pump, W.H.P.

$$= \frac{100\times L\times p}{60} = \frac{100\times1900\times9}{60} = 28,500\text{ W} = 28.5\text{ kW}$$

Since

$$E = \frac{\text{W.H.P}}{\text{B.H.P}} \times 100$$

$\therefore$ For the second pump $E = \frac{28.5}{40} \times 100 = 71.25\%$

Problem 29.52: A rectangular bund with vertical walls and level base surrounds two cylindrical oil tanks. The inner measurements of the bund are 70m and 55m and the wall is 4 m high. The diameter of the oil tankers is 30m and 20m respectively.

a) How many litre of water does the bund hold when full?

b) How long will it take to pump out half the water from the full bund using three pumps, each of which uses two lines of delivery hose with 25mm nozzle in each, all working at a nozzle pressure of 9 bar?

(Graduateship Exam — 1988)

a) The total capacity of the tank = $70 \times 55 \times 4 = 15400\ m^3$

The total volume occupied by the oil tanks $= \pi \times \frac{d^2}{4} \times h$

Volume of the first tank $= \frac{22}{7} \times \frac{30 \times 30}{4} \times 4 = 2828.6\ m^3$

Volume of the second tank $= \frac{22}{7} \times \frac{20 \times 20}{4} \times 4 = 1255.6\ m^3$

$\therefore$ total volume of the two oil tanks $= 2828.6 + 1255.6$
$= 4084.2 m^3$
$= 4084\ m^3$ (say)

Water held in bund when full will be $= 15400 - 4084 = 11316 m^3$ $= 11316000$ litre.

b) By applying the formula

$$L = \frac{2}{3} d^2 \sqrt{P}$$

We have, for the six nozzles

$$\frac{2}{3} \times 25^2 \times 3 \times 6 = 7500\ l/min$$

Water to be pumped is half of the bund capacity $= 11316000 \div 2$
$= 5658000$ litre

$\therefore$ time taken to pump out half of the water from the bund will be $= 5658000 \div 7500 = 754.4$ min $= 12$hr 34 min.

Problem 29.53: The breadth of a street between two houses A and B is 10m. A fireman operates a branch from the top of the house A, making an angle of depression of 45^0, striking the jet at the top of the house B. The height of the house B is 15m.

a) determine the height of the house A;

b) calculate the brake power of the pump in watt, taking efficiency of the appliance as 80%;

c) if the pump is capable of operating the branch fitted with 15mm nozzle at a pressure of 5 bar from the top of the house A, the loss of pressure due to friction in the hose pipe is of the order of 0.55 bar. Determine the jet reaction at the nozzle. (Graduateship Exam — 1983)

a) Let A and B be the top of the two houses and CD the width of the street as shown in the diagram.

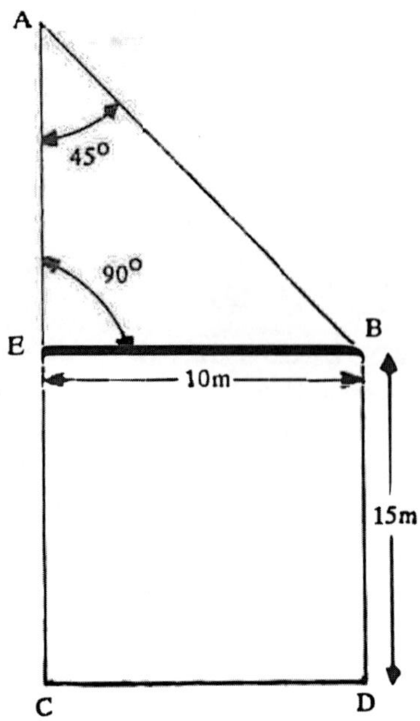

Fig.45

In Δ AEB, EB = CD (width of the street)

$\angle A = 45^0$ and $\angle E = 90^0$

$\therefore \angle ABE = 45^0$. Hence, Δ AEB is an isosceles triangle.

$\therefore$ BE = AE = 10m

Here CE = BD = 15 m (given).

Also, $\tan 45^0 = \frac{AE}{BE} = 1$

or

$\frac{AE}{10} = 1$

or

AE = 10m. Again, CE = 15m. Hence, height of the house A = AE + CE = 10 + 15 = 25m

b) Pressure at the pump is sum of the following:

pressure at the branch = 4.0 bar

loss of pressure, due to friction in hose pipe = 0.55 bar

loss of pressure due to height = 2.45 bar (since $\frac{25}{10.19} = 2.45$)

$\therefore$ preasure at the pump = 4.0 + 0.55 + 2.45 = 7.00 bar

Also, discharge from the nozzle $= \frac{2}{3} d^2 \sqrt{P}$

$=\frac{2}{3}\times 15^2\times\sqrt{4}$

$=300$ l/min

and W.H.P. $=\frac{100\times L\times P}{60}=\frac{100\times 300\times 7}{60}=3500$ W.

Efficiency $(E)=\frac{W.H.P}{B.H.P}\times 100=80$ (given)

Therefore, B.H P. $=\frac{3500\times 100}{80}=4375$ W $=4.375$ kW

c) Jet reaction $=\frac{1.57\,pd^2}{10}=\frac{1.57\times 4\times 15\times 15}{10}=141.3$ N.

Problem 29.54: A hollow truncated pyramid (frustrum) sloping at 45^0 angle has the following internal dimensions: Base = 20m each side; rim (frustrum edge) = 8m each side; height up to rim = 6m. If the frustrum is filled with a liquid of specific gravity 1.1, find out

a) total quantity it will hold when filled to the brim;

b) when filled up to 4m height;

c) what would be the height of the pyramid up to appex?

(Graduateship Exam – 1981)

a) Volume of the frustrum of a pyramid

$=\frac{h}{3}\times(A_1+A_2+\sqrt{A_1\times A_2})$

Substituting the values,

volume $=\frac{6}{3}(400+64+\sqrt{400\times 64})$

$=2(464\text{m}+160)=1248$ cu.m.

This is equivalent to 1248000 litre.

b) At 6m height, frustrum side is 8m. This will increase proportionately with lower height.

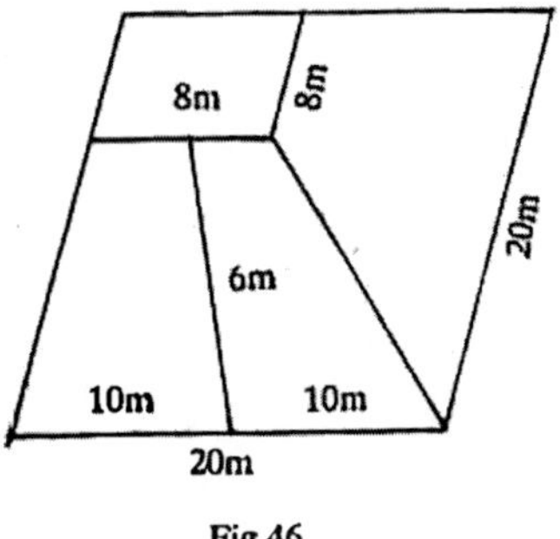

Fig.46

At 4m height, it will be $\frac{8\times 6}{4}=12$m

Now, applying the formula and susbtituting the values, the requisite volume at 4m height

$=\frac{4}{3}(400+144+\sqrt{400\times 144})$

$= \frac{4}{3}(541+240) = 1045.332\,m^3 = 1045332$ litre

c) Height of the pyramid is the perpendicular length from apex to centre of the pyramid at its base. Let it be hm.

Length form the centre of the pyramid to its end is 20/2 = 10m. With lateral surface of the pyramid, it makes a right-angled triangle. So

$h = 10\times \tan 45^0 = 10\times 1 = 10$m.

Problem 29.55: (a) A pipe 120m long and 150 mm in diameter is the outlet for a reservoir. The coefficient of friction is 0.05 and the pipe descends at a gradient of 1 in 12. If the issuing water shows no loss of head during the flow, determine its velocity in metre per second.

(b) A hollow cylindrical container 2m in diameter and 1m in height is being filled with foam having an expansion of 7 times. If the drainage rate of foam is uniform at the rate of 25% every minute, calculate the quantity of water drained at the bottom 3 minutes after filling.

(Graduateship Exam – 1988)

In this problem as the water coming out of the pipe along the gradient shows no loss of head, the loss of the metre head due to friction as a result of the flow of water in 120m of the pipe is made good due to the effect of gravity caused by the gradient of the pipe.

Hence, the loss of head due to gravity = 120/12 = 10m.

Now, for the loss of head due to friction, we have

$$H_f = \frac{2flv^2}{Dg}$$

By substituting the values we have

$$H_f = \frac{2\times 0.05\times 120\times v^2}{\frac{150}{1000}\times 9.81}$$

or

$$10 = \frac{2\times 0.05\times 12\times v^2}{0.15\times 9.81}$$

or

$$v^2 = \frac{10\times 0.15\times 9.81}{2\times 0.05\times 12} = 12.26$$

or

$$v = 3.5 \text{m/sec.}$$

(*b*) Volume of the foam in the cylindrical container $= \pi r^2 h$

Substituting the values, the volume of foam

$$= 3.1416 \times 1^2 \times 1 = 3.1416 \text{m}^3 = 3141.6 \text{ litre.}$$

Also, expansion = 7 times

$\therefore$ volume of water $= \dfrac{3141.6}{7} = 448.8$ litre

Now, drainage of the foam during the first 1 minute = 25%, i.e. 1/4th of the water in the foam.

During the second 1 minute time, 25% of the balance of 75% of foam, i.e. $\dfrac{25}{100} \times \dfrac{75}{100} = \dfrac{3}{16}$ will be the drainage.

During the third 1 minute time, 25% of the balance of 50% of the foam will be the drainage

$\therefore$ At the end of 3 minutes, the drainage will be $\left(\dfrac{1}{4} + \dfrac{3}{16} + \dfrac{1}{8}\right)$ of the volume of foam.

$$\therefore \text{ total water drainage } = \left(\frac{1}{4} + \frac{3}{16} + \frac{1}{8}\right) \times 448.8 \text{ litre}$$

$$= \frac{9}{16} \times 448.8 \text{ litre}$$

$$= 252 \text{ litre.}$$

Problem 29.56: A rectangular swimming pool, measuring 12 metre in length and 9 metre in breadth with a base which slopes uniformly, having a depth of 1.5 metre at the shallow end and 5.5 metre at the deep end, is full of water. Due to sedimentation, 8.1 metric tonne of sand has settled down in the pool occupying irregular shape.

A pump with a brake power of 40kW with efficiency rating of 75% working at a pressure of 8 bar is engaged to pump out water from the pool. If 1125 litre of water remains unpumped at the base of the pool, calculate the quantity of water pumped out and the time taken. (Specific gravity of sand is 1.44). *(Graduateship Exam – 1984)*

$$\text{Average depth} = \frac{5.5 + 1.5}{2} = 3.5 \text{ m}$$

$$\text{Capacity of the swimming pool} = 12 \times 9 \times \frac{7}{2} \times 1000 = 3{,}78000 \text{ litre}$$

Volume of sand = $\frac{8.1 \times 1000}{1.44}$ = 5625 litre

(since specific gravity of sand = 1.44).

Total quantity of water to be pumped out = 378000–(5625 + 1125) = 371250 litre (since 1125 litre of water were left in the tank)

Since $E = \frac{\text{W.H.P.}}{\text{B.H.P.}} \times 100$

substituting the values we have

$$\text{W.H.P.} = \frac{40 \times 75}{100} = 30 \text{ kW}$$

Now, by applying the formula

$$\text{W.H.P.} = \frac{100 \times l \times P}{60}$$

and substituting the values, we have

$$L = \frac{30 \times 60 \times 1000}{100 \times 8} = 2250 \text{ l/min}$$

$\therefore$ time taken to pump out water $= \frac{371250}{2250} = 165$ minute.

Problem 29.57: A fixed water monitor, when operated at an angle of 60^0, strikes the 15th floor of a building and when operated at 30^0, strikes the fifth floor of the same building. If the building is located at a distance of 30 metre from the monitor, calculate the difference in height between the 5th and the 15th floor. Also find out the jet reaction of the monitor (jet size 30mm and pressure 7 bar) (Graduateship Exam – 1984)

Let M be the position of the monitor, N the 15th floor and P the 5th floor, as shown in the diagram.

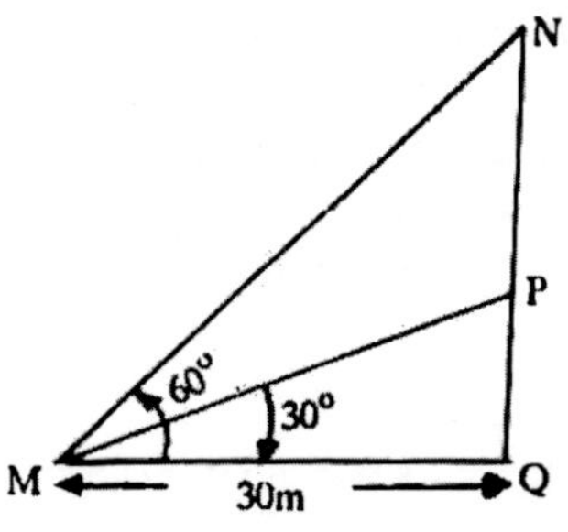

Fig.47

Now from the Δ MNQ, we have tan 60^0 $= \frac{NQ}{MQ} = \sqrt{3} = 1.732$

NQ (the height of the 15th floor) = 30 × 1.732 = 51.96m (since MQ = 30m)

Also, tan $30^0 = \frac{PQ}{MQ} = \frac{1}{\sqrt{3}}$

or

$$\frac{PQ}{30}=\frac{1}{\sqrt{3}}$$

Hence

$$PQ=\frac{30}{\sqrt{3}}=17.35$$

Hence the difference in height between 5th and 15th floor = 51.96–17.35 = 34.61m

The formula for the jet reaction $=\dfrac{1.57\times p\times d^2}{10}$

Substituting the values, we have

$$\text{jet reaction}=\frac{1.57\times7\times30\times30}{10}=989.1 \text{ newton.}$$

Problem 29.58: Calculate the height of the effective jet of a monitor fitted with 45 mm nozzle when operated vertically at a pressure of 9 bar. Also find out the jet reaction produced at the nozzle (1 metre head = 0.1 bar). *(Graduateship Exam – 1984)*

Effective maximum height of a jet $h_e=\dfrac{2}{3}\left(H-0.113\dfrac{H^2}{d}\right)$

Substituting the values, we have

$$h_e=\frac{2}{3}\left(90-\frac{0.113\times90\times90}{45}\right)=46.44\text{m.}$$

The formula for jet reaction $=\dfrac{1.57\times p\times d^2}{10}$

Substituting the values,

$$\text{the jet reaction}=\frac{1.57\times9\times45\times45}{10}\ 2861.3 \text{ newton.}$$

Problem 29.59: A centrifugal pump with an efficiency rating of 70% pumps foam solution of specific gravity 1.12, delivering 2400 litre/min at a pressure of 5.6 bar. In another occasion, the same pump was used to pump gasoline (specific gravity 0.7), keeping the same output and pressure. Taking the friction in vertical pipe as negligible, determine the head in metres of fluid to which foam solution and gasoline will be raised. Also calculate the brake power of the pump required to handle both the liquids separately. (Take 1 metre head as 0.1 bar for water).

(Graduateship Exam – 1986)

Efficiency of the pump = 70%
Output = 2400 litre min

Pressure at the pump = 5.6 bar
1 metre head = 0.1 bar for water.

If the pump is working with water only, then output of 2400l is equivalent to 2400 kg.

Also pressure of 5.6 bar = 5.6×10 = 56 metre head.

While pumping foam solution (specific gravity = 1.12), the head will be lowered in relation to water. The head will now be

$$56\times\frac{1}{1.12}=50 \text{ metre head.}$$

With gasoline (specific gravity 0.7), the head reached will be

$$56\times\frac{1}{0.7}=80 \text{ metre head}$$

Also, W.H.P. for the pump $= \frac{100\times L\times P}{60}$

Substituting the values

$$\text{W.H.P.} = \frac{100\times2400\times5.6}{60}=22400\text{W} = 22.4 \text{ kW}$$

Efficiency of the pump = 70%

$$\therefore \text{ B.H.P} = \frac{22.4\times100}{70}=32 \text{ kW}$$

$$\left(\text{since } E = \frac{\text{W.H.P}}{\text{B.H.P.}}\times100\right)$$

Now, as per the pressure head produced in both the extreme cases, the brake power will remain constant in both cases.

(a) Weight of foam solution pumped = 2400×1.12 = 2688 kg, i.e. 2688 litre.

Hence,

$$\text{B.H.P} = \frac{2688\times100\times5}{60\times1000}\times\frac{100}{70}=32 \text{ kW. (50 m head = 5 bar).}$$

(b) With gasoline, weight of gasoline pumped = 2400×0.7 = 1680 kg

$$\therefore \text{B.H.P} = \frac{1680\times100\times8}{60\times1000}\times\frac{100}{70}=32 \text{ kW (80 m head = 8 bar).}$$

(c) Weight of foam solution pumped = 2688 kg, i.e. 2688 litre.

Hence,

$$\text{W.H.P.} = \frac{2688\times100\times5.6}{60\times1000}=25.088 \text{ kW}$$

Also, B.H.P $= \dfrac{W.H.P\times 100}{E} = \dfrac{25.088\times 100}{70} = 35.840$ kW

(d) Weight of gasoline pumped = 1680 kg, i.e. 1680 litre

$\therefore$ W.H.P of the pump $= \dfrac{1680\times 100\times 5.6}{60} = 15,680$W

(since $p = 5.6$ bar)

$\therefore$ B.H.P. $= \dfrac{15680\times 100}{70} = 22400\text{W} = 22.4\text{kW}$

Problem 29.60: A rectangular static tank, measuring 9m in length and 5 m in breadth, is to be filled to a level of 3m by two pumps both working at a pressure of 7 bar and each pump is coupled to a prime mover of 40 kW brake power. If the tank is filled in 30 minutes and the first pump discharges 2400 litre/min, calculate the efficiency of both the pumps.

(Graduateship Exam – 1986)

Volume of the tank $9\times 5\times 3$ = 135 cu m.

Capacity in litres = 135×1000 = 135,000 litre.

As the time taken by two similar pumps to fill the tank is 30 minute, discharge from the pumps per minute

$= \dfrac{135000}{30} = 4500$l

$\therefore$ discharge from the second pump = 4500 – 2400 = 2100 litre/min.

Since output, pressure and brake power of each pump is given, we may substitute the values in the formula for W.H.P. of the 1st pump, viz.

W.H.P. $= \dfrac{100\times L\times p}{60} = \dfrac{100\times 2400\times 7}{60} = 28,000\text{ W} = 28\text{kW}$

Similarly, the W.H.P of the second pump

$= \dfrac{100\times 2100\times 7}{60}$

$= 24500\text{W} = 24.5\text{ kW}$

Hence, efficiency of the first pump

$= \dfrac{\text{W.H.P}}{\text{B.H.P}}\times 100$

$= \dfrac{28}{40}\times 100 = 70\%$

Similarly, efficiency of the second pump may be calculated as

$$\frac{24.5}{40}\times 100 = 61.25\%$$

Problem 29.61: A sphere 10 m in diameter and filled with water is connected from its base to a pump. If the pump supplies a 25 mm jet and the jet reaction is 700 N, how long will it take to reduce the contents of the sphere by 2/3 ? (Graduateship Exam – 1987)

Volume of the sphere $= \frac{4\pi r^3}{3}$ where r = radius of the sphere

Hence, volume will be $= \frac{4}{3}\times\frac{22}{7}\times 5^3 \text{m}^3$

Water contained in 2/3 of this volume

$$= \frac{2}{3}\times\frac{500}{21}\times 22\times 1000 = 349206.3 \text{ litre}$$

The nozzle pressure can be found out from the formula of jet reaction, i.e.

$$\text{jet reaction} = \frac{1.57\times P\times d^2}{10}$$

$$= \frac{1.57\times P\times 25\times 25}{10} = 700 \text{ newton.}$$

whence

$$P = 7.1333 \text{ bar}$$

Also, $L = \frac{2}{3}d^2\sqrt{P}$

Substituting the values,

L (Nozzle discharge) $= \frac{2}{3}25^2\sqrt{7.13}$ m $=$ 1112.5 litre/min

Therefore, time taken to reduce the contents of the sphere by 2/3 = 3492063 ÷ 1112.5 = 313.8 minute = 5.2 hour.

Problem 29.62: A pump is pumping 2 m³/min of water, the surface of which is 5 m below pump inlet. At the outlet, the pump has a diameter of 100 mm and at this point the pressure is 8 bar. From the nozzle (which is at the same level as the pump outlet) the jet rises 35 metre.

a) Calculate the energy/kg of water, (i) at the outlet of the pump; (ii) at the top of the throw of the jet.

b) Explain why (i) and (ii) are not equal (Acceleration due to gravity = 9.81 m/sec² and may be rounded off to 10).

(Membership Exam – 1977)

This is a problem based on Bernoulli's theorem, which states that the total energy/kg at two different points in the system during fluid transmission, when expressed separately, are equal to one another.

The total energy/kg at any point = pressure energy + potential energy + kinetic energy

$$\text{Pressure energy (in J/kg)} = \frac{\text{pressure (in pascal)}}{\text{density of fluid (in kg m}^3\text{)}}$$

$$\text{Pressure energy (in J/kg)} = \frac{\text{pressure in bar} \times 100000}{1000}$$

(Since density of water per m^3 = 1000 and 1 bar = 100000 pascal).

Substituting the values,

$$\text{pressure energy} = \frac{1 \times 8 \times 100000}{1000} = 800\text{ J}$$

$$\text{Potential energy} = g \times H$$

$$= 10 \times 5$$

$$= 50\text{ J}$$

where g = acceleration due to gravity = 10 and H = height in metre

Kinetic energy = $\frac{1}{2}mv^2$, for 1 kg of fluid

We also know

$$Q = vA$$

where Q = quantity in m^3, v = velocity in m/sec, A = area

Now $Q = 2m^3/\text{min} = \frac{2}{60}m^3/\text{sec}$

Also,

$$\text{area} = \frac{\pi d^2}{4} = \frac{\pi \times 0.1^2}{4} \text{ (100 mm = 0.1 metre)}$$

We have

$$v = \frac{Q}{A} = \frac{2}{60} \times \frac{4}{\pi \times (0.1)^2} = 4.24\text{ m/sec}$$

Hence,

$$\text{kinetic energy/kg} = \frac{1}{2} \times 1 \times (4.24)^2 = 9\text{ J}$$

The total energy per kg of water at the outlet of the pump is therefore the sum of the pressure energy, potential energy and kinetic energy = $800+50+9=859$ J.

(*ii*) At the top of the throw of the jet, all the energy is potential energy, i.e.

$$m \times g \times h \quad = \quad 1 \times 10 \times (35+5) = 400 \text{ J}.$$

as the surface from which water is pumped is 5m below the pump inlet.

b) At the top of the throw, all the pressure and velocity energy have been used to get the water up there. So all the energy is potential energy. Hence, this will not be equal to the energy per kg at the outlet of the pump.

Problem 29.63: The area of a cross-section of a horizontal nozzle tapers from 4 cm² to 1 cm². Water flows past each section of the nozzle at the rate of 400 cm³/sec. Calculate the difference in pressure between the two sections.

As per Bernoulli's theorom, we have

$$gh_1 + gH_1 + \frac{v_1^2}{2} = gh_2 + gH_2 + \frac{v_2^2}{2}$$

or

$$gh_1 - gh_2 = \frac{v_2^2}{2} - \frac{v_1^2}{2}$$

since the pipe is horizontal, potential energy $gH = 0$.

We now have to find the difference in pressure head, i.e. $h_1 - h_2$ as also v_1 and v_2. Since $v = Q/A$ (where Q is the flow in litre/sec and A, the area),

$$\therefore v_1 = \frac{400}{4} = 100 \text{ cm/sec} = 1\text{m/sec}$$

$$\text{and } v_2 = \frac{400}{1} = 400 \text{ cm/sec} = 4\text{m/sec}$$

Therefore

$$gh_1 - gh_2 = \frac{16}{2} - \frac{1}{2} = 7.5$$

or

$$h_1 - h_2 = \frac{7.5}{9.81} = 0.76 \text{ metre head (since g} = 9.81).$$

The pressure difference is

$\rho g\ (h_1 - h_2)$

$= 1000 \times 9.81 \times 0.76$ (ρ = density and ρgh is the pressure) = 7456 pascal.

$= 7.5$ kPa (app.).

Problem 29.64: Water is flowing in a vertical tapering pipe 2 m in length. The top of the pipe is 100 mm in diameter and the bottom is 50 mm in diameter. The quantity of water flowing is 1300 litre/ min. Calculate the pressure difference between the top and bottom of the pipe.

Q = the flow in seconds

$= \frac{1300}{60} = 21.67$ litre/sec $= 0.0217 m^3$/sec (since $1 m^3 = 1000$ litre).

Also, the area of the pipe at top $= 0.1^2 \times \frac{\pi}{4} = 0.00785\ m^2$

Area of the pipe at the bottom $0.05^2 \times \frac{\pi}{4} = 0.00196\ m^2$

Also, $v = \frac{Q}{A}$

So, v_1 (velocity at top) $= \frac{0.0217}{0.00785} = 2.76$ m/sec

and v_2 (velocity at the bottom of the pipe) $= \frac{0.0217}{0.00196} = 11.07$ m/sec.

Applying Bernoulli's theorem at both ends of the pipe, we have

$$gh_1 + gH_1 + \frac{v_1^2}{2} = gh_2 + gH_2 + \frac{v_2^2}{2}$$

or

$$gh_1 + 9.81 \times 2 + \frac{(2.76)^2}{2} = gh_2 + 0 \frac{(11.07)^2}{2}$$

since potential energy at the bottom = 0.

or

$$gh_1 + 23.43 = gh_2 + 61.27$$

or

$$gh_1 - gh_2 = 61.27 - 23.43 = 37.84$$

Hence the difference in pressure head $h_1 - h_2 = 37.84/9.81 = 3.86$m.

The difference in pressure

$$p_1 - p_2 = \rho g\ (h_1 - h_2)$$
$$= 1000 \times 9.81 \times 3.86$$
$$= 37.87 \times 10^3 \text{ pascal}$$
$$= 37.9 \text{ kPa (app)}.$$

Problem 29.65: (a) Write down the equaions giving the energy of 1 kg of water at (i) A, (ii) B, (iii) C, (iv) D, giving in each case the type of energy.

(b) h_1 is less than h. Explain in detail, why this should be.

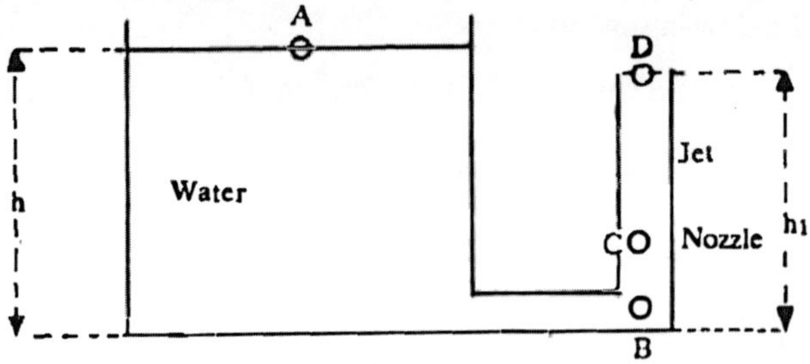

Fig.48

(*a*) *i*) At A, potential energy = g×*h* joule

ii) At B, there will be both pressure energy and kinetic energy. This will depend upon the diameter of the pipe leading to B. Hence

total energy = $gh + \frac{v^2}{2}$ (v is the velocity at B)

iii) At C, kinetic energy plus a small amount of potential energy, due to the height of C above datum B is given by

total energy = $\frac{v^2}{2} + gh_c$ (h_c is the height of C above B)

iv) At D, only potential energy = gh_1

(*b*) h_1 is less than h because of energy losses in the system. These are:

i) Friction losses:

From A to bottom of tank – very small because velocity is small.

In pipe to B – will depend upon the diameter of the pipe; if pipe is large, velocity will be low and friction loss low.

From B to nozzle – small diameter; so high velocity and high friction loss.

From C to D – air friction.

ii) Turbulence losses especially at nozzle C.

iii) Losses due to change of direction of flow.

APPENDIX 4

Formulae relating to area

Parallelograms (square, rectangle, rhombus)

= length × breadth or base × altitude

Trapezium $= \frac{1}{2}$ sum of parallel sides × altitude $= H \times \left(\frac{a+b}{2}\right)$

where ***a*** and ***b*** are the parallel sides.

Area of triangle = (*a*) $\frac{1}{2}$ base × vertical height $= \frac{b \times h}{2}$

Area of triangle = (*b*) $\sqrt{S \times (S-a) \times (S-b) \times (S-c)}$

where

$S = \frac{1}{2}$ sum of length of side $= \frac{a+b+c}{2}$

Equilateral triangle = 0.433 × side^2.

Hexagon = 2.6 × side^2.

Area of circle $= \pi \times r^2 = \frac{22}{7} \times r^2$ (r = radius) $= 3.1416r^2$

$= \frac{11}{14} \times d^2$ (d = diameter) $= 0.7854d^2$

Surface area (flat circular ring) $= 0.7854 \times (D^2 - d^2)$.

= area of outer circle–area of inner circle.

Circumference of circle $= 2\pi r = \frac{22}{7} \times 2r = \frac{22}{7} \times d = 3.1416d$

Sector of a circle $= \pi r^2 \times \frac{\text{contained angle}}{360}$

Diameter of circle $= \frac{\text{area}}{0.7854}$

Surface area of cylinder (without ends) $= 3.1416 \times d \times h$

Surface area of cylinder (with ends) $= (3.1416 \times d \times h + 2 \times 0.7854 \times d^2)$

Cone (convex area) $= 3.1416 \times$ radius of base $\times$ slant height

Pyramid, also cone (convex area) = Perimeter of base $\times \frac{1}{2}$ slant height.

Pyramid and cone (total surface area) = Convex area + area of base.

Frustrum (surface area) $= \frac{1}{2}$ sum of perimeters of two bases $\times$ slant height + areas of two bases.

Sphere (surface area) $= 3.1416 \times d^2 = 4 \times 3.1416 \times r^2$

Ellipse $= 0.7854 \times D \times d$ (product of two diameters, multiplied by 0.7854).

Formulae relating to volume

Cubic, rectangular, rhombic solid $= l \times b \times h$

Cylinder $= 0.7854 \times d^2 \times h = 3.1416 \times r^2 \times h$.

Volume of metal in hollow cylinder

$$= 0.7854 \times h \times (D^2 - d^2)$$

(D and d are the outer and inner diameters respectively)

$$= 3.1416 \times h \times (R^2 - r^2)$$

(R and r are the outer and inner radii respectively)

Hexagonal prism $= 2.6 \times \text{side}^2 \times$ height.

Pyramid = Area of base $\times \frac{1}{3}$ vertical height,

$$\text{Cone} = \frac{0.7854 \times d^2 \times h}{3} = \frac{3.1416 \times r^2 \times h}{3}$$

$$\text{Frustrum (pyramid or cone)} = \frac{h}{3} \times (A + a + \sqrt{A \times a})$$

$$\text{Sphere} = 0.5236 \times d^3 = \frac{4}{3} \times 3.1416 \times r^3.$$

$$\text{Volume of shell of Sphere} = 0.5236 \times (D^3 - d^3)$$

$$= \frac{4}{3} \times 3.1416 \times (R^3 - r^3)$$

$$\text{Volume of a tank with sloping bottom} = l \times b \times \frac{d_1 + d_2}{2},$$

where l and b are the length and breadth of the tank and d_1 and d_2 are the depth at the two ends of the tank.

Wedge

$$= \frac{\text{width} \times \text{vertical height} \times \text{Sum of three parallel sides}}{6}$$

$= \text{area of base} \times \frac{1}{2}$ vertical height

(for rectangular parallel wedge only).

Frustrum of wedge $= \frac{h}{6} \times \left(A + a + 4\left[\frac{l_1 + l_2}{2} \times \frac{b_1 + b_2}{2}\right]\right)$

where l_1 = length of base, l_2 = length of top, b_1 = breadth of base, b_2 = breadth of top.

Prismoid $= \frac{h}{6} \times (A + a + 4m)$

where m = area of middle section.

APPENDIX 5

Hydraulic calculations in metric units

It will be useful to remember the following relations while solving problems on hydraulics and others. Those marked with an * include approximations. Symbols used have been explained later.

i) Capacity of a rectangular tank $= l \times b \times h \times 1000$ litre.

ii) Capacity of a rectangular tank with a sloping base

$$= l \times b \times \frac{h_1+h_2}{2} \times 1000 \text{ litre.}$$

iii) Capacity of circular tank $= 0.7854 \times D^2 \times h \times 1000$ litre $= 800\, D^2h$ *

iv) Capacity of hose (litre per metre) $= \frac{8d^2}{10000}$ *

v) Capacity of hose (litre per 25m length) $= \frac{d^2}{50}$ *

vi) Pressure and head $p = H \times 0.0981$ bar. Also,

$$H = p \times 10.19$$

$$p = \frac{H}{10} \text{ * or } H = p \times 10\text{m.}$$

vii) velocity of a falling body from rest

$$v = gt \text{ m/sec}$$

or

$$t = \frac{v}{g} \text{ sec.}$$

viii) Distance through which a body falls

$$h = \frac{1}{2}gt^2 \text{ meters.}$$

ix) Head and velocity $= h = \frac{v^2}{2g}$ or $v = \sqrt{2gh}$ m/sec.

x) Quantity and velocity $Q = v \times A$ litre/sec

or

$$v = Q/A \text{ m/sec}$$

xi) Velocity and discharge $v = \frac{20L}{d^2}$ m/sec *

$$L = \frac{vd^2}{20} \text{ litre/min.}$$

FRICTION LOSS

xii) Loss of head $H_f = \frac{2flv^2}{Dg}$ metre head

xiii) Loss of pressure $p_f = \frac{20flv^2}{d}$ bar;

also,

$$p_f = \frac{9000flL^2}{d^5}$$

xiv) Nozzle discharge $= \frac{2}{3} d^2 \sqrt{p}$

xv) Jet reaction $= \frac{2pa}{10}$ newton

xvi) Jet reaction $= \frac{1.57pd^2}{10}$ newton

CALCULATION OF OUTPUT FROM WATER MAINS

xvii) Maximum output

$$= L \times \sqrt{\frac{\text{static pressure}}{\text{static pressure} - \text{running pressure}}}$$

xviii) Height of water jet:

Effective height of the jet $h_e = \frac{2}{3} (H - 0.113 \frac{H^2}{2})$

for effective fire-fighting stream, whereas actual height of the highest drop

$$H = H - 0.113\frac{H^2}{2}$$

CALCULATION OF HORSEPOWER, BRAKEPOWER, AND EFFICIENCY

Unit of power is watt and unit of work is joule.

Power = force × velocity.

$$\text{Water power} = \frac{100 \times L \times p}{60} \text{ watt}$$

$$\text{Efficiency of pumps} = \frac{\text{water power}}{\text{brake power}} \times 100$$

$$\text{or Brake horse power} = \frac{\text{water power}}{\text{efficiency}} \text{kW}$$

BERNOULLI'S THEOREM

This is important for calculation of flow in a pipeline and for calculating the difference of pressure at the top or bottom of the pipeline or between any two points of any moving fluid.

The theorem states that the total of pressure energy—due to pressure in the water or any flowing fluid, potential energy due to height above the normal datum line, and kinetic energy due to water or fluid being in motion—will always remain constant at any point of the pipeline. This may be expressed as follows:

$$gh_1 + gH_1 + \frac{v_1^2}{2} = gh_2 + gH_2 + \frac{v_2^2}{2}$$

where h_1 and h_2 are pressure head at points 1 and 2 of the pipeline, H_1 and H_2 are height above datum line at 1 and 2 respectively, and v_1 and v_2 are the velocities of the fluid at 1 and 2 respectively.

HYDRAULIC DATA FOR CALCULATION

One litre of fresh water has a mass of 1 kg.

One litre of fresh water exerts a downward force of 9.81 newton.

One litre of salt water exerts a downward force of 10.1 newton.

One cu.m of fresh water exerts a downward force of 9810 newton (force = mass × acceleration, and a newton is that force which when applied to a mass of 1 kg gives it an acceleration of $1 m/sec^2$).

One cu.m = 1000 litre.

1000 kg = 1 tonne (T).

One metre head of water equals 0.0981 bar.

One bar pressure of water equals 10.19m.

One bar = 100000 N/m^2 = 1 atmosphere (approximately) = 14.503 lb/sq. in. = 7 kg/cm^2.

CONSTANTS

g (acceleration due to gravity) = 9.81 m/sec^2.

Normal atmospheric pressure at 20^{0}C = 1.013 bar or 10.35 metre head of water.

Absolute zero = –273^{0}C

π=3.1416 = $\left(\frac{22}{7}\right)$

π^2=9.8696

$\frac{\pi}{4}$=0.7854

APPROXIMATE FIREGROUND CALCULATIONS

Loss of pressure due to height = 0.1 bar for each metre rise.

Friction loss in hose per 25 m length:

70mm non–percolating – 0.2 bar.

70 mm percolating – 0.4 bar.

Capacity of a pond or tank or lake

= $\frac{2}{3}$ (surface area × average depth)

Capacity of a circular tank:

$m^3 = 0.8D^2h$

$= \frac{8C^2h}{100}$

Litre = $800D^2h$

= $80C^2h$

SOME IMPORTANT RELATIONS FOR SOLVING PROBLEMS RELATING TO ELECTRICITY:

(For explanation of symbols, please refer to the chapters on electricity, Ohm's law and heating effects of current)

i) $I = \frac{E}{R}$ (Ohm's Law). Also $I = \frac{E}{R+r}$ (Ohm's law)

ii) $R = r_1 + r_2 + r_3 + r_4$ (total resistance for series circuit)

iii) $\frac{1}{R} = \frac{1}{r_1} + \frac{1}{r_2} + \frac{1}{r_3} + \frac{1}{r_4}$ (total resistance for parallel circuit)

iv) $H = 0.24ECT$ calories; also, $H = 0.24\, C^2Rt$ calories.

$$H = \frac{C^2 Rt \times 10^7}{J} \text{ cal} \quad (J = \text{Joule's constant for heat} = 4.2 \times 10^7)$$

v) 1 watt = 1 volt × 1 ampere (watt is the unit of power)

vi) kilowatt hour unit (domestic unit) $= \frac{\text{volt} \times \text{ampere} \times \text{hour}}{1000}$

v) 1 H.P. = 746 watt.

EXPLANATION OF SYMBOLS USED

A = cross-sectional area (sq.metre). m = mass (kilogram).
a = cross- sectional area (sq. millimetre).
p = pressure (bar). b = breadth (metre).
p_1 = pressure at entry to the pipe (newton/sq. m).
BP = brake power (watt).
p_2 = pressure at exit of pipe (newton/sq. m).
C = circumference (metre).
P_f = pressure lost in friction (bar).
D = diameter (metres). Q = flow (cubic metre/sec).
d = diameter (millimetre). E = efficiency.
R = reaction (newton). F = friction factor.
g = acceleration due to gravity.
r = radius.
H = metre head.
S = ½ the sum of the sides of a triangle.
H_f = head lost due to friction (metre).
t = time (second).
h = depth (metre).
v = velocity (m/sec).
L = flow (litre/min).
WP = water horsepower (watt).
l = length (metre).

CONVERSION FACTORS FOR S.I. UNITS

Basic unit	Approved unit of measurement	Conversion factor
Length (m)	kilometre (km) metre (m) millimetre (mm)	1 mile = 1.609 km 1 yard = 0.914 m 1 foot = 0.305 m 1 inch = 25.4 mm
Area Square metre (m^2)	sq.kilometre (km^2) sq.metre (m^2) sq.millimetre (mm^2)	1 $mile^2$ = 2.590 km^2 1 $yard^2$ = 0.836 m^2 1 $foot^2$ = 0.093 m^2 1 $inch^2$ = 645.2 mm^2

Basic unit	Approved unit of measurement	Conversion factor
Volume Cu.metre (m^3) Volume flow Cu.metre/sec (m^3/s)	cu.m (m^3) litre (l) ($10^{-3} m^3$) cu.m/sec (m^3/s) litre/min = $10^{-3} m^3$/min	1 cu.ft = 0.028 m^3 1 gallon = 4.546 litres 1 $foot^3$/s = 0.028 m^3/s 1 gallon/min = 4.546 l/m
Mass (kilogram) (kg)	kilogram (kg) tonne (t) = (10^3 kg)	1 lb = 0.454 kg 1 ton = 1.016 t
Velocity (metre/sec)	metre/sec (m/s) International knot (kn) kilometre/hour (km/h)	1 ft/sec = 0.305 m/s 1U.K.knot = 1.853 km/h 1 Int knot = 1.852km/h 1 mile/hr = 1.61 km/h
Acceleration	metre/sec^2 (m/s^2)	1 foot/sec^2 = 0.305 m/s^2 g = 9.81 m/s^2
Force (newton) (N)	kilonewton (kN) newton (N)	1 ton force = 9.964 kN 1 lb force = 4.448 N
Energy work	joule (J) kilo joule (kJ) kilowatt hour (kWh)	1 British Thermal Unit = 1.055 kJ 1 foot lb force = 1.356 J
Power (watt) (W) 1 J/s = 1 (Nm/s)	kilowatt (kW) watt (W)	1 horsepower = 0.746 kW 1 foot lb force/sec = 1.356 W
Pressure	bar = $10^5 N/m^2$	1 atmosphere = 101.325 kN/m^2 = 1.013 bar
Newton/$metre^2$ (N/m^2) = 1 pascal	milibar (m bar) = $10^2 N/m^2$ metre head	1 lb force/in^2 = 6894.76 N/m^2 = 0. 069bar 1 inch Hg = 33.86 m bar 1 metre head = 0. 0981bar 1 foothead = 0.305 metre head
Quantity of heat	joule (J)	1 British Thermal Unit = 1.055 kJ
Joule (J) Heat flow rate	kilojoule (kJ) watt (W)	1 British Thermal Unit/hr = 0.293 W
Watt (W)	kilowatt (kW)	1 British Thermal Unit/sec = 1.055 kW
Specific energy	kilojoule/kilogram (kJ/kg)	1 British Thermal Unit/lb = 2.326 kJ/kg
Calorific value Specific latent heat	kilojoule/m^3 (kJ/m^3)	1 British Thermal Unit/ft^3 = 37.26 kJ/m^3
Joule/kilogram (J/kg) Joule/m^3 (J/m^3)	Megajoule/m^3 (MJ/m^3)	

APPENDIX 6

Foam and Foam Branches, Classification of Foam, Rate of Application and Type of Foam Branches

Foam concentrates are classified in two ways:

i) Classification by expansion: low expansion (LX); medium expansion (MX); high expansion (HX)

ii) Classification by constituents: (*a*) Protein foam concentrate: Generally used as 4% concentrate, with low expansion (expansion ratio about 8:1). Effective on most hydrocarbon fuels. Makes a stiff foam with good resistance to burnback.

(*b*) Fluoroprotein foam concentrate: Generally used at 4% concentration for low expansion foam production having an expansion ratio of about 9:1. More fluid than protein foam, giving quicker control and extinction of fire. Good resistance to burnback and fuel contamination. Most suitable for sub-surface injection.

(*c*) Fluorochemical foam concentrate : Generally used at 3 to 6% concentration for low expansion foam production, having an expansion ratio of about 10:1. Effective on hydrocarbon fuels and some water-miscible liquids. This category of foam is very fluid giving rapid control and extinction of fire; but burnback resistance for this category is not as good as the protein or fluoroprotein type. Undiluted concentrate may strip paint and care should be taken not to allow contact with skin. Also known as Aqueous Film Forming Foam (AFFF) in combination with fluorocarbon surfactants. It is more expensive than other types.

(*d*) Synthetic foam concentrate : Generally used at 2% to 3% concentration for low and medium expansion foams and 1.5% to 2% for high expansion foam. Expansion ratios are 11:1, 75 to 150 : 1 and 750 to 1000:1 respectively. Particularly effective on low boiling point hydrocarbon fuels. Gentle surface application will give quick control and extinction but burnback resistance is not good and is susceptible to fuel–foam mixing and breakdown by radiant heat and hot fuel. Undiluted concentrate may strip paint and care should be taken not to allow contact with skin.

ALCOHOL RESISTANT FOAM CONCENTRATE

These are usually protein foams with additives used at 4% to 6% concentration for low expansion foam. It can resist water miscible liquids and is the only practical choice for many solvents.

COMPATIBILITY OF FOAM CONCENTRATES AND FOAM (BROAD GUIDELINES)

Different types of foam concentrates should not be mixed in the same equipment. In fact, different brands of the same type of foam concentrate are not to be mixed which includes different batches of the same brand. Normally, dry powder should not be used with foam unless otherwise advised.

FOAM EXPANSION RATIO

Low expansion : upto 50:1 (usually between 5:1 and 15:1). Medium expansion : between 50:1 and 500:1 and 1500:1 (usually between 75:1 and 150:1). High expansion : between 500:1 and 1500:1 (usually between 750:1 and 1000:1)

FIREGROUND FORMULA

a) Number of foam making branches/generators required -

For a circular tank, the tank diamater (D) = 10m. Output = 225 litre/min of foam solution. Therefore, the number of foam brances required

$$= \frac{4D^2}{\text{output of branch in litres perminute}}$$

$$= \frac{4D^2}{225} = \frac{4 \times 100}{225} = 1.77$$

i.e. number of foam brances required = 2.

b) High expansion foam concentrate required

1 litre produces appromimately 50 cu. m of high expansion foam. Therefore, foam concentrate required

$$= \frac{\text{cubic capacity(in cu.litres)}}{50} \text{ (app.)}$$

With this we add reserve for topping up due to natural breakdown and wastage.

FOAM BRANCH PIPES

Low expansion

Type	Water (litre/min)	Foam concentration (litre/min)	Pressure (bar)	Finished foam (litre/min)
5 x FMB	200–230	0–14	5-7	2000–2300
No. 2FB	225	5.78	7	2050
No.10FB	455	13.6	7	3640
No.20FB	909	27.3	7	7270
20.30FB	1360	40.9	7	10900

Medium expansion

Type	Foam solution (l/min)	pressure (bar)	Expansion rotio	Throw (m)
800F	200	7	100:1	10
2000F	535	7	100:1	12.5
KR4/75	200	5	75:1	6
KR2/150	200	5	150:1	3
SF225	225	7	85:1	9.5

HYDROCARBON FIRES—AMOUNT OF FOAM REQUIRED

Amount of foam-making equipment and foam required will vary depending upon the size of fire.

Area of fire (m^2)	Application rate at 5 l/sq.m (litre/min)	Foam conc. (l/min) at 4%		Foam branches with out puts (litre/minute)			Foam generators (Type nummbers)				
				225	450	900	5A	10	15	20	30
20	100	4	6	1			1				
40	200	8	12	1			1				
80	400	16	24	2	1		2	1			
100	500	20	30	3	2		3	1			
200	1000	40	60	5	3	2	5	2	2	1	1
400	2000	80	120	9	5	3	9	4	3	2	2

APPENDIX 7

Cryogenic gases – Liquified gases in cylinders and hazards associated with them.

CRYOGENIC GASES

Cryogenic gases are liquified gases which are stored in their containers at extremely low temperatures which are usually slightly above their boiling points at N.T.P., and correspondingly at low to moderate pressures. A gas in cryogenic form will occupy much less space and volume, facilitating easy transportation for commercial purpose. There are, however, certain specific risks associated with cryogenic gases.

Like all liquified gases, these gases expand very rapidly with rise in temperature, causing a rapid rise in pressure. However good the container design may be, heat from the atmosphere cannot be completely prevented from entering the container. The internal pressure in a container of cryogenic gas may build up to a dangerous level causing failure of the container and release of the gas.

Cryogenic materials must be handled in specified standardized containers and storage equipment designed for extremely low temperature operation. Since they vaporize with extreme rapidity and extract heat from objects at high temperature, they tend to displace air from enclosed spaces and when in contact with human body, may freeze and destroy tissue.

LIQUIFIED GASES IN CYLINDERS

There is a temperature above which a gas cannot be liquified by increase of pressure alone. This temperature is called the critical temperature and the pressure required to liquify a gas at the critical temperatue is called the critical pressure.

Liquified gases in cylinders do not obey the gas laws. The pressure in a cylinder of liquified gas will remain constant as the gas is drawn off, provided the temperature remains constant, since more liquid will evaporate to make up for the gas drawn off until all the liquid is evaporated. The pressure in the cylinder is therefore not any indication of the amount of gas in the cylinder.

When liquified gases are stored in cylinders, allowance must be made for expansion of the liquid and its ultimate conversion into vapour. If the temperature rises above the critical temperature, the pressure will rise probably to a critical level with a risk of explosion, and as a result, cylinders are never completely filled with liquid.

Filling ratio

The weight of a liquifed gas to be charged into a cylinder is determined by its filling ratio which varies from gas to gas, and amongst other things, depends upon the density of the liquid.

$$\text{Filling ratio} = \frac{\text{weight of liquified gas}}{\text{weight of water which completely fills cylinder.}}$$

The critical temperature and pressure of some of the commonly found gases are given below:

Gas	Critical temperature (°C)	Critical pressure bar	lb/sq.in
Sulphur dioxide	157	220	3200
Chlorine	144	78	1140
Ammonia	132	77.7	1120
Nitrous oxide	39	–	–
Carbon dioxide	31.1	73.1	1070
Oxygen	119	50	730
Nitrogen	147	34	493
Hydrogen	240	12.9	188

Before a gas cylindar is charged, it is important to know the filling ration of the gas to be charged. The following example will establish the importance of filling ratio. The filling ratio of ammonia is 0.5. This means that a cylinder capable of holding 10 kg of water may only be charged with 5 kgof ammonia. On the other hand, a cylinder of the same size could only be charged with 12.5 kg of sulphur dioxide for which the filling ratio is 1.25.

APPENDIX 8

Suction Lift at Different Temperature and Discharge Characteristics of Different Sizes of Hose

The suction lift of a pump decreases with the rise in temperature of water. At 21^{0}C it gives a lift of 7.3 m, and at 88^{0}C, it will give no suction lift when primed. The maximum theoretical suction lift of 10.3 m is obtainable only at comparatively low temperatures, i.e. in the region of 15.6^{0}C. This is because when water is subjected in this way to a vacuum and lifted through suction column, a small quantity tends to evaporate. This vapour fills the space above the liquid and the water does not rise so high in the suction hose. The higher the temperature, the greater the amount of evaporation at any particular vacuum reading. Thus, at a temperature of 65.6^{0}C the possible suction lift would be about 4.8 m, and at 80^{0}C it would come down to 2.43 m, and at 93.3^{0}C (slightly below boiling point of water) to nil.

Discharge characteristics of delivery hoses – graphical representation

It is important to know the discharge characteristics of the different sizes of non-percolating hose at varying lengths against varying pump pressures for water relay. Graphs can be used to determine the distance between pumps; if twin lines of hose are used, it should be remembered that the quantity delivered through each line is halved. Thus, if the total quantity to be delivered is 2273 l.p.m. through twin lines of 90mm hose at 7kg/cm^2 pressure, half this quantity can be delivered through a distance of 30m through a single line.

Graphs representing the discharge characteristics of different sizes of delivery hoses for varying distances, against different pump pressures for different makes and types of hoses should be obtained from the manufacturers to find out the best performances under different conditions. However, the best all-round performance is generally obtained in relay practice with a pump pressure of 7kg/cm^2 at the base pump in consideration of the characteristic of the pumps and the distance of relay between the pumps.

APPENDIX 9

Use of Logarithmic Tables

Problems on hydraulics and others involve a lot of calculations. Use of the common methods, viz. multiplication and division, is not only laborious but time killing too. Calculations using the log table lead to a quick solution of all the problems involving large multiplication or division.

The requisite information on the use of the logarithmic tables and the formulae expressing the relations on which the use of logarithms is based are discussed here. Attempts at treating the theory and the principles involved have, however, been omitted.

Points to note about logarithmic relations:

$$\log ab = \log a + \log b \tag{1}$$

$$\log \frac{a}{b} = \log a - \log b \tag{2}$$

$$\log a^{n} = n \log a \tag{3}$$

$$\log \sqrt[n]{a} = \frac{\log a}{n} \tag{4}$$

Formula (1) is used for logarithmic multiplication which is done by adding the log of individual numbers, and the product is obtained by consulting the antilog table. The same procedure is followed for the purpose of the division of a number by another, or obtaining the square or cube or their roots by using the formula (2), (3) and (4) respectively.

To find logarithm of a number

A common logarithm consists of an integer called the characteristic and an endless decimal part known as mantissa. The characteristic of a number will differ depending on the position of the decimal point in the number, but the mantissa will remain the same throughout. If the decimal point stands after the first figure of a number, counting from left, then the characteristic is 0; after two figures it is 1; after three figures it is 2 and so on. If the decimal point stands before the first significant figure, the characteristic is –1, usually written as $\bar{1}$; if there is one zero between the decimal point and the first significant figure, it is $\bar{2}$. For example:

Figure	Characteristic

$\log 2.222 = 0.3468$
$\log 22.22 = 1.3468$
$\log 222.2 = 2.3468$
$\log 0.2222 = \bar{1}.3468$
$\log 0.0222 = \bar{2}.3468$

The characteristics portion of the log of a number is determined by inspection but the mantissa portion has to be taken down from common logarithmic tables. To find log of 12.45, the characterisic becomes 1. Now for the mantissa, the first two digits (i.e. 12) is seen in the first column of the log tables and proceeding in that row, the mantissa is found under the column headed with the third digit, 4. This mantissa, 0934, is for 124 and to this is added 18, found in the different column (proportional parts) under the fourth digit 5. Thus the mantissa for 1245 is 0934 + 18 = 0952 and the log of 12.45 is therefore 1.0952. Similarly,

$\log 59.42 = 1.7739$
$\log 5.555 = 0.7447$
$\log 0.092 = \bar{2}.9638$
$\log 0.8231 = \bar{1}.9155$

To find the number corresponding to a given logarithm

When logarithm of a number has been found by taking into consideration its characteristic and the mantissa portion, the number corresponding to the logarithm will then have to be obtained from the antilog table. To find it, the mantissa portion is only taken into consideration.

The exact number is determined from the line with the first two figures from the decimal point of the number in the mantissa portion and under its third figure and to this is added the proportional parts, taking on the same line of the first two figures of the number under its fourth figure from the proportional parts. The decimal point is then placed according to the characteristics of the logarithm. If the characteristics is 2, the decimal point will be placed after the first three figures; if it is 1 or 0, the decimal point will be placed after two figures or one figure respectively. If, however, the characeristic is $\bar{1}$ then point will be placed just before the first figure; if it is $\bar{2}$, one zero will have to be placed between the decimal point and the first figure and so on. For exampale :

Numbers	Characteristic	Mantissa (from logarithm table)	Results (from antilog table)
log 792.4	2	0.8989	792.3
log 99.21	1	0.9965	99.20
log 8.502	0	0.9295	8.502
log 0.6002	$\bar{1}$	0.7783	0.6002
log 0.0594	$\bar{2}$	0.7738	0:0594

The use of log and antilog for long arithmetic calculation saves time and labour and gives the correct results quickly. A few illustrations are given below:

To find

(1) $5260 \times 0.0038 \times 2.74$

Now
$$\begin{aligned} \log 5260 &= 3.7210 \\ \log 0.0038 &= \bar{3}.5798 \\ \log 2.74 &= 0.4378 \\ \hline \text{Sum} &= 1.7386 \end{aligned}$$

Antilogarithm : 54.78

(The sum is the logarithm of the product, the mantissa of which is 7386. On looking up this mantissa in the logarithm tables, it is seen that it corresponds to the digits 5478. Now the characteristic is 1; hence the decimal point will be placed after two figures. The number corresponding to the logarithm, known as antilograthm, is 54.78)

(2) To find $5468 \div 231$

$$\begin{aligned} \log 5468 &= 3.7378 \\ \log 231 &= 2.3636 \\ \hline \text{Difference} &= 1.3742 \end{aligned}$$

Antilogarithm = 23.67

(The difference is the logarithm of the division, the mantissa of which is 3742. On looking up this mantissa in the logarithm tables, it is seen that it corresponds to the digits 2367. Now the characteristic is 1 hence the decimal point will be placed after two figures).

(3) To find $(3.488)^4$

As per formula (3)

$\log(3.488)^4 = 4\log 3.488$

$= 4\times 0.5426$ (log3.488 is multiplied by 4)

$= 2.1704$

$= 148.0$ (By antilog)

(4) To find $(0.0418)^3$

As per formula (3),

$\log(0.0418)^3 = 3\log 0.0418$

$= 3\times \bar{1}.3788$

$= \bar{4}.1364$ (log0.0418 is multiplied by 3)

$= 0.000073$ (by antilog).

(5) To find $\sqrt[4]{24.27}$

As per formula (4),

$$\log\sqrt[4]{24.27} = \frac{\log 24.27}{4}$$

Now $\log 24.27 = 1.3850$

Dividing by 4,

$$\log\sqrt[4]{2427} = \frac{1.3850}{4} = 0.3462$$

Hence antilog 0.3462 = 2.219

(6) To find $\sqrt[3]{0.02}$

As per formula (4),

$$\log\sqrt[3]{0.02} = \frac{\log 0.02}{3}$$

Now $\log 0.02 = \bar{1}.6989$

Dividing by 3,

$$\log\sqrt[3]{0.02} = \frac{\bar{1}.6989}{3}$$

$= \bar{0}.5663$

$= 0.2714$ (by antilog)

(7) Find the value of $\dfrac{(87.29)^2\times 4.139\times 0.0274}{12.98\times\sqrt{36.19}}$

$\log(87.29)^2 = 2\log 87.29 = 2\times 1.9409 = 3.8818$

$\log 4.139 = 0.6169$

$\log.0.0274 = \bar{1}.5622$

(A) log of product $= 2.9365$

$\log 12.98 = 1.1133$

$$\log\sqrt{36.19} = \frac{\log\ 36.19}{2} = \frac{1.5586}{2} = 0.77936$$

(B) log of product = 1.8926

Difference (A)–(B) = 1.0439

Antilog 1.0439 = 11.06

APPENDIX 10

Effect of Speed, Viscosity and Impeller Diameter on the Performance of Centrifugal Pumps

The capacity of a centrifugal pump can be determined by examining the pump's performance curve and the system requirement curve or the system head curve, under the system in which a centrifugal pump is installed. The capacity at which the pump will operate on that system is indicated by the intersection of the pump's performance curve and the system head curve. It is, however, interesting to note the following regarding the performance of a centrifugal pump under different conditions:

If the speed of a pump is doubled, then the head developed by the pump is quadrupled and the capacity which the pump can handle is also doubled, viz. a pump capable of developing 15m total head at 450 l.p.m. at 1750 r.p.m. with a given impeller diameter will develop 60m total head at a capacity of 900 l.p.m. when operating at 3500 r.p.m. The efficiency of the pump remaining the same, with the change of the speed, the horsepower increases by a factor of eight when the speed of the pump is doubled.

To get a rough idea of the pump's performance and with the efficiency of the pump remaining constant, the aforesaid relationship may be expressed as follows:

For a given pump and impeller diameter

$$\frac{RPM_1}{RPM_2}=\frac{GPM_1}{GPM_2}=\sqrt{\frac{Head_1}{Head_2}}=\sqrt[3]{\frac{BHP_1}{BHP_2}}$$

or to express it in a different way

$$\frac{RPM_1}{RPM_2}=\frac{GPM_1}{GPM_2}$$

or

$$\left[\frac{RPM_1}{RPM_2}\right]^2=\frac{Head_1}{Head_2}$$

or

$$\left[\frac{RPM_1}{RPM_2}\right]^3=\frac{BHP_1}{BHP_2}$$

It may, however, be also noted that these formula give only an approximation of the final performance of the pump since the efficiency does change slightly. However, the answer obtained is an excellent approximation.

Effect of change of impeller diameter

The effect of changing the impeller diameter in a given pump being operated at a constant speed can be expressed as follows:

For a given pump and speed

$$\frac{\text{Imp diam}_1}{\text{Imp diam}_2}=\frac{GPM_1}{GPM_2}=\sqrt{\frac{Head_1}{Head_2}}=\sqrt[3]{\frac{BHP_1}{BHP_2}}$$

i.e.

$$\frac{\text{Imp diam}_1}{\text{Imp diam}_2}=\frac{GPM_1}{GPM_2}$$

Also
$$\left[\frac{Diam_1}{Diam_2}\right]^2=\frac{Head_1}{Head_2}$$

$$\left[\frac{Diam_1}{Diam_2}\right]^3=\frac{BHP_1}{BHP_2}$$

These formulae are good for small changes of impeller diameter but they should not be applied when the impeller diameter changes by more than10% and, in that case, the test curves for the pump for the new impeller diameter should be referred to.

Effect of viscosity

The performance of a centrifugal pump changes with an increase in viscosity. An increase in the viscosity of the fluid decreases the capability of the centrifugal pump but increases the horse power. The head capacity curve drops off as viscosity is increased and the brake horsepower also increases sharply, but the N.P.S.H. (net positive suction head) requirement remains the same.

While handling viscous liquids it is advisable to ask for the correction curves for the pump from the manufacturer or his agents.

APPENDIX 11

Essential Requirements for Some Fire Appliances

(A brief guide based on relevant I.S. specifications)

1. 1 800 l.p.m. motor fire engine for use in towns and urban areas

To incorporate a fire pump of 1800 l/m capacity with extension ladder (10.5 m) mounted on gallows, capable of easy withdrawal by one man and towing a trailer pump when required.

a) Road speed of 72 km/hr without trailer on level ground;

b) Acceleration— 64 km/hr in 40 seconds; *c*) Capable of being started from rest up a gradient of 1 in 4 when fully laden; *d*) The brakes (foot operated) to stop the fully laden appliance whthin 17 metres from the point of application of the brakes at 48 km/hr speed, along a level dry road (55% brake effciency) and the hand brake to hold the fully laden appliance stationary on a dry surface gradient of 1 in 4 in neutral gear.

DESIGN AND CONSTRUCTION

Body

Any timber used for body construction to be of good quality, well seasoned and suitably treated. All metal parts, exposed to atmosphere or coming in contact with water shall be of corrosion-resisting material or be suitably treated.

Chassis : Shall be a four wheeler with rear axle drive only and rear axle to be fitted with twin wheels and capable of carrying not less than 250 kg over and above the maximum estimated load including the standard equipments. The wheel base and the overall width not to exceed 4.5 m and 2.30 m respectively.

Turning circle: not exceeding 17 m on either lock and ground clearance not less than 23 cm.

The gear box: Minimum of four speeds forward and one reverse with provision for a power take-off (overhead 'turret' mounted type), capable of transmitting full engine power.

Body work : Enclosed accommodation for seven men. The driving compartment to be so designed as to provide maximum possible vision to the driver. No part of the body work to reduce the road clearance to less than 23 cm or increase the width of the vehicle to more than 2.30 m. The height of the appliance with extension ladder mounted shall not exceed 3 m from ground level and the roof to be such as to support the weight of one man. Driver's seat: adjustable and all windows of safety glass. Doors on both sides of the appliance. Provision to be made in the crew's compartment for carrying three B.A. sets, lockers with internal lighting, preferably automatic. Hose lockers to be of sufficient size (depth and height not less than 58 cm, to accommodate 30 m lengths of unlined hose or 23 m lengths of R.L. hose.

Engine

Six or more cylinders of petrol or oil-fuel type, capable of developing not less than 56 kW brake power at maximum working r.p.m., capable of driving the fully-laden appliance at speed from starting up, without any preliminary running period, even under abnormally cold atmospheric conditions. Dual coil ignition for petrol engines. Engine cooling systems to provide for continuous stationary running without overheating, including running of the pump by providing 'Indirect Cooling System'.

Fuel tank

Not less than 90 l capacity with contents gauge and with two fuel pumps—one mechanically and the other electrically or manually operated.

Electrical system

12 or 24 volt with two heavy duty batteries, connected in series, being of a minimum of 180 Ah and 90 Ah capacity respectively at 10 hr rate for petrol engines and 108 Ah for oil engines. The dynamo to be of heavy duty type and the wiring shall be single pole with positive earth and with separate fuses for all important electric circuits.

Hose reel tank and pipe work

Hose reel tank of minimum 365 litres with water level indicator, being suitably baffled with a filling orifice of 15 cm diameter, removable strainer and cap and with a cleaning hole of 25 cm diameter and cover to be provided at the base as also with an overflow pipe (50 mm diameter).

The hose reel (60 m of 19 mm bore rubber hose in convenient lengths with crow's foot couplings, mounted as to be accessible from either side) shall be fed by the pump and the connecting pipes between the tank, pump and hose reel to be provided with 5-way control valves, viz. hydrant tank, hydrant reel, tank-pump reel, hydrant pump reel and off.

Pump

To be of centrifugal type, rear mounted or amidships, preferably of single-stage design with stainless steel pump shaft carried on antifriction bearings. The impller neck rings and impeller rings to be of high quality bronze and renewable. Glands of suitable type with drain plug at the bottom of the casing to be provided.

The pump at 16.6^{0}C and 760 mm pressure and 4000 r.p.m. of impeller shaft working with all internal and external strainers fitted shall be capable of the following performance subject to the allowance: (*a*) 1% for every 2.8^{0}C temperature rise, (*b*) 4% for every 300 m elevation above sea level, (*c*) 6% for maximum humidity (60%) as against the output and (*i*) 30 cm for every 300 m elevation above mean sea level; (*ii*) 1% for every 2.8^{0}C rise in water temperature as against the lift stated below:

	Minimum output at pressure and lift stated	Conditions
1.	1800 l/min (400 g.p.m.) at 7 kg/cm^2 (100 lb/sq. in) pressure with a suction lift of 3.0 m (10 ft) measured vertically from water level to suction eye.	Working through 5m, i.e. two 2.5 m lengths of specified suction hose.
2.	1450 l/min at 8.8 kg/cm^2 pressure with 3 m suction lift.	As above
3.	40% of 1800 l/min as output at a pressure of 7 kg/cm^2 with a suction lift of 7.3 m.	Working through 10m, i.e. four 2.5 m lengths of specified suction hose.

Suction inlet to be provided with a standard 100 mm suction hose connection with removable internal strainer and blank cap; also, minimum two deliveries with 63 mm quick release coupling and clack valves with standard hose connections.

Primer

Preferably fully automatic (except in the case of rotary primer). The primer to lift water at least to 7.3 m at a rate of not less than 30 cm/sec.

Stability

A fully-equipped appliance with full load (excluding crew) to be subjected to the tilting test and the point at which overturning occurs is not passed at an angle of 35 degrees from the horizontal and preferably not passed at 37.5^0 from the horizontal position.

Acceptance tests for the appliance

Road test: Acceleration, performance, braking test, turning circle and stability test to fulfil the requirements.

Pump test: The pump shall be run for a continuous period of four hours delivering the manufacturer's rated output at 3 m lift at 7.0 kg/cm^2 pressure when neither the water in the engine cooling system shall require replenishment nor the temperature of the engine lubricating oil shall exceed 90% of the maximum temperature recommended by the manufacturer and the engine shall show no sign of distress.

Primer test: The primer shall be tested with a vertical lift of 7.3 m measured from the water level to the centre of the suction eye to check the requirements in the output.

2. 1350 l.p.m. (300 g.p.m.) – small fire engine

A light transport vehicle with a front or rear mounted pump, driven by the road engine, capable of traversing rough and hilly terrain and easily manoeuvrable in the narrow streets of small towns or congested areas.

DESIGN AND CONSTRUCTION

F.A. tank

The appliance to carry a first-aid water tank of 270 litre capacity, made of 3.15 mm m.s. sheets, suitably baffled inside and treated to make it corrosion resistant, with a filling orifice (15 cm), a cleaning hole (25 cm), water level indicator and an overflow pipe.

Hose reel

Rubber hose reel (20 mm bore) of 20 m length to be mounted on the appliance and fed by the hose reel pump with a five-way valve, as stated under 1800 l/min motor fire engine.

Road speed

The fully-laden appliance (without trailer) shall be able to attain a maximum road speed of 100 km/hr on a level road, and with the warm running engine, the fully-laden appliance shall be capable of being accelerated to attain a speed of at least 65 km/hr in 40 sec from a standing start through the gears; also capable of being started from rest up a gradient of 1 in 4. With the trailer attached, the speed of the appliance not to exceed 50 km/hr.

Chassis

The chassis shall be a four wheeler with drive on all the four wheels. Wheel base to be within 3.0 to 3.2 m and the overall width shall not exceed 2.0 m. The turning circle should be as small as possible but not to exceed 17 m and the ground clearance not less than 20 cm. The total weight of the appliance, fully laden, shall not exceed the g.v.w. of the vehicle.

Engine

Petrol driven, capable of developing not less than 30 kW (or 40 B.H.P.) for continuous operation and 52 kW (70 B.H.P.) auto-rating, with arrangements to ensure reliable and quick starting up; also capable of driving the fully-laden appliance at speed from starting up without any preliminary running period even under abnormally cold atmospheric conditions. The clutch shall be of heavy duty type and gauges for indication of temperature of water and oil pressure to be provided.

Fuel system

Fuel tank of 50–70 litre capacity with fuel tank content gauge.

Electrical system

6 or 12 volt system – batteries of heavy duty type (lead-acid storage batteries) and heavy duty dynamo with separate fuses for all electrical circuits to be provided.

Pump

Centrifugal type, preferably of single-stage design, as light as possible with stainless steel shaft carried on antifriction bearing within the casing with self-adjusting type gland and a drain plug at the bottom of the casing. The pump to be tested at 16.6^0C temperature and at pressure of 760 mm of mercury subject to the allowances for 1800 l/min motor fire engine for the pump. At 3500 r.p.m. of the impeller shaft, with all the strainers fitted, the pump to give the following minimum output : (*i*) 1350 l/min with 7.0 kg/cm^2 pressure and 3.0 m lift, while working through two 2.5 m lengths of specified suction hose, and (*ii*) 1200 l/min with 8.5

kg/cm^2 pressure at 3.0m lift, working through four 2.5m lengths of specified suction hose.

Suction inlet : To be provided with a standard 100 mm suction hose connection with removable internal strainer and blank cap.

Primer : Preferably fully automatic and capable of lifting water at least 7.0 m at a rate of not less than 30 cm/sec.

Body work

All metal work of the body to be corrosion resistant. To provide seating accommodation for four men including driver and to enclose as much as possible of the appliance with necessary accessibility. Windows, if provided, to be of safety glass and lockers with automatic internal lighting for equipments as also a spare wheel complete with tyre and tube to be provided. Provision for carrying a 4.5 or 7.5 m extension ladder as specified by the purchaser to be made along with grab rails and non-skid steps. No part of the body work shall reduce the road clearance to less than 20 cm when the appliance is fully laden or increase the width of the appliance to more than 2.3 m.

Hose lockers – waterproof type and the height and depth of the locker shall not be less than 60 cm as measured from the bottom to the top.

Stability

Requirements same as that for 1800 l/min motor fire engines.

Special equipments

A trailer of approved design may be provided with the appliance to meet the special needs. The trailer to accommodate the following equipments: (*a*) Submersible pump (vertical, single-stage or multistage centrifugal pump rigidly connected to an A.C. motor complete with cable reel and flexible wire rope and adjustable tripod for wells up to 3 m in diameter) and capable of delivering water at 800 l/min (180 gallons/min) at 30 m head. (*b*) Portable generator of 230 volt A.C. single phase for driving the submersible pump and lighting up the searchlights. (*c*) Portable pump set, if required. (*d*) Three reels, mounted on the trailer, capable of paying out cable/hose in the same line simultaneously, viz. (*i*) one reel to carry 100 m of T.R.S. cable, the loose end being attached to the submersible pump motor, (*ii*) one reel to carry 100 m of flexible wire rope for suspending the pump, and (*iii*) one reel to carry 90 m of delivery hose in 30 m lengths coupled together by standard instantaneous couplings, the free end being coupled to the submersible pump outlet.

Acceptance tests

Road tests : The acceleration, performance, braking tests, turning circle, and stability test to satisfy the requirements, mentioned against each.

Pump and primer tests : The primer shall be tested with a vertical lift of 7.0 m measured from water level to the centre of the suction eye of the pump to check the fulfilment of the requisite output, which has to be run continuously for 4 hrs to deliver the minimum output against 3 m lift. During this test, the temperature of the engine cooling water and the lubricating oil shall not exceed 85^{0}C and 79.5^{0}C respectively.

Overturning test of trailer : The fully laden appliance with the trailer attached to be driven at 65 km/hr. No overturning of the trailer shall take place on a fairly straight road with normal traffic.

Submersible pump test : The submersible pump to be run for 4 hrs continuously, delivering not less than 800 l/min (or 180 galls/min) at 30 m head. This shall also satisfy the continuous running test for the generator and the searchlights are to be kept switched on during the test.

3. 1800 l.p.m. trailer pump

Capacity not less than 1800 l/min at 7.0 kg/cm^2 pressure, driven by an internal combustion engine or compression–ignition engine. Both the units are mounted on a trailer, with the pump at the rear, capable of being towed by a fire appliance.

DESIGN AND CONSTRUCTION

Engine

The engine, whether petrol or oil-fuel type (compression–ignition), shall have not less than four cylinders. For petrol engines, dual coil ignition with automotic cut-out and a generator for charging a 12 volt battery with capacity of 84 Ah at 10 hr rate shall be provided.

A permanently attached hand starting device which is easily accessible shall be fitted. A self-starting device, if required, to be provided. The engine shall be capable of running at speed from starting up without any preliminary running period even under abnormally cold atmospheric condition and indirect cooling system of the open circuit type to be provided for the engine cooling. An efficient filter of the type which allows cleaning while the pump is in operation when water passes through the cooling tubes shall be provided along with an external filter for the engine lubrication system and a tubed dip-stick to measure the oil in the sump while the unit is running. The engine exhaust to be so arranged as to discharge the gas as far away as possible from the pump operating position.

Fuel

Fuel tank to provide for 2 hr running on full load and fitted with contents gauge on the control panel and the filling orifice shall be positioned as far away as possible from the exhaust pipe, being marked for fuel and with an anti-flash device when the fuel is petrol. There shall be two fuel pumps—one machanically operated and the other electrically or manually operated.

Pump

Centrifugal type, preferably of single-stage and as light as possible. The design, construction, performance, output as also the priming system shall be the same as laid down for the 1800 l/min motor fire pump.

Transmission

The assembly of the pump and engine shall be as light as possible. The transmission between the engine and the pump may incorporate a clutch when so required to enable the pump to be disengaged and engaged when the engine is running at idling speed.

Trailer

The trailer to be fitted with two wheels with pneumatic tyres of suitable size (6.00× 16.6) and with efficient braking arrangement. The trailer frame shall be designed to meet the strenuous conditions while being towed at speed over rough ground; when the pumping unit is mounted on it, the C. G. shall be as low as possible and slightly forward of the axle when the towing eye is 66 cm from the ground. The weight of the trailer, including water, petrol and oil only, not to exceed 1000 kg. When being towed, the height of the towing eye of the trailer shall normally be 56 cm above the ground level and no part of the trailer unit shall have a ground clearance of less than 23 cm when the trailer is tilted to raise the height of the eye to 66 cm or lower it to 46 cm. Two handles of minimum 50 cm length capable of being folded and secured along the frame, to be provided at the front of the trailer frame and to be at least 15 cm above the level of the towing eye.

Stability

To check that under fully equipped and loaded condition, under normal towing position, if the surface on which the appliance stands is tilted to either side to an angle of 40^0 from the horizontal, the point at which overturning occurs is not passed.

Draw bar and towing eye

To be of high quality forged steel of not less than 63 kg/cm^2 ultimate tensile stress and of internal diameter of 75 mm for the towing eye. The design of the eye, housing and the means of fixing the housing to the trailer chassis frame shall take care of a draw bar pull of 2000 kg without being over-stressed.

Acceptance tests

Pump test : In addition to the requisite output at different pressures and lift being checked, the pump shall be run continuously for a period of four hours (with the engine cover closed) delivering the manufacturer's rated output at 3 m lift and at 7.0 kg/cm^2 pressure. During this test, the water in the engine cooling system shall not require replenishment and the temperature of the engine oil shall not exceed 90% of the maximum temperature recommended by the manufacturer.

Primer test : With a vertical lift of 7.3 m measured from water level to the centre of the suction eye, the primer shall be tested to check the requirements stated.

Road test : The trailer shall hold the road well while being towed and the height of the towing eye above ground level and the ground clearance under varying conditions to be checked. The tests shall be made at 64 km/hr speed.

Stability test : Tilting test to be made as per stability requirement unless the maufacturer furnishes a certificate that the appliance with full water and petrol tank and equipments carried in designed storage position, fulfils the requirements.

Schedule of equipments carried

(*i*) Four lengths of 2.5 m length of suction hose (100 mm size) with couplings of same size; (*ii*) One number suction hose collecting head (100 mm); (*iii*) Two suction wrenches; (*iv*) One metallic suction strainer along with a basket strainer; (*v*) One litre capacity fire extinguisher of the vaporizing type.

4. Water tender—Type A for fire brigades

DESIGN AND CONSTRUCTION

The appliance carries a water tank of minimum 2700 litre capacity (made of m.s. plates of 3.15 mm thickness suitably welded or rivetted and brazed) mounted on the chassis a self-contained portable pump and an extension ladder of 7.5 m mounted on the gallows. The appliance shall be capable of towing a trailer pump. The tanks to be oval shaped with convex heads and to be made corrosion resistant by suitable treatment. Tanks exceeding 600 mm in any horizontal direction shall be fitted with vertical baffle plates in both directions at intervals not exceeding 600 mm. Each baffle plate shall have a water-way of not less than 0.01 m^2 cross-sectional area to ensure that the level of water remains the same in the tank. Tanks to be provided with anti-static device, filling orifice (2.5 cm diameter) fitted with a removable strainer and a cleaning hole (4.5 cm diameter minimum). The drain cock and pipe shall be of not less than 50 mm clear water-way throughout. The drain pipe to go below the chassis without reducing the ground clearance (23 cm) when fully loaded. When more than one tank is used, each one shall be fitted with a separate filling orifice and cleaning hole. Two filling pipes (hydrant connection) of 65 mm diameter, each with 63 mm male instantaneous coupling with strainer, to be fitted to the tank.

Sparge pipe and road watering pipe

May be provided in the front and at the rear of the appliance to protect the tyres from ground fires and the control valves for which shall be accessible from the driver's seat.

Road performance

A fully-laden appliance shall be capable of attaining a road speed of 72 km/hr on level ground and the acceleration shall be such that it can also attain a speed of 64 km/hr from a standing start through the gears in a maximum time of 40 sec and is capable of being started from rest up a gradient of 1 in 4 without the use of auxiliary creeper gear. The braking system shall satisfy the same requirements as laid down for 1800 litre/min motor fire engine but shall be of the air-assisted hydraulic type.

Chassis

Capable of carrying a load not less than 250 kg over and above the estimated maximum load including standard equipments. Wheel base and overall width not to exceed 4.35 m and 2.3 m respectively. Turning circle to be small, not exceeding 20 m on either lock. Road clearance not to be less than 23 cm. Chassis to be either a four wheeler or a six wheeler with a fore-wheel drive arrangement for disengaging the drive to front axle to move over steep gradient on a rough terrain. Gear box to have four speeds forward and one reverse.

Engine

Six cylinder – oil or petrol. Same as under 1800 l/min motor fire engine.

Fuel tank

Same as for 1800 l/min motor fire engine.

Electrical system

Same as for 1800 l/min motor fire engine.

Portable pump

A 275 l/min portable pump to be mounted immediately behind the water tank on solid tyred road wheels of not less than 15 cm or not more than 30 cm diameter so as to bring the suction eye below the lowest point of the tank with the same being connected to the water tank.

Body work

Timber shall not be used for body contruction and body to provide accommodation for not less than seven men and to enclose as much as possible of the appliance without interfering accessibility. Rest of the requirements are the same as for 1800 l/min motor fire engine.

Ladder gallows, lockers and stability requirements

Ladder gallows to be designed to carry only 7.5 m extension ladder. As for lockers and the stability of the appliance, the requirements are the same as under 1800 l/min motor fire engine.

5. Water tender – Type B

DESIGN AND CONSTRUCTION

The appliance incorporates a fire pump of 1800 l/min capacity and carries 1800 litre water tank and an extension ladder of 10.5 m, mounted on the gallows, on rollers, capable of easy withdrawal by one man and it shall also be capable of towing a trailer pump.

General requirements

The requirements with regard to the road speed, acceleration, braking efficiency and starting up a gradient of 1 in 4 are the same as under 1800 l/min motor fire engine. So also are the choice of materials and corrosion-resistant treatment for parts coming in contact with water or exposed to atmosphere.

Chassis, engine, fuel system, electrical equipments, pump and primer

The requirements are the same, as laid down under 1800 l/min motor fire engine.

Water tank and pipe work

A water tank, oval in shape with convex heads for maximum strength, made of m.s. plates (3.15 mm thickness) of minimum 1800 l capacity shall be mounted on the chassis. The design of the tank and its mounting shall be the same as laid down under water tender Type A.

Hose reel

The tank shall be connected to the pump and hose reel, holding not less than 60 m of 20 mm bore rubber hose in such a way that pressurization of water tank or water tank pump connection shall not be possible when pumping water from an outside source of supply. A five-way control valve, between the tank, pump and reel, as stated under 1800 l/min motor fire engine to be provided to control the five different operations. The plumbing between the pump and the tank shall provide a clear water-way of not less than 100 mm throughout without any restriction and arrangements to be provided also for venting the tank to atmosphere when water from it is being drawn.

Sparge pipe and road water pipe

The requirements are the same, as laid down under water tender Type A.

Body work, stowage, stability and acceptance tests

The requirements for these items are the same as laid down under 1800 l/min motor fire engine.

6. Portable chemical fire extinguisher (soda acid type)

The extinguisher shall be of the invertible design, being painted 'Fire Red' with the nozzle incorporated with the top end and shall be of 9 litre capacity. The shape of the extinguisher to be cylindrical with an outside diameter of 175 mm.

MATERIAL OF CONSTRUCTION

M. S. sheets used for the manufacture of body to be not less than 1.25 mm thick and not less than 1.60 mm for the cage of the acid bottle. Leaded tin bronze shall be used for neck ring, cap, nozzle and extruded brass section for plunger rod. Brass sheets used for strainer and cage for acid bottle shall be not less than 1.60 mm in thickness. Rubber used for washers shall be acid and alkali resistant.

BODY

The body of the extinguisher shall be constructed of steel sheets by either rivetting, swagging and soldering or welding.

DISCHARGE FITTING

The discharge nozzle shall be fixed to the body by means of a union and nut. The union shall have not less than 10 mm bore. The size of the holes in the strainer fitted at the end of the discharge fitting inside the body shall be less than that of the orifice of the nozzle and the aggregate area of the holes shall be not less than six times that of the nozzle union orifice.

Nozzle

The design of the nozzle and the area of the orifice shall be such that under normal temperature condition, viz. at $27^0 \pm 2^0$C, the solution shall be expelled in the form of a jet which shall maintain an effective throw of not less than 6 m for the minimum periods of time given below. The solution shall also be completely discharged from the extinguisher within maximum periods specified : (*a*) Minimum period during which the jet shall be maintained at a length of not less than 6 m – 60 sec. (*b*) Maximum period for 95% discharge of solution – 120 sec.

Expansion space

This should be sufficient in volume to ensure that when the discharge nozzle is temporarily closed and the extinguisher put into operation at a temperature of $21^0 \pm 2^0$C, the pressure exerted shall not exceed 14 kg/cm^2.

CHEMICAL CHARGE

(*a*) Bicarbonate of soda shall be of such strength that no precipitation of solids take place at 7.2^{0}C. (*b*) The acid (sulphuric acid) and the alkali shall be so proportioned that the discharge liquid is alkaline.

TESTS

Every extinguisher when constructed shall be capable of withstanding an internal hydraulic pressure of 25 kg/cm^2 for a period of 5 minutes without leakage or visible distortion and every extinguisher shall be tested by the manufacturer to the said pressure for a continuous period of 5 minutes.

In any destruction test, when so required, ultimate failure shall not occur at a pressure of less than 32 kg/cm^2 and if below 32 kg/cm^2, the same shall not occur in any joint, seam, casting or fitting.

7. Portable chemical extinguisher (foam type)

CAPACITY

9 litres.

MATERIALS USED

Same as described for soda acid type.

DESIGN

Invertible design. Nozzle incorporated with top end (dome) in the break-seal with plunger type and with cap in the double seal type. Painted fire red.

BODY

Construction either rivetted and soldered or welded type.

MARKING

The extingusher to be marked with letter 'B', indicating suitability for class 'B' fires.

CHEMICAL CHARGE

(*a*) For outer container, carbonate or bicarbonate of soda in solution together with a stabilizer, and for (*b*) inner container, an acid or an acid salt like $Al_2(SO_4)_3$ in such proportion that when the inner and outer solutions are brought into conjunction, the resulting solution shall not be acidic and shall be expelled, as per performance stated below:

Performance

At 27 ± 2^{0}C, the foam solution shall be expelled in the form of a jet, maintaining a throw of not less than 6 m for the minimum period of 30 sec and maximum period of 90 sec of complete discharge of minimum 95% of the expellable foam. The film of foam expelled shall cover an area of 1.5 m to a depth of 5 cm.

EXPANSION SPACE

Same as laid down for soda acid type, except that when the discharge nozzle is closed, the pressure exerted shall not exceed 17.5 kg/cm^2.

ANTI-CORROSIVE TREATMENT

The internal surfaces of the body are to be completely coated with lead tin or lead alloy by hot dipping or by elctrical deposition. The external surfaces are to be thoroughly subjected to anti-corrosive treatment to prevent wear and tear.

TESTS

Same as for soda acid extinguisher.

8. Portable fire extinguishers (dry powder type)

The dry powder used shall be non-toxic and shall retain its free flowing properties under normal storage conditions in the extinguisher.

SHAPE AND BODY

The shape of the body shall be cylindrical and the sizes shall be as follows for 2, 5 and 10 kg extinguishers:

Capacity of extinguisher	Outside diameter of body	Size of filler opening
2 kg	100 mm	60 mm
5 kg	130 mm	75 mm
10 kg	160 mm	75 mm

The top end (dome) and bottom end (dish), if formed from sheet or solid drawn, shall be dished outwards (convex) without reverse of curvature to a radius not exceeding the internal diameter of the body. Any circumferential or longitudinal joint shall be rivetted and soldered, brazed or welded. In invertible type of extinguishers, a cross bar or strip of adequate strength shall be welded to the bottom rim of the body at right angle to the nozzle to facilitate holding of the extinguisher during operation.

GAS SPACE

A gas space to be provided above the specified dry powder level in the body. It shall be of sufficient volume to ensure that when the discharge nozzle is temporarily closed and the extinguisher is operated at 27 ± 2^0C or at such other temperature as may be specified by the purchaser, the internal pressure shall not exceed two-third of the hydraulic test pressure specified.

PIERCING MECHANISM

Where the gas cartridge is fitted inside the extinguisher, a spring loaded piercing mechanism shall be provided in the cap for piercing the seal of the gas cartridge. A safety clip to be provided to prevent accidental operation of the piercing mechanism.

DISCHARGE FITTINGS

The extinguisher outlet shall be fitted with a rubber or braided hose of 75 cm length and 10 mm internal diameter for a 5 kg capacity extinguisher and of 100 cm in length and 12.5 cm internal diameter for a 10 kg capacity extingusher. The bursting pressure of such type of hose shall not be less than 84 kg/cm^2.

PERFORMANCE REQUIREMENTS

The design and construction of the extinguisher to be such as to discharge not less than 90% by weight of the actual rated capacity of dry powder, when the extinguisher is operated at an angle of 45^0 from horizontal position at a temperature of 27 ± 2^{0}C. At this temperature, the contents to expel in the form of a continuous discharge as stated below:

Capacity	Minimum period for throw of jet	Maximum period to discharge 90% of contents	Range of throw of jet	Requirements
2 kg	10 sec	15 sec	3 to 4.5 m	For 2 kg extinguishers, the whole of the powder to fall beyond 1.5 m from the nozzle. For 5 to 10 kg of the same, the whole of the powder to fall beyond 3.0 m from the nozzle.
5 kg	15 sec	20 sec	3.5 to 5.5 m	
10 kg	23 sec	30 sec	5 to 7.5 m	

Tests

a) The body of the extinguisher to be tested to an internal hydraulic pressure of not less than 1.5 times its working pressure or 42 kg/cm^2, whichever is higher, for 5 minutes and there shall be no sign of leakage during the test.

b) The body shall be tested for an internal gas pressure of 14 kg/cm^2 for assembly and there shall be no sign of any leakage.

c) In any destruction test, when so required, ultimate failure shall not occur at a pressure of less than 52.5 kg/cm^2.

9. Recommended scale of portable fire appliances for different types of fire risks

a) Class 'A' fires—light hazard (schools, offices, engineering workshops, etc. as also for storage for wood, textiles, papers, rubbish and the like): One 9 litre water bucket for every 100 m^2 of floor area or part thereof and one 9 litre water type (soda acid, gas pressure or bucket type) extinguisher to be provided to each six buckets or part thereof, with a minimum of one extinguisher and two buckets per compartment of the building, The appliances to be so distributed over the entire floor area that no person to travel more than 90 metres from any point to reach the nearest appliance. In special cases, approved by the appropriate authority, buckets may be dispensed with, provided the supply of extinguisher is doubled.

Class 'A' fires – ordinary hazard (sawmill, carpentry shops, small timber yards, book-binding shops, etc.) : Same as above, but the distribution to be such that no person to travel more than 15 m from any point to reach the nearest appliance.

Class 'A' fires – Extra hazard (large timber yards, godowns, flour mills, godowns storing fibrous materials) : Same as for 'ordinary hazard' plus extra appliances as recommended by the inspecting authority.

b) Class 'B' fires (oil, petrolem products, grease, paints, solvents and the like): Foam type or CO_2 or dry powder type portable extinguisher, as recommended by the inspecting authority to be provided in addition to the requirements of extinguishers for class 'A' fires (light hazard). Each individual case has to be separately examined but a minimum of one extinguisher of the type recommended per 50 m^2 of floor area to be provided.

Where the total area of occupancy presents wholly class 'B' risk, all extinguishers shall be for class 'B' risk only with the provision of at least one extinguisher for 50 m^2 of floor area and the travel distance shall not exceed 15 m.

c) Class 'C' fires (gaseous substances under pressure): CO_2 or dry chemical powder extinguishers to be provided near each plant or group of plants.

d) Class 'D' fires (reactive chemicals, active metals and the like): Special dry powder type of extinguishers (viz. chloride based) or sand buckets to be provided at the scale recommended for class 'B' fires. The inspecting officer may, however, require a higher scale of appliances, depending upon the risk involved.

e) Class 'E' fires (electrical equipments, delicate machines and the like): Extinguishers with B.C.F., C.B.M., B.T.M. or dry chemicals or CO_2 as the extinguishing media to be provided near each plant or group of plants as per risk involved.

10. Foam Compound for producing mechanical foam

GENERAL

Foam compound is defined as a clear homogeneous liquid, free from suspended matter and visible impurities, without any corrosive effect on the container, also non-poisonous and innocuous and free from any objectionable odour to the extent practicable. It shall be a concentrated homogeneous colloidal suspension of hydrolysed protein, containing suitable stabilizers and sufficient preservative to prevent decomposition.

PERFORMANCE

The foam produced shall consist of an aggregation of bubbles of lower specific gravity than oil or water and to have tenacious qualities for clinging to vertical or horizontal surfaces and covering the same. It shall be capable of cooling hot surfaces and flowing freely over the surface of a burning liquid and to form a blanket, sealing off volatile flammable vapours coming in contact with air or oxygen. It shall be dense, resisting disruption due to wind, draught, heat and flame and shall be capable of resealing in the event of mechanical rupture, and also, should be compatible with other foam compounds without any reduction in the quality of the fire-extinguishing properties.

STORAGE—DETERIORATION OF QUALITY

a) No physical, chemical or microbiological changes shall occur, when foam compound is stored either in original containers or kept in the foam compound tanks of fire-fighting appliances for a minimum period of five years from the date of delivery under tropical conditions.

b) It shall also not form scum, sediment or any precipitate which is likely to interfere with its flowing characteristics in the fire-fighting equipments or choke it.

c)Foam compound to be stored in original leak-proof containers at temperatures not exceeding 50^0C or below 0^0C and the store house to be free from damp and should be well ventilated, but the stores not to be exposed directly to sun's rays.

d) Metal drums or barrels to be stacked over wooden dunnage and the barrels to be stacked in single layer only but polythene jerrycans can be stacked in not more than five layers.

e) In case of leakage from the containers, the contents should be immediately transferred to a good leak-proof container and sealed.

f) Each batch of the foam compound supplied to be stored separately and the batches supplied earlier to be consumed first.

g) Metal containers being corroded and found rusty internally shall not be re-used for packing foam compound.

ESSENTIAL REQUIREMENTS

			Requirements Minimum	Maximum
1.	*pH at 27±1°C*			
	a)	Original sample	6	7.5
	b)	After storage at 65±1°C for 72 hrs, followed by storage at –5° ±1°C for 36 hrs	6	7.5
2.	*Specific Gravity at 27°C*			
	a)	Original Sample	1.13	1.18
	b)	After storage for 72 hrs at at 65 ± 1°C, followed by storage for 36 hrs at –5±1°C	1.13	1.18
3.	*Miscibility with water*		Miscible in all proportions	
4.	*Viscosity*		Centistokes	
	a)	At 27 ±1°C	25	40
	b)	At 0±1°C	70	120
5.	*Residue on evaporation* Per cent by weight		35	50
6.	*Sludge content*			
	a)	Original sample		0.25%
	b)	After storage at 65°±1°C for 72 hrs, followed by storage at –5±1°C for 36 hrs		0.50%
7.	*Expansion factor at 27±1°C*			
	a)	With 3% solution	6	–
	b)	With 5% solution	7	–
8.	*Drainage factor at 27±1°C* (Time for drainage of 25% of the liquid in the foam)		5 min	10 min

	Requirements Minimum	Maximum
9. *Fire extinguishment*		
a) Control time (to extinguish the fire except for licks of flame at the edges of foam blanket)	–	4 min
b) Extinction time (For complete extinguishment)	–	5 min
10. *Thermal stability*	7 min	
11. *Fluidity*	Shall maintain a satisfactory flow for a minimum distance of 40 cm.	
12. *Sealability of foam blanket overburning liquid/ cohesion*	15 min	–
13. *Adhesion to vertical or horizontal surfaces*		
a) With 3% solution	15 min	–
b) With 5% solution	10 min	–
14. *Burn-back area inside the opening in the foam blanket after fire extinction*	–	50 cm^2

CONTAINERS

Three types are normally available, viz. 20 litre (polythene jerrycan); 20 litre (m.s.drum); 200 litre (m.s. barrel). A minimum of 5% of the volume of the container to be left vacant and the containers shall be secured for air-tightness after filling.

11. Unlined flax canvas hose for fire-fighting

MATERIAL

Dry spun long line flax yarn of best quality, boiled to an alkali solubility of not more than 10%, free from any weaving defect and dirt, knot or lump, etc. shall only be used for manufacture of hose.

SIZES

Normally three sizes are available with internal daimeter of 50, 63 and 70 mm and in lengths of 23 m and 30 m.

REQUIREMENT

Diameter	Weight (gm/metrelength)	Flow (l.p.m)	Loss of pressure (kg/cm^2)	Percolation during 6th to 10th min after reaching maximum pressure	Percolation during 15th to 19th min after reaching maximum pressure
50 m	260 (300 max)	450	2.3	11 litres	4.5 litres
63 m	350 (400 max)	750	2.0	12.5 litres	5.75 litres
70 m	400 (470 max)	900	1.8	13.5 litres	6.00 litres

FLEXIBILITY

The hose to be sufficiently flexible to be laid in 2m flakes without kinking and when dry to be made up into a smooth roll, i.e. without flats, after being subjected to 7 kg/cm^2 prassure for 30 minutes.

PROOF TEST

This test is to be carried out on the full length after the percolation test. The pressure to be built up not exceeding 7kg/cm^2 per minute to 21 kg/cm^2 and the maintained for 5 mts. The hose shall not show any sign of serious defects, except pin holes (without breakage of yarn) but not at 12 kg/cm^2 and those due to broken warp threads which are easily repairable and considered as not serious defect.

BURSTING PRESSURE

The bursting pressure shall not be less than 32 kg/cm^2.

APPENDIX 12

Broad Principles of Fire Prevention in Multistorey Buildings above 24M

Practice in the U.K.

The fire prevention of high rise buildings is achieved in the U.K. by in-built structural constructions, viz. fire-resisting stairs with pressurized staircase and smoke lobby with complete segregation of the floors by fire-resisting constructions. Each flat on the floor is made completely fire-resisting with F.R. doors, so that there is little chance of any fire travelling from one flat to the other. In addition to this, there are rising mains (preferably wet riser installation) with landing valves and hose reels at each floor, apart from other fixed fire-fighting installations.

The efficiency of the entire fire prevention system, hinges on an automatic fire alarm system, called Sound Diffuser Mark IV System, fitted on the ground floor, which gives visual indication on its indicator panel as to the location of the fire on the floor concerned with intermittent fire alarm ringing throughout the building (e.g. C.I.S and Plaza buildings in Manchester which are nearly 140m in height including three basements). The control panel and the indicator board of the sound diffuser system are connected with thermally sensitive Automatic Fire Detectors, installed on the ceilings of the rooms on each floor. The detecting head has a thermal link, which fuses at a fixed temperature during a fire and causes an electric circuit to be completed through the indicator board, simultaneously starting the electric motor of the pump and, boosting up the pressure in the Wet Rising Installation and at the same time, sending an alarm to the nearest fire station.

The fire officer, on his arrival, immediately checks the indicator panel at the building end and inserts the jack into the plug point for other floors on the indicator board to ensure if there has been any other fire in the building other than the flat indicated on the panel. There are automatic electric lifts, connecting the different floors rising upto different heights being separately energized, apart from a lift, called 'Goods lift', used by the fire brigade during any emergency, which alone can go up to the topmost floor and can be fully controlled by the firemen from the ground floor or from the cage inside without being operated by the inmates of the building from any intermediate floor. This lift is energized by two separate sources of power from different generating stations to ensure the availability of power at all times.

The lifts and the staircases are enclosed within walls of a minimum 4 hr fire resistance and with self-closing fire-resisting doors in the central core of the building with two separate exits at the two ends of the buildings, accessible from each floor. The cables for power, light and communications are located within this fire-resisting central core. The doors on both entrances of the lobby and the pressurized staircase are equipped with a heat- and smoke-sensing element preventing the doors from opening, when the temperature reaches 120^{0}C or smoke obscuration is 0.098 optical density per metre or more at ceiling height or at an elevation of 3.5 m, whichever is lower, at the lobby entrance.

This fire prevention system for high rise buildings in U.K. can also be adopted in our country with certain adjustments.

General

It is important to see that sufficient open space on all sides is also left and the height of the building is restricted to the width of the street. The maximum height of building shall not exceed 1.5 times the width of the road abutting plus the front open space. For heights of buildings above 25 m and upto 30 m, there shall be a minimum open space of 10 m. For heights upto 30 m, there shall be a minimum open space at the rate of 1 m for every 5 m or fraction thereof for heights above 30m, subject to a maximum of 16 m.

It is interesting to note in this connection the recommendations of the Tall Building Committee appointed by the Government of West Bengal. According to the Committee, a minimum clear open space of 6 m both at the front and rear and 3.5 m on the two sides should be left for all tall buildings to be constructed. No building over six storey in height can be constructed, if the width of the street is less than 9.75 m and for construction of buildings which are nine storey or above, the width of the street should be 19.8 m at least.

Details of certain important requirements as per relevant I.S. specification

1. HYDRANT INSTALLATION AND WATER SUPPLY

Hydrants (preferably wet riser installation, permanently charged with water under pressure) are to be installed in all buildings over 24 m in height with arrangements for automatic starting up of the pumping to boost up the pressure as soon as water is drawn from a hydrant landing valve at any floor. The minimum pressure at each of the topmost hydrants shall be 3 kg/cm^2. For buildings over 60 m in height, special pressure-reducing arrangements in some of the lower hydrants and hoses should be provided. There shall usually be at least one riser to each 1000 m^2 of floor area and the risers should be located within a lobby approach staircase or within the staircase where there is no lobby. The inlet diameter of the riser shall not be less than 150 mm. One or two hydrants may be taken up on each floor for each 150 mm riser.

Each wet hydrant installation to be fed by a pump rated to deliver 2275l/min. The pump is to draw its water from a storage tank of not less than 2,00000 litre in capacity, arranged in equal sections of 1,00000 litre each, interconnected through a valve to permit cleaning of the tank from time to time, without putting the hydrant installation completely out of commission, with provision for replenishment from the town's main or with arrangements for filling up at least 2275 l/min into the tank by means of four 63 mm instantaneous inlets and a 150 mm fire brigade pumping connection. As a measure of emergency water supply connection, four 63 mm instantaneous inlets direct to each hydrant riser shall also be provided, so that the fire brigade may pump to the hydrants, in the event of the hydrant pumps being out of commission. The connection to each riser is to be fitted with a sluice valve and reflux valve.

Hydrant pump

Each wet hydrant installation to be supplied with water by an automatic pumping set coming into operation on a predetermined drop in pressure in the hydrant mains by means of a specially devised starting equipment. The pressure for this is to be maintained by an air vessel. Each pumping set shall be capable of delivering 2275 litre/min and generating a pressure at flow, which will ensure a minimum pressure of 3 kg/cm^2 at the highest landing valve outlet.

Standby pumping set

A standby pumping set shall also be provided unless there is alternate standby generator available to supply electricity in the event of public supply failing. Each pumping set shall be capable of delivering 2275 l/min and to ensure a minimum pressure of 3 kg/cm^2 at the highest landing valve outlet.

The hydrant pumps should be of the Squirrel Cage direct-on started electric motor, provided with a drip-proof type of enclosure. The standby pump should be driven by an automatic diesel engine.

2. LOBBY APPROACH STAIRCASE AND FIRE-LIFT

In buildings over 24 m in height, a lobby approach staircase with fire-lift should be provided for. The fire-lift (capable of carrying at least 6 men, fully automatic with emergency switch at ground floor) is to facilitate fire-fighting and rescue operations, particularly from top floors. In general, there shall be a lobby approach staircase to every 1000 m^2 of floor area of each storey, positioned at or near the block.

3. FIRE ALARM AND COMMUNICATION WITH THE NEAREST FIRE SERVICE

In the event of a fire in any flat or block, the same shall be indicated by both audible and visual alarm with automatic starting of the hydrant pump and the nearest fire station should be informed by a permanently installed 'fire-line' connected with the fire station wherefrom a predetermined attendance of appliance and crew should be turned out immediately.

Fire prevention inspection

Regular inspection of the fixed fire-fighting installations, including the hydrants, water supply, landing valves, hose reels, automatic fire detectors and their periodical test by a competent person is essential and the test reports should be properly logged.

Proper cleanliness, good house-keeping, periodic testing of all electric circuits and equipments, stopping leakage from gas pipes are other points which should be taken into consideration in connection with fire prevention.

APPENDIX 13

Metric System in Fire-Fighting – Conversion of the Units

Useful hints

Calculating a kg to be 2.2 lb and a cm^2 to be 0.155 of a square inch, the following table could be regarded as representating the water pressures of the pumps:

kg/cm	p.s.i
1	14
2	29
3	43
4	57
5	71
6	85
7	100
8	114
9	128
10	142

The following may be noted for ladders:

Feet	Metre
30	9
35	10.5
40	12
45	13.5
50	15
55	16.5
60	18
100 (Turntable ladder)	30

As for delivery hose, the relevant units are the following:

Feet	Metre length
50	15
60	18
75	22.5

The conversion figures are approximately as follows :

1.56 in	4 cm
1.95 in	5 cm
2.35 in	6 cm
2.73 in	7 cm

With suction hose:

Length	
8 ft	2.4 metre
Diameter	
3.93 in	10 cm

For the extinguishers, the 2 gal types have been superseded by those of 9 litre capacity. The same applies to the fire buckets also. The sizes of the rescue and other lines have also undergone the following conversion:

100 ft to 30 metres in length.

130 ft to 40 metres in length.

220 ft to 65 metres in length.

120 fathoms grass or coir lines carried on fireboats may as well be classified as 215/220 metre (for comparison of the circumference, the diameter of the delivery hose, stated before, may be referred to).

APPENDIX 14

Fire Retardant Compounds to Prevent Rapid Spread of Fire, Involving Textiles, Paper, Timber, etc.

The records of fires in theatres, hotels, dance halls, departmental stores show that tragic loss of life and valuable property is due to the rapid spread of fire in draperies, curtains, scenery and inflammable decorations, It is impossible to make materials, having cellulose base or composition, completely fire-proof. Treatment with suitable chemicals or compounds may, however, have the effect of preventing flaming or reducing very considerably both the liability to combustion and its rate of progress.

Fabrics may be made fire retardant either by impregnation (by soaking or immersion in a bath containing the agent and drying) or by surface coating by painting or spraying followed by drying.

Timber should be impregnated to obtain a sufficient depth of penetration of the fire-retardant compound. There are two methods of doing it :

1. Open tank method

Here the timber is immersed in the solution which is heated to boiling point and then allowed to cool to ordinary temperature. Penetration takes place largely during the cooling stage.

2. Closed cylinder process

The timber is introduced into large cylinders which are exhausted of air. While being evacuated, the solution is run into the cylinder and a pressure of up to 12.5 bar is applied.

A number of formulae for fire-retardant solutions are known, some of which are reproduced below:

a) U.S. Bureau of Standards

24 parts of sodium tungstate, 6 parts of diammonium phosphate and 100 parts of water.

b) Others

i) Boric acid 60% and borax 40% in water.

ii) Solution of mono-ammonium phosphate 33% and borax 67% in water.

iii) Diammonium phosphate 80%, boric acid 20% in water.

A loading of about 30% is obtained by hand wringing of the fabric and subsequent drying.

The following table gives details of the requisite amount of borax–boric acid solutions to be applied to various materials:

	Borax (gm)	Boric acid (gm)	Water (litre)
For woodwork	850	680	9.0
For domestic articles	198	85	2.25
Stage, scenery, etc.	283	227	4.5
For fire-retarding straw	453	652	9.0

Note: The drying of treated materials must be carefully carried out and preferably done with the material in a horizontal position in order to maintain even distribution of the agent.

For treating thatched roofs, the following mixture has been found quite effective: ammonium sulphate 12.6 kg, ammonium carbonate 6.3 kg, Borax 3.2 kg, Alum 6.3 kg, water 180 lit. A standard formula for fire-retardant paint is sodium silicate (water glass) 50kg, kaolin (China clay) 67.5 kg, and water 45 litre. Of late, the use of antimony oxide, sodium tungstate, sodium stannate and diammonium phosphate have found applications in various formulations.

Numerous chemicals have been investigated for fire-retarding paper and similar cellulosic materials and these include most of the substances mentioned in connection with the cotton fabrics above. The preparations employed are usually added to the finished pulp or stock before the addition of any filler, which may be used. Examples of the preparations used are (*i*) a mixture of ammonium phosphate, ammonium chloride, sodium phosphate and borax, and (*ii*) zinc chloride dissolved in water, excess of ammonium hydroxide added and then ammonium chloride. Magnesium chloride may, however, be used instead of zinc chloride.

Recent advancements

Recently a chemical formulation based on antimony oxide with halogenated co-polymer binder has been successfully developed to impart flame retardancy to canvas cloth with a view to reducing fire hazard in tents and pandals. The solvent suspension is prepared by mixing borate salt and finely divided antimony oxide and this mixture is dispersed in a solution obtained by dissolving the halogenated co-polymer binder and phosphate salt in an ester or ketone organic solvent as per the formulation below:

Name of the chemical	Weight
Antimony oxide	7–15%
Halogenated co-polymer binder	2–8%
Borate salt	4–8%
Phosphate salt	1–5%
Phthalate salt	0.01–2%
Ester of carboxylic acid as solvent	75–88%

This solvent suspension does not allow the flame to spread and it also renders the fabric self-extinguishing when involved in a fire.

APPENDIX 15

Salient points on Petroleum Act 1976 with Petroleum Rules 1976

Petroleum refers to any liquid hydrocarbon or mixture of hydrocarbons and any inflammable mixture (liquid, viscous or solid) containing any liquid hydrocarbon.

Petroleum Class A : Petroleum having a flash point below 23°C.

Petroleum Class B : Petroleum having a flash point of 23°C and above but below 65°C.

Petroleum Class C: Petroleum having a flash point of 65°C and above but below 93°C.

Notes

a) The word petroleum includes kerosene and it is included in 'Non-dangerous petroleum'.

b) No license is required for import, transport or storage of Petroleum of Class A which are not intended for sale, if the total quantity in possession does not exceed 30 litres.

Petroleum of Class A, should be kept in securely stoppered receptacles of glass, stoneware or metal, which in the case of glass or stoneware should not exceed one litre in capacity, or in the case of receptacles of metal, exceed 25 litres in capacity.

Petroleum of Class A, exceeding 30 litres in capacity, shall be stored in an isolated place which does not communicate with any room where any person may reside or work, or in any room where people assemble.

c) Petroleum having flash point not below 93°C is exempted from the purview of the Petroleum Act 1976.

d) Whenever there is any accident by explosion or by a fire as a result of the ignition of petroleum vapour, attended with loss of human life or serious injury to a person or property, the occupier of the place or the person in charge shall immediately report the matter in full detail to the nearest magistrate or to the officer-in-charge of the nearest police station and to the Chief Inspector of Explosives.

e) Containers of Petrolueum of Class A shall be constructed of tinned, galvanized or externally rust proof sheet iron or steel as approved by the Chief Inspector of Explosives and shall not exceed 300 litres.

f) Air space of not less than 5% of its capacity shall be kept in each container.

g) Containers of petroleum of Class B or C shall also be constructed of steel or iron as approved. An air space of not less than 5% of its capacity shall be kept in each container for Class B and 3% of its capacity for Class C.

h) All empty tanks or containers of Class A or Class B which contain petroleum shall be kept securely closed until they have been thoroughly cleaned and freed from petroleum vapour. No repair work to such container (hot work) shall be carried out unless it has been thoroughly cleaned and freed from petroleum vapour.

i) Due precautions are to be taken at all times to prevent escape of petroleum into any drain, sewer, or harbour, river or over any public road or railway line.

j) No child under the age of sixteen years and no person in a state of intoxication shall be employed for the loading or unloading or transport of petroleum or in any premises licensed under these rules.

k) No person shall smoke and no matches, fires, lights or articles or substances capable of causing ignition of petroleum shall be allowed at any time in proximity to a place where petroleum is refined, stored or handled or in any vehicle in which petroleum is transported.

l) Petroleum in bulk shall not be transported in a barge or flat unless the barge or flat is self-propelled or is in tow of or otherwise attended by a steamer or tug and carrier. (*i*) At least four fire extinguishers suitable for extinguishing oil fires, and a covered sand box containing 0.20 cu.m of sand to be provided; (*ii*) a suitable hammer of non-sparking metal to be provided; (*iii*) a red flag shall also be provided.

m) No ship or other vessel shall carry petroleum in bulk if it is carrying passengers or any inflammable cargo other than petroleum or coal. No country craft shall carry petroleum Class A if it is carrying passengers.

n) The loading and unloading of petroleum in bulk shall be by armoured hose and metal pipes and all such hose or pipes shall be electrically continuous and free from leakage.

o) No fire, naked light, matches or other appliances for producing ignition or explosion, and no smoking shall be allowed on board any barge, flat or vessel used for the transport of petroleum Class A.

p) Vessels unloading or loading petroleum shall have adequate fire extinguishing appliances so disposed that they can be put into immediate use.

q) The following will apply to any mechanically propelled vehicle, used for transport of petroleum by road, which is other than of Class B, other than in bulk, or petroleum of Class C: (*i*) the engine shall be of internal combustion type; (*ii*) the exhaust shall be wholly in front of the tank or the load as the case may be and shall have ample clearance from the fuel system and combustible materials and shall not be exposed to leakage or spillage of the fuel or product or accumulation of grease or oil. The exhaust pipe shall be fitted with an approved spark arrestor; (*iii*) The muffler or silencer shall not be cut off from the exhaust system; (*iv*) The engine air intake shall be fitted with an effective flame arrester or an air cleaner having effective flame arrestor characteristics substantially installed and capable of preventing emission of flame from the side of the engine in the event of backfiring; (*v*) the cab of the vehicle shall be of all metal construction and its near window shall be fully covered with wired glass; alternatively the cab and the engine shall be separated from the tank or the load, as the case may be, by a fire-resisting shield which shall fully cover the tank or the load; (*vi*) For all electric light or electrically operated equipment employed or where any vehicle, including a trailer, is used in the transportation by road of pertroleum other than petroleum of Class C,

(1) the voltage not to exceed 24 volts.

(2) The electric wiring shall be heavily insulated and to be provided with suitable over-current protection in the form of fuses or automatic circuit breakers.

(3) The generator, battery, fuses and circuit breakers shall be in the cab of the vehicle or in the engine compartment with a heavy duty switch close by to cut off the battery.

(4) All vehicles used for transport of petroleum by road shall be constantly attended by at least one person who is familiar with the provisions of the Petroleum Act and the emergency procedures. The vehicle shall not be parked on a public road or in a congested area or at a place within 9 metres from any source of fire. It shall also be provided

with appropriate type of portable fire extinguisher at easily accessible position.

(5) All petroleum pipe lines entering any tank vehicle for loading or unloading shall be electrically continuous and be properly earthed.

(6) No mechanically propelled vehicle carrying petroleum shall be loaded or unloaded until its engine has been stopped and the battery is isolated from the electrical circuit.

(7) No tank vehicle shall be loaded at a rate exceeding 1 metre per second at the delivery end of the filling pipe until the filling pipe is completely submerged in petroleum and thereafter the loading rate may be gradually increased; but it shall, at no time, exceed 6 metre/sec at the delivery end of the pipe line.

Storage of petroleum

CLASS A (FOR STORAGE NOT EXCEEDING 300 LITRES IN A STORAGE SHED)

i) Petrol of this category is to be stored in a storage shed constructed of suitable non-combustible material on isolated ground· the doors or windows of this shed may be of wood; it may be strored in a properly ventilated iron bin of a design approved by the Chief Inspector of Explosives.

ii) The storage shed shall have to be adequately ventilated near the ground level as also near the roof. The ventilators shall be provided with two layers of non-corroding metal wire gauze having not less than 11 meshes per linear centimetre.

iii) The storage shed shall not form part or be attached to any building in which any person resides or works or where persons assemble for any work unless it is separated therefrom by a substantial roof and partition wall of masonry construction, having no openings therein.

iv) The storage shed, if in any building, shall not be situated under any staircase or under any other exit.

v) Any two storage sheds or bins or other storage premises not more than 6m apart shall be deemed to be one storage shed.

vi) All empty receptacles shall be kept securely closed unless they have been thorougly cleaned and freed from petroleum vapour.

vii) Containers shall not be repaired on the premises unless all reasonable precautions are taken to ensure that these are free from such petroleum. Also, care shall be taken at all times to see that petroleum of Class A does not escape into any drain, sewer, harbour, or water-course or a public road.

i) To be stored in the licensed storage shed contructed of suitable non-combustible material, but the beams, rafter columns, doors and windows may be of wood. The floor of the storage shed shall be suitably finished to form a sump or enclosure not more than 30 cm deep and capable of receiving and retaining, in case of any accident or emergency, a volume of not less than half the quantity allowed under the licence.

ii) The storage shed shall not form part of or be attached to any building in which any person resides or works or where persons assemble for any purpose, unless it is separated by a substantial floor or partition which is constructed of non-inflammable material and has no openings in it.

iii) It should also be not situated under any stair case or under any other means of escape.

iv) Any two storage sheds not more than 3m apart shall be deemed to be one storage shed.

STORAGE OF PETROLEUM (CLASS A) IN A TANK

i) Every tank shall be outside any building and placed in a masonry or concrete pit and packed round with sand, earth or clay so that no air space is left between the tank and the masonry or concrete pit; the tank shall be visible.

ii) Every tank shall be fitted with an independent vent pipe leading into open air. The vent pipe shall be securely supported and shall not be less than 4m in height and 4m from any adjoining land or from the nearest opening of the sales room/kiosk or any other facility in which sources of fire are likely to be present. Vent pipe of one tank shall not be interconnected with the vent pipe of another. The open end of every vent pipe shall be covered with two layers of non-corrodible metal wire gauze having not less than 11 meshes per linear centimetre and shall be further protected from rain by a hood or by suitably bending it downwards.

iii) Every tank before being repaired or exhumed shall be cleaned of all petroleum and of all flammable vapours. When a tank is opened for cleaning or repair, no electric or other lamps, electric cable fans or appliances or equipments capable of igniting flammable vapours shall be brought near the man-hole of the tank until the tank is certified to be 'gas free' by a competent person.

iv) No artificial light capable of igniting flammable vapours shall at any time be present in the immediate vicinity of the tank, lorry/wagon during the transfer of the petroleum to the tank, and no person engaged in such transfer shall smoke. When the underground tank is being filled with petrol, no smoking shall be allowed within a distance of 9 m from the barrels.

v) No license is needed for transport/storage of limited quantities of petroleum of Class A, B, or C. The quantities are: for Class A – 30 litres (not intended for sale); for Class B – up to 2500 litres and none of it contained in a receptacle exceeding 1000 litres in capacity; for Class C – up to 45,000 litres when such petroleum is transported or stored in accordance with the rules u/s 4 of the Petroleum Act.

Electric installation

With the exception of what has been stated below no electric wiring shall be installed and no electric apparatus shall be used in any refinery installation, storage shed, service station, or other places where petroleum is refined, blended, stored, loaded or unloaded.

Hazardous area

An area shall be deemed to be a hazardous area where :

i) Petroleum having flash point below 65^{0}C or any flammable gas or vapour in a concentration capable of ignition is likely to be present.

ii) Petroleum or any flammable liquid having flash point above 65^{0}C is likely to be refined, blended, handled or stored at or above its flash point.

CLASSIFICATION OF HAZARDOUS AREA

Hazardous areas are classified as:

i) Division 0 area, where flammable gases or vapours are expected to be continuously present.

ii) Division 1 area, where flammable gases or vapours are likely to be present in the area under normal operating conditions.

iii) Division 2 area, where flammable gases or vapours are likely to be present in the area only under abnormal operating conditions of failure or rupture of an equipment.

a) No electric apparatus shall be allowed in a Division 0 area except that an intrinsically safe apparatus of an approved type with an intrinsically safe circuit may be used where use of such an apparatus cannot be completely ruled out.

b) All electric apparatus installed or used in a Division 1 area shall be either :

1) flameproof or instrinsically safe apparatus, as approved by the Chief Controller of Explosives, or

2) must be of industrial-type apparatus housed in an enclosure or a room which has been made safe by pressurizing or purging with a plenum of atmosphere free from significant concentration of any flammable gas or vapour and so arranged or interlocked that in case of the failure of pressurizing or purging agent, the electric supply is automatically cut off or a warning is automatically given to a person in attendance who shall take suitable measures to prevent a hazard.

c) All electric apparatus installed or used in Division 2 area shall be either:

1) a non-sparking apparatus of a type approved by the Chief Controller of Explosives, or

2) An apparatus of any of the types as prescribed for Division 0 or Division 1 area.

Electric wiring

All electric wiring, other than the conductors of an intrinsically safe circuit, shall be effectively sealed at all joints, mechanically protected and adequately supported and shall consist of:

i) approved armoured cable with correctly designed terminations complete with armour clamps. The armouring and the electrical clamps are to provide mechanical support to the cable and electrical continuity, or they should be metal sheathed cable with correctly designed and installed terminations, or

ii) single or multicored insulated cables accomodated in solid drawn heavy gauge screwed galvanized conduits used in conjunction with approved flameproof fitting, the conduit being sealed at both ends and installed in such a manner as to permit internal condensation to drain at a point or points from which it may be removed;

iii) Single or multicored mineral insulated cable of approved type in conjunction with approved flameproof-type glands at all joints and terminations.

Earthing and bonding

All electrical system and equipments shall be efficiently earthed. The resistance value of an earthing system to the general mass of the earth shall not be less than,

i) 4 ohms in the case of electrical systems and equipments or a value that ensures the operation of the protective device in the electrical circuit, whichever is lower, and

ii) 10 ohms in the case of all non-current-carrying metallic parts of major electrical apparatus or any major metallic object;

iii) All joints in pipelines, valves, plants, storage tanks and equipment for protection shall be made electrically continuous by bonding or otherwise; the resistance value between each joint shall not exceed 10 ohms.

Portable electric apparatus

i) No portable lamp or apparatus other than a portable lamp, as approved by the Chief Controller, shall be installed or used in a hazardous area.

ii) No mains operated portable lamp shall be operated at a voltage exceeding 25 volts above the earth provided that the Chief Controller may allow higher operating voltage not exceeding 55 volts above earth.

Precautions against fire

i) No person shall smoke in any installation, storage shed, or service station, save in places specially authorized by the licensing authority for the purpose.

ii) No person shall carry matches, fuses, or other appliances capable of producing ignition or explosion in any installation or storage shed which is used for the storage of petroleum.

iii) No fire, furnace or other source of heat or light capable of igniting flammable vapour shall be allowed in any installation or storage shed or service station, save in places specially authorized by the licensing authority.

iv) An adequate number of portable fire extinguishers capable of extinguishing oil fires shall always be kept in every installation, storage shed, or service station at strategic points and all persons employed in such installations shall be conversant with the use of such extinguisher.

Precautions against fires including fire control at refineries

i) Every refinery shall be fully protected against fire by a well organized and trained fire-fighting service with necessary materials and fixed, mobile and portable equipment for fighting fires.

ii) An adequate supply of water should be available at all strategic points in the refinery by means of an independent ring main or grid provided with isolating valves. The mains shall be kept constantly pressurized by two or more boosting pumps of adequate capacity, preferably working automatically as soon as any significant loss of pressure in the main occurs. One of the boosting pumps, at least, should be independent of the normal power supply.

iii) All mains shall be fitted with hydrants at convenient places not more than 30m apart; such hydrants shall be of a design suitable for operating conditions and for connecting mobile pumps.

iv) Static water supply of adequate capacity shall be provided when mains water supply may be subject to interference.

v) All refinery personnel shall be conversant with the use of first aid fire-fighting appliances and a select refinery personnel shall be trained in all aspects of fire-fighting.

vi) The Chief Inspector may relax any of the provisions as stated above or require additional fire-fighting provisions to be made, if he deems such relaxation or provisions are necessary for any refinery.

APPENDIX 16

Explosives – Some Important Points Quoted from the Explosives Act and the Rules

Under the Explosives Act and the Rules framed thereunder, explosives have been classified under eight categories, viz. (*i*) gunpowder, (*ii*) nitrate mixture, (*iii*) nitro compound, (*iv*) chlorate mixture, (*v*) fulminate, (*vi*) ammunition, (*vii*) fireworks, and (*viii*) L. O. X. (liquid oxygen explosives).

Notes

a) Fulminate means any chemical compound or mechanical mixture which, from its great susceptibility to detonation, is suitable for employment in percussion caps or any other appliances for developing detonation or which, from its extreme sensibility to explosion and from its great instability, is specially dangerous. Of all the explosives, the fulminates, due to their readiness to undergo rapid decomposition from very small stimulus, are most hazardous.

b) L. O. X. refers to an absorbent carbonaceous material such as wood pulp, carbon black, metal powder, coal dust etc., impregnated with liquid air or liquid oxygen with or without the addition of other substances.

Some important points

i) No explosive shall be imported, tendered for transport, possessed or sold unless it is properly packed as prescribed under the Explosives rules. The outermost package shall be marked in conspicuous character with the word 'Explosive', the name of the explosive, the number of the class and of the division to which it belongs, and the name of the consigner or manufacturer.

ii) The floor of any place over which the explosive is to be laid should be throughly cleaned and swept both before and after use so that nothing which may endanger the safety of the consignment is left behind.

iii) The casks or packages containing the explosives should not be thrown, dropped, rolled or pulled along the ground or floor, but should be passed from hand to hand and carefully deposited and stored.

iv) After the handling of explosives has commenced, the operation shall proceed with due diligence and without unnecessary stoppage.

v) No person shall smoke and no fires, lights or articles of an inflammable nature, or liable to spontaneous ignition or capable of causing any fire or explosion shall be allowed at any time in proximity to a place where an explosive is stored or handled.

vi) No person should go near any place where explosives are handled, shall have in his possession any matches, fuses or other appliances capable of causing ignition or explosion, or carry knives or other articles made of iron and steel or wear boots or shoes with iron nails or strengthened with iron nails (unless such boots or shoes are covered with leather, India-rubber or felt or other materials in the form of overshoes or otherwise).

vii) If any explosive escapes from the package in which it is contained or is spilt, such explosive shall immediately be carefully collected and destroyed.

Fire-fighting classification of explosives

Class I explosives are those which must be expected to explode en masse as soon as fire reaches them.

Class II explosives are those which are readily ignited and burn with great violence without necessarily exploding.

Class III explosives are those which may explode en masse. But compared with Class I explosives, these may be exposed to a fire for sometime before exploding. There will, however, be a blast and fragment hazard.

Class IV explosives are those which burn fiercely and give off dense smoke which in certain cases has toxic effects. There is no risk of mass explosion.

Class V explosives are those which contain toxic substances.

Class VI explosives are those which may be exposed to a fire for sometime before exploding. The risk of mass explosion is not involved but small sporadic explosions occur with increasing frequency as the fire takes hold. There will be a fragment hazard but not a serious blast risk.

Class M.P. comprises of substances of the non-explosive, dangerous goods class, containing metallic powders such as magnesium, aluminium or zinc powders, either in ammunition or in bulk. When these are stored by an explosives establishment, provision for fire-fighting must be made.

Fire-fighting procedure

It may be remembered that under no circumstances fighting fire involving explosives should be carried out in accordance with practice and technique adopted for ordinary risks. The key to correct fireground tactics and procedure in these circumstances lies in an intimate knowledge of the behaviour of the different types of explosives. The staff of the explosives establishment are experts in this field and it is, therefore, a must that the officer-in-charge of the public service units be present, should be guided by, and act in close cooperation with the explosives establishment.

FIGHTING FIRES IN ABOVE-GROUND SITES

Success in fighting fire involving explosives is largely dependent on actions being taken before the fire can develop. Copious amount of water must also be available.

Class I explosives fire

If detected early, the prompt application of first aid fire-fighting measures may prevent development of a serious fire. The fire alarm must be operated immediately and all non-essential staff evacuated to a safe position. Action should be taken to prevent the explosives from being involved. Fire-fighting operation are to be carried out from behind adequate cover such as provided by intervening mounded building or high ground.

If fire reaches the explosives, an explosion is to be expected, the external effects of which will depend upon the quantity and type of explosives and the design of the building and its protecting traverses. Action in such cases should be confined only to prevent the fire spreading to adjacent buildings or stacks. Roofs and walls of the adjacent buildings should be thoroughly sprayed with water to counteract the effect of heat, burning debris or sparks. The offcer- in-charge will decide whether the explosives contained in these buildings or stacks are also to be sprayed, especially if the number or size of fragments falling on such buildings is large. If drenchers or sprinklers are fitted in the buildings, they should be operated directly, when the risk is apparant.

Class II explosives fire

If a fire occurs in a building of an explosive factory containing such explosives, it will spread rapidly and burn fiercely. There is no risk of mass explosion. The fire-fighting service should attempt to subdue the fire and prevent its spread to adjacent buildings, as stated for Class I explosives.

If a fire occurs in a filling factory or an above-ground storage site, first aid fire-fighting staff can fight the fire before or after the explosives become involved, as there is no great risk of explosion. The fire is likely to be fierce.

Class III explosives fire

If detected early, the prompt application of the first aid fire-fighting measures will prevent the development of a serious fire. The fire alarm should be operated immediately and all non-essential personnel evacuated from the vicinity. If the explosives have become involved, fire-fighting should be continued when substantial cover is afforded by intervening mounded building or high ground. The spread of fire to neighbouring buildings should be dealt with as stated under Class I fires.

Class IV explosives fire

If detected early, the prompt application of first aid fire-fighting measures may prevent the development of fire. The fire alarm should be operated immediately and the fire-fighting services are to fight the fire, whether the explosives are involved or not, as there is no risk of mass explosion. Dense smoke will be given off and the use of breathing apparatus is essential for personal safety. When incendiary fillings are involved, a fierce fire with intense heat is to be expected and to prevent the spread of fire to other buildings, actions suggested under Class I explosives fire are to be taken.

If phosphorus fillings are involved, loose phosphorus will ignite spontaneously when it dries out and special precautions are necessary in proper removal of the residue. The affected packages and loose residue should be removed to a safe spot and isolated into small groups and allowed to dry where they will burn out.

When the fire has been subdued, the building should be strewn with wet sand and thoroughly cleaned. All residues will have to be removed to a safe place and allowed to burn out. The building should be dried out and carefully inspected in the dark for signs of phosphorus before being used again. Special care should be exercised by fire-fighting personnel to avoid contact between phosphorus and fire-fighting equipment, clothing, or human body. Phosphorus causes severe flesh burns.

Class V explosives fire

If detected early, prompt application of first aid fire-fighting measures may prevent the development of the fire. The fire alarm should be operated immediately. The fire-fighting services may fight the fire whether the substances are involved or not as there is no risk of mass explosion. The toxic effects may, however, be very serious. The bursting charge of the weapons are liable to explode in a fire and scatter the toxic fillings. Protective clothings and self-contained B.A. sets are essentially required by the fire-fighting staff to avoid liquid contamination with body and the toxic effects in the form of a cloud of lethal gas. The fire should be fought from the windward side. A general alarm must be sounded to put the police and the civilian population on the alert to enable them to proceed in accordance with the prearranged scheme.

Class VI explosives fire

If detected before the explosives are involved, prompt first aid fire-fighting measures will prevent the development of the fire. The alarm should be operated immediately. Once the explosives have become involved, all non-essential personnel are to be evacuated from the vicinity, but fire-fighting to be continued from behind light cover such as brick buildings. The spread of fire to adjacent buildings should be dealt with as for Class I explosives fires.

Class M.P. fire

If detected early, prompt application of first aid fire-fighting measures may prevent the development of the fire. The fire alarm should be operated immediately.

To deal with the burning metallic powders, extinguishers of eutectic chloride type or those containing powdered talc, asbestos, asbestos graphite or dry-sand are to be used. Care should be taken to avoid agitating the powder. Water, foam or CO_2 extinguishers should not be used, except in the case of ammunition in this class, which, if involved in the fire, may be fought at early stages with water.

FIGHTING FIRES IN UNDERGROUND SITES

a) The term underground sites means storage sites where the whole of the storage space is below the natural ground level.

b) Self-contained B.A. sets are essential for personal protection in underground fire-fighting.

c) The fire-fighting procedure should be, in general, similar to that of the above-ground fires, with the following exceptions:

Class II

If these explosives are involved, the flames are likely to sweep through the entire place. The available oxygen will be quickly exhausted and the chances of escape or fire-fighting are very small.

Class IV

Explosives belonging to this class are not stored in underground sites because of the difficulties in fire-fighting which would arise from the flames or smoke given off by the substances when they are seriously involved in a fire.

Class V

These explosives will only be held in underground sites in very exceptional circumstances. In case they are involved underground, the fire can be fought so long as it is clear that only the packages are involved. When there is a risk of the weapons bursting through heat or explosion, fire-fighting should be suspended. Full protective equipment should be worn in all operations of this nature. During fire-fighting, the personnel in close proximity to the fire should be sprayed with water to prevent the protective clothing getting ignited. The site can be entered after an interval of two or three days after the fire ceases and inspected by fully protected personnel.

High and low explosives

Explosives are sometimes referred to as high and low explosives. The difference lies in their reaction speed. In the case of high explosives, the reaction can be so instantaneous that the process of explosion may be termed as detonation. Low explosives have a slower development in their explosion and the term deflagration (literally 'flaming off') is used to describe them. The principal member of the low explosives group is gun powder (black powder). From a fire point of view, this is one of the most noteworthy explosives since it is extremely sensitive to ignition from sparks, heat and friction. It burns very violently even when quite free and not compressed and releases volumes of smoke on exploding. It is used in blasting fuse and pyrotechnic compositions. Following are some of the main characteristics and uses of common high explosives:

NITROGLYCERINE

A very powerful and sensitive explosive with qualities that make it difficult to use in unmixed form but excellent for many purposes in combination with other explosives. It forms the basis of dynamites and blasting gelatine.

DYNAMITES

These are not individual susbstances as popularly supposed. Dynamites are a very considerable group of powerful explosives embodying nitroglycerine and absorbent often with gelatines and other ingredients like ammonium nitrate.

NITRATES

Ammonium nitrate, though used as a fertilizer, is one of the commonest constituents of nitrate mixture although it is not classed as an explosive. When used in combination with selected other substances, it has a wide variety of civil and military uses (e.g. slurry explosives). The well-known Amatol, for example, which combines ammonium nitrate with T.N.T. (trinitrotoluene), burns very rapidly and fairly harmlessly (except in very large masses), but is a very powerful explosive when compressed and suitably initiated. Its principal uses are in propellent mixtures for shotgun and small arms and in nitroglycerine explosives.

T.N.T.—TRINITROTOLUENE

Powerful explosive, used for blasting and as bursting charges for some types of ammunition. They are relatively safe to handle and, in bulk, may burn to detonation.

CHLORATES

Principally used in fireworks. They are not used in blasting explosives. They have limited use in cap and detonator composition. They are normally used in the form of salts of sodium or potassium.

FULMINATES, AZIDES AND STYPHNATES

They form very sensitive and dangerous mixtures with sulphur, phosphorus and carbonaceous materials. The duration of their explosion is short and violent. They are commonly used with other substances as initiators in the form of caps and detonators. As a measure of safety, they are normally made wet with not less than 20% of water and packed in double packing so that the inner container, when closed, should not lose any moisture or allow any escape of explosives.

PENTAERYTHRITOL TETRANITRATE (P.E.T.N.)

Another dangerous explosive used as detonator; sensitive to shock; should be handled very carefully and to contain not less than 25% of moisture for safety. The containers should have a double packing. The inner package should be a polythene bag, closed at the top with twine thread.

Causes of fire and methods of protection

In most cases, fires occur in the use, manufacture or storage of explosives, including fireworks, from inadvertant ignition of a material or component containing explosives. There may be rapid or intense fire of short duration, or a more steady fire of variable persistance. Such fires are normally accompanied with violent explosions with projectile of debris which may cause other fires. Damages may vary between minor effects within the building itself to complete destruction by fire or explosion. Personnel may also suffer from burns or injuries, which, in some cases, may be fatal. Serious outbreaks of fire or conflagration are, however, rare from such explosions.

The cause of ignition during manufacture is often impossible to determine, but may be due to inadvertant inclusion of foreign bodies, grit or dust in the materials themselves or in the processing machinery; causes of ignition may also include variations in the compositions, too low atmospheric humidity, friction, mishandling, whereby explosives are accidentally dropped or struck.

Prevention and protection

Protective procedures are elaborate and far-reaching. They depend on a very high standard of control, cleanliness and fire protection and on weeding out a source of ignition by the use of special clothing and footwear, flooring, tools and other equipment. They also include the provision of first aid fire-fighting appliances and, in larger establishments, the usual resources of a factory fire brigade. Few fixed fire-fighting installations are normally provided since in most cases their actions would be too late to be of any benefit and, in others, might itself produce very dangerous conditions. In many of the processes, automatic explosion protection and suppression are incorporated. Means of escape plays a larger part than any fire extinguishing measures in ensuring the safety of works people.

APPENDIX 17

General Guidlines on Fire Prevention in Chemical Industries

1. Basic principles of fire prevention

a) Segregation of hazardous material from sources of ignition.

b) Elimination of all avoidable sources of ignition and confining all unavoidable sources of ignition.

c) Design features to ensure limited spread of fire or effects of explosion if it occurs.

d) Provision of sufficient and suitable detection system, alarm and extinguishing devices.

e) Protection of personnel and provision of the means of escape to avoid being exposed to or being trapped in fire or toxic fumes.

f) Training of personnel in safety procedures.

2. Site preparation

a) ADJACENT FIRE RISK

The effect of the radiated heat from a fire can be minimized by providing a clear space, between building and the neighbouring premises, of at least 90m and in no case less than 30m.

b) ACCESS TO SITE

The site must be accessible to fire brigade with sufficient working space and it must not be obstructed by parked car or other vehicles or due to storage of miscelleneous articles like empty drums or other similar articles.

c) WATER SUPPLIES

The water supply must be sufficient without being diverted from process work. It may be stated that fire in large chemical works easily require 18,000 litre/min or even more.

Hydrants to be installed at all suitable and convenient points at intervals of 90m to provide adequate coverage to all the areas within the factory.

d) SITE DRAINAGE

Drains to be clear of buildings, railways and built-up areas, Drain capacity to be sufficient to cope with the water used for fire-fighting, as well as for normal process work. Pollution of drainage by flammable materials must be prevented by suitable traps and interceptors.

e) LAYOUT OF BUILDINGS AND STRUCTURES AS PER THE DEGREE OF FIRE RISK

Intelligent layout of buildings and structures can reduce the danger of fire spread, especially from radiated heat or explosions. A necessary part of the planning is that all plants, buildings, structures and materials and processes should be assessed for the susceptibility to fire and explosions and the requisite firebreaks with proper type of construction incorporating the safety requirements to be provided. Radiated heat from large fires has been known to ignite combustible materials over 30m away.

f) SITE SERVICES

Pipelines conveying flammable liquids and gases can constitute a fire hazard. Electrical cables can be an ignition source and so can be steam pipes. Electrical lines should be kept separate from pipelines conveying flammable liquids/materials; also, adequate separation has to be provided between pipelines carrying flammable materials and pipelines which carry hot or corrosive substances. Careful attention has to be paid for routing such services especially to see if they should be routed overhead, underground or within culverts. The routing should be so as not to approach hazardous areas unnecessarily.

3. Buildings and structures

a) Design engineers/architects are to consider first how fire is likely to behave, and if it breaks out at any particular location, then how it could be contained in buildings. A fire might occur due to radiated heat, sparks or flying brands from nearby burning buildings. Roof covering of all buildings are to be of non-combustible materials. The risk of fire spread between buildings is affected due to the presence or siting or arrangements of the windows and other openings in the outside walls in addition to the separation of one building (fire break) from another, as also the nature of the contents stored or processed. Compartmentation of the buildings will prevent the fire from spreading from one compartment to the other, depending upon the grading of the fire resistance of the walls/floors in addition to the supporting steel work (columns/beams) being adequately protected.

Fire-resisting walls are to be provided at vulnerable points (i.e. between the processing and the storage section) and all the openings or doorways in these walls are to be fitted with shutters or doors having fire resistance equal to that of the wall.

b) LIGHTNING PROTECTION

Buildings and structures which do not require protection against lightning are built of conducting materials or in which conducting materials form a substantial and prominent part of the structure, provided the metal parts of the structure are adequately earthed. Other buildings or structures can be protected by a vertical earth conductor which gives protection within a 45^0 cone, of which the tip of the conductor is the apex.

c) VENTILATION

Adequate ventilation is an important safeguard against fire and explosion. In chemical industries, during the processing stage, small quantities of gases, vapours and dusts which present flammable explosive hazards are normally released into the atmosphere and ventilation must be adequate to reduce the concentration to a safer level.

Normally natural ventilation, which is dependent on the vapour density of the gas/vapour released, is adequate. Where the gas is less dense than air, high level extraction is required with air inlets situated at a low level. As a rough guide, there should be 0.46 sq.m of inlet per 9.29 sq.m of floor level. Particular attention should be paid to possible accumulation of flammable gases or vapours in pockets. Ventilation should be sufficient under normal working condition to keep the concentration of the vapour–air mixture well below the lower flammable limit.

4. Movement and transport of materials

a) Pipelines for flammable liquids should be as straight as possible without sharp bends and should be of sufficient diameter to allow adequate flow of liquid without exceeding the critical velocity, above which static electricity may be generated (the accepted velocity for hydrocarbons is 1m/sec approximately). Pipelines should possess electrical continuity and to be earthed properly.

Tanks of flammable liquids should preferably be located below the ground level and the liquid is to be moved by pumping or by pressure system using inert medium. Pumps are to be located in pits to retain leaks and should be well maintained. In the event of a leak or fracture in the pipeline, the pump should be capable of being shut off automatically.

Flame arrestors should be inserted in long lengths of pipework where there is possibility of ignition. Care should be taken to ensure that air is not drawn into pipework containing flammable gases and it should be ensured that the concentration of flammable gases is maintained above the upper limit of flammability in air. Where pipelines can transfer flame from one part of the plant to another, it may be practicable to use automatically operated suppression systems or quick-acting valves to isolate sections of the plant.

b) TRANSPORT OF DUSTS/PULVERIZED PRODUCTS

Some solid organic materials, as also certain metals and inorganic susbtances, can produce explosive dust clouds (particle size greater than 1 micron, but less than 76 micron) when dispersed in the form of dust (20 to 40 gm/m^3). Adequate ventilation is essential to reduce the concentration of the dust level below the lower limit and explosion reliefs to be provided by means of explosion vents or bursting discs in the casing of the equipment concerned.

c) VEHICLES

Vehicles used in hazardous areas should have flameproof fittings with spark arrestors fitted in the exhaust pipe with fire extinguishers of the appropriate type.

5. Plant safety

By adopting proper safety measures in advance, much can be done to forestall fire and explosions and to limit the effects. Plant is to be designed to prevent the escape of flammable gases/liquids or dusts. They can be instrumented to give warning of rise in temperature, liquid level or pressure. Other instruments can be used to detect leaks, excess flow or stoppage of flow in pipelines and cooling coils. Explosimeters can be used to detect dangerous concentration of flammable vapours. Fail-safe and interlocking processes can be arranged so that before a critical operation is started up, certain safeguarding operations are already in progress, e.g. plants may be designed not to operate until the ventilation has been functioning for a specified time.

Relief of explosion or over-pressure can be designed and employed to prevent damage to the plant and building ($0.09m^2$ of vent area for every $0.56m^3$ of the plant, i.e. 1sq.ft of vent area for every 20 cu.ft of the plant). The explosion relief should be so positioned as to vent the explosion products into a safe place so that life and property are not endangered.

APPENDIX 18

Some Useful Information

(A)

AIR SUPPORTED STRUCTURES

Air supported structures (pneumatic building construction) are of comparatively recent origin and are being developed for many commercial and industrial applications such as temporary garages, radar equipment protection, mobile hospitals and workshops, enclosures for swimming pools, tennis court etc. There are three types of air supported structures:

i) An air inflated structure in which air is contained within ribs formed of P.V.C. or other plastic or fabric membrane. These ribs form the structural elements, i.e. the columns and beams, which in turn support the roof and walls.

ii) An inflated double-walled structure in which air is contained between the membranes.

iii) An air supported structure which consists of a single membrane supported by a small pressure above atmosphere (inflation) over the whole of the internal surface of the structure.

These structures are firmly anchored to the ground and to achieve sufficient air pressure differential, low pressure fans supply air in sufficient quantity to compensate for losses through the fabric and through the doors. Air locks are used to reduce the amount of loss through the doors. The fabrics used are inherently flameproof, but most would probably melt in a fire. Any holes formed by such melting would allow the membrane to sag with possible collapse on to the fire which may lead to disastrous consequences.

AIRFIELD CRASH TENDER

As per latest specifications, the airfield crash tender is to carry 6500 litre of water, 800 litre of foam, with a midship mounted pump capable of delivering 4000 lit/min at 8.5 kg/cm^2 and 3000 lit/min at 10.5 –12.5 kg/cm^2. The output of monitor to be at 3000 lit/min and effective throw of foam at 55m, and 500 litre of water/foam solution, each from the two headlines.

The monitor and headlines should be able to work simultaneously. The appliance shall be capable of producing foam while creeping or moving. The appliance, when fully loaded, should have an acceleration from 0–80 km in a maximum time of 40 seconds and also a maximum speed 100 km/h and braking efficiency to stop dead within a maximum of9m from a speed of 32 km/hr.

AERIAL EXTENSION LADDERS

These are of various types for use in fires or rescue work involving high-rise buildings. Among the latest types suitable for operation even in narrow streets with a cluster of tall buildings are types like Simon Snorkel with 30.5m working height, Bronto Skylift with a reach of 52m and a cage of 500 kg carrying capacity and Ruthman Stigger with a working height of 60.6m with cage of 500 kg capacity with lateral out-reach on either side of 29.3 metres. These may be inconvenient for operation in narrow streets.

These may be compared with Turn Table ladders or Telescopic Boom type ladders of 30m height, as may be available with most of the metropolitan fire service.

AQUEOUS FILM FORMING FOAM (AFFF)

Aqueous film forming foam or air foam contains fluorocarbon surfactant in small quantity (not more than 6%) with a water-soluble high polymer. This reduces the surface tension of water and, as a result, a thin film of aqueous film forming foam float on the burning oil. This causes an immediate extinction of fire but the film of water/foam is liable to be broken down within a short interval of time unless followed by the application of a stable thick blanket of hydrolysed protein foam, thereby eliminating all chances of re-ignition. This is also referred to as Light Water.

AUTOMATIC FIRE DETECTORS

These are designed to automatically detect any fire or abnormal heat and sound an alarm indicating the outbreak of fire. They are of following types:

a) Fixed temperature detectors: a form of fire detector that responds only when a predetermined temperature is reached (normally 77^{0}C), by closing an electric circuit which incorporates a battery and an electric bell.

b) Line detector: a form of fire detector which responds to a rise of temperature anywhere along the length of a hollow copper tube of very small diameter fixed on the ceiling, usually fitted with a temperature-sensitive liquid. The ends of the tube terminate on diaphragms which are pushed due to expansion of the liquid in the tube and operate the alarm through an electrical circuit.

c) Point fire detector : this type of fire detector responds to an abnormal rise in temperature, detected at a fixed point, as against line detector.

d) Rate of rise detector: these detectors incorporate bimetallic strips, one end of which is suitably shielded and protected to reduce its rate of expansion when exposed to fire conditions, and so designed as to respond when the temperature rise is abnormally rapid.

Besides heat detectors, there are other types of detecting devices which work on the principles of smoke detection, infra-red and ultra-violet ray detection (radiation detectors). Some of these are:

a) Smoke detectors: These are of two types, viz. the ionization type and the optical type. The ionization type is very sensitive in the early stages of fire when there is emission of smoke. They are recommended for protection of computer installations, control rooms for telecommunication, underground cable in the cable ducts, libraries, archives etc. The ionization type detector head contains a small radioactive source which continuously emits alpha particles within the ionization chamber, and as a result, a small electric current flows in the external circuit, which, being very small, is amplified and can be readily monitored. In a fire condition, the smoke particles entering the chamber causes a reduction in the current flow. When the current falls below a predetermined level, the amplifier, which forms a part of the circuit, initiates an alarm. The ionization detector heads are mounted on the ceillings and each head provides adequate coverage for 100 sq.m of floor area.

The optical type, on the other hand, is sensitive to light. This type of detector head comprises a light source and a photo-electric cell within a chamber. When smoke enters the chamber, the steady beam of light falling on the photo-electric cell is affected and thereby the light is scattered and there is a fluctuation of current, which after being amplified activates a relay coil to sound an alarm. The coverage for these detectors is 93 sq.m per head.

b) Radiation detectors: There are two types of detectors in this category:

i) Infra-red detectors: These are radiation detectors and detect the infra-red radiation which is produced from any flame or source of heat. Normally, the flame produced from a fire has a distinctive flieker in the frequency range of 4 Hz to 15 Hz. Infra-red fire detectors will activate the alarm, if the incoming signal is in the frequency of 4 to 15 Hz, and if the signal persists for a pre-set period of 2 to 15 seconds.

Mode of detection

The signals (infra-red radiation) are passed through a series of lens and filters on to a photo-electric cell, which gets activated to produce impulse of current corresponding to the signals received. The current is filtered, amplified and fed to the integrator timer circuit which scans the signals and activates the alarm. An infra-red detector must 'see' a flame before it can raise an alarm. Hence, there should be no obstruction between the flame and the detector. Individual detector heads can protect each compartment and may be placed in a strategic position facing the potential hazard. Alternately, scanning infra-red detectors are also available with a deflector which continually scans the protected area every 20 seconds and monitors 360^0 degrees in the horizontal plane and a wide angle on the vertical plane.

ii) Ultraviolet detectors: Like the infra-red detector, the ultraviolet detector also needs to 'see' the flame before it is activated. The principle of operation is similar to the ionization-type detector. When ultraviolet radiation strikes the gas-filled tube, it ionizes the gas in the tube and a small current is set up between the two electrodes. When the current flow is greater than the set point of the amplifier, the circuit closes immediately and causes the alarm to sound. An integrator can be incoporated in the circuit which will effectively delay the alarm for 10 to 15 seconds and also can reduce false alarm. The detector is not affected by sun light or artificial light but is sensitive to electric arcs, and hence, should not be used in areas where welding work is being done.

Ultraviolet detectors are most commonly used for specialized applications such as for monitoring of aircraft engine nacelle. They can also be used to protect fuel storage tanks, oil drilling rigs, paint spray booths etc. One amplifier can cater to as many as four detector heads which can be mounted up to 300m from it. The detector has a 90^0 angle of vision and will detct 1.8 sq.m of flame at a distance of 12 m.

General comments

Radiation detectors have a quick response capability, as they are not dependent on combustion products coming in contact with the detector head; they can also be used out of the doors. Radiation detectors, need a clear view of the area to be protected and all lenses or covers must be kept clean if efficiency is not to be impaired.

iii) The laser beam fire detection system: This is the latest development in the field of automatic fire detection though it has not been used in this country. It requires a careful maintenance and adjustment of the system. Low power pulsed infra-red beam is used. The receiver unit is tuned to accept the pulsed frequency, and in this case, critical alignment between the two units is not necessary because the beam of radiation is relatively wide. On the other hand, the laser beam has a unique advantage in that it provides a coherent band of light and does not diffuse or fan out as it travels. The beam is thrown across the protected area fairly close to ceiling level to fall on a photo-electric cell.

In the event of a fire, the turbulance caused by the hot rising air produces a 'dancing effect' in the beam. The photo cell is designed to react to this and raise the alarm. The photo cell is usually fronted with a checker-board mask which makes it easier to discriminate between 'dancing' due to normal vibration and the more 'rapid dancing' arising from a fire condition.

B.

BRAKE HORSE POWER

The power developed by an engine is referred to as the 'brake horse power' and it varies according to the engine, type, size and efficiency. This is also known as brake power (B.P.) and measured in kilowatts (kW). The efficiency of an engine depends upon its brake horse power.

B.C.F. AND B.T.M.

These are the two florinated extinguishing agents of comparative recent origin which are now being used throughout the world. They are also known by their Halon numbers, viz. 1211 and 1301 for B.C.F. (brome-chloro-difluoro-methane) and B.T.M. (brome-trifluoro-methane). Both these agents possess a relatively high degree of fire-fighting effectiveness and can knock out a flame very quickly. They can be stored easily as dense liquids and vaporize either before or during application on a flame to leave no appreciable residue. The comparative efficiency of these two extinguishing agents are more or less similar. The most obvious difference between these two agents is in their boiling points, viz. 4^{0}C for B.C.M. and–57. 6^{0}C for B.T.M. with corresponding vapour pressure of about 2.2 and 16.2 bar at 24^{0}C.

Due to the very low boiling point of B.T.M., it is necessary to pressurize a hand extinguisher or the reservoir of an automatic system with nitrogen to a higher value. The container of a B.T.M. hand extinguisher is therefore quite heavy as compared to the corresponding type of B.C.F. extinguisher. Also, because of the very low boiling point of B.T.M. it is impossible to get a liquid throw from a B.T.M. extinguisher.

B.T.M. (Halon 1301) is suited for use in total flooding system particularly for normally occupied areas while Halon 1211 (B.C.F.) seems to be more suitable for use in local application. Both B.C.F. and B.T.M. can very quickly knock out a flame and can be used for any type of fire specially for electronic equipments, transformers, switch-gears, gaseous and highly flammable liquids, hazardous solids etc. The high liquid densities of Halon 1301 and 1211, coupled with their high extinguishing effectiveness, results in a dramatic reduction of storage space requirements for systems using these agents compared to those using carbon dioxide. The table gives the details :

Performance and characteristics

Extinguishing agent	Extinguishing concentration by volume		Maximum discharge duration	Dangerous concentration
	For surface flaming (%)	For deep-seated burning (%)		
Carbon dioxide	34–40	60–70	1–4 min	10% for 1 min
Halon 1211	5–8		10 sec	4% for 1 min
Halon 1301	4–8		10 sec	7.5% for 4–5 min

C.

CRYOGENIC GASES

Cryogenic gases are liquified gases which exist in their containers at extremely low temperatures, slightly above their boiling points at N.T.P. and correspondingly at low to moderate pressures. For industrial purpose, a gas may be termed cryogenic if it can be liquified at or below–74^{0}C.

COMPARTMENTATION

To prevent a fire in a building from spreading from its origin to other parts of the building, the walls and floors enclosing each part of the building concerned are so constructed with adequate fire resistance as to form effective barriers to fire. This breaking up of a building into fire-tight cells is termed compartmentation. For institutional and other residential buildings (single storeyed hospitals, hotels etc), the floor area is usually limited to 3000 sq. metre.

CONCRETE

This is a mixture of cement, sand and broken stone chips. Spalling of the surface material is likely if hot concrete is suddenly chilled by a jet of water. To make the concrete fire-resistant, lime stone should not be used as aggregate. Normally a mixture of cement, sand and broken brick chips (18 mm size) in the ratio of 1 : 3 : 5 has good fire-resisting quality.

REINFORCED AND PRE-STRESSED CONCRETE

Reinforced concrete

Ordinary concrete can withstand very high compressive stress as against its poor tensile strength. To compensate the lack of tensile strength, concrete is reinforced with high tensile steel rods. For beams/joists, the reinforcing bars are positioned close to the bottom edge. Fire resistance is dependent upon the cross-sectional area of the beam and the amount of concrete cover provided for the reinforcing bars.

Pre-stressed concrete

Pre-stressed concrete is a form of structural concrete in which high tensile steel tendons are stressed against the length of the concrete which is thus put into compression before imposed loads are applied.

Fire resistance of structural concrete, whether reinforced or pre-stressed is determined primarily by the protection against an excessive rise in the temperature of the steel, afforded by the concrete cover. Generally, the greater the amount of cover the longer is the period of fire resistance.

Structural concrete, unlike steel, does not usually collapse suddenly. It may deflect considerably under load and floors may suffer local breakdown; but even after a severe fire most concrete structures are normally safe enough to be reinstated to perform their original functions.

D.

DUST EXPLOSION

An explosion caused by the dispersal of finely divided dusts of certain organic or metallic origin, e.g. flour, sugar, shellac, magnesium, aluminium etc. The force of explosion depends, among other things, upon the density of dust cloud. The lowest concentration of dust required for explosion is 20 to 40 gm/m^3 in air.

The pressure generated is of the order of 690 kN/m^2 (100 p.s.i.) and a 22.86 cm brick wall can withstand 3.5 kN/m^2 pressure. It is therefore quite likely that a massive wall of 38 cm thickness will be completely disintegrated by the force of the explosion in no time.

E.

EXTINGUISHING MEDIA – RECENT ADVANCEMENTS

Halogenated hydrocarbons

As a result of progressive research and practical tests, certain halogenated hydrocarbons, specially bromo-choloro-difluoro-methane (B.C.F.) and bromo-trifluoro-methane (B.T.M.) are now available and their use has been well established. As per halon number, these two agents are known as Halon 1211 and Halon 1301 respectively. They react very fast, with extremely quick knocking out effect on the fire, by interfering with the chain reaction especially for Class B, C and E fires. Halon 1301 is the most effective gaseous extinguishing agent.

The need for a highly efficient, low toxicity, three dimensional extinguishing agent with high dielectric strength is particularly felt for protection of sophisticated electrical and electronic equipments like control room, switching section, electronic computer and data processing section, etc and Halon 1301 is ideally suited for all such risks. But due to its very low boiling point (–57^{0}C at 760 mm Hg) it may not be very useful in tropical countries unless correctly installed or applied. On the other hand, Halon 1211 due to its comparatively higher B.P. (–4^{0}C) is more suitable in tropical countries. The peak flammability concentration for B.C.F. is 9.3% in air as compared to 6.3% for B.T.M. Halon 1301 is less toxic (7–10% for 1 min) as against Halon 1211 (4–5% for 1 min).

Dry chemical powders

As against ordinary sodium bicarbonate based powders, potassium bicarbonate based powders are far superior for class A or class B fires. They are at least twice as effective as the best sodium bicarbonate powders and are called purple K due to the lilac flame colour produced by potassium ions.

a) Monnex dry powder: The recent advancement in the field of dry powder extinguishing agent is most significant, and as a result, Monnex dry chemical extinguishers have been introduced for fighting fires in class A, class B, or Class C with a very quick knocking out effect. Monnex dry powder is a product from the reaction of urea and potassium bicarbonate. It has the unique property of breaking up into small particles (or decrepitating) when heated, or when spread over a fire from an extinguisher of suitable design.

'Monnex' is about five times more effective as compared to sodium bicarbonate based powders, and three times as compared to potassium bicarbonate powders. It has been seen that a fire area of 28 m^2 using aviation fuel (F.P. 30^0 F or roughly – 1.2^0C) could be completely extinguished by using a single 9 kg Monnex D.C.P. extinguisher. The critical rate of application is 140 gm/sec, as against 500 gm/sec for sodium bicarbonate based powders. Monnex is the trade name of the powder and it is manufactured under a patent obtained by I.C.I. of UK.

Toxicity of extinguishing agents

Agent	Approx LCo 15 min rate %	U.L (group)	classification
B.T.M.	80.0	6	
B.C.F.	30.0	5A	
D.T.E.	9.0	4	
D.D.M.	5.5	4	
C.B.	2.8	3	
C.T.C.	1.3	3	
CO_2	65.0	5a	

Notes: LCO is the maximum concentration that will cause no death during or after the exposure. U.L. classification is the American Underwriters Laboratory classification. According to this classification, group 1 is the most toxic, and group 6 is the least toxic based on animal experiments.

EXPANSION RATIO

A term normally used to determine the quality of foam produced for fire-fighting. This refers to the ratio of the volume of foam produced as against the water used initially. Expansion ratio of 1 : 8 for chemical foam means 2 gallon of water solution is capable of producing 16 gallon of a foam. The ratio for medium expansion foam is 1 : 400, and for high expansion foam, it is normally 1 : 1000 but may vary from 600 to 1000.

EFFICIENCY OF ENGINES

The efficiency of an engine or a motor fire pump depends upon the water horsepower developed and the brakepower of the pump, in other words, on the output and the input of the pump. It can be calculated as:

$$E\,(\text{efficiency}) = \frac{\text{Output}}{\text{Input}} \times 100$$

EC 50

Effect concentration 50%. A concentration statistically calculated to cause an effect (e.g. incapacitation) in 50% of the animals exposed to it. This has significance to the exposure hazard while using halogenated hydrocarbon extinguishing agent.

ECT 50

The mathematical product of time of exposure and concentration, statistically calculated to cause a toxic effect in 50% of the animals.

F.

FOG NOZZLE

The latest type of these nozzles can produce 0.35 mm size droplets producing fog and they are so constructed that just by turning the nozzle slightly, one can change over from solid jet to water curtain and then to fog.

In one model, the flow rate is controlled by operating a large handle, on the top, which in its first position gives an output of 100 litre/min at 6 bar, and when the handle is pulled back, the flow rate is increased to 300 litre/min. The automatic pressure control valve incorporated inside the nozzle keeps the jet form and nearby fog droplet size constant, even if the flow is suddenly reduced by an inadvertent pump variation or hose kink. Fog nozzles can extinguish a fire quickly with less wastage of water and are invaluable in cutting off radiant heat and cooling the atmosphere.

FIRE DAMPER

A mechanical device fitted in the air-conditioning or ventilation ducts to isolate smoke or toxic fumes from entering a compartment, and thereby isolate the AC system in an air-conditioned building. They are mostly automatic and incorporate a fusible link (set to operate at 68^0C) or an electromagnetic device (a solenoid).

FOAM

Normally two types are available, viz. chemical and mechanical foam. Chemical foam is produced from extinguishers by the reaction of a solution of sodium bicarbonate and aluminium sulphate and the resulting foam consists mainly of aluminium hydroxide. Mechanical foam is produced by aeration of water, under a pressure of not less than 7 kg/cm^2 along with a small quantity protein based foam compound, by means of a specially designed branch pipe. The approximate composition of foam produced is 90% air, 9.7% water and 0.3% foam compound.

FEEDER PILLAR

A pillar containing switches, links or fuses for comnecting feeders with distribution mains.

G.

GEIGER COUNTER

An instrument for detection of ionizing radiation (chiefly alpha, beta or gamma radiation). An unknown source of radiation which cannot be seen or physically felt on the fireground, can be easily detected by this portable instrument and persons engaged in fire-fighting can take precautionary measures for personal protection as also to reorient the fire-fighting strategy involving radioactive substances, atomic research centres etc.

H.

HALF LIFE

This is the time taken for the activity of a radioactive isotope to decay to half its original value. Half lives vary from isotope to isotope and they may vary from a fraction of a second in some cases to millions of years in others. By knowing the half life of a radioactive isotope, one can estimate the relative active strength of the material and take requisite precautionary measures as stated under Radiological Safety.

HALON NUMBER

The halogenated hydrocarbons, as used in the fire service for extinguishing fires, are sometimes indicated by code numbers in arithmetical figures as stated below:

The first digit of Halon number represents the number of carbon atoms in the molecule of the compound. The second digit indicates the number of fluorine atoms, the third digit shows the number of chlorine atoms, the fourth digit the number of bromine atoms and the fifth dight reflects the iodine atoms. Thus, B.C.F. (bromo-chloro-difluoro-methane) is indicated by 1211 and B.T.M. (bromo-trifluoro-methane) by 1301.

I

ISOTOPE

Atoms of the same element (i.e. having the same atomic number) which differ in mass number are called isotopes of that element. The isotopes of an element are identical in chemical properties except those determined by the mass of the atom. The different isotopes of an element contain different number of neutrons in the nucleus.

L.

LOBBY APPROACH STAIRCASE

Normally, in buildings over 24m in height, lobby approach staircases are provided with fire lifts to provide efficient means of escape and facilities for fire-fighting. It is so called because the entrance to the staircase/ fire lift is through a lobby (enclosure) of fire resistant material with self-closing doors on both entrances to the lobby and the fire lift. A small amount of positive pressure (of about 5 mm water gauge) is maintained inside the lobby, thereby rendering the staircase and the fire lift smoke free.

LIGHT WATER FOAM

This material behaves like foam. By combining a foam of per-fluoro surfactants with a water soluble high polymer, a foam of reasonable stability with extremely rapid knock down property and a self-sealing floating aqueous film is obtained. It is still in a class of its own in effectiveness. In speed of action and effective utilization of available water, it is claimed as even superior to fluoro-protein foam. Light water foam is more fluid and it has faster drainage than protein foam, though it is similar to fluoro-protein foam in drainage. Expansion ratio ranges from 8 to 10 with normal foam-making equipment. Its self-sealing film is longer lasting (say about 20 minutes) than that of fluoro-protein foam. It is used in 6% concentration, making it suitable for use in extinguisher and foam-generating equipment designed for protein foam.

A skilled operator can extinguish about 4 sq. m (40 sq.ft) of burning petrol with 9 litre of such extinguisher. A 100 litre (20 gallon) wheeled extinguisher of this type can effectively deal with large spill fires. Light water concentrate is not toxic, but slightly acidic and irritating on the skin (pH = 4.2). It is stored in stainless steel or polyester fibreglass containers.

LATENT HEAT OF FUSION

This is the heat required to convert a solid at its melting point into liquid at the same temperature. It is expressed in joule/kg.

LATENT HEAT OF VAPOURIZATION

This is the heat required to convert a unit mass of liquid at its boiling point into vapour at the same temperature. It is expressed in joule/kg.

LIMITING OXYGEN INDEX (L.O.I.)

This is measured by a standard test (BS 2782). In this test, a candle-like specimen of the material to be tested is placed in a vertically mounted tube. A mixture of oxygen and nitrogen is passed up the tube. The concentration of oxygen, at which the specimen will just extinguish, after attempted ignition with a small gas flame is the L.O.I.

Cotton, rayon, cellulose all have L.O.I. in the 17–18 region, i.e. they will burn even when there is less oxygen than there is in air. Whereas, wool and many varieties of wood have L.O.I. just above 21.

M.

MULTISTOREY CAR PARK

In such a building of maximum permitted size, all the structural elements would be required to have a fire resistance of four hours, and its size would be restricted so that only about 400 cars could be accommodated. Under such specifications, the fire load is considered to be low, compared with other storage buildings of this class. Relatively few people are in this kind of a building at any one time, and therefore, life risk is not high. The open sides would facilitate fire-fighting and the means of escape is generally good. The structural problems involved in attempting compartmentation and continuous ramping are required from the point of view of safety.

P.

POLYURETHANE FOAM

They are a sort of foamed plastics containing isocyanates. The material is quite soft with air bubbles and spongy in appearance. Because of their softness and cushioning effect, they are extensively used in the production of upholstered furniture, beddings and cushions etc. Polyurethane foam is generally thermoplastic, and when involved in a fire, will melt and burn with thick black smoke giving out carbon monoxide and poisonous hydrocyanic acid gas.

PYROPHORIC METELS

Pyrophoric metals are those which ignite spontaneously upon exposure to air. Phosphorous and finely divided dusts of uranium, aluminium, magnesium are examples of pyrophoric metals. Special care and handling procedures are needed to store, collect and dispose off such materials usually under a nitrogenous atmosphere.

POWER TAKE-OFF

This is a device by which the full power developed at the gear box of an appliance can be diverted, when required from its normal path, down the transmission to the rear axle and used instead to drive a fire pump. In fire brigades, a power take-off is used to drive the main fire pump and a hose reel pump and also to drive the operating mechanism for turntable ladders.

PRESSURIZATION OF ESCAPE ROUTES

Pressurization is the technique adopted for protection of stairs and lobbies from invasion of smoke and toxic gas by creating a higher pressure in an escape route by mechanical ventilation. The most common means of achieving pressurization is by centrifugal or axial fans driven by an electric motor. The fans are connected to a duct system with output grilles. The grilles can be sited at each floor level, alternate floors or say every fifth floor, depending on the requirements of the particular building. There are two basic considerations when designing a pressurization system. They are : *(a)* the pressure required in the staircase and/or lobby, which is normally 5 mm water gauge, and *(b)* the leakage paths (gaps around doors and windows, which allow air to escape – the maximum recommended gap is 3 mm). For effective pressurization, good fitting doors are essential.

PROSCENIUM WALL

As the fire risk in the stage/area of a theatre is considerable, it is isolated from the auditorium by a substantial wall (the proscenium wall) having considerable fire resistance. The opening in the wall is further protected by a fire-resisting curtain and a drencher system.

PREMIXED FLAME

When some flammable vapour and air has already been mixed in appropriate concentration before the application of any ignition source, and if any flame is propagated through this premixed layer, then this is a premixed flame. Premixed flames are far less frequently seen by a fireman. Propagating premixed flame is an explosion. Premixed flames in explosive mixtures of gas/air will travel away from the source, at a characteristic speed called the burning velocity.

PYROLYSIS

This is chemical breakdown of a material by heat. The large complex molecules in wood, for examle, are pyrolysed to simpler things like methanol vapours, carbon monoxide and hydrogen.

pH VALUE

Number of grams of hydrogen ions per litre of solution gives the pH value. As pure water at ordinary temperatures dissociates slightly into hydrogen ions and hydroxyl ions, the concentration of each type of ion being 10^{-7} gram-molecules per litre, the pH of pure water will be 7. This figure indicates neutrality on the pH scale. If acid is added to water, its hydrogen ion concentration will increase and its pH will therefore decrease. Thus a pH below 7 indicates acidity and pH in excess of 7 indicates alkalinity.

PYRO ELODUR CABLE

A special type of fire-resisting cable manufactured and sold under this brand name by a German firm. The speciality of this cable is that, in case of a fire, the conducting cables, if melted due to heat, will not cause any short circuit as is the case with ordinary cables. The short circuit will be interrupted locally.

The insulating and the jacketing materials in this type of cable will neither pyrolyse nor burn as they are self-extinguishing and flame retardant. There is also no emission of corrosive gases.

PNEUMATICALLY OPERATED RESCUE EQUIPMENT (AIR BAG)

A special type of inflatable air bag, very strongly built with reinforced Neoprene and capable of withstanding very high payload. According to the manufacturers, the payload may exceed 50 tonne and may even carry a steam roller.

This equipment is specially useful for rescue purpose. It may be used for lifting big trucks or motor vehicles that have overturned. The empty bag is inserted under the chassis. Air is pumped into the bag from a compressor and it swells up and lifts the vehicle for rescuing trapped persons very quickly, without any mechanical effort as in other types of equipments.

R.

RADIOACTIVE MATERIALS

Such materials are in a continuous process of degeneration, emitting, alfa, beta or gamma rays, leading to the formation of isotopes of new elements. These are quite hazardous and adequate protective measures in case of accidental release should be taken along with provision of sufficient water supply for decontamination as also safe disposal of contaminated materials.

RADIO-ISOTOPE

These are isotopes of radioactive materials which are constantly undergoing disintegration and decay due to atomic radiation. The radiation may consist of gamma radiation, or simply alpha or beta particles, depending upon the isotopes of the element. Radio-isotopes may be encountered in laboratories, nuclear reactors, power stations etc., and are considered to be hazardous. Fire officers coming across such substances should take proper precaution. (Please see Radiological Safety.)

RADIOLOGICAL SAFETY.

Radiological safety depends upon three factors : *(i)* half life period of the source, *(ii)* distance of the source from the operator (the more the distance, less will be the effect of radioactive emission), and *(iii)* type of the shielding employed for protection.

R.M.S. VALUE

In A.C. circuit, the current attains a maximum value (peak value) in course of its positive or negative swing as per root mean square value. The effective value of the current and voltage will be $=(1/\sqrt{2})\times$ peak current and $(1/\sqrt{2})\times$ peak voltage respectively (i.e. 0.7 of the peak current, and 0.7 of the peak voltage). The R.M.S. value of the current is important for determining the amount of heat generated.

RAPID INTERVENTION VEHICLE

An essential requirement for crash fire-fighting involving aircrafts. The vehicle should be capable of an acceleration of 80 km/h in well under 25 seconds and then cruise at 100–110 km/ hr. It should carry mainly A.F.F.F. in pre-mixed solution (1000 litre) at 6% and should also carry B.C.F. extinguishing agent. All major international airports are obliged to have one or two R.I.V. depending upon the category. The vehicle is to carry all rescue equipments.

R-FACTOR

The ratio of extinguishing concentration (EC) to dangerous concenrration (DC) in relation to vaporizing liquid extinguishing agents. If the value of R exceeds 1, then the agent is not considered ideal for total flooding system in enclosed areas where life risk is involved. Again, if the value of R exceeds 4, it is not considered safe for use in hand extinguishers. Some examples are:

For C.T.C $\frac{EC}{DC}=\frac{9.7}{1.2}$ and $R=8.1$

For M.B. $\frac{EC}{DC}=\frac{7.1}{0.6}$ and $R=11.8$

For B.C.F. $\frac{EC}{DC}=\frac{5.2}{24}$ and $R=0.22$

Among the three, the B.C.F. is therefore the safest.

S.

SEPARATING WALL

A fire-resisting wall or part of a wall which is common to two adjoining buildings.

SIEVERT (SV)

Equivalent dose rates of radiation is measured in sieverts per hour (Svh). This is a measure of rate at which damage is done to tissues.

SINGLE PHASE

Alternating current flowing through a single circuit.

STOICHIOMETRIC MIXTURE

Between the lower and upper limit of flammability, there is a point where the vapour–air mixture is ideal for the propagation of flame. This ideal mixture is the stoichiometric mixture. For methane, the limits of flammability is between 5.3 and 14%, and 9% mixture is the stoichiometric mixture.

T.

THERMISTOR

This is a heat-sensitive resistor which has a high negative temperature coefficient of resistance. Thus, its resistance decreases appreciably with temperature rise. It is used as a safeguard against current surges in any circuit, where this could be harmful, and as a basis for certain types of temperature measurement.

THERMOCOUPLE

This is a device consisting of two dissimilar metals such as iron and copper joined at two places so that when a difference of temperature exists between the two joints, a voltage is produced which can be used to measure the temperature difference.

TRANSISTOR

An electronic device using the flow of electrons in a semiconductor junction to control the flow of electric current through the device.

THRESHOLD LIMIT VALUE (T.L.V.)

It indicates the average concentration of a gas in air beyond which it is considered dangerous. T.L.V. for carbon monoxide is 50 ppm (parts per million) and that for phosgene is as low as 0.1 ppm.

U.

U.V.C.E. (UNCONFINED VAPOUR CLOUD EXPLOSION)

In chemical industries, flammable liquids are processed and stored at temperatures above their boiling points. A sudden uncontrolled release of such liquids in atmosphere can rapidly vaporize, creating an explosive mixture diffusing in air. Fine mist from such a release remains suspended in air in droplet sizes of 0.5 to 10 microns which readily ignite. Invariably, such vapours are denser than air and drift over a wide area covering plant, equipment and buildings.

Usually vapour clouds released from high elevation under pressure have caused greater havoc than when released at the ground level. The vapour cloud moves horizontally with snow-ball effect. Where the releases are massive, under pressure, and in a very short time, ignition occurs within 15 to 20 seconds from the periphery of the vapour cloud where the vapour–air mixture is just flammable. There is rapid flame propagation through the vapour–air mixture (premixed flame) which attains deflagration velocity, with severe shock wave from blast, resulting in widespread damages. Where large tanks of flammable liquids are involved, large sections of the tank are hurled to a great distance by the force of explosion, causing widespread damages and destruction to the adjoining property with loss of life. This is unconfined vapour cloud explosion or, in short, U.V.C.E.

The force of explosion from U.V.C.E. has been estimated to be similar to that from 15 to 45 tons of T.N.T. Buildings in the plant may be demolished. Large columns and other parts of the plant collapses with pipes, tanks and containers being ruptured with a big devasting fire, surrounding an area of 10 acres or more.

B.L.E.V.E. (boiling liquid expanding vapour explosion)

This is similar to the above in effect and is also caused due to sudden release of flammable liquid or liquified flammable gas under pressure from a closed/confined container. The released liquid will boil in atmosphere and vaporize rapidly to develope a B.L.E.V.E. Already ignited from fire, it makes the B.L.E.V.E. a huge fire ball, flashing and tending to move downwind with intense heat radiation and a huge combustion pressure wave.

U.V.C.E. and B.L.E.V.E.

A B.L.E.V.E. fire ball of 10,000 cu.m is not uncommon. There are instances of fatal burns from B.L.E.V.E. at a distance of 400 metres, blistering of paints in houses at 1,000 metres, and some degree of burns to spectators more than 12,000 metres away.

If the boiling liquid expanding vapour release (B.L.E.V.E.) does not light up but drifts and ignites subsequently, is termed as U.V.C.E. and not B.L.E.V.E. It is only this difference in time lag for ignition which differentiates between the two, as, otherwise, both have the same properties and characteristics. Both B.L.E.V.E. and U.V.C.E. normally take place under the following conditions:

1) Flammable liquids or liquified flammable gases must be there in a confined container under high pressure.

2) The contained liquid must be at a temperature above its normal boiling point at atmospheric pressure.

3) There must be a failure of the container, due to some reason, resulting in the flammable liquid to flow out and form a gas cloud and the quick ignition of the same.

V.

VAPORIZING LIQUID

A fire extinguishing agent, e.g. halon, which is stored in liquid form and released in such a way as to vaporize rapidly in a fire zone.

VAPOUR PRESSURE

The pressure exerted at any particular temperature by a vapour in equilibrium with its solid or liquid. The vapour pressure of water at 20°C is 0.023 atm, and at 100°C, 1 atm.

V.F.A. (VOICE FREQUENCY REMOTE CONTROL SYSTEM)

This is the most up-to-date fire brigade remote control communication system suitable for large centralized mobilizing schemes. It is simply a monitored-line system, designed for the remote control of all types of fire stations, and call-out systems consisting of a double wire network. One circuit is normally used for transmission of voice frequency tone signals, and the other provides two-way special facilities.

W.

WATERSPRAY PROJECTOR SYSTEMS

They are normally of two types – medium or high velocity systems.

Medium velocity projector system is considered suitable for desired cooling effect on L.P.G. tanks of spherical or bullet type whereas high velocity projector system is used for quenching fires involving petroleum products or oils having flash point above 65°C and specially for fires involving oils used in transformers. The extinction of oil fires is achieved by the waterspray projector system by *(i)* emulsification, *(ii)* cooling and *(iii)* dilution of the oxygen available by the water vapour formed.

The system incorporates specially designed sprinkler heads placed at different angles, near the transformer or L.P.G. tanks to be protected. In case of fire, a very fine spray of water travelling at high velocity is discharged through specially designed high velocity projectors. These are made in various sizes and are designed to give an even distribution of water over the area covered. The projectors are arranged in small groups to cover the risk. Each group being connected by pipe work to a control (detector head) which operates automatically in case of a fire and allows water to be discharged simultaneously through all the projectors in the group. The pipe work between the controlling valves (automatic deluge valve) and the automatic controls is charged with compressed air and, in the event of a fire, the compressed air being released, water enters the pipeline through the deluge valve and finally comes out in the form of a spray.

WATER GEL

A sort of a thick emulsion in water containing some proprietory ingredients, which has been kept a trade secret by the manufacturers. It is a TRL (U.S.A.) patented product. The gel is kept absorbed by a thick woolen blanket, kept in a container, at a convenient place near the risk to be covered. In case of a fire at the preliminary stage, especially involving chemicals, oils, fats (class B), electrical appliances or burning gas etc., the blanket is placed over the burning substances and the fire is quickly extinguished.

When a person's clothings have caught fire, flames can be easily put out by simply putting the fire blanket soaked in water gel over the person. The manufacturers claim that the water gel fire blanket provides emergency burn therapy and it is also a medical device for burns/scalds against hot liquids, chemical or gas fires; for this, special burn dressings soaked in the gel are also available in different sizes. The water gel heat shield, a blanket soaked in the gel (2.43m × 1.82m), is also used to protect an individual from radiant heat and thereby to provide an escape path. It also allows a rescuer to safely enter a fire and evacuate trapped individuals from a fire – as claimed by the manufacturers – by providing an effective heat shield and eliminating the effect of radiated heat.

WATER

a) Hard water

Water which does not form an immediate lather with soap due to the presence of carbonates or bicarbonates or other compounds of calcium, magnesium or iron dissolved in water. Temporary hardness is due to the presence of bicarbonates of the metals and it can be removed by boiling; but permanent hardness cannot be removed by boiling. This can be removed by the addition of washing soda, i. e. sodium carbonate. Permanent hardness is due to the sulphates of the metals in water. All hardness can be removed by the use of geolites.

b) Heavy water

This is deuterium oxide (D_2O) and it is present in natural water to the extent of 1 in 5000. Here, hydrogen of water is replaced by deuterium. Heavy water is used as a moderator in some nuclear reactors.

c) Wet water

Water in which some wetting agent like fluorocarbon surfactant (usually 6%) is added to reduce the surface tension of water to enhance the penetrating power of water for fires involving highly compressed bales of jute or cotton. On the other hand, application of wet water may damage the exposed stocks of goods due to high absorption of water and thereby increase the load on the floor.

WATER HORSEPOWER (WATER POWER)

This refers to the useful power developed in a pump, measured in watts. It will vary depending on the output from the pump and the corresponding pressure. It is an important factor for determining the efficiency of a pump.

WATER HAMMER

If the flow of water is suddenly cut off in a pipe, its kinetic energy is converted into pressure energy. Water hammer refers to the absorption of this pressure by the pipes and fittings.

SOME ADDITIONAL INFORMATION

DEMAND REGULATOR

Unlike the Reducing Valve Assembly in oxygen B.A. set, all compressed air sets have the demand regulator, which is a single-stage reducer comprising a tilt valve and a diaphragm housed in a suitable casing.

Inhalation causes partial vacuum on one side of the diaphragm in the regulator, causing the diaphragm to move inwards and press against the tilt valve spindle. This tilts the valve off its seating and permits flow of air from the cylinder.

Exhalation, on the other hand, causes the diaphragm to move outwards, away from the tilt valve spindle, allowing the tilt valve to reseat and cut off the air supply. The exhaled air is exhausted to atmosphere.

The demand regulator operates in such a way that an adequate supply of air-irrespective of the working condition-is always available to the user.

FIRE LIFT

A lift designed to have additional protection with controls that enable it to be used under the direct control of the fire brigade in fighting fire. Such a lift is fully automatic and is provided with an emergency switch at the ground level. It can carry a minimum of six persons.

MONOMER

A substance made up of small molecules which are capable of joining together in very large numbers to form a polymer of high molecular weight, e.g. ethylene, vinyl chloride.

PANIC BOLT

A locking bolt with a hinged bar, fitted on the inside of an exit door in public auditoria. In case of an emergency, a door can always be opened from the inside.

P.U.V.C.E.

P.U.V.C.E stands for Percussive Unconfined Vapour Cloud Explosion and is a hazard related to mass storage of LPG. This may cause widespread destruction.

APPENDIX 19

Requirement of Pumps, Ladders, Setting up of Fire Stations, Water Supply Requirements and Staffing Pattern

Requirement of pumps for fire stations

As per recommendations of the sixth meeting of the standing Fire Advisory committee appointed by the Government of India, the number of pumping units required for a town should be calculated, on the basis of population as given below:

Population	Number of pumping units
Half lakh	1
One lakh	2
One and half lakh	3
Two lakhs	4
Two and a half lakh	5
Three lakhs	6

Notes: *(i)* From 3 lakhs upwards, there should be one additional pumping unit per lakh of population, or a fraction thereof. In addition to the above, a reserve of 20% of total pumping units, subject to a minimum of 1 should also be provided.

(ii) In industrial cities and areas of high fire risk, the scales and types of additional fire-fighting appliances should be determined by an actual survey of the areas to be protected.

(iii) A pumping unit means a self-propelled motor fire engine or a trailor fire pump, complete with towing vehicle or a jeep fire engine. The pumping unit should have a capacity of approximately 2250 litre/min. Self-propelled fire engine like Jeep/Landrover fire engines are preferable to trailor fire pumps and towing vehicles.

(iv) There should be one rescue van for each place having a population of 3 lakhs to 10 lakhs, while it should be augmented by additional rescue vans for every additional 10 lakhs. This does not cover the requirements of special areas, like docks, air-fields, mines etc., which may require special equipment to cover the risk factors involved.

Ladders

Extension ladders (10.6m, preferably wooden) are to be provided in places where the buildings have a ground and two upper floors only; and where there are more than two upper floors, i.e. 15 to 18m, fire escapes and hook ladders should be used. The use of 30m. Snorkel (hydraulic platform) or turntable ladder (TTL) may be considered where the height of the buildings exceed 18m. In general, a snorkel is considered more useful than a TTL, as with a snorkel both fire-fighting and rescue can be done simultaneously and upto 4 persons at a time can be rescued from a burning building with the application of a powerful jet on to the fire. The only drawback with the snorkel is its big size and the difficulty in its manoevrability in narrow streets or lanes.

Water supply for urban areas

The general requirement is 450 litre/min pumpingcapacity for every 1000 population plus a reserve of 4.5 litre per head for fire-fighting purpose for towns/cities having population of 2 lakhs and above. This may be augmented on the basis of special requirements like the types and construction of buildings, special fire risks, accessibility of fire engines, communication system etc, which are is to be assessed by actual survey of the area by fire experts.

Manpower requirement for fire stations (operational and communication staff)

(1) STATION OFFICERS AND SUB-OFFICERS

They are to be provided, on pump basis, as stated below:

Size of station	Strength of officers
2 pump station	1 station officer and 1 sub-officer

3 pump station	1 station officer and 2 sub-officers
4 pump station	2 station officers and 2 sub-officers
5 pump station	2 station officers and 3 sub-officers
6 pump station	2 station officers and 4 sub-officers

Note: Depending upon the fire risk to be covered, sub-officers may be replaced by station officers.

RESERVE STAFF

(*i*) Fifty percent reserve of the total staff of station officers and sub-officers on duty are to be provided for periodical relief, depending upon the duty system, e.g. 24 hours off after every 48 hours on duty.

(*ii*) Ten percent of the total staff— on duty and on periodical relief— are to be provided as training reserve.

(*iii*) A leave reserve of 15% of the total staff on duty will have to be kept.

LEADING FIREMAN

One leading fireman per fire appliance and one for station and out-door duty at all times to be provided.

DRIVER CUM PUMP OPERATORS

One driver/operator per motor vehicle plus a duty reserve to be provided at each station to ensure the following minimum number as required:

Number of motor vehicles	Number of drivers
2	3
3	4
4	6
5	7
6	9

FIREMEN

Six firemen per appliance to be provided apart from one fireman for fire alarm duty, 2 firemen for hydrant and water resources inspection and 1 fireman for despatch duty per station.

WATCH-ROOM OPERATORS

Four watch-room operators for each station to be provided, of which one to be on duty for every 8 hours and the fourth man as spare to be kept for relief work. In addition, 25% as overall reserve should also be provided.

(The information given above are based on the recommendations of the standing Fire Advisory Committee, under the Government of India, Ministry of Home Affairs, New Delhi, vide Compendium of Recommendations of the S.F.A.C.)

APPENDIX 20

Annual Depreciation and Normal Life of Fire Brigade Equipment

According to the author, the normal life of a fire service equipment would depend on proper care and maintenance and use of the equipment, as also whether the equipment is capable of meeting the prescribed periodical tests.

Category A

Equipment	Normal life	Annual depreciation	Residual value	Remarks
Portable pumpset (275 litre/min)	5000 hrs stationary operation or 10 years whichever is completed earlier	10%	2%	For-self propelled vehicles, every 28 km run on road to be considered as 1 hour stationary operation. Thus, 5000, hrs of stationary operation is equal to 138900 km running.
Trailer fire pump (680 litre/min)	"	"		
Trailer fire pump (1800 litre/min)	"	"		
Motor fire engine (3200 litre/min)	"	"		
Water tender: Type A	"	"		
Water tender : Type B	"	"		

Equipment	Normal life	Annual depreciation	Residual value	Remarks
Mechanically operated turntable ladder for fire brigade	"	"		
Jeep fire engine	"	"		
Emergency tender	"	"		
Foam and CO_2 crash tender (combined and individual)	"	"		
Dry powder crash tender	"	"		
Rescue tender	"	"		
Trailer-mounted tanker	"	"		
Category B				
Suction hose	2 years or 200 hrs of use, whichever is earlier	50%	Nil	Use means operation on fire practice or tests.
Flax canvas hose	"	"		
Hose reel tubing	"	"		
Category C				
Ladders: all types except turntable ladders	5 years	20%	Nil	–
Wooden or metal extension ladders	5 years and 7 years respectively	20% (wooden) 15% (metal)	" "	– –
Wheeled fire escape (metal or wooden)	10 years	10%	"	–
Scaling ladders	5 years	20%	"	–
First floor ladders (wooden)	5 years	20%	"	–
First floor ladders (metal)	5 years	20%	"	–
Category D				
Branch pipes, knap-sack tank, nozzles,	Metal: 10 years,	Metal 10%,	Metal 2%, otherwise nil	–

Equipment	Normal life	Annual depreciation	Residual value	Remarks
nozzle spanner, strainer and suction collection head	wooden: 5 years, and rubber, leather and canvas 1 year	wooden 20%, rubber, leather or canvas 100%		–
Hose and hose fittings, including suction and delivery hose, breachings (dividing and collecting), stand pipe, suction hose wrench, hand pump, spades, shears, chain pulley block, hammer, spreaders for iron railings and other cutting in tools	Metal: 10 years, wooden 5 years, and rubber, leather and canvas: 1 year	Metal 10%, wooden 20%, rubber, leather or canvas 100%	Metal 2%, otherwise nil	–
Category E				
Fire extinguishers (all types) and Stirrup pump	5 years for all types, except for dry powder type for which life is 10 years	Dry powder type 10% and for others 20%	Nil	–
Category F				
Self-contained breathing apparatus for fire service (oxygen or compressed air type)	4 years	25%	Nil	–
Resuscitation apparatus	4 years	25%	Nil	–

(The aforesaid information is based on the recommendations of the Standing Fire Advisory Committee, Government of India, Ministry of Home Affairs, as per Compendium of Recommendations of the S.F.A.C.)

Bibliography

1 J.B. RAJAM, *A Text Book of Heat for Degree Students.*
2. M.M. THATTE, *A Text Book of Inorganic Chemistry.*
3. P.DE, *A Text Book of Inorganic Chemistry.*
4. W. KINGSLEY, *Chemistry for Fire Engineers.*
5. A.M. CAMERON, *Chemistry in Relation to Fire Risk and Fire Extinction.*
6. D. B. SINHA, AND J.M. DAS SARMA, *College Physics.*
7. E.S. HODGES, *Electricity and Fire Risk.*
8. B.S. BAHL AND G.D. JULI, *Essentials of Physical Chemistry.*
9. *Facts and Figures for Firemen,* Institution of Fire Engineers.
10. *Fire Protection Handbook,* N.F.P.A., Boston, Mass.
11. *Fire Technology (Electricity),* Institution of Fire Engineers (London).
12. *Focus on Fire,* Hotspur Publishing Co. Ltd., Manchester 1.
13. D.N. VASUDEVA, *Fundamentals of Magnetism and Electricity.*
14. J.J. WILLIAMSON, *General fire Hazards and Fire Prevention.*
15. *Handbook of Industrial Loss—Prevention,* Mac Graw Hill Book Co (Inc), London.
16. JOHN BOWMAN, *Hydraulics for Fire Engineers.*
17. B. NEKRASOV, *Hydraulics.*
18. RONALD V. GILES, *Hydraulics and Fluid Mechanics.*
19. CECIL SMART, *Industrial Fire and Explosion Hazards.*
20. PARTINGTON, *Inorganic Chemistry.*
21. L.M. MITRA, *Inorganic Chemistry.*
22. N.M. BOSE AND J. CHATTERJEE, *Intermediate Physics.*
23. Institution of Fire Engineers Quarterlies.
24. *Manual of Firemanship,* H.M. Stationery Office, London.
25. *Manual of Firemanship* (Appendix on Metrication).
26. *Mathematical Problems for Firemen,* Institution of Fire Engineers.
27. *National Fire Code,* N.F.P.A. Boston, Mass.
28. J.N. ROY AND R.N. DAS GUPTA, *Outlines of Physics.*
29. J.H. DUBOIS, *Plastics.*
30. W. W. DIGGLE, "Hazards of Static Electricity."
31. A.S. MINTON, *Toxic Fire and Explosion Hazards in Industry.*
32. R. KILLEY, *Water problem in Fire Fighting Explained.*
33. D.M. WHARRY AND R. HIRST, *Fire Technology Chemistry and Cmbustion.*
34. P.A.D. SHEEN AND A. GREY, *Fire Technology Calculations.*
35. EDGRLY AND ROBINSON, *Handbook of fire engineers.*

Index

ADDENDA

NEW DEVELOPMENTS IN FIRE PROTECTION TECHNOLOGY

1. Early Suppression Fast Response Sprinkler (E.S.F.R.)

It is a revolution in Fire Protection Technology. The E.S.F.R. sprinkler quickly discharges a large volume of water in the form of a very fine spray directly into a fire and suppresses it. The time of response is also much faster, as against an ordinary sprinkler head.

With normal sprinkler, the upward draft to the fire upon actuation, is generally 41 ft/sec (12.3 metres/sec), with the use of less water as compared to ordinary sprinkler heads.

Within a year of its introduction, the E.S.F.R. sprinkler protection limits were extended to include even more challenging occupancies such as, Aerosol storages, Rolled papers, Idol palets etc.

These high performance sprinklers can protect virtually any stored commodity in warehouses upto 30 ft (9 m) high. E.S.F.R. sprinklers have been found to be effective for most common materials, including unexpanded plastics in cardboard cartons, in single row, double row and multiple rows, racked storages or in solid piled or open frame storages.

Other big advantages are the elimination of the need for in-rack sprinklers and the need for a smaller water supply.

E.S.F.R. sprinklers at 50 lbs/sq. in (3.5 bar) can protect cartoned expanded plastics, commodity stacked at upto 25 ft (7.6 metre) high in a 30 ft (9 mt:) buildin

Uncartoned expanded plastics require E.S.F.R. sprinkler at 75 P.S.I. (5 bar) pressure with storage heights upto 20 ft (6 m.) in a 25 ft high (7.6 m) building.

2. Double Knock System

In double knock systems, two detectors from two different locations need to be triggered independently to raise an alarm. This system eliminates the possibility ot any false alarm, as also the automatic discharge of extinguishants, specially in the case of false alarm.

3. VESDA (Very Early Smoke Detection Apparatus)

One major development in the field of smoke detection is VESDA. The object is to detect a fire at the early stages, through VESDA smoke detecting system and apply water, if possible, before flaming combustion occurs. It is an extremely effective smoke detection system, which draws a continuous air sample from the risk area into a very sensitive optical chamber. This system is 100 times more sensitive than a standard optical smoke detector.

4. Analogue/Addressable Systems

Analogue/Addressable systems transmit data from the sensor to the control panel and back again, providing constant information on the current state of each detector connected to the panel.

By analogue addressable systems we can provide precise source of fire, pin pointing its location during a fire emergency.

This incorporates Emergency Voice/Alarm Communication System (EVCS), which are originally developed as the means to ensure safe evacuation of large amount of people from the increasing number of "High Rise" structure.

EVCS system provides a distinct electronic tone which is unmistakable as an emergency warning. Pre-recorded messages offer precise instruction to occupants of a multistoreyed building automatically upon alarm and a live voice microphone allows the system operator to update instruction at any time to the occupants trapped in the upper floors.

Hazardous escape routes can quickly be identified and the occupants redirected to come out safely.

However, the advantages of an EVCS are more widely applied in factories, office and shopping mall.

5. Thermostat

It is a device for maintaining a constant temperature. It cuts off the supply of heat, when the required temperature is exceeded and automatically restores the supply, when the temperature falls below the pre set temperature.

It usually consists of a bi-metallic strip, so arranged that when it is heated (or cooled), the power supply contacts are opened (or closed).

6. Thermister

It is a semi-conductor, the electrical resistance of which decreases rapidly with increase of temperature, e.g. the resistance of a circuit may be of the order of 10^5 ohms at 20°C, and only 10 ohms at 100°C. It is used as a sensitive temperature measuring device and also to compensate for temperature variations of other components in a circuit.